D0806955

Covenant Documents

Reading the Bible again for the First Time

Revised Second Edition

By Wayne Brouwer

Hope College

cognella®
academic publishing

Bassim Hamadeh, CEO and Publisher
Michael Simpson, Vice President of Acquisitions
Jamie Giganti, Managing Editor
Jess Busch, Senior Graphic Designer
David Miano, Acquisitions Editor
Monika Dziamka, Project Editor
Natalie Lakosil, Licensing Manager
Sean Adams, Interior Designer

First published in the United States of America in 2015 by Cognella, Inc.

Trademark Notice: Product or corporate names may be trademarks or registered trademarks, and are used only for identification and explanation without intent to infringe.

Printed in the United States of America

ISBN: 978-1-63189-190-8 (pbk)/ 978-1-63189-191-5 (br)

cognella
academic publishing
www.cognella.com   800-200-3908

Contents

COVENANT MAKING (2) 223

The Creator establishes a covenant relationship with a missional community by way of a redemptive act

Foreword

The second edition of *Covenant Documents: Reading the Bible again for the First Time* is a gift to us all! It is a huge gift for the young follower of Jesus who needs to learn more about the book loved by the new family that he or she has joined. And it is an equally huge gift for those who have walked with the Lord for a long time and are called to teach or disciple those who haven't. I will be proud to have this book in my library, and it won't be long before my copy shows its wear.

The subtitle of this book tells you everything you need to know about it and its author. We are actually always reading the Bible again for the first time whether we know it or not, and Wayne Brouwer helps us to understand that. The Bible bears witness to itself that it is "living and active" and that necessarily means that each recurring reading of it is as fresh as the morning dew. Rabbi Abraham Joshua Heschel says that the Bible, "... is the perpetual motion of the Spirit ... Irrefutably, indestructibly, never wearied by time, the Bible wanders through the ages, giving itself freely to (all), as if it belonged to every soul on earth." And if he is right about that, and I for one have found it to be true, then we need a faithful guide for each successive reading. Wayne Brouwer and his latest book are that guide.

Wayne Brouwer has the mind of a scholar, the heart of a pastor, and the eye of an eagle! You will thrill to see what this uncommon anatomy has produced in *Covenant Documents: Reading the Bible again for the First Time.*

—Dr. Timothy Brown
President and Henry Bast Professor of Preaching
Western Theological Seminary
Holland, Michigan

Introduction

Approaches, Genres, and Interpretive Options

A s he was about to set out on a long journey, a traveler was asked by a friend if he was packed and ready. "Almost," he said. "There is still a little corner in my suitcase in which I need to cram a guidebook, a lamp, a mirror, a telescope, a book of fine poetry, a number of biographies, a bundle of old letters, a hymnal, a sharp sword, and a small library of sixty-some volumes."

"How will you manage that?" the traveler's incredulous friend queried.

"Easily," he replied. Taking his Bible, he placed it in the few inches of remaining space, and with that he closed his suitcase.

That old story reminds us of the unique and varied character of the Bible. It is indeed a collection of writings that span multiple genres. Included between the covers of this book of scripture for billions of Christians there are cosmogonic myths, heroic ancestor stories, historical reviews, social and legal codes, ethical pronouncements, worship songs, versified dramas, educational and instructional materials, wedding entertainment, sermons and prophecies, biographies, teachings and exhortations, letters to individuals and groups, doctrinal dissertations, and apocalyptic visions.

Moreover, while these writings are manifold in their literary types, they were also authored over thousands of years. The Pentateuch, for instance, is variously pegged to timelines that begin as early as 1400 B.C. and continue as late as 400 B.C. What we call the "Former Prophets" spell out historical scenes ranging between 1100 and 400 B.C., with a number of theories as to when the documents themselves came into being. The "Latter Prophets" are only slightly jiggered on the calendar, with dates spanning 1000–300 B.C. Meanwhile, the poetry of the Hebrew Bible, along with the various "Writings," seems to have been produced from around 1200 B.C. to somewhere in the Hellenistic era, perhaps as late as 300 B.C. When we turn to the New Testament, the dates collapse into about five decades. Most of the letters appear to have been written between about 48 and 70 A.D. The four gospels emerge, depending on the chronological criteria used, from the late 50s to the late 90s A.D. The book of Acts follows events that took place over the years from 30–60 A.D., and was likely written before 70 A.D. Hebrews and Revelation are harder to pin down, but both were in distribution in the latter decades of the first century. Thus, in a single volume, there are writings from sixteen centuries of literary output.

Obviously, such a collection could not have been penned by a single human author. Moses is connected most closely with the first five books that open our Bible libraries today, although a host of theories exists as to who really wrote or collected or edited or interpolated these pages. Although much of the literature of ancient Israel was produced without references to authors, Joshua, Samuel, and David are thought to be significant writers of earlier documents, while Isaiah, Jeremiah, and other prophets add great sections to later Hebrew Bible literature. Among these voices are court historians, poets, and dramatists, many of whom acknowledge that they are also relying on other sources for information or inspiration. In the New Testament age, we can be a bit more certain about many of the letter and gospel writers, followers of Jesus from various walks of life, but even here there is a great deal of ambiguity.

What adds further drama to the mix is that the Christian Bible is clearly the product of two great religious traditions, each of which is distinct from the other in our world. What is known today as the "Old Testament" forms the complete "Hebrew Bible" of Judaism. Furthermore, this grouping of documents was canonized by first-century rabbis who were themselves a remnant of but one of the ethnic and cultic streams that originally constituted the Hebrew nation of Israel. Meanwhile, the "New Testament" is distinctly Christian, even though its core writings emerge from the first-century Jewish community. These, in turn, are supplemented by others which transcend the early Jewish Christian religious or ethnic parameters, and even mark theological distinctions against it.

In broad summary, the Bible is a collection of writings emerging from within and shaped by two specific religious traditions. But to that must be added a further qualifier: Both these communities understand the Bible to be a book that carries in its pages something transcendently significant—purporting, in fact, to be divine revelation.

Worldview Choices

It is at this point, when considering the character of the Bible and its unique function within certain religious traditions, that fundamental choices have to be made regarding worldview. The Bible has in it the contours of a philosophic understanding of all that exists, and what it should mean, which is at odds with other foundational points of view. These dissonant perspectives cannot be readily harmonized, though we are always looking for points of contact and possible elements of overlap or integration. Nor can the various cosmological understandings be proven valid or invalid by any objective means available to us. We do not hold to a worldview that shapes the rest of our thinking because it is verifiable beyond all doubt or opinion; instead, we believe *out of* certain frames of reference because (1) they are familiar to us (background or culture); (2) they provide the greatest cohesive systemization of our experiences (philosophic paradigm); or (3) they respond most deeply to our questions and needs (religious hunger). It is our worldview that informs our research and investigations and constructs and interpretations of daily life. While our worldview may be changed or altered or honed or manipulated over time to more fully reflect our ongoing experiences or more recent philosophic inquiries, it cannot be proven scientifically precisely because we are confined to a "system," a biosphere bound by the incessant ordering of time with expanding, but not infinite, limits, that prevents us from stepping outside and looking back at the world and reality from a transcendent perspective.

Non-Intelligent Closed System

Each religion of the human race, and every scientific, cultural or philosophic paradigm for reality, is a reflection of a foundational worldview. While these exist around us in plethora, they may be reduced to three large groupings. First, there are Non-Intelligent Closed System perspectives. These understand the meaning of the universe in which we live to be accessible only from within. There is no external source of information available to us, no "God" or gods, and no revelation other than that which we discover from the nuanced clues embedded in the matter and energy that swirl around us. Human life, from this viewpoint, is accidental and not necessary to the system. We have no more meaning than any other object or substance on our planet. Were chemicals to have been combined in other ways and acted upon by differing forces or energies, there might not be any human race whatsoever, or there may well have developed a species or several which differed wildly from what we have become familiar with as we look in the mirror. Within this worldview, the Bible is as much a historical curiosity open to the social sciences, as is any other book of mythology that seeks to bring meaning to a merely chaotic and random environment. Any "revelation" connected to scripture is, at best, a kind of widely affirmed insight which seems to be in tune with many cultural experiences; at worst, it is a mighty hoax devised deviously by some to subject and exploit the fears and knowledge limitations of the masses in efforts at gaining power, prestige, or pelf.

Intelligent Closed System

A second major grouping of worldviews, which we might call Intelligent Closed System perspectives, shares the belief that our world is indeed a closed system. What we see is what we get. There is no godlike spirit hovering outside and above and beyond the universe accessible to us. But unlike the undirected randomness found in the previous worldview collection, this perspective believes that Life itself, probably combined with Time, forms the intelligence that drives the system. Think of it—we are bound by Time as the great organizer of all that we experience. We cannot return to yesterday except in our memories, and these do not allow us to change anything that has already taken place. Human (and, for that matter, universal) existence is hung on the sweeping hands of Time. We do not understand Time. We cannot control Time. Even when we explore the relativity of our experiences of Time, we are unable to alter its massive grip and pull on our existence. Similarly with Life itself. While we can make machines that imitate the functionings of our legs and arms and teeth and fingers and even our brains, we cannot infuse into these robotic contraptions that essential spark of Life itself. There is something mysterious and magical about Life. It propagates itself in the cells of our bodies and the mutable genetic material by which we engender replacement beings in our communities, but we cannot create it *ex nihilo*. We know whether a flower is alive or dead, but we cannot bring the former out of the latter. We sit at bedsides, unable to reverse the draining of Life from a body, powerless to do more than prolong the exit strategy. So it is, from this collective worldview family, that Life and Time are understood together to be the intelligence which shapes the universal system. We are always on the cutting edge of their development, for it is only in the immediate *now* that they operate on us and on the world around, so that all is constantly changing, growing, accumulating, and learning. Life and Time together are the creative edge that shapes existence in a closed system. And from this perspective, human life is meaningful insofar as it plays out its role and obeys its "designed" purposes—aligning with activities that sustain Life and refraining from any nonsense that would pretend to circumvent Time. In this context, the Bible is seen to be a record of human reflection of how best to live with and understand Life and Time. If it carries any "revelation," this is merely a more profound insight into how Life and Time actually function. Also, we might even name Life and Time as "God," since they control the system in which we find ourselves, but we should not understand this "God" to transcend either Life or Time. "God" is our way of talking about the fundamental mechanics or energies of the system. And in that respect, "God" actually can change. For if "God" is the intelligence that drives the system, the accumulated experiences of the system in turn alter the options, which can then be manipulated again by "God." So, while the greater universal system is closed to anything transcendent outside of it, the power of Life and Time is the internal energizing wild card that continues to evolve and develop the system itself, and thus we have understandings of "God" which grow over time. That is why we "moderns" are more sophisticated in our religious perspectives than were our "primitive" ancestors. They had fewer experiences through which to learn about Life and Time, and their "God" reflections on these were not nearly so developed as are ours today. "God" has changed because Life and Time have served to infuse that term with more and varying meanings.

Creator/Creature Open System

We recognize these worldview perspectives around us, the former linked to various forms of absolute naturalism or fatalism, and the latter speaking through great Asian religious traditions, Process Theology, and varieties of Animistic Spiritism. They are ultimately irreconcilable with one another, and are also in competition with one other worldview collection, which might be labeled as Creator/Creature Open System. This third worldview group believes that there is a creator God who exists outside and before the system of reality in which we are housed, and that this God shaped the system so that it has inherent meaning and purpose. Existence is planned and intended by God. Human life is honored as a unique facet of created reality, formed to occupy a place of primary influence in the world as we know it, and reflecting attributes of the character of the creator. Moreover, human life has been compromised in some way, and this accounts for the tragic and senseless elements of our daily walk. Furthermore, the creator did not—and does not—abandon this world system to chance or fate, but invests in the renewal and redemption of all things: human life and also the other expressions of reality. Within this worldview, the Bible is understood to be one dimension of the divine-human redemptive link, ensuring that whoever God is will not be forgotten among us, and that whatever God is doing will not be lost in the hectic shuffle of human social shifts.

We must acknowledge these worldviews as we enter a study of the Bible. We cannot prove one worldview over another. Nor can we force someone to shift from the paradigm of one perspective to that of another. But we cannot talk with meaning about the Bible without at some point admitting our philosophic stance. One may not say that Jesus is Savior or Redeemer and at the same time aver that the Bible is merely the product of human reflections about the problem of evil.

This does not mean that we are not able to talk with one another as scholars or students of biblical literature if we hail from differing worldviews. We are able to investigate the same historical data, rely on the same linguistic information, and probe the same cultural references together with a great deal of camaraderie. But at the end of the day, we will use the Bible differently if we are part of communities holding to competing worldviews.

Revelation and Human History

To be sure, there are significant problems which trouble all who are sensitive biblical investigators, whatever worldview community nurtures them. On the one hand, historical conundrums arise when we ask certain questions, for there are limits to the data we can obtain in order to verify some dates and events that exist within the testimonies found in the Bible. Indeed, there is even obvious internal evidence that the Bible itself was shaped and altered over time, so that some of its writings depend on earlier sources, some of its documents were adapted and edited from literary production that preceded them, and some of its pages appear to have experienced later interpolations of injected passages.

On the other hand, each reader of the Bible travels with the constant companion of religious agnosticism: How and what and why does God "reveal?" What are we to take from this passage, and on what grounds? Is there a deeper meaning? How can we know? Is the revelation of God found in the magic of the words? Is it contained in the testimonies of the participants in the biblical record? Is it to be abstracted from syllogistic statements of doctrinal fiat? Are some passages (like the red-lettered quotations of Jesus in various translations) more important than others? How or why?

In order to gain deeper access to the mysteries and meanings of the Bible, the heritage of scholarly interpretation has devised a number of tools:

Source Criticism attempts to separate the distinctive sources behind the current text of the Bible, so that the earliest cultural understandings which created the seminal writings might inform us how we view the text in its development.

Form Criticism spends time analyzing the unique literary genres that are found in the Bible, and assesses how these function in shaping the current message of the text.

Redaction Criticism focuses on gaining a greater understanding of how and why the various genres and source texts were edited and compiled into the received or final stage of literary development.

Literary Criticism keeps its primary attention on the text in its current or received form, and probes how its shape, form, or literary patterns invests its words with additional meaning.

But these are only tools of investigation. They help us analyze the text without giving us more clarity as to why the Bible exists in the first place.

Revelation versus History

Here again, there are fundamental religious choices to be made. Those who view divine revelation as intrusive to the closed system of our experiential environment tend to talk about the Bible in one of four ways. Some, like Schleiermacher, adopting the Kantian philosophic distinctions, believe the transcendent is off-limits to our scientific inquiry, so the Bible must be received as a book of testimonies from those who have felt the impinging power of the divine upon their lives. Others, like Gerstner, believe the Bible is a supernaturally produced volume of essentially divine dictation, using prophets and apostles a bit like dehumanized tape recorders in order to communicate in human language the transcendent doctrine that becomes enscripturated. Albright and Wright went another route, within this same family, and saw scripture as the record of divine actions in human history; only the former (God's redemptive deeds) were truly revelatory by their interruption of natural orders and phenomena, but the Bible lingers as inspired insofar as it correctly recounts and interprets these redemptive events. Finally there is the "witness" solution of Barth, who believed that divine revelation was always immediate and personal, and saw scripture as the earliest attempts by humans to talk about where one might encounter God, and thus set a context within which, through continued preaching, people of successive generations might seek other such revelatory rapprochements with God.

Revelation as History

Another family of investigators does not set divine revelation and human history against each other. Instead, scripture is either a record of our progress in understanding God (Wellhausen, Von Rad), or it is a chronicle of the unfolding process of "God" in becoming actualized as the name for the intelligence which drives the system (Ogden, Ricoeur).

In the former, there is a progression to our understanding of God. So, for instance, the theology of the Old Testament ought to differ somewhat from that of the New Testament, simply because our awareness of God's character and activities has changed and grown over the centuries. Even within the Old Testament, reflecting upon the huge span of time in which its ideas develop, the perspectives of the post-exilic community are likely to be very different from those of the patriarchal societies, simply due to the progression of time and the insights that change and grow through this unfolding. Furthermore, we today, these many centuries later, have continued to learn many things about God or spirituality or values, so our theologies do not need to confine themselves to mere explication of the doctrines of the biblical text. Our theology keeps evolving as a reflection of our mutating perceptions.

In the latter view, it is not only our understandings of God that develop more fully over time, but more essentially, "God" is always revising itself as well. Since "God" is the term we give to the energizing force that pulsates as the intersection of Life and Time, "God" is constantly absorbing and creating adumbrations of identity simply through the process of process. Theology is not so much about gaining a clearer understanding of God and created reality by way of analyses of texts, traditions, and encounters; rather, it is the means by which we constantly seek to keep abreast of the changing nature of "God"—that is, the essential energizing force which drives change in our realm of experiences as shaped by the emanations of "God" we call Life and Time.

Revelation in History

In distinction from these is a perspective which sees the Bible as part of an Open System world, in which a Creator continues to interact with the Created in meaningful ways. Within this point of view, the scriptures are formulated out of certain redemptive events, but exist as the accessible documents which shape the communities of faith flowing from these initial experiences. In other words, the Bible is begun and developed as the documents that describe the Creator's actions within human history to reassert the divine presence and perspectives, and continues to grow as spiritually insightful wisdom is granted to some, who help others understand the Creator's ways and will through changing times. Since the Creator is sovereign over all the creation, these redemptive actions and the inspiration which shapes reflections on them give the Bible unique authority. And because the Bible itself began as an attempt by God to create a community of witness and testimony within human history, a commonly understood covenant structure appears to have been used to form the early dimensions of this redemptive relationship. In this way, the Bible begins and continues to grow as what might be termed "covenant documents." This will be the thesis underlying the pages that follow. In brief overview, it can be outlined in this fashion:

> **Covenant Making**: The Creator establishes a covenant relationship with a missional community by way of a redemptive act

> **Old Testament**: The Pentateuch   **New Testament**: The Gospels

Covenant Living: The Creator guides the covenant relationship with a mission community by way of authorized spokespersons

Old Testament: The Former and Latter Prophets

New Testament: Acts and the Epistles

Covenant Questions: The Creator nurtures the covenant relationship with a missional community by way of spiritual wisdom and insight

Old Testament: Poetic Literature and Psalmody

New Testament: Hebrews and Revelation

Such a view is not the only way to look at the Bible, of course, but what is presented here is coherent and consistent with the Bible's own internal testimony. Some may read these pages as encouraging and illuminating. Some may engage these reflections to find fault and disagreement. So be it. My intent is to share beyond my classrooms a lifetime journey of investigation that has brought clarity to my own reading of the Bible and sense to my worldview quests, and which a great many students have found helpful as they sought meaningful grounding for their faith in an ever-changing and challenging world.

Wayne Brouwer

Discussion Points

- What criteria should we use when comparing the Bible to the authoritative texts of other religions? What is it that we look for when explaining their similarities or differences? Why?
- What expressions of religion that we observe around us might be found as subsets of the various worldviews described above? How do they share these fundamental worldview perspectives, and where do they differ from other religions precisely in worldview matters?
- What, in your opinion, is the nature and content of "revelation?" What might we need to know that we cannot find without divine intervention? How might we know which insights are inspired and authoritative, and which others are not so?
- What makes the Bible a cohesive collection of literature? Why these writings and not others? What is the glue, the binding, that has kept them together over the centuries?

For Further Investigation

Bavinck, Herman (2010). *Philosophy of Revelation*.

Brouwer, Wayne (1985). *Revelation and History: An analysis of approaches to the relationship between revelation and history in recent theological systems* (Hekman Library, Calvin College: Unpublished Master's Thesis).

Covenant Making

The Creator establishes a covenant relationship with a
missional community by way of a redemptive act

1.

Where the Bible Begins

Starting at Sinai

Where does the Bible begin? Where does any story begin? At the beginning, of course!

For the Bible, it would seem most obvious that this beginning is the opening chapters of Genesis. After all, Genesis is at the front of the book with which we all have become familiar. Moreover, Genesis deals with origins, as its very name implies. In fact, Genesis ferrets out the original Big Bang beginning, when from nothing (or out of primeval chaos), God blasted the universe into existence. After that, Genesis goes on to describe beginnings of all other sorts—the origins of fauna and flora, the elemental steps of the human race, the critically disruptive entrance of evil, the formation of communities, nation states, cultures, and races, and even the birth of the tribal grouping called Israel, which will dominate the rest of the Bible's pages.

But, as logicians caution, simply because pages currently are found in a certain order does not mean that the first ones we encounter necessarily came into being prior to those that follow. There are many theories about the origins of the Pentateuch which suggest that what we see today may be an end product that actually differs significantly from the composition and chronology of its parts. While we will pursue this in more detail later, for now it is critical to look deeper into the Bible's own understanding of its origins. Did someone sit down one day and decide to write about the creation? Was the Bible initiated by an obscure scribe with too much time on his hands who was exploring the family tree, and then hit upon the idea of writing a best-seller about Abraham and kin, only to be bested over the centuries by others who turned the tale into an endless serialization with subplots that finally destroyed the original narrative? Or were there ethicists in collegial dialogue who despaired of the condition of their societies and together formulated a new code of behavior, surrounding it with a mythical world to give it staying power?

While speculations might swirl, the Bible's own pages are quite clear about its presumed beginnings. If by "Bible" we mean a book of writings that purport to have revelatory or religiously shaping significance (i.e., "scripture"), then we must ask where such writings first happened and under what conditions within the Bible's own literary self-understanding. With this in mind, it becomes apparent that we need to start by looking at the events reported to have taken place at Mt. Sinai, in the middle of the book of Exodus.

Why? Because none of the stories reported in the Bible about events occurring prior to the Sinai event make mention of or imply the presence of a written source of revelation or inspiration. For instance, important as he was to biblical history, Adam had no "Bible." Nor did Noah, during all those years that he tried to hear a voice speaking of impending world destruction. Even Abraham, whose story is so central to the biblical record in both Testaments, was not guided by a collection of sacred writings to which he could turn for devotional reflection each morning.

In clear and unambiguous testimony, the Bible's own internal evidence expresses that the writing down of important ideas or history as a sourcebook of revelatory insight was begun when the Israelites encountered God in a unique way at Mt. Sinai. It was there, according to the pages of Exodus, that God and Moses collaborated to create written documents which would travel with the community that eventually became the settled nation of Israel.

So, it is imperative to understand more clearly what was taking place at Mt. Sinai. To do that, we need to know something of the broader history of the second millennium B.C.

Suzerain-Vassal Covenant Documents

One of the dominant civilizations of the second millennium was the Hittite kingdom. Somewhat secluded in the mountainous plateaus of Anatolia (eastern Turkey today), the Hittites shaped a vast web of international relations which, at the height of their power in the 14th century B.C., encompassed most of the ancient Near East. While they were companions of other similar civilizations that shared commonalities of culture, conquests, and cities, the Hittites linger in archaeological and historical studies for, among other things, their standardization of a written code used extensively in the normalization of international relations. In order to establish appropriate structures that would spell out the Hittites' ongoing interactions with subjected peoples, a prescribed treaty form appears to have been widely used. The parameters of the typical Hittite suzerain-vassal covenant included:

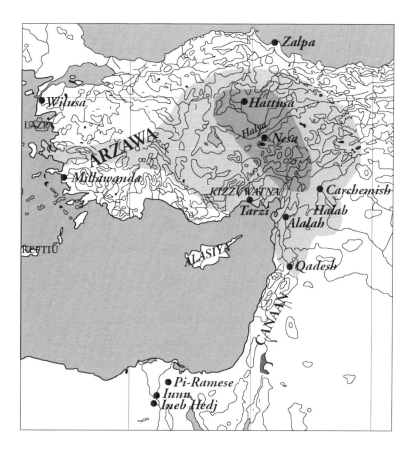

Figure 1.1 Hittite Kingdom.[1]

A **Preamble**, which declared the identity and power of the ruler responsible for establishing this relationship.

A **Historical Prologue** outlining the events leading up to this relationship, so that it could be set into a particular context and shaped by a cultural or religious frame.

Stipulations, which specified the responsibilities and actions associated with the relationship.

Curses and Blessings that evoked the negative and positive outcomes if this covenant were either breached or embraced by the parties.

Witnesses, who were called to affirm the legitimacy of this covenant-making event, and who would then hold the parties accountable.

Document Clauses, which described ratification ceremonies, specified future public recitations of the treaty, and noted the manner in which the copies of the covenant were to be kept.

---

1 Adapted from: Copyright © Dbachmann (CC by 3.0) at http://commons.wikimedia.org/wiki/File:Hittite_Empire.png

What makes this bit of ancient historical trivia so intriguing for biblical scholars is the uncanny correspondence between the elements of this Hittite covenant code and the literature at the heart of Israel's encounter with God at Sinai. Note the following:

> When God is first heard to speak from the rumbling mountain, the words are essentially the **Preamble** of a suzerain-vassal covenant: "I am the Lord your God" (Exodus 20:1).
>
> Immediately following is a brief **Historical Prologue** reminding the people of the events that precipitated this encounter: "... who brought you out of the land of Egypt, out of the house of bondage" (Exodus 20:2).
>
> Then comes a recitation of **Stipulations** that will shape the ethics, morality, and lifestyle of the community (Exodus 20:3–23:19).
>
> Following these are the **Curses and Blessings** (Exodus 23:20–33) of a typical covenant document. What is unusual in this case is that the order is reversed so that the blessings precede the curses. This provides the same rigors of participatory onus, but gives it a freshness of grace and optimism that are often absent from the quick condemnation of the usual ordering.
>
> The **Witnesses** are the Elders of the Israelite community (Exodus 24:1–2), bringing authentication of this process and these documents into the human realm, when it was often spiritualized in other covenants by listing local gods as moderators of these events.
>
> Finally there is the **Document Clause** (Exodus 24:3–18) that spells out the ratification ceremony. It will be followed by a further reflection on the repositories of the covenant document copies once the Tabernacle has been built.

The striking resonance between the usual form of the Hittite suzerain-vassal covenant and the essential first speech of Yahweh to Israel at Mt. Sinai makes it difficult not to assess the beginnings of conscious Israelite religion in terms other than that of a suzerain (Yahweh)-vassal (Israel) covenant-making ceremony. Furthermore, this appears to elucidate the mode and function of the first biblical documents. They were not intended to be origin myths, ancestor hero stories, mere legal or ethical or civil codes, sermons, prophecies, or apocalyptic visions (though all of these would later accrete to the initial writings of the first community encounter with Yahweh); they were initially the written covenant documents formulating the relationship between a nation and the (divine) ruler who earned, in battle, the right to order Israel's world.

This is why the word "covenant" becomes an essential term for all the rest of the literature that will be garnered into the collection eventually known as the Bible. The Bible begins with a covenant-making ceremony that produces certain documents, and then continues to grow as further explications of that covenant relationship are generated. One can read theology or ethics or politics or history out of the Bible, but one cannot do so while ignoring the essential role of the Sinai covenant between Yahweh and Israel. Even the idea of "kingdom," so prevalent and pervasive in the Bible, is predicated on the covenant, for it is by way of the Covenant that Israel becomes the dominion of the great King. The Kingdom of God is the context for all that is portrayed in the Bible, but the Covenant is the administrative document through which the Kingdom takes hold and adheres in the human societies which form the front ranks of Yahweh's citizenry.

The Battle of the Superpowers

This perspective is further confirmed in the rest of the writings that surround Exodus 20–24. First, Exodus 1–19 forms an extended "historical prologue" to the Sinai Covenant by declaring Israel's precarious situation in Egypt (chapter 1), the birth and training of the leader who would become Yahweh's agent for recovering Yahweh's enslaved people (chapter 2), the calling of this deliverer (chapters 3–4), and the battle of the superpowers (the pharaoh and Yahweh) who each lay claim to suzerain status over this vassal nation (chapters 5–19). Second, Exodus 25–40 focuses on the creation of a suitable residence for Israel's suzerain. Thus, the whole of Exodus may be quickly outlined as Struggles (1–19), Stipulations (20–24), and Symbols (25–40) surrounding the Sinai covenant-making event. Each of these deserves some further reflection.

The struggles of Chapters 1–19 involve a number of things. At the start, there is the nasty relationship that has developed between the pharaoh of Egypt and the Israelites. An editorial note declares that "Joseph" has been forgotten, and this small reference forms the bridge that later draws Genesis into an even more broadly extended historical prologue to the Sinai covenant. We will find out, by reading backward, that Joseph was the critical link between the Egyptians and this other ethnic community living within its borders. When the good that Joseph did for both races was forgotten, the dominant Egyptian culture attempted to dehumanize and then destroy these Israelite aliens.

> **Exodus in Literary Sections** 📖
>
> 1–19 **Struggles** to Obtain Covenant Identity
>
> 20–24 **Stipulations** of the Covenant Relationship
>
> 25–40 **Symbols** of the Covenant Expressions

The deadly solution proposed by the pharaoh in dealing with the rising population of his slave community may sound harsh, but it was likely a very modest and welcomed political maneuver among his primary subjects. Because there is virtually no rain in Egypt, with most of its territory lying in or on the edge of the great Saharan desert, the Nile is and was the critical source of water that sustained life throughout the region. The Nile "miraculously" ebbed and flowed annually, responding to the rains of central Africa, thousands of miles away. Far removed from Egypt's farmlands and cities, this process was attributed to the gods that nurtured Egyptian civilization. Thus, it was fitting for the people to pay homage to these gods, especially by giving appropriate sacrifices to the power of the Nile. In that manner, having the boy babies of the Hebrews tossed into the Nile's currents would not have been considered genocide, but instead it would be deemed a suitable civic and cultural responsibility. Such a practice provided the Nile god with fittingly dear tribute, and at the same time allowed the bulk of the Egyptian population to save its own babies by substituting those of this surrogate vassal people living within their borders.

Moses's own name ties him to the royal family of Egypt and its influence (note the frequent occurrence of the letters MSS in the names of pharaohs of the eighteenth through twentieth dynasties—*Thutmoses*, *Ramses*, etc.), and his training in the palace schools would provide him with skills that set him apart from the rest of the Israelites in preparation for his unique leadership responsibilities. Moses's time in the wilderness, on the other hand, made him familiar with

Moses's Egyptian Name

The meaning of Moses's name is derived from the ancient Egyptian word describing the action of "emerging" or being "drawn from," which connects Moses to the story of his discovery by the pharaoh's daughter (Exodus 2:10). But it also links Moses to the royal family of his era. Several generations before Moses's birth, *Aakheperkare* (1520–1492) established a dynasty that ruled for nearly a century, with three successive males in the leadership line identifying themselves as *Thutmose*. This name meant "drawn from …" or "born out of *Thot*," one of the more important gods of the ancient Egyptian pantheon. Greater still was *Ra*, the sun god, for whom *Thot* acted as a primary guardian or emissary, and whose identity the pharaohs of Moses's own day took upon themselves: *Menpehtire Ramses*—"drawn from …" or "born out of Ra" (1292–1290) and *Usermaatre-setpenre Ramses* (*Ramses* II or *Ramses* "The Great," 1279–1213).

Bedouin life, and similarly fortified his ability to stand at the head of a wandering community once Israel was released from slavery.

In Moses's unique encounter with God at Mt. Horeb (Chapters 3–4), he experienced the power of the forgotten deity of Israel, and learned a name by which this divinity would soon become known again to the people. "Yahweh" (יהוה) is a variation on the Hebrew verb of existence, and that is why translators bring it into English with terms like "I am" or "I will be." Furthermore, through the voice from the burning bush, this God immediately connected the current events with a specific past through a historical recitation that would later be explained at length in the extended Genesis historical prologue to the Sinai covenant: Yahweh is the God of Abraham, Isaac, and Jacob. Because of the promises made to that family, Moses is now to become the agent through whom the Israelites will be returned to the land promised to their ancestors. Of course, this is what triggered the battle for control of the nation, and eventually set the stage for Yahweh to claim suzerainty over Israel at Mt. Sinai.

The conflict intensifies in Exodus 5:1–6:12, when Moses makes his first dramatic appearance back in Egypt. The pharaoh's initial reaction is disdain; why should he listen to the apocalyptic ravings of a wilderness wild man, even if he seems unusually aware of Egyptian language and protocol?

At this point, the famous plagues enter the story. While these miracles of divine judgment make for a great Hollywood screenplay, the reason for this extended weird display of divine power is not always apparent to those of us who live in very different cultural contexts, especially when it is interspersed with notes that Pharaoh's heart was hardened, sometimes, in fact, seemingly as an act of Yahweh. Could not Yahweh have provided a less destructive—and deadly—exit strategy for Israel?

The plagues begin to make sense when viewed in reference to Egypt's climate and culture. After the initial sparring between Moses and the pharaoh's sorcerers (Exodus 7:10–13) with snakes to show magical skills, the stakes are raised far beyond human ability merely to manipulate the natural order. First, the waters are turned to blood; then, the marshes send out a massive, unwelcome pilgrimage of frogs; next, the dust is beat into gnats, soon to be followed by even peskier flies; subsequently, the livestock gets sick from the dust, and this illness then spreads to human life in the form of boils and open sores; penultimately, the heavens send down mortar shells of hail, transport in a foreign army of locusts, and then withhold the light of the sun;

finally, in an awful culmination, the firstborn humans and animals across Egypt die suddenly.

Strange. But not quite as much when seen in three successive groupings. Among the many deities worshipped in ancient Egypt, none superseded a triumvirate composed of the Nile, the good Earth, and the heavens, which were the home of the sun. So it was that the initial plagues of bloody water and frogs both turned the Nile against the Egyptians, and showed the dominance of Yahweh over this critical source of national life.

The ante was then upped when Yahweh takes on the farmland of Egypt, one of the great breadbaskets of the world. Instead of producing crops, Moses shows, by way of plagues three through six, how Yahweh could cause these fertile alluvial plains to generate all manner of irritating and deadly pestilence, making it an enemy instead of a friend. Finally, in the third stage of plagues, the heavens themselves become menacing. Rather than providing the sheltering confidence of benign sameness, one day the heavens attack with the hailstone mortar fire of an unseen enemy. Next, these same heavens serve as the highway of an invading army of locusts. Then old

> ### The Ten Plagues 📖
>
> *First*: Water to Blood
>
> *Second*: Overrun by Frogs
>
> *Third*: Gnats from the Dust
>
> *Fourth*: Flies from the Dust
>
> *Fifth*: Livestock Disease (at this point the community of Israel is distinguished from the Egyptian society, and will not suffer directly the impact of the rest of the plagues)
>
> *Sixth*: Boils
>
> *Seventh*: Hail
>
> *Eighth*: Locusts
>
> *Ninth*: Darkness
>
> *Tenth*: Death of Firstborn

friend *Ra* (the sun), the crowning deity of Egyptian religion, simply vanishes for three days. The gloom that terrified the Egyptians was no mere fear of darkness, but rather the ominous trepidation that their primary deity had been bested by the God of the Israelites.

All of this culminated in the final foray of this cosmic battle, when the link of life between generations and human connectedness with ultimate reality is severed through the killing of Egypt's firstborn. The Egyptians believed that the firstborn carried the cultural significance of each family and species, so in a sudden and dramatic moment, the very chain of life is destroyed. Furthermore, since the pharaohs themselves were presumed to be deity incarnate, descending directly from the sun by way of firstborn inheritance, cutting this link eviscerates the life-potency of the Egyptian civilization, not only for the present, but also for the future. It is a true cultural, religious, political, and social knockout punch.

This explains why the plagues originally served not as gory illustration material for modern Sunday school papers, but rather as the divine initiatives in an escalating battle between Yahweh and the pharaoh of Egypt over claims on the people of Israel. The plagues were a necessary prologue to the Sinai covenant because they displayed and substantiated the sovereignty of Yahweh as Suzerain not only over Israel, but also over other contenders. Israel belongs to Yahweh, both because of historic promises made to Abraham, and also by way of chivalrous combat, in which Yahweh won back the prize of lover and human companion from the usurper who had stolen her away from the divine heart. Furthermore, Yahweh accomplishes this act *without* the help of Israel's own resources (no armies, no resistance movements, no terrorist tactics, no great escape plans), and in a decisive manner that announces the limitations of the Egyptian religious and cultural resources.

This is why the final plague is paired with the institution of the Passover festival (Exodus 12). The annual festival would become an ongoing reminder that Israel was bought back by way of a blood-price redemption, and that the nation owed its very existence to the love and fighting jealousy of its divine champion. In one momentous confrontation, Egypt lost its firstborn and its cultural heritage, while Israel became Yahweh's firstborn and rightful inheritance.

These things are further confirmed in the reiteration of the importance of circumcision (Exodus 13:1–16). The rite of circumcision was practiced by a number of peoples of the ancient Near East, but invariably as either a mark of elitism (only those of a particular class in the community were circumcised), or as a rite of passage (boys or young men who did heroic deeds in battle or the hunt would be circumcised to show that they had become part of the adult warrior caste). What is unique about the commands regarding circumcision for Israel is that it is egalitarian (all males are to be circumcised, and through them, all females gain the right to be called the people of Yahweh), and that it is to be done typically on babies or young boys prior to any efforts on their part to perform deeds of valor. This transforms a regional practice that had been identified primarily as a badge of honor earned, into a mark of ownership given, as expressed in the patriarchal antecedent found in Genesis 17. It is through this lens that the New Testament practices of baptism must also be viewed; John's baptism (along with many purification rituals among, e.g., the Essenes and Pharisees) carried with it the flavor of a ritual of passage leading to earning the colors of heightened spiritual maturity, while the use of baptism in the church followed the ownership markings of Israel's practice of circumcision (see, for instance, Jesus' command regarding baptism in Matthew 28:18–20 and Paul's connection of baptism and circumcision in Colossians 2:11–12).

Related to this divinely initiated ownership theme is the miraculous deliverance of Israel through the Red Sea, coupled with the annihilation of the Egyptian army and its national military prowess in the same incidents. While Exodus 14 narrates the episode in the nail-biting urgency of a documentary, chapter 15 is given over largely to the ancient song of Moses, which unmistakably identifies the entire exodus event as divine combat against Pharaoh over the possession of Israel. Furthermore, the victory ballad also clearly anticipates the effect of this battle on the other Near Eastern nations,

---

Who Was the Pharaoh of the Exodus?

Many theories have been proposed, but two are prominent. If one assumes an early date (fifteenth century) for the Exodus, a likely candidate would be Amenhotep II. His father, Thutmose III, was recognized as a strong leader who harshly oppressed enslaved peoples in vast building programs. Moreover, Amenhotep II's reign (1427–1400) is somewhat adumbrated in the annals of ancient Egypt, with fewer references to his deeds than that of his father. Also, he was succeeded by his son, Thutmose IV, who, interestingly, was not his *firstborn*! Detracting from this perspective is a complete lack of evidence that the events of Exodus 1–19 could have happened during Amenhotep II's life.

More often suggested is that Ramses II was the pharaoh of Exodus. He had a very long rule (1279–1213), and gave his name to the building projects noted in Exodus 1:11.

with the result that Yahweh is able to march the Israelites through many hostile territories, and eventually settle the nation in Canaan as an ongoing testimony to Yahweh's rightful prestige. So it is that the exodus itself is not the divine goal, but only the first stage toward something else.

A House for God

What this further divine intention might be is then illumined by the singular event which follows from the covenant making-ceremony of Exodus 20–24: the construction of the Tabernacle. The narrative of Exodus 25–40 has three major sections. In chapters 25–31, preparations for the Tabernacle are made, and detailed plans are formulated. Then comes the intruding and jarring incident of the golden calf (chapters 32–34), in which not only Israel's loyalty to Yahweh, but also Yahweh's loyalty to Israel, are tested. Finally, the architectural initiatives of Exodus 25–31 are resumed in the actual construction of the Tabernacle and its dedication (chapters 35–40), almost as if the dark blot of the interlude had never happened.

Why all this emphasis on building the tentlike Tabernacle? Why invest in a movable shrine, rather than rally around some sacred hilltop (Mt. Sinai, for instance)? The answer is intrinsically related to the covenant-making event itself. If Israel is now the (reclaimed) possession of Yahweh, then Yahweh must take up visible residence among the people. The Tabernacle is not a strange phenomenon of the natural order, like an unfailing spring or a volcanic vent or a residual

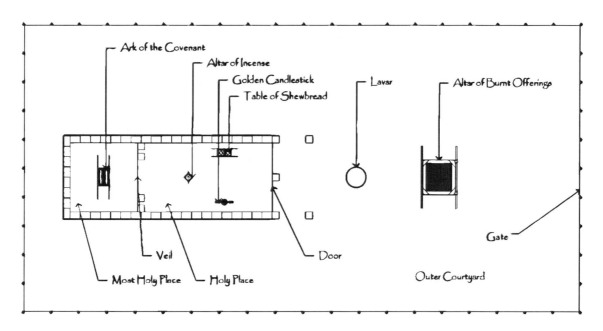

Figure 1.2 Tabernacle Plan.[2]

---

2   Copyright © Gabriel Fink (CC by 3.0) at http://commons.wikimedia.org/wiki/File:Tabernacle_Schematic.jpg

Figure 1.3 Tent living as the Israelites might have experienced it.[3]

meteor rock. Instead, it is the fabrication of a civilization that is intentionally on a journey, guided by an in-residence deity who travels with them. These people do not make pilgrimage to a shrine and then return to their homes; rather they move about in consort with the source of their identity actually residing within the center of their unwieldy sprawl.

Testimony of this is contained within the very architectural plans for the Tabernacle. Although parts of the facility will be off-limits to most of the people (and thereby somewhat mysteriously remote), the basic design is virtually identical to that of the typical Israelite portable residence and the living space that surrounds it. First, the cooking fire of any family unit was situated in front of the tent. Second, there would be vessels for washing located near the door of the tent. Third, while many meals might be taken around the fire, some were more ordered and formal, and occurred in the initial spaces within the tent. These required atmospheric accoutrements like dishes, lamps for lighting, and the aromatic wafting of incense. Finally, the privacy of the intimate acts of marriage and family were reserved for the hidden recesses of the tent, where visitors were not allowed.

This, then, became the plan for the Tabernacle. Its courtyard was public space for meals with God and others of the community around the Altar of Burt Offerings (see Leviticus 1–7). The Laver, or Bronze Basin, held waters for washing and bodily purification. In the closest part of the Tabernacle itself was found the hospitality area, where Yahweh figuratively dined more formally with guests at the Table, in the soft ambience created by the Lamp and Altar of Incense. To the rear of the Tabernacle, Yahweh reserved private space, yet had it fashioned with all of the symbolism of royalty. The Ark of the Covenant was essentially a portable throne upon which Yahweh was carried with the people, for its uppermost side was designated as the Mercy Seat. Furthermore, this throne was under the guard of two representative heavenly creatures simply called *cherubim*. In a manner akin to the sentries posted at the Garden of Eden in Genesis 3, these beings stood watch to ensure that the holiness of the deity was protected.

Thus, the Tabernacle existed uniquely in its world, representing the physical home of the community's deity as a residence within its own spatial and temporal context. Israel was

---

3   Copyright in the Public Domain.

not a people who needed to create representations of powers that it then idolized; instead, the very society in which it lived emanated from the identity of the chief citizen who lived at its heart.

It is in this context that the golden calf incident of Exodus 32–34 must be understood. Moses's delay on the mountain, talking with Yahweh on behalf of the people, bred frustration and anxiety within the community. So, they begged Aaron for symbols around which to rally, and what emerged was a bull calf made of gold. The Israelites were probably not seeking to worship something other than the God who brought them out of Egypt so recently; rather, they were trying to find a representation of that God within their cultural frame of reference, so that they could cajole (or manipulate) this deity into further meaningful actions, rather than wasting time in the seeming stall of their current lethargy. Since the bull calf was revered among the Egyptians for its ability to portray the liveliness of sentient power, it could well serve the Israelites in their quest to display national adolescent brash energy.

The problem for Yahweh, however, is twofold. First, the calf was an *Egyptian* symbol, and thus essentially blasphemous in light of Yahweh's recent decisive victory over all aspects of Egyptian power and civilization. Second, the calf reflects brute strength in the natural order, and of a kind that could be controlled by human will. A bull is meant to be yoked and harnessed and guided by whips and goads. True, it is more powerful than its human driver, but at the same time, it became a tool in service to the human will. For Yahweh to be represented in this manner undermines the significance of the divine defeat of Egypt and its culture, and appears to turn Yahweh into a mighty—albeit controllable—source of energy serving the Israelite will.

Under Moses's leadership, his own tribe, the Levites, rally to avenge Yahweh's disgrace. Because of that action, they are appointed to the honored position of keepers of the House of God. Meanwhile, Yahweh himself wishes to break covenant with Israel and instead start over with Moses's family; after all, Moses and Yahweh had become great partners and almost friends over the past few years, and especially through their time on the mountain. Moses argues against this divine turnabout, however, for two reasons. First, he reminds the Great One that Yahweh had sealed this suzerain-vassal covenant with Israel, and it could not so easily be discarded or broken. Yahweh had deliberately invested Yahweh's own destiny into this people, and while they might wrestle with the chafing fit of the new relationship, Yahweh no longer had a right to deny it. Second, Moses raises the card of shame. What would the nations say if Yahweh quit this project now? The peoples of the ancient Near East had begun to tremble because of Yahweh's decisive victory over Pharaoh; if the God of Israel was able so clearly and

Figure 1.4 The Ten Commandments in Hebrew.[4]

convincingly to topple the deities of Egypt and their power in both the natural and supernatural realms, what hope could there be for any other mere national interest or powers? But if Yahweh now suddenly leaves the Israelites to die in the wilderness, the nations around would see that this god was no more than a flash-bang, a one-hit-wonder, a dog with more bark than bite. Moses

---

4   Copyright in the Public Domain.

uses Yahweh's own covenant to make the deity toe the line and get back into bed with Israel on this honeymoon night.

All of this is affirmed in various ways through the text of these chapters. For instance, prior to the construction of the Tabernacle Moses seeks to commune with Yahweh, not only on the mountain, but also in a small structure called the "Tent of Meeting," which is located slightly outside the camp (Exodus 33:7–11). Once the Tabernacle is built, however, this designation of the "Tent of Meeting" is transferred to that newer edifice (Exodus 39:32–40:38). Furthermore, the term used to describe the grander "Tent of Meeting" is *mishkan*, which means place of dwelling. The same root is also found in the Hebrew term *shakhen*, which means neighbor (so the significance of Yahweh moving into the neighborhood), and again in the *shekina* ("presence") cloud of glory that settled on the Tabernacle as its divine occupant moved in.

Similarly, Moses was to chisel out two tablets of stone (Exodus 34:1, 4) on which Yahweh would inscribe the summary of the covenant stipulations (Exodus 34:27), which were identified as the Ten Commandments (Exodus 34:28). Most of our representations of the Ten Commandments today picture them as too large to fit on one stone surface, so two tablets are needed to contain all the words. Furthermore, since the first four commandments seem to focus on our relationship with God, while the last six have the human social arena in purview, the Ten Commandments are typically arranged on the two stone tablets to reflect this division. This is not the intention of the ancient text, however. There were always two copies made of a suzerain-vassal covenant: one to remain with the subjected people in their homeland and the other to take up residence in the distant palace library of the king. What is unique about Israel's situation is that the two copies of the covenant were to be kept in the very same place—within the Ark of the Covenant. While we might miss the significance of this because of our lack of sensitivity to the ancient customs, the impact on the Israelites would be nothing short of astounding—the king was planning to live in the same place as his people! Both copies of the covenant could be kept in the same receptacle (which also functioned as the king's throne) because Israel's monarch was not a distant absentee landlord. As went the fortunes of Israel, so went the identity of Yahweh, for Yahweh committed the divine mission to the fate of this nation via the Covenant.

This is why the Tabernacle was more than a religious shrine for Israel. It was different than a mere ceremonial place for offerings. It was, in fact, the home of Yahweh at the center of the Israelite community. When the sun settled behind the horizon and the cooking fires were banked to save wood as the people traveled through the wilderness, one tent continued to have a light on all night. In the heart of the camp, the Lamp glowed in the fellowship hall of the Tabernacle; Yahweh kept vigil while the community slept. In the morning and evening, a meal could be taken with Yahweh (the sacrifices, burnt so that Yahweh might consume the divine portion by way of inhaling the smoke), and constantly, the feasting room was made ready for the King to meet with his subjects.

What happened at Mt. Sinai? God formally claimed Israel as partner in whatever the divine mission was for planet Earth. Israel, in turn, owned Yahweh as divine King and Suzerain. In effect, Yahweh and Israel were married, and their starter home was built at the center of the camp.

The Beginning of the Bible

Thus, the literature of the Bible began as the documents of a divinely initiated covenant-making ceremony, using the formulae of the common Hittite suzerain-vassal treaty to shape its words. Added to this, almost immediately, were the plans for the divine residence within the community, and an extended covenant prologue which rehearsed the very recent context in which Yahweh had battled the pharaoh of Egypt for the right to dance with Israel. So it is that in its literary origins, at least as portrayed in the text of the Bible itself, the purpose of scripture is to identify the parameters of the covenantal partnership between God and the people who share God's life and mission. It exudes ethical pronouncements—not because it is a book of morality, but because it functions as the shaper of a culture where Yahweh has chosen to move into the neighborhood and breathe through Israel an ethos of witness in a world that was no longer consciously aware of its Creator or of its own truest character.

Discussion Points

- Briefly retell the story of Moses's life, outlining its various major sections, and indicating how these uniquely prepared him for the leadership role he was to assume in the last third of his years.
- What is the political significance of the series of plagues in Exodus 7–12, and what are its implications for Israel's identity before and after leaving Egypt?
- Explain the covenant-making ceremony between God and Israel described in Exodus within the context of general covenant-making practices in the ancient Near East.
- Explain the contents of the Tabernacle and their meaning or significance for Israel. How is the Tabernacle a source of religious identity different from other shrines or holy sites?

Why is it significant that the Sinai Covenant summary was etched onto two stone tablets, and that these were both kept in the same location?

For Further Investigation

Kline, Meredith. (Grand Rapids: Eerdmans, 1972). *The Structure of Biblical Authority.*

2.

Origins and Worldview

How Genesis Answers Four Postmodern Questions

I f the Bible begins at Mt. Sinai, as the initial documents of the Covenant between Yahweh and Israel, what is the purpose of Genesis? In order to answer that question, we must first probe carefully the literary development of the text of the Bible's sequentially first book.

When reading Genesis in a single sitting, it is fairly obvious that there is a marked shift in the text between chapters 11 and 12. The first eleven chapters of Genesis are further removed from our day-to-day experiences, having more of a mythological character to them, somewhat similar to the cosmological origins stories found in many ancient societies. At the same time, although chapters 12–50 seem to enter our historical arena more fully, because of their attention to extended descriptions of the daily lives and interactions of people we might know, they still feel something like the ancestor hero stories that are told in nearly every community as a means to define social or ethnic identity.

Competing Worldviews

The "mythical" qualities of Genesis 1–11 ought not to be interpreted as synonymous with either "untrue" or "nonhistorical." Myths are stories that summarize worldviews in elided prose, giving snapshots of the value systems that drive a culture, or providing hooks on which to hang the unspoken—but ubiquitous—understanding of a social group's values and self-perception. This is why the stories told by way of myths may sometimes appear to be cartoonlike fairy tales, or at other times, they may be a selection of emblematic events from the actual unfolding of a community's early history. In fact, many times they appear to be a combination of both. Myths, by their very nature, are not scientific descriptions or journalistic documentaries, and should not be read in that manner. Myths serve, instead, to carry the fundamental values and worldview understandings of a culture in a manageable, memorable collection of tales.

It is in this way that Genesis functions as an extended historical prologue to the Sinai Covenant. The stories of Genesis answer a number of important questions that arise, simply because Israel has been shaken loose from four hundred years of enslaved slumber, and is now being reshaped as the marriage partner of God in a divine mission that has not yet been fully

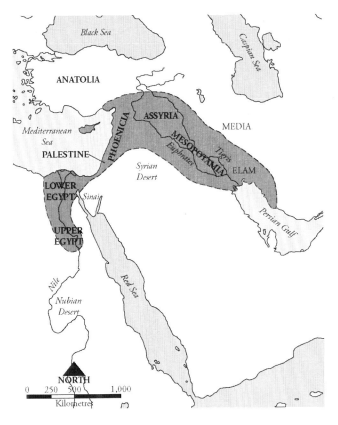

Figure 2.1 The Ancient Near East.[1]

---

1 Adapted from: Copyright © NormanEinstein (CC by 3.0) at http://commons.wikimedia.org/wiki/File:Fertile_Crescent_map.png

clarified. Genesis gives the context to the suzerain-vassal treaty formed in Exodus 20–24. It takes important moments from both Israel's distant and recent past, and uses these as the shepherding banks by which to direct the flow of the people's river of identity into their new and uncertain future.

Because there is no authorial self-disclosure within the pages of Genesis, we are left to speculate about its specific origins. An interesting and important clue emerges from the text itself when the Hebrew nomenclature for God is analyzed. Most often, especially beginning with the stories of Abram in Genesis 12, "Yahweh" (יהוה) is used to name the divinity. According to the book of Exodus, this name emerged in Israel through the deity's self-disclosure to Moses in the encounter between them at Mt. Horeb (Exodus 3). This would indicate that whoever wrote Genesis and whenever the writing happened, this book was created no earlier than the lifetime of Moses, and functions within the scope of the covenant-making events of Exodus. Thus, if one is to listen to the internal testimony of the literature of the Bible, Genesis must be understood to function as a companion volume to the covenant documents of Israel's national identity formation at Mt. Sinai. Therefore, Genesis must be read not as a volume preexisting in a disconnected primeval world, but rather as the interpretation of events leading up to the engagement of Yahweh and Israel at Sinai in the suzerain-vassal covenant established there. Genesis is the extended historical prologue of the Sinai Covenant.

Viewed this way, the message of Genesis is readily accessible. To begin with, the cosmo-logical origins myths of chapters 1–11 are apologetic devices that announce a very different worldview than that available among and within the cultures which surrounded Israel. The two dominant cosmogonies in the ancient Near East were established by the civilizations of Mesopotamia (filtered largely through Babylonian recitations) and Egypt. Cosmogonic myths describe the origins of the world as we know it, providing a paradigm by which to analyze and interpret contemporary events. Scattered across these cosmogonic myths are four methods of creation:

> **Fabricating**: Divine acts upon undifferentiated primordial matter that result in elements of the world as we know it.
>
> **Conflict Resolution**: Deities battling with one another or with the original powers of chaos, with the result that the winners get to shape natural elements out of the losers.
>
> **Sexual Generation**: Either the intragender replication of a god to form other gods or natural substances, or the sexual interaction between gods and goddesses, bringing into existence offspring, who give name or shape or power to visible entities.
>
> **Declaration**: Creation through the spoken word.

The Genesis account of creation contains a small nod toward the first of these, but expends the bulk of its energy using the last. The world as we know it, according to the perspective of Genesis, was produced by the divine creative word.

While this may raise eyebrows in a modern world shaped significantly by monotheistic views and theologies, such an understanding of the world was resoundingly different from and overtly challenging to the Egyptian origins myths. Distilled from the various records that are available to

Figure 2.2 Ancient Babylonian Origins diagram.[2]

us, the generalized creation story of ancient Egypt goes roughly like this. *Nun* was the chaos power pervading the primeval waters. *Atum* was the creative force which lived on *Benben*, a pyramidical hill rising out of the primeval waters. *Atum* split to form the elemental gods *Shu* (air) and *Tefnut* (moisture). *Tefnut* bore two children: *Geb* (god of earth) and *Nut* (goddess of the skies). These, in turn gave birth to lesser gods, who differentiated among themselves and came to rule various dimensions of the world as we now know it. Humanity was a final and unplanned outcome, with these newly produced weaklings useful only to do the work that the gods no longer wished to do, and to feed the gods by way of burning animal flesh (and thus transferring it from substance to smoke in order to make it accessible to the deity).

Similar, and yet uniquely nuanced, are the cosmogonies of ancient Mesopotamia. The name *Mesopotamia* literally means "between the waters." It denotes that region of the Near East encompassed by the combined watersheds of the Tigris and Euphrates rivers. Early civilizations here, enveloped by a somewhat different climatic environment than that found in Egypt, reflected this uniqueness in their origin myths. *Apsu* was the chaos power resident in the primeval waters. *Tiamat* was the bitter sea within the primeval waters upon which earth floated. *Lhamu* and *Lahamu* were gods of silt (at the edges of Earth) created from the interaction of the primeval waters and the bitter seas. The horizons, *Anshar* and *Kishar*, were separated from one another by the birth of their child, *Anu* (sky). *Anu* engendered *Ea-Nudimmud*, the god of earth and wisdom. All of these gods were filled with pent-up energy, and this caused them to fight constantly. Since they existed within the belly of *Tiamat*, *Apsu* got indigestion and made plans to destroy all his restless

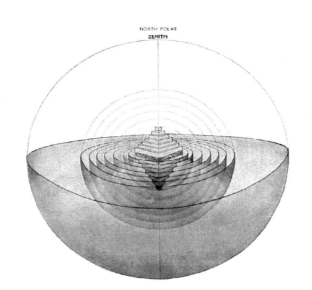

Figure 2.3 Ancient Babylonian Origins diagram.[3]

---

2 Copyright in the Public Domain.
3 Copyright in the Public Domain.

and noisy children (i.e., the rest of the gods). In order to survive, *Ea* cast a spell which put *Apsu* to sleep. Then *Ea* killed *Apsu*, but his remains formed new gods, all of whom were now in a bitter struggle with each other and with their older relatives. Among the gods, *Marduk* rose as champion, quelling the fights and resurrecting order. To celebrate his success, *Marduk* created Babylon, which thus became the center of the universe and the source of all human civilization. These late-on-the-scene beings were created from the spilled blood of the gods, and they were deliberately fashioned as slaves who would do the work that the gods no longer wished to do.

When placed alongside these other cosmogonic myths, the Genesis creation story is very spare and poetically balanced. In brief testimony, it declares that God existed before the world that is apprehended by our senses was brought into being. It also asserts that creation happened by way of divine speech rather than through the sexual interaction of deities, or as the animation of guts and gore left over and emerging out of their conflicts. Moreover, creation was an intentional act that took place by way of orderly progression:

> Day 1: Arenas for Light and Darkness
> Day 2: Arenas for Sky and Sea
> Day 3: Arenas for Earth's dominant surfaces
> Day 4: Inhabitants of Light and Darkness
> Day 5: Inhabitants of Sky and Sea
> Day 6: Inhabitants of Earth

In the balanced rhythm of poetic prose, the Genesis creation story shows how divine planning and purpose brought the world into being specifically as a home for humanity. These creatures are not the by-products of restless fighting among the gods. Nor are they a slave race produced in order to give the gods more leisure. In fact, according to the Genesis account, human beings are the only creatures made in the image of God, thus sharing the best of divine qualities.

It is obvious from the careful structuring of the Genesis creation account that it is neither a journalistic description of sequential events, nor the scientific report of an unfolding lab experiment. "Light" is the first "creation," cutting through and overturning the power of darkness and chaos that otherwise precluded meaningful existence. Yet the sources of light that actually make illumination happen in our world do not begin to exist until the fourth "day" of creation. What is going on? Why are things about creation expressed in this manner?

The answer seems to be a combination of contrast and organization. All other ancient stories of cosmological beginnings also start with chaos, but none of them ever fully emerges from it. Elements of random functionality may present themselves at times in or out from chaos, but behind and above and around such moments of meaningful structure, the cosmos remains a chaotic entity. In some civilizations, competing forces within chaos (such as *yin* and *yang*) may actually balance one another enough to provide temporary stability, and even creative energy. Yet they remain the restless tentacles of chaos, which pervades everything.

The Genesis cosmological myth sees the world very differently. Before existence and chaos, there is/was God. Existence itself is not the roiling of quasi-independent powers, but the expression of thoughtful divine intent. The manner in which things came into being had purpose and organizational structuring from the start.

A comparison of the values that underlie these various creation myths reveals the differences that are fundamental for shaping distinct worldviews:

Egypt and Mesopotamia	Genesis
Divinity exudes throughout the natural order	Divinity is separate from the natural order
There is an eternal dualism of good and evil	All is created good, and evil only enters later as a usurper
All things originate by devolution, with successive generations of creatures always crasser, baser, or less important than earlier ones	All things originate by intentional divine plan and are developed into species that occupy unique homes in the natural order
Humanity is an afterthought, a bother, and a slave race	Humanity is the reason for all the previous creative activity and alone shares divine character and purpose
The purpose for humanity's existence is toil	The purpose for humanity's existence is creativity, relationship, and rest

Two Creation Stories?

It is sometimes suggested that there are two creation stories (1:1–2:3 and 2:4–25) in Genesis, each emphasizing a unique mythological purpose, and perhaps even contradictory to one another. Such a view fails to take into account the deliberate literary structure of Genesis as a whole. Genesis 2:4–4:26 is clearly identified as the first of what will be ten "genealogical" sub-units of the book as a whole. Each of these is prefaced by the Hebrew word תולדות (toledoth), and contains the unfolding of a morally weighted story that will press ahead the larger arc of the Genesis narrative. Genesis 1:1–2:3 stands outside of and prior to the genealogical series, setting the stage and context for everything that follows. In the Gospel of John, mimicking the literary development of Genesis, 1:1–18 functions in the same manner.

If, as the literature itself requires, the creation stories of Genesis 1–2 are part of a lengthy historical prologue to the meeting of Yahweh and Israel at Mt. Sinai, these cosmogonic myths are not to be read as the end product of scientific or historical analysis. They are designed to place Israel in an entirely different worldview context than that which shaped their neighbors. Humanity's place in this natural realm is one of intimacy with God, rather than fear and slavery. The human race exists in harmony with nature, not as its bitter opponent or only a helpless minor element. Women and men together share creative responsibility with God over animals and plants.

Moreover, there is no hint of evil or sin in the creation stories themselves. In fact, the recurring refrain is that God saw the coming-into-being of each successive wave of creation and declared it to be good. There is no eternal dualism of opposing forces that in their conflict engendered the world as we know it. Nor is the creative energy of human life itself derived from inherent and coequal powers of good and evil which, in their chasing of one another, produce the changes necessary to drive the system. Instead, evil appears only after a fully developed created realm is complete, and then enters as a usurping power that seeks to draw away the reflected creativity of the human race into alliance with forces which deny the Creator's values and goals. Evil and sin are essentially linked to human perspectives that are in competition with the one declared true and genuine by the creation stories themselves.

In Genesis 3–11, following the devastating effects of evil that leach their way through the world, there appear to be two divine attempts to recover the pristine qualities of the original creation. First, after the initial humans step out of the worldview of the Creator and enter the perspectives of the tempter, the Creator displays graciousness in delaying the sentence of death upon them, and also by way of providing promises that this conflict need not end their existence. Instead, the human creatures are driven out of the Garden of Eden, in what seems to be a divine desire to pull them to their senses through the restlessness of homelessness. They become exiles, and their descendants, in order to compensate, build cities as an apparent attempt to regain civility. All these efforts fail, however, and the cancer of disobedience explodes in acts of killing and violence.

Then comes the second recovery effort. Just as his name seems to imply, Noah is heralded as one who will bring "comfort" from the afflictions of both sin and the curses of God that accompany it (Genesis 5:29). What takes place, however, is the famous flood story (Genesis 6–9), in which God designs a massive "do-over." The natural realm is destroyed, except for a floating biological bank called the ark. Noah and his family are spared the ravages of a massive flood intended to wipe out the terrestrial dimensions of the universe created in Genesis 1. All that survive are the few humans and the species restorers that have been kept safe in the big boat.

Three Kinds of Covenants

In ancient Israel's world, there were three dominant covenantal structures that shaped relationships locally and internationally: **Parity Agreements** were made between equal parties for mutual benefit (cf. Jacob and Laban in Genesis 31:36–54)

Royal Grants were the gifts of kings to those on whom they wished to show favor, and did not, by themselves, require a long-term reciprocal behavior (cf. God's gifts and promises in Genesis 9:8–17)

Suzerain-Vassal Covenants were social constructs shaping a reciprocal relationship between a ruler and people (cf. Exodus 20–24)

No Lingering Religious Racism

The "Curse on Canaan" and its corollary, "Blessing on Shem" (Genesis 9:24–27), do not allow for religious racism on the part of modern interpreters. The words of reaction to the responses of Noah's sons when confronted by his naked drunkenness only speak to the immediate context of Israel at Sinai. The next divine initiative would be to bring them to the "Promised Land" of Canaan, where they would displace the current occupants. This text provides theological grounds for the invasion.

Figure 2.4 The sign of the "bow."[4]

In God's instructions to Noah following the flood (Genesis 9:1–7), there are clear echoes of the divine mandate given to Adam and Eve in the Garden of Eden (Genesis 1:28–30). In other words, the tale of the flood is as much a story of re-creation as it is of judgment and destruction. A new element is added however, one which would be vital for Israel to understand as it stood before God at Mt. Sinai. After the words of blessing by which Noah and his family are given earth again as their home, there are words of self-reflection by the Creator (Genesis 9:8–17). For the first time, chronologically speaking, the idea of a "covenant" enters the biblical record. Interestingly here, though, it is shaped in the manner of a Babylonian royal grant rather than a Hittite suzerain-vassal treaty.

The Babylonian royal grant was a formula by which kings could record their acts of benefi-cence. Unlike the suzerain-vassal covenant, it did not bind the receiver of the gift into some form of specific responsive obedience. Instead, it assured the one who had received the gift that this was intended by the king, and could not be revoked by others. Sometimes, in fact, a maledictory oath accompanied the donation, assuring the recipient that the burden of following through on the gift remained the responsibility of the giver. The maledictory oath was a promise, made at the expense of personal well-being, that the king would guarantee the gift.

This is clearly expressed in the divine promise of protection and continuation of earth's natural order in Genesis 9:8–17. There will never again be a catastrophic destruction on the scale of the great flood just finished, nor will any other initiative be launched either by the Creator or by any other threatening power to attempt the annihilation of life on planet Earth.

A sign accompanied this assertion, but not as a reminder to humanity. Instead, God declared that the bow in the heavens will frequently appear as a recurring memory jogger *for the deity*. There is no word for "rainbow" in the Hebrew language; the term used in this divine speech is simply "bow," like the weapon a hunter brought into the forest after his prey or an archer stretched with arrows on the field of battle. Understood as it was initially intended, the "bow" thus takes on sinister significance. Whenever God viewed the bow, it was curved with tension, ready to release its projectile toward heaven. The implication would be clear to the ancient Israelites. God was taking a self-maledictory oath as part of this royal grant to spare creation; in it, the deity professed self-annihilation if no other solution was found to bring safety and everlasting continuity to the natural order, including the human race. This, in anticipation, heightened the significance of the role of the divine mediator, both in its Israelite context and beyond.

In the end, neither remedy intended to countermand the intrusion of evil into the world order, which had been created "good," had any lasting merit. On the one hand, Eden's exiles fabricated cities where, rather than finding a return to the garden, they compounded the menace and suffering of sin. Similarly with the other initiative: the re-creation attempted through Noah failed, as the stories immediately following show. Noah's son, Ham, ridiculed his drunken father,

---

resulting in a sharp curse placed upon his descendants (Genesis 9:20-25). Then the entire human community gathered itself into a monolithic empire that threatened to become self-sufficient (Genesis 11:1-9). Suddenly, evil resided not only in specific individuals who did bad things, but took on a corporate face. As God challenged this power play, the story turned in a new and decisive direction.

Three Story Cycles

If Genesis 1-11 is analogous to the cosmogonic myths that informed the societies among which young Israel was wrestling for a place, the rest of the book has a character not unlike that of the ancestor hero stories that also shaped other national cultures. Once again, comparing the tales of Abraham, Isaac, Jacob, and Joseph to the mythology of neighboring civilizations does not imply that these biblical tales are false or untrue. Rather, it is helpful to see the manner in which the literature functions in defining the identity of the emerging culture; ancestor hero stories provide a genre of comparison. In other words, the narratives of the patriarchs are not merely documentary history through which Israel could fashion a set of lively bedtime stories. Instead, the very heart of Israel's identity was shaped as the nation reflected on certain aspects of the lives of its forebears. For this reason, there is no complete history of Abraham, or entire biography of Isaac, or fully developed life of Jacob. Indeed, one would be hard pressed to formulate these from the limited amount of historical information given about each.

Instead, the purpose of these stories, particularly since they appear to emerge from the Sinai Covenant-making events of Exodus, is to provide a basis for Israel to understand who she is as a nation. This becomes more apparent when the essential focus of each major story cycle is probed.

Although later references to Israel's ancestral parentage would emerge as the standardized phrase "Abraham, Isaac, and Jacob," in reality, the second part of Genesis contains three major story cycles, in which Isaac is only a footnote to those of Abraham and Jacob, and Joseph is added as a key player in the larger drama. In rough overview, Genesis 12-50 may be outlined in this manner:

>Abraham Story Cycle (chapters 12-25)
>Jacob Story Cycle (chapters 26-36)
>Joseph Story Cycle (chapters 37-50)

The Unresolved Questions of Genesis 1-11

There are so many questions that emerge from reading these early chapters of Genesis. Unfortunately for us, the text never tells us:

- *Where evil originated*
- *Why the serpent was more crafty and could tempt Eve*
- *Why there were trees for temptation and for eternal life in the Garden of Eden*
- *Where the other people came from*
- *Why people then lived so long*
- *Who were the "Sons of God" (6:2) or the "Nephilim" (6:4)*
- *How all the animals could get on one boat*
- *What happened to the fish and sea creatures during the flood*
- *How extensive the flood was*

These issues remain open to general and scholarly discussion, but are not essential to the message of Genesis or the Bible as a whole

Each of these story cycles adds a unique element to Israel's self-identity when read backward from the covenant-making ceremony at Mt. Sinai. In this way they form, with Genesis 1–11, a deliberate, extended historical prologue to the suzerain-vassal treaty by staging that event against the prevailing worldviews of the day, and within a certain missional context, that illumines the purpose of Israel's existence—and the reason why Yahweh takes such interest in this tiny nation.

Melchizedek

Though mentioned only as a kind of offhand reference in Genesis 14:18, Melchizedek returns in growing significance twice in subsequent biblical literature. In Psalm 110, he will serve as the enigmatic greater role model for a royal son of David, who will transcend petty politics and truly serve God and God's people in righteousness, justice, and peace.

Then, in the New Testament book of Hebrews (Chapter 7), the myth of Melchizedek will mushroom into a paradigm for Jesus as true universal king, beyond merely a stint as a ruler in Jerusalem, like Israel's previous monarchs.

The Abraham Story Cycle

Abram is an Aramaean from the heart of Mesopotamia, whose father Terah begins a journey westward, which Abram continues upon his father's death. Whatever Terah's reasons might have been for moving from the old family village—restlessness, treasure-seeking, displacement, wanderlust—Genesis 12 informs us that Abram's continuation of the trek was motivated by a divine call to seek a land which would become his by providential appointment. This is the first of four similar divine declarations that occur in quick succession in chapters 12, 13, 15, and 17. Such repetition cues us to the importance of these theophanies, but it ought to also cause us to look more closely at the forms in which the promises to Abram are made.

In brief, Abram's first three encounters with God are shaped literarily as royal grants. Only in Genesis 17 does the language of the dialogue change, and elements are added to give it the flavor of a suzerain-vassal covenant. This is very significant. When Abram receives royal grant promises of land or a son, he seems to treat these divine offerings with a mixture of indifference and skepticism. He immediately leaves the land of promise in Genesis 12, and connives with his wife, Sarai, and her handmaid, Hagar, to obtain an heir in Genesis 16. Even in the stories of Genesis 13–14, where Abram sticks with the land and fights others to regain his nephew Lot from them after local skirmishes and kidnappings, Abram turns his thankfulness toward a local expression of religious devotion through the mystical figure of Melchizedek (Genesis 14:18–20). Only when God changes the language of covenant discourse, bringing *Abram* into the partnership of a suzerain-vassal bond, does *Abraham* enter fidelity and commitment to this new world, new purpose, and new journey.

Genesis 12—Royal Grant: Land	*Abram's Response*: Leave the Land
Genesis 13—Royal Grant: Land	*Abram's Response*: Fight over the Land
Genesis 15—Royal Grant: Son	*Abram's Response*: Connive to get Ishmael as Son
Genesis 17—Suzerain-Vassal: Land, Son; Renaming, Circumcision	*Abraham's Response*: Faith and Trust (cf. chapter 22)

For Israel, standing at Mt. Sinai in the context of a suzerain-vassal covenant-making ceremony, the implications would be striking. First of all, the nation would see itself as the unique and miraculously born child fulfilling a divine promise. Israel could not exist were it not for God's unusual efforts at getting Abram to make Sarai pregnant in a way that was humanly impossible. Second, the people were the descendants of a man on a divine pilgrimage. Not only was Abram en route to a land of promise, but he was also the instrument of God for the blessing of all the nations of the earth. In other words, Israel was born with a mandate, and it was globally encompassing. Third, while these tribes had recently emerged from Egypt as a despised social underclass of disenfranchised slaves, they were actually landowners. Canaan was theirs for the taking because they already owned it! They would not enter the land by stealth, but through the front door; they would claim the land, not by surreptitious means or mere battlefield bloodshed, but as rightful owners going home. This would greatly affect their common psyche: They were the long-lost heirs of a kingdom, returning to claim their royal privilege and possessions. Fourth, there was a selection in the process of creating their identity. They were children of Abraham, but so were a number of area tribes and nations descending from Ishmael. What made them special was the uniqueness of their lineage through Isaac, the miraculously born child of Abram and Sarai's old age. Israel had international kinship relations, but she also retained a unique identity fostered by the divine distinctions between branches of the family. Fifth, in the progression of the dialogue between Yahweh and Abram, there was a call to participation in the mission of God. As the story of Abram unfolded, it was clear that his commitment to God's plans was minimal at best until the change from royal grants (Genesis 12, 13, 15) to the suzerain-vassal covenant of chapter 17. Each time Abram was given a gift, he seemingly threw it away, tried to take it by force, or manipulated his circumstances so that he controlled his destiny; only when God took formal ownership of both Abram and the situation through the suzerain-vassal covenant of Genesis 17 was there a marked change in Abram's participation in the divine initiative. The renaming of Abram and Sarai to Abraham and Sarah was only partly significant for the meaning of the names; mostly, they were a deliberate and public declaration that God owned them. To name meant to have power over, just as was the case when a divine word created the elements of the universe in Genesis 1, and when Adam named the animals in Genesis 2. Furthermore, in the call to circumcise all the males of the family, God transformed a widely used social rite-of-passage symbol into a visible mark of belonging now no longer tied to personal achievements like battlefield wins or hunting success, but merely to the gracious goodness of God, and participation in the divine mission.

Abraham and His Sons

Ishmael ("God is hearing")
Born to a slave concubine
Loved by Abraham
Not chosen to carry the direct Covenant blessing
Father of many Near Eastern tribes and peoples

Isaac ("Laughter")
Born to a chosen and free wife
Loved by Abraham
Chosen to carry the direct Covenant blessing and responsibility
Father of Esau and Jacob; the latter became "Israel"

Abraham and the Sacrifice of Isaac (Genesis 22)

This incident is identified as a test of Abraham's faith. In light of his response to earlier royal grant promises (12—leaves the land; 13—tries to take the land by force; 15—connives to get a son), Abraham is now called to declare his loyalty to the God who has ratified a suzerain-vassal covenant with him (Genesis 17). While the test may seem overly demanding (kill your only son, the one given miraculously and the heir to your identity and promises), there are mitigating factors that help us understand it better. First, it was not out of the ordinary for people at that time to believe that deities required human sacrifice. The unusual twist in this story is that Yahweh, by stopping the bloodshed of Isaac, chooses deliberately to distance himself from these other deities, and shows that he does not delight in human sacrifice. Second, Yahweh provides an alternative offering, a ram divinely placed on the scene. Third, the place is named "Moriah," which can ambiguously mean either "Yahweh sees" or "Yahweh will be seen," both of which are correct (Yahweh sees the faith of Abraham; Yahweh is more clearly seen by Abraham), and thus illuminates the idea presented in the text that, "Yahweh provides" the sacrifice. Fourth, this idea is further confirmed by later references to the location of the site. In 2 Chronicles 3:1, this mountain is specified as the future location of Solomon's Temple. Such a designation would tie the animal sacrifice to the Temple rituals of a later century. It would also put the events of Genesis 22 on the very spot where Jesus would be crucified some twenty centuries hence, in another intense Father/Son engagement.

But what was that divine mission? Only when Israel heard the rest of the Covenant prologue, and then followed Moses to the Promised Land, would it become clear. Still, in recalling the tale of father Abraham in this manner, Genesis places before Israel at Sinai a very important element of its profound identity: We came into this world miraculously as a result of a divine initiative to bless all the nations of the earth; therefore, we are a unique people with the powerful backing of the Creator, and participating in a mission that is still in progress.

The Jacob Story Cycle

Only a few details of Isaac's life are told on the pages of Genesis, and they occur in the transitional paragraphs from the Abraham story cycle (Genesis 12-25) to the Jacob story cycle (Genesis 26-37). Isaac is to have a wife from within Terah's larger family back in the old country, and this is accomplished through clear divine intervention and leading (chapter 24). To Isaac and Rebecca are born twins who are opposites in character, and always in competition with one another (chapter 25). Rather than emerging with an identity of his own, Isaac seems doomed to repeat his father's mistakes (chapter 26).

After those few notes, Jacob takes center stage. He is a conniver from birth (Genesis 25:21-34); favored by his mother (Genesis 25:28; 27:1-28:9); cheats his family (father Isaac—27:1-39; brother Esau—25:29-34, 27:1-39; uncle Laban—30:25-43; daughter Dinah—34:1-31); works for his uncle Laban to earn wives Leah and Rachel (Genesis 29:15-30) and cattle (Genesis 30:25-43); is cheated by his uncle (Genesis 29:25-27); afraid of his brother (Genesis 32:3-21); a cowardly wrestler with God (Genesis 32:22-32); and finally receives the covenant blessing and mandate (Genesis 35:1-15).

While all of these stories are fascinating in themselves, there are two significant themes that emerge as dominant. First, in the character of Jacob, the nation of Israel will always find herself reflected. After all, it is Jacob who bequeaths his special Covenant name, "Israel," to the community formed by his descendants. Hearing about Jacob and his exploits would be like reading a secret diary mapping Israel's psychological profile. Even before leaving Egypt, the people were wrangling with Moses about burdens and responsibilities, seeking ways to shift workloads and blames elsewhere. Once the wilderness trek began, a variety of conniving subterfuges showed up, including complaints about who really had a right to lead. The spirit of Jacob remains with his namesakes.

Second, the meaning of the name "Israel" and the circumstances surrounding it become a defining moment in Israel's theology. Rarely does the text of Genesis crack open to reveal an origin outside of its narrative timeline, but as the tale of Jacob's nightlong wrestling match concludes, there is indeed a note that identifies the organized nation of Israel as the audience reviewing these matters (Genesis 32:32). The story itself is more sordid than it appears at first glance. Jacob and his amassed company are heading back home to Canaan. Jacob hopes that his brother, Esau, has miraculously had a bout of amnesia and is excited to welcome him, with no dark thoughts about Jacob's nasty subterfuge a few decades earlier. But Esau has a good memory, and the report quickly arrives that the maligned brother is racing toward Jacob's retinue at the center of an aggressive army seeking revenge.

Always the manipulator, Jacob strategizes ways to save his skin. First he splits the caravan in two, hoping Esau will target the wrong camp. Then, large gifts are sent ahead in the expectation that Esau will be slowed by the herds offered, and his men distracted by the feasts of fresh roasted meat they take. Perhaps a little drunkenness might accompany the barbecue rituals, and because of these subterfuges, Jacob's group will be able to slip past in the night.

But Jacob knows the depth of his guilt, and his manic attempts at self-preservation continue. He sends his wives and children and remaining possessions across the Jabok River while he remains behind. This is a sinister and cowardly move, for it exposes Jacob's family to the possible onslaught of Esau's army, without the moderate natural moat of the river to make their position more defensible. Meantime, Jacob himself would be sitting in the protection of the rearward hills, and will have the advantage of hearing the screams of his children and wives while they are slaughtered as a warning order to escape, even if they do not. Jacob is always the conniver, and a master of self-preservation.

Yet it is here, in the quarters where he has taken such pains to make himself safe, that he becomes most vulnerable. "A man wrestled with him till daybreak" (Genesis 32:24). We know even less about this figure than the little that Jacob seems to know. Nevertheless, both he and we are to infer that this was a divine engagement, and that God would not allow Jacob's hiding to keep him aloof from the court of heaven or a confrontation with himself and the tests of righteousness. At the same time, there is a graciousness in the story which reminds us that the divine messenger does not overpower or overwhelm Jacob, but continues to grapple with him, and even provides a blessing he does not deserve. This, then, is the meaning of "Israel"—one who wrestles with God.

Looking back at Jacob, Israel at Mt. Sinai would see herself. She carries the conniving DNA of her forebear in her social makeup. But here at Mt. Sinai, she also carries his divinely appointed name. In the suzerain-vassal covenant Yahweh formulated with her, the wrestling continues. Yahweh and Israel are bound in an embrace that would change them both.

The Joseph Story Cycle

Although Abraham hears a disembodied voice, and Jacob has a vision of heaven one night at Bethel, it is Joseph whose Genesis record is entirely shaped by dreams. He enters the narrative as a self-absorbed, privileged son, who foolishly antagonizes his family by reporting nighttime revelations that he is the most important among them, destined to become their lord and master (Genesis 37:2–11). His arrogance precipitates a plot among his siblings to get rid of him (Genesis 37:12–35), and this brings him to Egypt as a slave (Genesis 37:36; 38:1–6). Now the dreaming takes center stage again as Joseph is unjustly thrown in prison (Genesis 39:7–23), where he meets two men from the pharaoh's court who are awaiting adjudication on treason charges (Genesis 40:1–4). They each have dreams (Genesis 40:5–8), which Joseph is able to interpret (Genesis 40:9–19) in a way entirely consistent with the events that follow (Genesis 40:20–22).

Joseph's unique skills come to the attention of the pharaoh two years later, when the ruler's nighttime reveries plague him like a nightmare, and Joseph is brought in to make sense of it all (Genesis 40:23–41:36). This earns Joseph a spot as co-regent of Egypt (Genesis 41:37–57), and it is from this position that he becomes savior of his family during the ensuing famine (Genesis 42–46). Joseph's tale ends with his sons, Manasseh and Ephraim, gaining equal status with Jacob's other sons in the inheritance distributions (Genesis 48–49) and Joseph burying his father with honors in Canaan (Genesis 50:1–14), while keeping alive the dream of having the whole family return there one day when the current crisis has passed (Genesis 50:15–26).

In its focus on dreams, the Joseph story cycle that concludes Genesis deals with two issues. First, it answers the question of how this nation of Israel, springing from such illustrious stock, become an enslaved people in land not their own. Second, it creates a vision for the way in which the future is brighter than the past: Along with their forebear, Joseph, they need only take hold of the dream of God for them.

The Meta-Narrative of Genesis

When viewed through its obvious literary development, the book of Genesis is reasonably perceived as an extended historical prologue to the Sinai Covenant. It provides the information necessary for Israel to understand why Yahweh is establishing this treaty with this particular people, and what will be the outcome of it. In its pages are described the divine explanations about the character of reality, including creation's original goodness and the devastating effects of sin. Genesis informs Israel of God's long-standing plan to reassert divine connections with all the races of humanity, and that this is now to be done through a particular community shaped by way of the Sinai suzerain-vassal covenant. Furthermore, Genesis describes Israel's unique, miraculous origins, and spells out something of her edgy character. Finally, it unfolds the more recent history that tells why Israel was in Egypt rather than in Canaan, where she belonged.

In effect, the literary design of Genesis, in its largest arcs, has this shape:

> 1–11 Origins Story Cycle
> > What is the nature of reality?
> > > It is divinely good, but thoroughly contaminated by evil.

12-25 Abraham Story Cycle
>   Who are we as a unique people?
>   We are miraculously born to be God's witness to the nations.

26-36 Jacob Story Cycle
>   What is our character as a people?
>   We are deceitful connivers who nevertheless wrestle with God, and God with us.

37-50 Joseph Story Cycle
>   How did we get to Egypt?
>   By dreaming our own dreams.
>   How did we get out of Egypt?
>   By dreaming the dreams of God.

Genesis, then, cannot be separated from Exodus, because it is first of all addressed to the nation of Israel standing at Mt. Sinai, gaining its new identity through the suzerain-vassal covenant being made there. Furthermore, Genesis is not an independent text of either mere ancestor stories or chronologies of creation and national origins. Because it is literature that illumines the Sinai Covenant, it only gives information relative to that event. Chapters 1-2 are not so much about the documentation of time lines and details in the divine creative activity as they are a clearly articulated worldview against the current understandings of humanity, and the natural realm found in neighboring nations. The Sinai Covenant only makes sense if there is a sovereign creator who still has a stake in human society. Furthermore, although sin and evil are part of the pervasive common earthbound experience, these are not coequal or coeternal with God or good or the way things are supposed to be. Finally, in Israel's unique patrimony is a story that separates this nation from the rest of humanity, not in anthropological superiority, but only in mission and mandate.

The four worldview questions addressed on the pages of Genesis linger throughout history as critical issues of human life and society. As modernism swept the sacral world out of the heavens, postmodernism continues to look for meaning somewhere in the clouds of dust below. The four questions of Genesis serve as a link between the biblical record and current quests for meaning.

What is the nature of the universe in which we are living? Is it a random collection of happenstance occurrences that is, at best, the provenance of chaotic fate, and at worst weighted against us by vindictive unseen powers? Or is it the product of a loving and intelligent and personal deity, who is still seeking restoration and renewal with the human race after our centuries of bratty willfulness that have nearly annihilated civilization?

What is the unique purpose and meaning of the "Church" or the "people of God?" Does religion (or at least Christianity) make one deluded and irrelevant? Is there meaning that goes beyond repetitive ritual to be found in becoming part of a religious movement? Why is "mission" so important to the Church, and what is the truest nature of that mission? Are we still on the journey of Abraham? And what is the blessing we are holding out to the nations of this world?

Who are we in our core beings? Just because we were born and raised in the Church, does that mean we are more noble, more pious, more godly, more deserving, than others who did not have the same heritage? What does it mean to be a scrapping human being? Who are we fighting for, even in our "religious wars?" What happens to us when God comes down to wrestle with us?

Who is winning? Who is losing? And what does the wrestling itself mean for how we understand our nature and our place in life?

How did we get to Egypt? How did we get to Chicago, to New York, to Johannesburg, to Moscow, to Des Moines, to Mexico City, to Kyoto, to La Paz, to Padunkaville? What are the dreams we are chasing in our mad pursuit of self? In what prisons do we find ourselves the morning after we've seen our names in bright lights? Is there another dream to see, a vision to grasp, a world still waiting to be born that gives us a context in which to live and move and breathe and grow again? How are we going to get out of Egypt? When will we begin to dream the dream of God?

The Morally Weighted Genealogies of Genesis

This grand perspective of Genesis is confirmed by another literary overlay that subtly weaves together all of the smaller sections of Genesis. A recurring textual device in the book is the phrase, "These are the generations of ..." (2:4, 5:1, 6:9, 10:1, 11:10, 11:27, 25:12, 25:19, 36:1, 37:2). When surveying the book through this grid, several ideas emerge. First, the initial story of the creation (Genesis 1:1–2:3) does not begin with this phrase, and therefore stands apart from the rest of the sections that follow. Second, these subsequent ten sections, which each begin with the phrase, appear to be morally weighted, so that the dominant evaluation in each is either positive or negative, with respect to responsive obedience or disobedience to God. Third, there is a progression to the series that highlights the unique character and role of the group that will ultimately emerge as the nation of Israel.

The outcome is an unfolding explanation of human history which moves from original perfection (the creation story of Genesis 1:1–2:3), through the corrupting influence of individual expressions of sin and rebellion (the "generations" of "heaven and earth" and "Adam"), into a divine response that targets an individual for salvation (the "generation" of "Noah"); this is followed by a communal rebellion (the "generation" of the "Sons of Noah"), precipitating a divine counteraction, which produces a community designed for obedient witness (the "generations" of "Shem" and "Terah"). Along the way, this family experiences separations tracking the line of the missional community (the "generations" of "Isaac" and "Jacob") in distinction from others (the "generations" of "Ishmael" and "Esau").

Creation Plus Ten "Generations"

One literary device that shapes Genesis is the initial statement of the moral goodness of God's creative activity (1:1–2:3), followed by the explication of ten "generations," each of which is morally weighted as seeking original goodness (+) or not (-):

- 2:4-4:26 "Heaven and earth" (-)
- 5:1-6:8 "Adam" (-)
- 6:9-9:29 "Noah" (+)
- 10:1-11:9 "Sons of Noah" (-)
- 11:10-26 "Shem" (+)
- 11:27-25:11 "Terah" (+)
- 25:12-18 "Ishmael" (-)
- 25:19-35:29 "Isaac" (+)
- 36:1-37:1 "Esau" (-)
- 37:2-50:26 "Jacob" (+)

By the time Genesis ends, Israel at Mt. Sinai is placed into an interpreted natural order shaped by a particular worldview, has been informed about its unique calling and character, and understands the reason for Yahweh's recent political battle and victory over the pharaoh of Egypt in order to reclaim Israel as a redemptive community of witness. In response to the failed attempts at winning back humanity by way of the homeless restlessness of Adam and Eve and their early descendants just outside the Garden of Eden, and again through the re-creative efforts to restart the human race through Noah following the purging flood, Israel now can see its place as a nation with a peculiar identity that is intended to become a city on the hill, providing a divinely inspired lifestyle and religion—in contrast to those which are more or less the products of human invention gone bad.

When distilled into a diagram, Genesis may be portrayed in this manner:

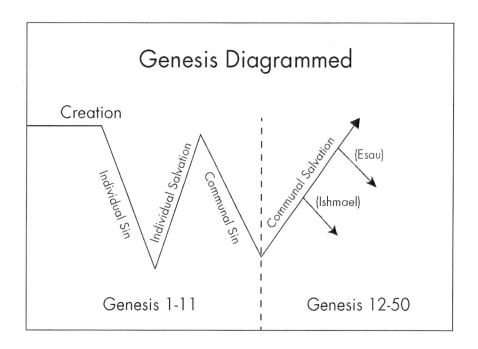

Figure 2.5 Genesis Diagrammed.

All of this initiates another question. What does it feel like to have God move into the neighborhood? What is life like when God is the chief resident at the heart of the community?

Answering these questions necessitates further Covenant documents. The books we know as Leviticus and Numbers probe those issues.

Discussion Points

- Review the dominant origins myths of ancient Egyptian and Mesopotamian societies, and in light of them, explain the theological meaning of the Genesis creation story for Israel.
- How does the flood story in Genesis 6–9 show evidence of divine grace, even as it relates a tale of judgment?
- Why is the use of the name "Yahweh" when identifying God in conversation with Abraham significant for linking the stories of Genesis with the Exodus records of divine covenant-making?
- Describe the various types of covenants in ancient Israel's world, and tell how these play a critical role in understanding the events of Abraham's life described in Genesis 12–17.
- How does the Genesis account of the renaming of Jacob as "Israel" link his life and character to the nation that would later bear his name? Outline the contents of Genesis in broad sections, and explain how these help us understand the Covenant between God and Israel formed at Mt. Sinai.

For Further Investigation

Brandon, S. G. F. (London: Hodder and Stoughton, 1963). *Creation Legends of the Ancient Near East.*

Thury, Eva M., and Margaret K. Divinney. (New York: Oxford, 2005). *Introduction to Mythology: Contemporary Approaches to Classical and World Myths.*

3.

Living with God

Testing the Elasticity of Marriage in Leviticus and Numbers

I f the Bible begins at Mt. Sinai as the initial documents of the Covenant between Yahweh and Israel, and Genesis functions as the extended historical prologue to that Covenant, what other literature might be necessary to flesh out covenant matters? Leviticus and Numbers provide essential addenda, explaining what life is like when God lives in the house next door.

Leviticus: Life with Yahweh

Although readers might quickly get bogged down in the seemingly endless list of commands and regulations found in Leviticus, if one steps back to view the book as a whole, there are clear groupings of materials. The collection might be outlined like this:

> *Instructions regarding offerings (1–7)*
> *Instructions for the priests in their ritual activities (8–10)*
> *Instructions regarding general hygiene in the community (11–15)*

Instructions about the Day of Atonement (16)
General instructions about clean and unclean living (17–25)
Curses and blessings (26)
Appendix: Instructions concerning dedications (27)

Leviticus in Summary 📖

Theme: "Be holy, because I, the Lord your God, am holy." (19:2)

1–7: Through Internal Substitutionary Cleansings

8–10: Through Symbolic External Cleansings

11–15: Through Active Community Hygiene

16: Through Annual Religious Renewal

17–25: Through Daily Cleansing Practices

26: Through Normative Religious Ethical Grounding

27: Through Dedication Rituals

While these instructions are understandable for the most part, and provide a general outlook on life in the Israelite camp, they remain somewhat arbitrary until viewed in light of what appears to be the primary rationale undergirding the entire social ethos. In Leviticus 19:1–2, Moses receives this command: "The Lord said to Moses, 'Speak to the entire assembly of Israel and say to them: "Be holy, because I, the Lord your God, am holy."'" Holiness is a lifestyle that is intrinsic to the Creator's character. So, naturally, when Yahweh moves into the camp of Israel as her Suzerain, some behavior modification is necessary among the vassals. In essence, the commands and regulations of Leviticus explore and explain the unique culture of Israel's modified society, now that she is under new authority, and her champion has chosen to identify closely with this people.

In this light, the various sections of Leviticus take on new and vibrant meaning. Rather than merely cataloguing certain rituals or practices (because these are the way things have always been done and are now simply being codified), there is a new and pervasive dynamism akin to something like getting a town ready for its recently elected mayor, or the inauguration of a new president in a superpower nation, or the affirmation of a new constitution and governing body after a great revolution. The lack of any significant historical narrative or context-setting materials at the outset of Leviticus indicates that these instructions are elaborations upon the big covenant declarations of Exodus 20–24, along with the raising of the Tabernacle at the center of the community (Exodus 25–40). Now the day-to-day operations are explained and nuanced. In fact, the instructions about offerings in chapters 1–7 form a perfect bridge between finishing the Tabernacle and getting on with life. The five types of sacrifices commanded and explained may be seen as vehicles for communicating inward "cleansing" or "holiness," both to Yahweh and also to others in the newly reshaped community. These offerings are visible prayers, and may, in fact, picture the idea of a mealtime with God. Notice that these offerings take place in the courtyard of the Tabernacle (similar in location to the place where informal meals were eaten in front of the Israelites' family tents) at the same time as the typical meals in Israelite custom were eaten.

The ritual purification of the priests, in their special role as caretakers of the house of Yahweh and the rites practiced in it, are explored next (chapters 8–10). Since the clan of Moses and

Aaron had been particularly vigilant for Yahweh's honor (Exodus 32:25-29) in the recent horrible golden calf incident (Exodus 32–34), these Levites become symbolic in their functionary cleansing rituals for the washing of the entire nation. By vicarious extension, the people together, through the Levites, practice hospitality at this tent at the center of the camp. This is particularly seen through the negative lesson given by the events surrounding the death of Aaron's sons, Nadab and Abihu (Leviticus 10:1–11); they apparently wrote their own rules for how the rituals were supposed to take place, and through their folly, the entire nation was warned to take note.

[1]The Levites thus take center stage within the community. They care for the House of Yahweh on behalf of the Israelites; the family of priests is contained within their numbers; they process the approach of the community as a whole to Yahweh through their administration of the sacrifices of Leviticus 1–7; and they are to oversee the details of the "cleansing/holiness" practices throughout the camp. For these reasons, the collection of regulations, in its later Greek (*Septuagint*) translation, is fittingly titled "Leviticus," or the activities pertaining to the Levites in the administration of Yahweh's holiness among his people.

This is how the concerns about mold, mildew, and foods, and blood flow and sores and diseases in chapters 11–15 should be viewed. They are more than simply good sanitation practices for forty years of camping. Instead, they reflect the fully orbed *shalom* that is part of the Creator's understanding of how things are to operate in the realm that was divinely designed. When Yahweh moves into the neighborhood, the place ought not to look, feel, or smell like a dump.

All of this is made explicit in chapter 16, with the yearly prescription of the Day of Atonement. This highly ritualized annual event is to be a national time of quick, thorough, and pervasive

Figure 3.1 A modern recreation of the Tabernacle[1]

A Closer Look at the Offerings of Leviticus 1–7

Burnt Offerings (1)

Animal offerings only, totally consumed (no meat for priests or offerers)

To provide regular renewal with God

Cereal/Grain Offerings (2)

Either raw grain or baked loaf, token part burned, the rest for priests/Levites

Indicates thankfulness

Peace Offerings (3)

Animal offerings only; only certain organs and fat burned

The rest appears to be available to eat as a symbol of relationships restored

Sin Offerings (4:1–5:13)

Animal offerings only; only certain organs and fat burned

Atones for wrong actions in social contexts

Guilt Offerings (5:14–6:7)

Animal offerings only; only certain organs and fat burned

Atones for wrong actions in specifically cultic religious contexts

---

1 Copyright in the Public Domain.

Day of Atonement Rituals

Priests are cleansed:

–Washings (external contamination removed).

–Bull sacrificed (internal contamination removed).

Two male goats selected:

–One sacrificed as sin offering for the nation.

–One declared the scapegoat, loaded symbolically with the sins of the nation and sent out of the camp, into the wilderness to die as alien and enemy

High priest enters the Holy of Holies with much incense, sprinkles blood on Yahweh's throne.

High priest bathes for a final time.

---

symbolic cleansing, which encompasses the ongoing and regular concerns for holiness/cleansing that have already been mentioned. First the priests go through a ceremonial purification that involves both washings (external cleansing) and the offering of a bull (internal cleansing). Then, two male goats are selected, with one becoming the sin offering for the people (symbolic national cleansing) and the other transformed into the scapegoat, which carries any residual pollution outside of the camp. Next, the high priest alone enters the Most Holy Place (the throne room of Yahweh), fills the room with a cloud of incense (hiding either Yahweh or the priest or both from the sins that have just been addressed through offering and displacement), and sprinkles blood from both offerings on the throne of Yahweh (the Mercy Seat of the Ark of the Covenant). Finally, the high priest bathes again, washing away even the splattering of sin or pollution that might have come back upon him in the business of the day. Through this ritual the nation is cleansed, and the "holiness" of Leviticus 19:1-2 reigns.

Rounding out these rituals and regulations, chapters 17–25 contain a miscellany of commands, all of which relate in some way to the general themes already found in Leviticus 1–15. What is particularly interesting about the "headings" or "captions" within the text itself are the notes at the beginnings of chapters 18 and 19, which clearly express the idea that Israel has moved from one suzerain to another, and thus must live by the beat of a different social drum. It is precisely here that the summary command to holiness or clean living, which thematically encapsulates the book as a whole, is found (19:1-2). Some of the dominant groupings of materials within the larger section include these:

- **The Sanctity of Blood** (17:1-16). Paralleling the opening of Leviticus, with its serialized explanations of the five primary offerings, this group of commands explains in greater detail the treatment of both animals and humans with reference to the unique role of blood, and how all of life must be respected.
- **Proper Social Intimacy** (18:1-30; 20:1-27). This chapter opens with a clear instruction about suzerainty and the obligations of the Israelites to their new King (18:1-5). They used to be owned by the pharaoh of Egypt, and had to live according to his culture and commands. But now they belong to Yahweh, and the practices of their new lives are shaped by a different social order—the holiness of heaven. Since the primary relational intimacy of humankind happens in the act of sexual intercourse, clear fences of propriety are drawn

in these commands, with the cumulative effect of safeguarding marriage, and holding all individuals in honor in such a way that sexual shame or hidden relationships might not mar honest daily interactions.

- **Sourcing the True Powers** (19:1–37). While most of these short commands may seem unrelated, there is a pervasive common theme among them. It has to do with social power, which was (and remains) a major factor in relational perceptions. How does one manipulate power and events toward one's own prestige or advantage? How does one tie into the elemental auras of the natural order so that one's craft and influence might rise? Countervailing such values brings a host of little prohibitions and preferred behaviors that seek power, not in other creatures or creations, but in the Creator alone. Divination, sorcery, manipulation, spiritism, and even gossip or various other forms of social hierarchy with the prejudices and oppressions created by them, are strictly forbidden.
- **The Leadership Challenge** (21:1–22:33). Taken as a whole, biblical religion identifies a unique shift in leadership responsibility with the general outpouring of the Holy Spirit of God at Pentecost (Acts 2). Old Testament social fidelity to Yahweh is often pinned on the moral character of specific point-persons in the community (e.g., Moses, Joshua, Aaron and the high priestly family, and later the kings). With the broad dissemination of God's Spirit in the New Testament age, leadership continues to remain a significant component giving shape to the ecclesiastical community, but is not as critical as is found in the Old Testament, where the Spirit of God is given primarily to leaders (note Numbers 11:16–30; 1 Samuel 10 and 15; Joel 2:28–29). For that reason, the general routines of priestly preparations and activities found in Leviticus 8–10 are here clarified through specific instructions and practices.
- **The Rhythm of Life** (23:1–26:2). Most significantly, perhaps, the very structure of daily life was changed by the calendar of covenant living. Replacing the Egyptian ten-day week of slave labor is the new creation-tied seven-day week aimed toward the Sabbath rest. Rising above this foundation is a superstructure of monthly and yearly festivals designed to remind Israel constantly of her identity, her

> ### Numbers in Summary 📖
>
> **1–10:—Signing on the Dotted Line:** Affirmation and inclusion of those who are part of this covenant relationship by way of clan registration
>
> Structure of community organization
>
> Special functions for certain families
>
> Provisions for unique situations
>
> **11–25—Covenant Breaking and Renewal**
>
> Complaints and rebellion among the people (11)
>
> Complaints and rebellion among the leaders (12)
>
> Failure to trust Yahweh for victory in Canaan (13–15)
>
> Clan uprising and aftermath (16–19)
>
> Encounters with other nations, including Midian (20–25)
>
> **26–36—Covenant Reaffirmation** (including a summary of the covenant calendar) **and a final push toward Canaan**

history of redemption, and her ongoing relationship with Yahweh. Time itself reflects God's marriage to Israel.

One of the most striking things about the book of Leviticus is chapter 26, which is essentially the "curses and blessings" section of a typical suzerain-vassal covenant. Located as it is at the conclusion of the various stipulations found in the book, this standardized formula draws the instructions of Leviticus back into the formal covenant documents begun in Exodus 20. The direct implication of 26:46 is that Leviticus 1–25 is another set of stipulations that are essential to the Sinai Covenant. Furthermore, as in Exodus 23:20–33, the usual order of "curses and blessings" is reversed, hinting at the gracious disposition of the Suzerain who is establishing this covenant relationship. In fact, contrary to the typical absolutes of other "curses and blessings" lists, the Leviticus version ends with notes on how the people may regain their covenant status and blessings, even if they have broken its stipulations (Leviticus 26:40–45). Provisions are made for failure, repentance, and covenant renewal.

Hebrew Calender			
Name	Number	Length	Gregorian Equivalent
Nissan	1	30	March-April
Iyar	2	29	April-May
Sivan	3	30	May-June
Tammuz	4	29	June-July
Av	5	30	July-August
Elul	6	29	August-September
Tishri	7	30	September-October
Cheshvan	8	29 or 30	October-November
Kislev	9	29 or 30	November-December
Tevet	10	29	December-January
Shevat	11	30	January-February
Adar	12	30	February-March
Adar II (leap years)	13 (leap years)	29	February-March

Figure 3.2 The Hebrew Year Calendar.

The final chapter of Leviticus (27), as it has been passed down for many centuries, is a kind of liturgical appendix, giving instructions about how some of the ritual practices hinted at in the earlier commands and stipulations are actually to take place. There are also a few specific codes of operation or behavior which seem to have been added on after the initial collections were written down.

Numbers: In and Out and In Again

While Leviticus describes the mood, climate, and atmosphere in the community where Yahweh has taken up residence, Numbers functions more like the outtakes of marriage counseling. First come lists of family trees and social responsibilities (chapters 1–10), which prepare the nation for travels toward their final destination (Numbers 10:11–36). Then there is a series of specific tests of covenant loyalty (chapters 11–25), many of which deeply trouble the community and its divine partner. The final section (chapters 26–36) exudes the feel of an anniversary celebration for a couple that has weathered a lot of storms. Vows are renewed (hence the list of those who are indeed participants in the Covenant, like the identification of extended family sitting for a picture), the parameters of married life are spelled out (so the reiteration of the calendar in chapters 28–29), and progress in the lives of the partners is noted (e.g., the summary of the journey in chapter 33).

The calendar of daily, weekly, monthly, and yearly markers was not for Israel so much a schedule of holidays that broke up the work seasons into manageable pieces. Rather, it was the rhythm of married life with Yahweh. It was the way in which the covenant relationship was acknowledged daily and weekly, and then encouraged the deep

---

The Covenant Challenges in Numbers

As soon as the Sinai Covenant has been declared and instituted, a series of challenges to its structures and authority takes place:

- General complaining is punished by divine fire (11:1–3)
- Lack of meat is answered by quail gluttony (11:4–34)
- Moses's leadership is challenged by his siblings (12:1–15)
- The wisdom of Yahweh in choosing Canaan as Israel's homeland is denied (13:1–14:45)
- A Sabbath-breaker is condemned (15:32–36)
- Moses's leadership is challenged by others from his tribe (16:1–40)
- Moses's and Aaron's leadership is challenged by the rest of the nation (16:41–17:13)
- Lack of water is answered by a gushing rock (20:1–13)
- General grumbling is punished by venomous snakes (21:4–9)
- The Amorites challenge Yahweh's authority and are defeated (21:21–35)
- The Moabites challenge Israel's identity and are defeated (22:1–25:18)

Each challenge is answered with Yahweh proving himself to be both Israel's true sovereign and the world's true Creator God. Furthermore, as Yahweh declares in Leviticus 26:44–45: "I will not reject them or abhor them so as to destroy them completely, breaking my covenant with them. I am the Lord their God. But for their sake I will remember the covenant with their ancestors whom I brought out of Egypt in the sight of the nations to be their God. I am the Lord."

Hebrew Calender

Cycle	Name	Meaning	Date	Note
Day	Evening & Morning Offerings	Connect with God		
Week	Shabbat Rest	Purpose of Life		
Month	New Moon Offerings	Refresh Relationship with God	First of each month	Trumpets; Solemn Assembly
Year	Passover	Deliverance/ Identity	14 Nisan (Spring)	Pilgrim Feast
Year	Unleavened Bread	Extension of Passover	Immediately following Passover	
Year	Weeks / Harvest / Firstfruits	Provision	6 Siwan (Early Summer)	Pilgrim Feast
Year	Rosh Hashanah (New Year)	Shabbat Rest	1 Tishri (Late Summer)	
Year	Day of Atonement	Renewal	10 Tishri (Early Fall)	
Year	Tabernacles / Booths	Harvest Celebration	15-22 Tishri (Fall)	Pilgrim Feast
Life	Sabbatical Year	Rest, Renewal	7th Year	
Life	Year of Jubilee	Restoration, Liberty	50th Year	

Figure 3.3 The Hebrew Festival Calendar.

permeation of the relationship as a kind of living testimony through the multiple anniversary remembrances throughout the year.

It is important to remember at this point that the authority granted these writings by Israel had little to do with modern theological discussions about "inerrancy," "infallibility," or "inspiration." These documents held significance in the community because of the Sinai Covenant and its implications for the life of the nation. An analogy to life in the United States might be something like this: Which is more important—the Constitution or the Declaration of Independence? A reasonable answer is that neither is more important, but that both presuppose the other. There cannot be a unique national community unless it has defined itself in contradistinction from other powers and civilizations (i.e., the Declaration of Independence), but that separation from other cultural groups carries no weight unless it is translated into the common practices of peoplehood (i.e., the Constitution). The authority in each document is not based upon exact and accurate grammar and punctuation and historical recall, although each of these things comes into scrutiny as scholarship attempts to ferret out nuances and hidden assumptions. Instead, the staying power of the documents is premised on their ability to reflect the initial actions that created the unique social, political, and cultural identity of the people.

In this way, the authority of the documents that become "scripture" for Israel (and then are transferred into the Christian Church) is rooted in the assumption that the suzerain-vassal covenant between Yahweh and Israel is a true historical reality. Remove this premise, and the literature of the Hebrew Bible becomes merely a fairly-tale wish at best, devised by later generations to support a particular cultural ethos, or at worst, the insidious propaganda of one or more of ancient Israel's kings or religious parties projecting their recent emergence into a more distant past for validation.

If, indeed, the written documents we now call Exodus, Genesis, Leviticus, and Numbers began as the actual stipulations of a clearly intended, divinely initiated suzerain-vassal covenant articulated through Moses at Mt. Sinai, the piecemeal and collected character of the literature we now have in the Pentateuch makes a great deal of sense. After the national encounter with Yahweh that produced the Exodus, a Declaration of Independence (from Egypt) and Dependence (upon Yahweh) was needed (hence the summary statement now known as the Ten Commandments). Then a more rigorously developed Constitution, based upon the divinely initiated escape from Egypt and its implications for new national identity, was necessary (so the tightly worked out suzerain-vassal covenant of Exodus 20–24). Finally, as this critical relationship and the implications of life in the wilderness and its growing goals of resettlement took shape, documents like the Bill of Rights and other amendments, along with further historical reflections and laws interpreting the Constitution for specific situations, would be crafted.

All of these, however, derive their authority not from the careful wording of the documents themselves, but from the redemptive event that first created the nation, and the all-enveloping "marriage" relationship which ensued when Yahweh joined the divine mission of reclamation and blessing (as elicited in the stories of Abraham) to the national life of Israel. This perspective continues to underlie the purpose and significance of the other biblical books that follow.

Discussion Points

- Explain why Leviticus 19:1–2 serves as a kind of "theme verse" for Leviticus, and explain in overview the contents of the book in light of that divine declaration.
- Identify at least four different types of sacrifices as outlined in Leviticus 1–7. Tell what kind of specific devotional acts they are meant to express.
- Describe some of the key social behaviors regulated in Leviticus 17–25, and suggest reasons for Yahweh's instructions about Israel's ethical standards.
- Outline and describe the rhythm of feast days and festivals that shaped the calendar of Israel's existence, explaining what aspects of the relationship between the nation and her God each explores or expresses.
- Briefly outline the contents of Numbers and explain their primary significance for Israel in light of the Sinai Covenant.

- Identify half a dozen specific challenges to the structures and authority of the Sinai Covenant found in Leviticus 11–25. Indicate how Yahweh responded in each instance, and explain the general principles at stake.

For Further Investigation

Gorman, Frank H. (Grand Rapids: Eerdmans, 1997). *Divine presence and community: A commentary on the Book of Leviticus.*

Wenham, Gordon. (Grand Rapids: Eerdmans, 1979). *The Book of Leviticus.*

4.

Extending the Franchise

Deuteronomy—the Gospel According to Moses

If the Bible begins as the covenant documents confirming the suzerain-vassal treaty between Yahweh and Israel, Exodus exists as the "what" of the covenant parameters, Genesis as the "why" of the covenant background, Leviticus as the "how" of the covenant lifestyle, and Numbers as the "who" of belonging in the covenant, particularly through some difficult efforts at stretching, breaking, and renewal. Deuteronomy, which rounds out the "Pentateuch," "Books of Moses," or "Torah" of the Hebrew Bible, functions within this covenant literature orbit as well, but addresses the issue of "how long?" How long will the Sinai covenant remain in effect? Was it active only for the generation that stood at the mountain? Or does it have continuing impact on the generations that follow from its first engagement? The answer that Moses gives is that Yahweh intends the Sinai Covenant to be the shaping tool in what he supposes to be a never-ending marriage relationship.

Where Does the Name "Deuteronomy" Come From?

In Deuteronomy 17:14–20, Moses anticipates Israel's distant, but looming, monarchy. At verse 18, he instructs future kings to make a copy of "this law" as a ready reference and guide to governing. When the Hebrew text of the Old Testament was translated into Greek (the *Septuagint*), the reference to this copy in Deuteronomy 17:18 became "second law" (*deuter onomos*), and since then, the book has been called *Deuteronomy*.

There are a number of things to consider when reading Deuteronomy. First, its literary "feel" is personal, passionate, and poignant. Deuteronomy is very personal because it is the last will and testament of Moses as he finds the third of his incredible careers (forty years in training to be a government official in Egypt, forty years of Bedouin family life in the Sinai wilderness, forty years as leader of this nation, and mediator between it and Yahweh) drawing to a close. It is passionate, since Moses wants to cram into a few short speeches the entire theology, worldview, mission, and lifestyle that has pressed itself upon Israel through the exodus and covenant encounter at Sinai. It is poignant because it emerges as a dying man's testimony delivered with deep meaning to the people he has come to love. Some have called Deuteronomy the "gospel" of Moses because it is filled with the tenderness and goodwill that is truly good news for Israel and the Christian Church, which finds its roots in the Sinai Covenant. According to the New Testament gospels, Jesus quoted Deuteronomy more than any other Hebrew Bible book, except for the Psalms. Particularly striking was Jesus' use of Deuteronomy in refuting the devil in his wilderness temptations.

The literary unfolding of Deuteronomy is similar to a genre sometimes identified as "Farewell Testament." Other biblical examples include Jacob's address to his family in Genesis 48–50; Joshua's final words to both the elders and the gathered nation of Israel in Joshua 23–24; Jesus' farewell discourse with his disciples, as recorded in John 13–17; Paul's brief parting address to the elders of the Ephesian church in Acts 20; and what appears to be the final letter of Paul to his young protégé, Timothy (2 Timothy). Each of these testimonials expresses the hopes and sentiments of a man facing imminent death, and compacts into a tight frame a great amount of summary teaching, exhortation, prayer, and visioning. What is unique about Deuteronomy is its additional layers of literary development that give evidence of careful crafting of the document into its final form.

There are, for instance, six distinct textual units that begin with the formulaic phrase "this is" or "these are" to reference the words or speeches of Moses, or a summary of the Covenant stipulations. These literary units are then arranged in the form of three major

Distinct Textual Units in Deuteronomy

Each begins with a variation on the formula "this is/these are"

1:1–4:43

4:44–11:32

12:1–26:19

27:1–28:68

29:1–32:52

33:1–34:12

addresses by Moses, followed by a concluding appendix of the final events in Moses's life. Furthermore, when all of this organizational development is viewed as a whole, Deuteronomy appears to be shaped very much like the general outline of a typical suzerain-vassal covenant document. In other words, the literature of Deuteronomy functions on several levels at the same time: it is Moses's personal last will and testament to Israel; it is also a summation of the most important elements of the entire Sinai Covenant; and, at the same time, it is an actual Covenant renewal document that is now the possession of succeeding generations within Israelite society. As a Covenant document, Deuteronomy can be viewed in this way:

> Covenant Prologue (1–4)–Preamble plus
>   Historical Prologue
> Covenant in Summary (5–11)–Stipulations
> CoreCovenantStipulations(12–26)–Stipulations
> Covenant Curses and Blessings (27–28)–Curses
>   and Blessings
> Covenant Renewal (29–32)–Document Clause
> Epilogue–(33–34)

In Deuteronomy, the Sinai suzerain-vassal covenant is summarized and reiterated as a working document for future generations. This is particularly seen in the mandate Moses gives for a Covenant renewal ceremony at Shechem (Deuteronomy 27:11–26), to be fulfilled once the Israelites have crossed over the Jordan River into Canaan. The "Curses and Blessings" section of the suzerain-vassal Covenant are reiterated (Deuteronomy 27:15–26), drawing the book of Deuteronomy into the corpus of Covenant literature that will function as Israel's normative constitution.

While the bulk of Deuteronomy is a restatement and summary of materials otherwise scattered throughout Exodus and Leviticus, in particular, there are a number of minor elements that are newly considered. For instance, when Moses repeats the Ten Commandments in Deuteronomy 5:6–21 (cf. Exodus 20:1–17), the basis for the fourth

---

Speeches of Moses In Deuteronomy

Plus Concluding events

First Speech (1:1–4:43)
Second Speech (4:44–28:68; except for chapter 27)
Third Speech (29–30)
Concluding Events (31–34)

When Was Deuteronomy Written?

The internal testimony of Deuteronomy claims that it is composed of Moses's final speeches to Israel, given and written down shortly before the end of his life (around 1250 B.C.). But theological discussions sometimes suggest other occasions for its inception. First, because Moses appears to anticipate a number of aspects of Israelite life after settling in Canaan, some claim that Deuteronomy is a much later document reflecting on the times of the monarchy, and attempts to give them historical revelatory authorization by placing these ideas in the supposed speeches of Moses before he died (2 Kings 22 is often cited). Second, because of some literary nuances (particularly that of naming God either "El/Elohim" or "Yahweh") that seem distinctive in different sections of the Pentateuch, some divide these documents into at least four groupings, asserting that each was produced at a distinct stage in Israel's history by complementary or competing factions in the society:

J—"Yahwist" (Exodus and Covenant stories)
E—"Elohist" (Creation narratives and older tales woven into the literature of "J")

P—"Priestly" (Leviticus and other ceremonial codes developed by the priests, probably during the Exile)

D—"Deuteronomist" (Deuteronomy and later writings incorporated into the final editing of the Pentateuch, probably after the Exile).

While these discussions help us understand the character and function of Pentateuch writings, they do not prove Deuteronomy's origins to be anything other than what is asserted by the text itself: Moses's final instructions to Israel on the eve of her entrance into Canaan as the covenantally created people of Yahweh.

The Strange Fortunes of Mt. Gerizim

An interesting conflict would eventually emerge from the intersection of Moses's statements in Deuteronomy 12 and 27 and the political fortunes of central Canaan. In 722 B.C., the Assyrians conquered and displaced the leftover Israelites living in what would then be called "Samaria," or the hill country north of Jerusalem (2 Kings 17). Other similarly conquered peoples were resettled into this region, only to find that they were ravaged by lions. In superstitious desperation, they petitioned the king of Assyria to send them religious leaders from among the former inhabitants, assuming that these priests or holy men would be able to teach them how to worship the God they evidently were slighting, the deity who was obviously punishing them. The Israelite priests who returned to the land were well acquainted with the Pentateuch, but because of the rift between Israel and Judah following Solomon's reign, they did not believe that the Jerusalem Temple was legitimate. Instead, based upon Moses's instructions for the Israelites to shout

commandment is altered slightly. In the original Sinai version, Sabbath rest was predicated on the rhythm of the creative expressions of God, so that after six days of work, rest is given to reflect and renew. Here in Deuteronomy, Moses asserts that Sabbath rest is necessary because of the exodus from Egypt; as slaves there, the Israelites were nearly consumed by the Egyptian worldview that they were made for drudgery, but now Yahweh has reaffirmed the divine design for humans to enjoy life beyond mere toil.

Also, the foundational monotheistic testimony of the Hebrew religion is clearly articulated in Deuteronomy 6:4-5 in a manner never before expressed: "Hear, O Israel: The Lord our God, the Lord is one. Love the Lord your God with all your heart and with all your soul and with all your strength." This will become the bedrock confession of Israelite monotheism, and will be recited by Jesus (Matthew 22:37) as the foundation upon which all of the rest of the Covenant literature and exhortations are built.

Third, there is in Deuteronomy the anticipation of Israel's settled life in Canaan as now coming very close, in a way that did not emerge in earlier documents of the Pentateuch. The battles of the conquest are mentioned (Deuteronomy 7:1–11), along with the unique character of Israel's social environment, once the nation is established in the land (Deuteronomy 7:12–26; 11:1–32). A single cultic shrine is anticipated (Deuteronomy 12:1–7), along with the establishment of a monarchy (Deuteronomy 17:14–20) and an entire national judicial system supported by "Cities of Refuge" (Deuteronomy 19). Finally, the specific covenant renewal ceremony at Shechem is outlined and described (Deuteronomy 27).

If indeed, as Deuteronomy assumes, the history and divine initiatives of Genesis through Numbers are factual, Moses is certainly one of the greatest leaders ever to live. His personal life was an incredible story of rescue, training, and triple transformation. His unique role as the mediator between Israel and Yahweh, producing the foundational literature of this religiously charged community, made him pivotal for all civilizations, since the worldview perspective outlined in the Bible became the evangelistic mandate dominating the majority faith group in the human race yet today. Thus, the concluding sentences of Deuteronomy are no exaggeration:

> Since then, no prophet has risen in Israel like Moses, whom the Lord knew face to face, who did all those miraculous signs and wonders the Lord sent him to do in Egypt—to Pharaoh and to all his officials and to his whole land. For no one has ever shown the mighty power or performed the awesome deeds that Moses did in the sight of all Israel (Deuteronomy 34:10–12).

Although the rationale for Moses not being able himself to go into the Promised Land seems somewhat arbitrary and disproportionate (cf. Numbers 20:1–13; Deuteronomy 34:4), it was probably a very wise move to initiate the conquest of Canaan under the leadership of a fresh commander. Moses was 120 years old at his death, and certainly needed to be relieved of his responsibilities, with the nation's blessing and appreciation.

Where to from Here?

Deuteronomy forms the conclusion to the Pentateuch, and for good reason. While the book of Joshua is sometimes included as a sixth volume in a presumed "Hexateuch," things change, both for Israel and for the documents associated with the Sinai covenant following the first five books. For one thing, there is no new revelatory insight about the covenant in either Joshua or the rest of the documents of the Old Testament. These writings, whether historical, poetic, wisdom, or prophetic, presuppose the Sinai covenant, but do not provide new covenant stipulations. Mostly, they wrestle with

the blessings of the Sinai Covenant from Mt. Gerizim near Shechem, this mountain began to take on holy overtones. For that reason, when the Samaritans made plans to set up the single cultic shrine which Moses anticipates in Deuteronomy 12, they build it on Mt. Gerizim. This rival temple to that in Jerusalem would become an ongoing source of tension between the Samaritans and the Jews, as reflected in the conversations between Jesus and the woman at Sychar (the first century A.D. name for Shechem) in John 4.

The Fourth Commandment

Exodus 20:8–11—"Remember the Sabbath day by keeping it holy. Six days you shall labor and do all your work, but the seventh day is a Sabbath to the Lord your God. On it you shall not do any work, neither you, nor your son or daughter, nor your manservant or maidservant, nor your animals, nor the alien within your gates. For in six days the Lord made the heavens and the earth, the sea, and all that is in them, but he rested on the seventh day. Therefore the Lord blessed the Sabbath day and made it holy."

Deuteronomy 5:12–15—"Observe the Sabbath day by keeping it holy, as the Lord your God has commanded you. Six days you shall labor and do all your work, but the seventh day is a Sabbath to the Lord your God. On it you shall not do any work, neither you, nor your son or daughter, nor your manservant or maidservant, nor your ox, your donkey or any of your animals, nor the alien within your gates, so that your manservant and maidservant may rest, as you do. Remember that you were slaves in Egypt and that the Lord your God brought you out of there with a mighty hand and an outstretched arm. Therefore the Lord your God has commanded you to observe the Sabbath day."

Bible "Big Picture"

Covenant Making: God establishes a covenant relationship with a missional community by way of a redemptive act.

Old Testament: The Exodus and Sinai Covenant
  Genesis—Why?
  Exodus—What?
  Leviticus—How?
  Numbers—Who?
  Deuteronomy—How Long?
New Testament: The Person and Work of Jesus

Covenant Living: God guides the covenant relationship with the missional community by way of authorized spokespersons.

Old Testament: The Prophets, with Their Interpreted History and Sermons

New Testament: The Apostles, with Their Ecclesiastical History and Letters

Covenant Questions: God nurtures the covenant relationship with a missional community by way of spiritual wisdom and insight.

Old Testament: The Poetry and Wisdom Literature

New Testament: The Comparison of Covenants and the Apocalypse

the implications of what the Sinai covenant means for Israel's life in new and changing situations. Also, they frequently make use of the "Curses and Blessings" section of the Sinai covenant documents, in order to evaluate the moral fiber of the community as it excels or fails in its billing as Yahweh's missional face among the nations. In light of the change of biblical literature following Deuteronomy, it might be helpful to know in part, at this point, the large contours of the perspective used in this study. For reasons which will continue to emerge, the view being developed is that there are three sections of literature in the Old Testament, each with its unique origins, purpose, and source of authority. The first section, "Covenant Making," contains Genesis through Deuteronomy, and asserts that these documents are the direct product of the suzerain-vassal covenant God made with Israel at Mt. Sinai. In an attempt to regain recognition and moral influence on the nations of the ancient world, God chose a method that would be familiar to Israel, and which would enlist her support in creating a visible community of witness at the crossroads of the major civilizations of that day. The authority of the documents produced in this interaction was not found in their unique moral insights or their unusually brilliant revelations, nor even in the towering personality of Moses. Instead, the authority that gives these documents revelatory significance is the redemptive event by which God reached into human history and established the nation of Israel as the terrestrial residence of the Deity. Thus, the Pentateuch would always have primary authority among the scriptures of the Old Testament, while the others derived their authority from the events and instructions recorded in these documents.

Within this section of biblical literature, Exodus stands at the heart, beginning as the actual text of the Sinai suzerain-vassal covenant itself, and then growing with the reports of the battle of the superpowers that transferred Israel's loyalty from the pharaoh of Egypt to Yahweh, culminating in the instructions for Yahweh's home within the community. Genesis extends the historical prologue of the covenant backward to explain why this action was necessary on the part of the Creator, and how Israel's deep past sets the stage for its recent history. Leviticus is the elaboration of the Covenant stipulations, especially explaining how they impact the lifestyle of Israel, now that Yahweh has moved into the neighborhood. In Numbers, the elasticity of the Covenant is measured, first by identifying its human participants, and then by walking with the nation through a variety of trials where Yahweh's authority is questioned, and the Covenant is ultimately renewed. Finally, in Deuteronomy, the Sinai Covenant is given a fresh reading for succeeding generations and affirmed as the guiding authority for Israel's future existence.

The next section of biblical literature will be about "Covenant Living." It will explore the impact of the Sinai Covenant on the actions and lifestyle of the nation of Israel. The immediate source of authority in these writings will be a growing community of prophets or leaders who are uniquely in tune with Yahweh's designs and desires, and who are able to articulate these by referencing the covenant documents of the Pentateuch.

Finally, there will be a section of biblical literature ("Covenant Questions"), in which all of the worldview of the Sinai Covenant will be presupposed, as issues of practical meaning in life are explored. These writings will probe questions related to that worldview, suggesting spiritual wisdom for changing times.

Discussion Points

- How does Deuteronomy function as Moses's "Farewell Discourse?" What are other instances of similar literature, and how does Deuteronomy compare to them?
- What is the meaning of the name "Deuteronomy?" How does this fit as the title for that book of the Bible?
- What are some of the unique elements of teaching that Deuteronomy gives as it presses the Covenant documents and instructions of Exodus and Leviticus into a new shape for a new generation?
- How does Deuteronomy articulate monotheism in a manner that will become a foundational testimony for Judaism and Christianity?
- Outline the contents of Deuteronomy, and explain how these reinforce the Sinai Covenant, particularly as they shape the document on several literary levels.
- How might the cohesive relationship between the books of the Pentateuch or Torah be explained? What holds these books together? How are they dependent upon one another for themes, ideas, and worldviews?

For Further Investigation

Craigie, Peter C. (Grand Rapids: Eerdmans, 1976). *The Book of Deuteronomy.*

Covenant Living (1A)

The Creator guides the covenant relationship with a missional community by way of authorized spokespersons

5.

Why Is the "Holy Land" Holy?

Living on the Busiest Intersection in Town

Now the literature of the Bible changes dramatically. Instead of focusing primarily on what Yahweh has done and is doing to stake a missional claim in the ancient Near East, the vantage point shifts to terrestrial action. True, it is still Yahweh who serves as Israel's commander in chief, but the emphasis is refocused toward how the army itself is faring on the battlefield.

The book of Joshua is clearly all about the land of Canaan. The Israelites presume to own it, even though they have never lived there. Yahweh declares it to be their homeland, even though in order for this to become a reality, bloody battles will ensue, and current settled communities will have to be displaced or destroyed. The promises made to Abraham (Genesis 12, 13, 17), owned by Jacob (Genesis 28, 35, 50), and claimed by Joseph (Genesis 50) serve as the theological justification for taking by force what, from a human point of view, belongs to other people. This is the critical issue that must be faced when reading Joshua. Either Canaan, as a specific piece of territory, has a deeply religious significance, which is used by Yahweh and Israel in a certain way for ends that are meant to bless the surrounding nations, or it is a scandalous record of cruelty done by nasty people who wash their defiled consciences in a horrible pious testimony, "The Deity made me do

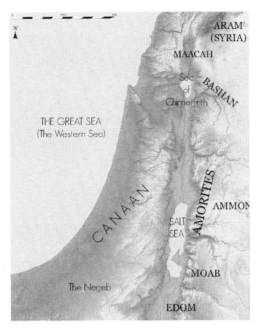

Figure 5.1 Topography of Canaan.[1]

it!" Only if the Pentateuch is indeed a revelation of God with a missional intent that is to be accomplished through the nation of Israel, does this sordid chapter in Israelite and human history make sense. Even facing this matter head on does not make the conquest of Canaan easily palatable. No serious student of the Bible ought to dance lightly through these pages and make facile judgments. Either Yahweh is engaged in a crucial galactic civil war battle to wrestle humanity back to its creational senses, and Israel is to play a part in that decisive conflict, or the religions of Judaism, Christianity and Islam are built upon a scandalous foundation of inflated self-important delusion. The book of Joshua forces us to face the desperation of biblical religion: Is this simply another moralistic ethic among the do-gooder philosophies of the nations, or is there a unique and all-encompassing polarizing choice engendered by this worldview that demands allegiance or condemnation?

At stake, in answering this dilemma, is an understanding of the unique location and purpose of a small piece of real estate. There are four major literary sections to the book of Joshua, and each is focused on "the Land":

Penetrating the Land (chapters 1–5)
Purging the Land (chapters 6–12)
Possessing the Land (chapters 13–21)
Promising the Land (chapters 22–24)

The identity of Israel will become inextricably connected to this land. It is ineradicably intertwined with Hebrew theology. It is essential to Israelite self-perception, so it is very important to ask why. Why this land, and not some other, better paradise? Why this piece of property, rather than an uninhabited region of northern Europe, or a tropical island in the South Pacific? What is so terribly important about this land, that it has become a constant source of theological embarrassment to generations of biblical scholars and the enemies of Judaism and Christianity?

Penetrating the Land (Joshua 1–5)

We need to see the land first through the eyes of Joshua and the participants in the stories found in the book named after him. Who was this man, bursting onto the scene with full command of Israel? The name his parents gave him was *Hoshea* (Numbers 13:8), which meant "Salvation." When Moses took him under his tutelage (Numbers 13:16), Moses began to call him

---

1   Copyright © Eric Gaba (CC by 3.0) at http://commons.wikimedia.org/wiki/File:Dead_Sea_terrain_location_map.jpg

Joshua, meaning "Yahweh is Salvation," and the name stuck. There are a number of references to Joshua throughout the Pentateuch that help define the character of this man. He was chosen by Moses to serve as the great leader's personal attendant (Exodus 33:11). This indicates that Joshua gave evidence of leadership gifts at an early age, and that he was likely part of a family already positionally recognized as dominant among the clans of Israel. When Moses ascended Mt. Sinai to receive the Covenant instructions, Joshua went along, at least part of the way (Exodus 24). At Rephidim, Joshua commanded the soldiers who were sent out to repel the Amalekites (Exodus 17:9), suggesting that he was already an acclaimed leader among the strategists of the nation. This is confirmed when Joshua is chosen as the appointed representative of Ephraim to serve with the other trusted persons, one gathered from each of the tribes, as a company of advance scouts, on Israel's first approach to Canaan (Numbers 13:8). Joshua's religious trust becomes obvious when he and Caleb are the only two among the twelve spies who speak confidently of Yahweh's ability to give the nation success in battle against seemingly stronger enemies (Numbers 14:30). On account of their pious optimism, these two are permitted to enter Canaan, while the rest of their generation dies away during the next forty years of wilderness wanderings. So, Joshua must have been older than virtually everyone else among the Israelites when he was commissioned by both Yahweh and Moses to succeed Moses as the leader of the people (Deuteronomy 31:14, 23).

The commissioning of Joshua, told briefly in Deuteronomy 31:23, is reiterated and expanded in Joshua 1 in a very unusual way. Yahweh addresses Joshua, confirming his leadership role and gifts (Joshua 1:1–9). Rather than responding directly to Yahweh, however, Joshua instead instructs the "officers" of the nation to call the people into readiness for the crossing of the Jordan and the beginning of the looming conquest (Joshua 1:10–15). Only after this chain of command has been established is there a direct response of loyalty and affirmation, coming now from the people themselves all the way back to both Joshua and Yahweh (Joshua 1:16–8), echoing the words that Yahweh had issued to Joshua at the beginning of the dialogue loop. Thus, in a few short sentences, Joshua's appointment is affirmed both from above and below, and his leadership tied to the fate of the people in the next series of moves on the Middle Eastern chessboard.

The restless energy at the close of Joshua 1 is almost palpable. After forty years of promises and delays, the final fight for the homeland is on! So the story of the spies in Joshua 2 seems at first chronologically misplaced. After all, in Joshua 1:11 the command to cross the Jordan begins a three-day countdown, while the full scope of the action described in Joshua 2 could not possibly fit into that time frame. It is precisely in this seeming anomaly that the clear intentionality of the literature of Joshua is seen. There is more than meets the eye initially in both the development and placement of chapter 2.

This story of the spies sent to Jericho is told chiastically. "Chiasm" is the name given to reflexive enveloping repetitions that are frequently found in Hebrew poetry and storytelling. Whereas Western linear thought tends to flow either inductively (with the information proffered building toward a concluding climax), or deductively (with a thesis declared at the beginning, followed by supporting evidence and implications), chiasm flows out from a normative center. The name "chiasm" is derived from the Greek letter *chi*, the form of which is sometimes used to describe the literary movement of the lines or themes in chiastic section.

"Chiasm"

Reflexive mirror parallelism in Hebrew poetry and storytelling:

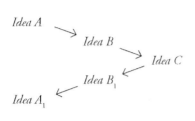

The main idea or implications are declared at the center of the passage ("C").

When diagrammed, the Greek letter *chi* (χ) is often used to show the movement of the ideas; hence "chiasm."

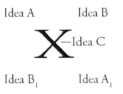

While we are not accustomed to hearing or reading literature that is shaped in this manner, the ancient Hebrews had both an eye and an ear for it, as is evident in the wide use of chiasm throughout the Old Testament. Here in Joshua 2, the impact of chiastic literary flow would be immediately apparent. For our untrained senses, a diagram will help us see what was obvious then:

Spies commissioned (2:1)
    Officers of the king [of Jericho] address Rahab (2:2–3)
        Rahab saves the spies (2:4–7)
            Rahab declares Yahweh's victory (2:8–10)
                Rahab's great testimony (2:11): "Yahweh your God is God in heaven above and on the earth below."
            Rahab declares Yahweh's victory (2:11–13)
        Rahab saves the spies (2:14–16)
    Officers of the King [of Heaven and Earth] address Rahab (2:17–21) Spies debriefed (2:22–24)

When read or heard in this manner, the literary purpose of the story becomes much more obvious, and the placement crucial. Although the events that are reported may have happened a week or two prior to the actual crossing of the Jordan River, the meaning of the spies' encounter in Jericho is of paramount significance to those who are suddenly stepping into the churning waters, fearing both its tumult and the turmoil that waits on the other side. Rahab is a representative of the people of Canaan, and as such she gives a testimony that would bolster Israel's challenged nerve. She declares that the peoples of Canaan already know the power and domination of Yahweh, Israel's God. This is a particularly striking statement coming from Rahab, whose occupation of prostitution may well tie her to the religious shrines of Jericho and its official priesthood. Whatever her station in that city's society, she gives an unequivocal report, as a member of the enemy community, that Yahweh has already crossed into the land and possessed it. All Israel has to do is follow Yahweh.

Rahab's testimony is a reminder that Yahweh is not merely a tribal god owned by Israel. Instead, Yahweh is the Supreme Divinity over both territory and lesser gods. Every nation ought to bow to Yahweh, as Rahab has already begun to do. Israel need only go into the land to perform the mopping-up operations, for the decisive battle has already been won.

This message is confirmed in several ways in the next three chapters. First, the crossing of the wild waters of the Jordan River is told in a way reminiscent of Israel's movement through the Red Sea a generation earlier (Exodus 14). Both situations required a divine act to overcome a natural barrier. The single significant difference between the former story and this one is that then, Moses was the vehicle for dispensing the power of Yahweh as he stood with arm and staff outstretched over the Red Sea, and now it is the visible portable throne of Yahweh (the Ark of the Covenant) which moves ahead of the people to stem the flow. In both instances, it was the power of Yahweh that parted the waters; now there is the added luxury of having that royal action expressed in a more direct manifestation of Yahweh's local movements through the furnishings of the house of the Deity resident among the people.

Second, a memorial is created out of twelve stones gathered from the riverbed. These stones would be rounded and smooth from years of polishing as the currents pushed and tumbled them along the riverbed. Therefore, they would look strikingly different from the rocks that littered the torrent's banks and formed the cliffs at its edges. The Israelites were supposed to take family outings to this site in the subsequent years, and have picnics next to the pile. The unusual monument was to be used as a teaching tool, reminding the next generations what Yahweh had done to create their unique identity and settle them in this land.

Third, the report of this miraculous act of crossing the Jordan River at flood stage zipped along the gossip channels of the nations and tribes living in Canaan, until a great fear of Israel and her God enveloped all of them. This is the only reason why Joshua can then command what has to be either

"When Your Children Ask"

For the nation of Israel, education was to be rooted in the historical realities that created the nation. This phrase is repeated at key times to underscore the critical elements of instruction. *When your children ask* ...

About the Passover (Exodus 12:24–27)

About Circumcision and Firstborn Redemption (Exodus 13:11–16)

About Manna (Exodus 16:31–35)

About the Jordan Stone Memorial (Joshua 4:1–9)

When Did the Israelites Enter Canaan?

There are three theories as to when and how the Israelites went into the land of Canaan and set up residence or became a nation in their own right:

By Invasion—This is the story told in the book of Joshua. If true, the events took place around 1350–1250 B.C.

By Infiltration—There were bands of runaway slaves and wandering peasants noted in the records of several ancient Near Eastern civilizations. They are called the *Habiru*. If there is a correlation between these people and the *Hebrews* of the Bible (scholarly opinion is divided about this), the infiltration of Canaan was a gradual process, taking place roughly between 1850 and 1350 B.C.

By Internal Struggle—Some scholars believe that the whole "Exodus" and "Conquest" were late projections backward, after competing clans and tribes original to Canaan began to unite with one another against external foes. According to this theory, the formation of a national identity would have taken place from around 1250 to 1000 B.C., and is reflected in the writings of the Judges and the struggles between David and Saul for domination of the emerging Israelite nation.

The position taken in this study is the first, with the book of Joshua reflecting events as they actually happened, rather than developed as the fiction of a later royal court attempting to legitimize itself through rewriting history for its own purposes.

the greatest act of leadership lunacy in the history of warfare, or its ultimate act of confidence and faith: On the west bank of the Jordan, standing on enemy territory, in full sight of the great sentinel city of Jericho, Joshua orders all Israel's males to be circumcised. Such an act would effectively render the entire army of Israel helpless for about a week. Only if there was absolute certainty that Yahweh was, in fact, in control of this land already, as Rahab had testified, would this debilitating decision make sense. In the days ahead, as the Israelites were going to go into battle stripped down and naked, their circumcision might be the only armor they would wear. It would remind them of the promises of their covenant Suzerain, and serve as identifying markings for their fellow comrades on the battlefield, where all men would otherwise look alike.

Fourth, the Israelites cross the Jordan River at exactly the same time of the year as when the nation, a generation before, left Egypt (Joshua 5:10). This "coincidence" effectively ties together the exodus from Egypt and the entrance into the Promised Land, as if no time at all had elapsed between the two. In effect, the waywardness of the wilderness generation is dismissed from the history books like it never happened. This seems to be the implication of the note in Joshua 5:9: *Then Yahweh said to Joshua, "Today I have rolled away the reproach of Egypt from you."*

Fifth, the miraculous food (*manna*), divinely dispensed during the wilderness wanderings, suddenly ceases (Joshua 5:11–12). Now that the Israelites are "home," they have a right to eat from the food provided by the divine inheritance.

Sixth, there is the strange and powerful story of Joshua and his midnight restlessness that causes him to wander sleepless on the plains of Jericho, the night before the confrontation with the residents of Canaan is to take place (Joshua 5:13–15). Out of the black night suddenly looms a mighty warrior who blocks Joshua's path. Reaching for his sword, Joshua demands to know which side this brute soldier is on: "Are you for us or them?" The stranger's response seems odd at first: "Neither!" (In Hebrew, it is actually simply the strong word "No!") Yet when he introduces himself, it all makes sense. He is, he declares, the "commander of the army of Yahweh." This information puts everything else into perspective. Joshua may be called and commissioned by Yahweh to serve a mighty leadership purpose, but he is not the field of operations commander. Yahweh has deployed several regiments to fight the war ahead, and Israel, under Joshua's leadership, is only one of those divisions. Even Joshua must respond to a general with more stars, as the theater of operations erupts. Thus, it is clear that Yahweh is the great Suzerain, not just over Israel, but throughout the universe; Israel's part in the battle is only a single facet of a larger engagement God is waging in the cosmic civil war, where only one Creator-Divinity can ultimately be sovereign.

This reminder, at the start of the conquest of Canaan, recapitulates the message of both Genesis and Exodus, that the world has lost its bearings and has come under the sway of evil forces. The mission of God is the game plan outlined in the Bible—to reclaim the territory and beings created good at the beginning of time, but to do so in a way that enlists a human community shaped by the Covenant in the enterprise, and maintains general human freedom of choice when calling all back to the Creator.

Purging the Land (Joshua 6–12)

The conquest of Jericho seems very odd when first read. Why would Yahweh order that a huge contingent of Israelites march around the city, led by armed warriors and priests blowing trumpets, and followed by another weapons-ready contingent? And why would Yahweh wish, in this strange foray, to have the Ark of the Covenant lifted to shoulder height, bobbing around at the center of the swarm that circles the city? Furthermore, why should the walls of Jericho fall of their own accord in this encounter, rather than be left to the usual siege tactics that will be employed by the Israelite army throughout the rest of the conquest battles?

There are several unique things about Jericho and its situation that called for unusual action in bringing it down. First, this is the initial battle on the soil of Canaan itself. For that reason, it is likely that Yahweh wanted to make perfectly clear to both Israel and the nations of the region that this was a divine engagement. Israel needed to experience the power of a conquest that was not pinned on its ability to produce, by way of military strength, and the other city-states and nations of Canaan had to learn quick fear of the God who energized this invading horde. Both were accomplished through the unusual battle tactics at Jericho.

In this regard, it is helpful to visualize the manner in which the citizens of Jericho would have observed the week-long march of the Israelite armies. In effect, it would look like a mighty flood rippling and flowing around the city, with all the individual marchers disappearing into a kind of tidal wave. Meanwhile, the Ark of the Covenant would appear to be floating on top of this undulating "liquid," at its very center. The correspondence between the name for Noah's boat in Genesis 6–9 and that given to the portable throne of Yahweh in this era can hardly be a coincidence. What the people of Jericho were to imagine was a fright similar to that experienced by the ancient civilizations when the waters of judgment roiled about them, and the Ark floated above them in anticipation of the next stage in human civilization. Indeed, it is the tumult of Yahweh's judgment against this land that will wipe the slate clean and start a new human community where the old one disappeared. As Noah and his family rode the Ark in safety above God's judgment on the nations of earth, so now Joshua and Israel are in the care of the Ark, as a new tide of divine condemnation sweeps through.

Second, the site of Jericho was no accident. There were several major trade routes crossing the ancient Near East, and Jericho sat on the gateway to Canaan from what was called "the King's Highway." This dominant artery of commerce, communication, and conquest ran from Damascus to Egypt just east of the Jordan River. One of the reasons for Jericho's wealth and strength was that it controlled access to any trade entering the land from the east. In other words,

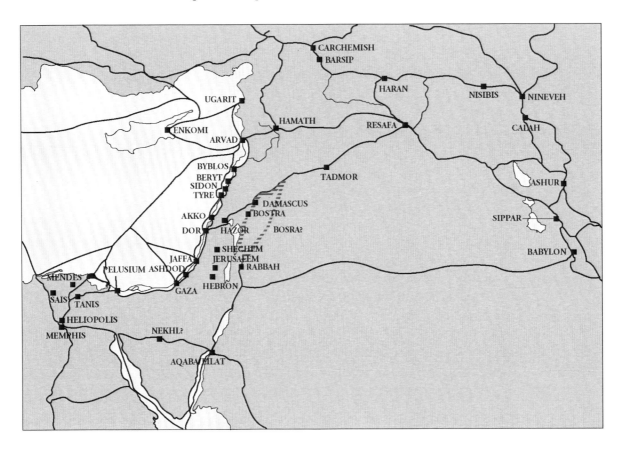

Figure 5.2 Major trade routes of the ancient near east.[2]

Jericho formed the door and welcome mat into Canaan. If Israel was to give the land a new identity, the old door and welcome mat had to be thrown out. This appears to be the significance of the curse against Jericho in Joshua 6:26. Since it had been established by peoples oblivious to the great Creator, and dedicated to lesser gods and purposes than the true grand design of the original creation, it must now make way for Yahweh's redemptive intents. All would be welcome in the new Zion to be established by God through Israel. But woe to any who wished for the old ways and the old gods and the darkness of a world where the Creator was neither acknowledged nor wanted.

Once Jericho was out of the way, the Israelites headed straight for the mountains of Ebal and Gerizim in order to renew the Sinai Covenant, as Moses had commanded (Deuteronomy 27; see Joshua 8:30–35). The next town on that route was a much smaller city than Jericho, a place called Ai. Scouts reported to Joshua that a quick campaign with fewer soldiers was all that was necessary because of its limited size and fortifications. But Israel's strength to act as Yahweh's champion had been compromised, because Achan had prevented the total destruction of Jericho.

---

2   Adapted from: Copyright © Briangotts (CC by 3.0) at http://commons.wikimedia.org/wiki/File:Ancient_Levant_routes.png

This transgression and its severe consequences are not the norm for divine punishment in the rest of the Old Testament. The incident seems to function as a warning sign for those witnessing it, so that they would understand the seriousness of what was taking place, and not seek quickly to deviate from the divine mission in order to pick up personal gain. A similar anecdote is recorded in Acts 5 at the very beginning of the New Testament Church's existence. There, Ananias and Sapphira used the concept of total devotion of goods as a means to gain public recognition, while hiding contrary deeds that would benefit their own economic station. In both instances, death is the divine judgment, and a great fear or awe consumes each community.

When Achan's sin and the city of Ai have both been dispatched, the suzerain-vassal covenant formulated at Mt. Sinai is renewed. The mountains of Gerizim and Ebal were roughly in the center of Canaan, and stood closely enough to one another that it was indeed possible to shout back and forth between them, as the recitation of Covenant curses and blessings required.

As soon as the renewal ceremony was accomplished, the story of Canaan's conquest was quickly told in three literary sections. First, the Gibeonites, terrified by the unstoppable onslaught of the Israelites, deviously made an alliance with Joshua and the people, pretending to be from far away (Joshua 9). The neighbors of the Gibeonites were incensed at their defection to these intruders, and mounted a battle against them. Since the Gibeonites were now allied with Israel, Joshua was required to go to their aid, and this became the excuse for the southern military campaign, which netted Israel more than half of Canaan by the time the fighting ceased (Joshua 10). In quick response, the city-states of northern Canaan banded together to keep Israel out. The strategy failed, however, and soon the entirety of the land belonged to Israel (Joshua 11).

All of these wars make for great military reading, but they also raise a huge theological question. Why was Israel sent into battle to destroy cities and civilizations, old men and young babies, and cultures and economies? There is no easy way to respond, or to find quick harmony with the near-pacifist perspectives of the New Testament. Several ideas enter the conversation, however, and while these are not fully satisfying, they are helpful in refocusing the questions. First, although there is an ongoing covenant relationship between Yahweh and a human society throughout the Bible, the nation of Israel in the Old Testament is formed as a political entity, in contrast to the other countries and

Figure 5.3 A panoramic view of modern Nablus, which stands on the site of ancient Shechem, where the Covenant renewal ceremony took place. Mout Ebal is on the left and Mount Gerezim is on the right.[3]

---

3   Copyright © Asad112 (CC by 3.0) at http://commons.wikimedia.org/wiki/File:Nablus_-_eastern_panorama.jpg

communities of the ancient world, while the Church of the New Testament is commissioned to be a pervasive influence within other societies, without becoming a political state in its own right. This means that there are aspects of Israel's existence that cannot be equated with the lifestyle promulgated for the early Church, and vice versa. While the Church is not to engage in slaughter and bloodshed, the nation of Israel was required to establish boundaries and control over civilian populations. In this respect, there is a close correspondence between the "Just War" theories explored by theologians of the New Testament Church and the manner in which Israel would promote and defend her statehood existence. While the mission of Yahweh through Israel demanded a particular covenant lifestyle, just as it does in the New Testament era of the Church, the actual formation of the national territorial existence required other means, including war and international diplomacy, to establish and maintain it.

Second, there are several hints that at least a portion of the warfare commanded in the settling of Canaan was understood to be merely a restoration of the rightful claims of Abraham's descendants to the land. After all, they had buried their honored ancestors in these hills, and had never sold off rights to the land owned by their forefathers. In effect, some say, Israel held a type of manifest destiny, which required them to reassert ownership entitlement over the squatters who came later and dwelt surreptitiously in *their* land. This was a nasty and bloody business that could not be easily accomplished through neighborliness or negotiation (although, as the story of the Gibeonites affirms, it was sometimes possible).

Third, there is a hint that the conquest of Canaan was, in part, a judgment against the wickedness of the peoples living there. While the social conditions that prevailed among the tribes and clans of ancient Canaan are beyond a complete ethical assessment, the manner in which Yahweh commands the razing of Jericho in dramatic parallel with the flood of Noah's time seems to indicate that the conquest was, at least in part, a declaration of judgment against the Canaanites.

Fourth, it is clear that the skirmishes of battle were one way of revealing Yahweh's strength to those who opposed Israel's existence. Just as the plagues in Egypt unquestionably declared the astounding and unparalleled military capabilities of Israel's God, so in these subsequent battles a clear message was sent that "our God is bigger than your god." The miracles that accompanied Israel's battleground activities would provide incontrovertible evidence of Yahweh's power for those who observed. Hopefully, these peoples would give up their smaller deities and find new camaraderie with Israel and her God. In this way, the blessing for all nations, promised to and through Israel's founding patriarch, Abram (Genesis 12), would come to pass, and the missional intent of the Creator to regather the crown of creation into new fellowship would be accomplished.

Cities of Refuge

East of the Jordan River:
  Kedesh (north)
  Shechem (central)
  Hebron (south)
West of the Jordan River:
  Golan (north)
  Ramoth (central)
  Bezer (south)

Figure 5.4 Map of Israelite tribal allotments.[4]

Fifth, there may well have been a need for Israel to experience a fairly sterile environment in its formative years, in order for it to become the community of Covenant witness that Yahweh intended. This seems to be confirmed when Israel's failure to completely destroy other civilizations within its borders is declared, in Judges 2, to be sinful, and in violation of Yahweh's intentions. Earlier encounters with other nations, like that with the Moabites in Numbers 25, had proved how quickly the Israelites could be led away from their unique Covenant commitments

---

4   Adapted from: Copyright © Richardprins (CC by 3.0) at http://commons.wikimedia.org/wiki/File:12_Tribes_of_Israel_Map.svg

to Yahweh. If this young nation was to get started as a community of witness, it would need some time to grow in independence from other national and religious influences.

All of these reasons do not fully satisfy a Christian reading of the bellicose events in Israel's early existence, especially when considering that along with Judaism, it emerges from the same religious tradition and divine initiatives. These suggestions do, however, provide a basis upon which to understand the uniqueness of Israel's situation, particularly when the political theocracy, national geography, and religious mission get inextricably intertwined for Israel in a way that is not experienced by the Church of the New Testament.

Possessing the Land (Joshua 13–21)

Although Israel was in control of Canaan after the battle against the northern coalition, there remained pockets of resistance and competing claims for specific territories within its borders (Joshua 13). Part of the reason for the allocations of boundaries for the tribes of Israel was to manage the final push for total dominance over residual alien clans. The general distribution is outlined over several chapters (Joshua 14–19). Then provision is made for six "Cities of Refuge" (Joshua 20), which would support a judicial system that provided a fair hearing for all who had been involved in major civil tragedies or crimes. Along with that, the Levites, who were not allotted a specific tribal territory, were given residences in a number of towns (Joshua 21). This allowed the Levites to share in the economic fortunes of the nation, and also dispersed these families, who were very closely connected with the religious rituals and ceremonies, throughout the land, providing a kind of visible leavening to influence the people to stay true to Yahweh.

Why was it necessary for the Israelites to become landowners rather than bedouins like their ancient ancestors? Partly, it seems to be a reflection on their changing role from slavery in Egypt. After all, when Moses restated the Ten Commandments in Deuteronomy 5, he tied together release from slavery and respect for other peoples as the basis for the Sabbath command. But the laws given about restoring family property after seven years and again in the Year of Jubilee (Leviticus 25) seem to indicate a deeper connection between land ownership and religious identity. We will explore this further at the end of the chapter.

Promising the Land (Joshua 22–24)

Three incidents round out the literature of this book, each of which addresses some dimension of the future of the land and Israel's place in it. First, there is the story of the tension produced when the warriors from the trans-Jordan tribes return home. While the early intent of taking and settling Canaan seems to have been limited to the area between the Jordan River and the Mediterranean Sea (cf. Numbers 32), several tribes found the lands just east of the Jordan to be to their liking. They requested the right to settle in this territory that had previously belonged to the Ammonites and Moabites. Moses gave them permission, with the stipulation that their soldiers must first accompany the rest of the tribes in the looming conquest of Canaan proper. This they agreed to do.

Now, in Joshua 23, these warriors go back to their settlements east of the Jordan. As they forded the river, they built a huge altar and ignited a great blaze on it. Neighboring Israelite tribes grew suspicious, thinking that these trans-Jordan relatives were already bowing to other gods. In the ensuing conversations, all fears were quelled, and Joshua heard their testimony that they were not seeking a shrine for worship other than the Tabernacle. Instead, they only wanted to set up a monument that would help them remember their ties with the rest of the tribes. In this way, a pledge was made for national unity, which transcended tribal identities.

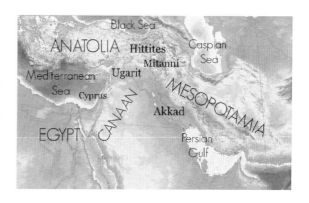

Figure 5.5 Israel's world; notice the strategic importance of its location among the nations.[5]

[5]Second, as he grew old and neared death, Joshua called together the elders who had shaped community life for the Israelites at his side (Joshua 23). He took them on a verbal tour of their remembered history, and called from them a pledge to keep their villages and cities true to the identity promulgated in the Sinai Covenant.

Third, in a final covenant renewal ceremony, Joshua gathered the whole nation together shortly before he died (Joshua 24). Once again, he reminded them *who* they were and *whose* they were. The Israelites did not exist as an independent tribe negotiating its own way among the other nations of the ancient Near East. Nor were they free agents, determining their religious allegiance by taking offers from the open market. They were the people of Yahweh, the nation of the Sinai Covenant, the human agency of God's mission to recover a relationship with the residents of planet Earth, as communicated to Abraham many centuries before.

The concluding appendix to the book (Joshua 24:28–33) lists three graves: those of Joshua, Joseph, and Eleazer. Each is uniquely significant. Graves are a symbol of settlement and home-land. Abraham and his wives were buried in this land, as were Isaac and his wives. When Jacob died in Egypt, his family made sure to bring his body back to Canaan to bury it here. Now the generations are passing again, and upon their deaths, Joshua the leader, Joseph the ancestor, and Eleazer the religious head are all buried in this land. It is a fitting reminder that the land has finally achieved its intended rest, and its rightful owners can rest here as well. They are truly home.

It is in this light that the location of the Promised Land must be considered. Why was Canaan the land promised to Abraham? Why did Israel wrestle these acres away from other clans in order to establish its own settlements?

Without question, there are many geographical areas of the world that would have appeared to be far more desirable. Mesopotamia, with its well-watered valleys surrounding the Tigris and Euphrates rivers, had a much better agricultural base than did Canaan. Egypt experienced both a more stable climate and a more secluded location. Anatolia was better suited to permanent

5   Copyright © Sémhur (CC by 3.0) at http://commons.wikimedia.org/wiki/File:Middle_East_topographic_map-blank.svg

Is the "Holy Land" Still "Holy"?

Because the history and legacy of ancient Israel is tied to "Canaan" or "Palestine" (a term derived from the Philistines, who occupied the coastal plains for many years), and because of the resurgence of a call for a Jewish homeland following the atrocities of the Holocaust, there is lingering debate as to how the divine promises about this land are to be understood today. Is this inheritance a God-given right in perpetuity? Does the current nation of Israel have a right to this territory forever by virtue of divine appointment? What about the Palestinians? Do they have political right to this territory because of long occupancy?

The answers to such questions depend, at least in part, on theological interpretations of both Old and New Testaments:

- If the promises about the land are strictly held as eternal inheritance rights, descendants of ancient Israel (today's Jews) remain the proper owners and primary inhabitants of present-day Palestine.

- If, however, the land was strategic for divine witness during the millennium prior to Jesus, and that mission was transferred to the Christian church at Pentecost, there is no ongoing divine appointment about who owns the land.

According to New Testament/Christian theology, the mission of God shifted from a centripetal center in Jerusalem toward which all nations would be drawn (cf. Isaiah 2:1–5) to a centrifugal spreading of the witnessing community to all nations (cf. Acts 1:8). In this view, the "Holy Land" is no longer "Holy," and its occupation today needs to be determined by other methods than theological divine right.

settlement, because of its mountain-ringed highlands, than was the open strip of countryside between the Jordan River and the Mediterranean Sea. In fact, Canaan was largely a rock pile, very indefensible, lacking any natural harbor for trade, and geographically splintered, so that it would be very difficult to forge a national identity across high mountainous ridges and deep separating valleys.

What made this piece of property so valuable, at least in Yahweh's eyes? In the words of every real estate salesman: location, location, location. Canaan was the unparalleled single piece of territory in the ancient world that connected the various civilizations with each other. It was the bridge between Africa and Asia. It was the rest stop on the trade routes from what would become Europe to both the Orient and Egypt. It served as the primary highway for marshaling troops in the military campaigns of its world, and formed a key segment in every major communication line or caravan trek.

Canaan was precisely the one spot in the world of that day where the nation of Israel could not be hidden from other tribes, countries, and clans and peoples. In other words, the Promised Land was, for Israel, not a secluded sanctuary or retreat where the pastoral scenes of Eden could be replayed, but rather the busiest street in town. Here, Israel was placed as the divine billboard, calling all nations back to a relationship with the Creator. Here, Israel's unique community character and moral ethos were on display to attract other civilizations to inquire and seek after the God of this people.

The choice of Canaan as the Promised Land was no accident, when seen in the larger perspectives of the Sinai Covenant and its missional foregrounding provided by the book of Genesis. If the Creator was going to find a way back into the hearts of the races of humans who had long ago forgotten their Maker, it would require the formation of a community shaped by the Sinai Covenant, and then displayed in the most prominent location possible in the world of the day: Canaan. In this sense, the mission of God was not first built out of Jesus and the New Testament Church, but was resident in the religion of the Bible from its very beginning. This is why Jesus would says that his disciples were to be like a city set on a hill (Matthew 5:13–16), for that is exactly what his ancient kin, the Israelites, were intended to be.

Discussion Points

- How are the contents of Joshua structured in broad sections, and what is the theological significance of the book for Israel's identity?
- What are some of the reasons why Israel's warfare might have been divinely condoned? How do these explanations intersect with perspectives on war, violence, and killing put forward in other sections of the Bible, or by the religions based upon these scriptures?
- Why is the location of the "Promised Land" so significant for Israel? What role did it force upon the nation among its neighbors?
- What parallels can be drawn between the Exodus from Egypt and the entrance of Israel into Canaan? What implications might these comparisons hold for the Israelite self-perception and identity?
- How is the story of Rahab and the spies shaped? What is its theological significance in the book of Joshua?
- Trace and explain the covenant renewal ceremonies from Deuteronomy through the end of Joshua.
- Whose graves are mentioned at the close of Joshua, and what is their theological significance?

For Further Investigation

Brouwer, Wayne. (Atlanta: SBL, 2001). *The Literary Development of John 13–17: A Chiastic Reading.*
Craigie, Peter C. (Grand Rapids: Eerdmans, 1979). *The Problem of War in the Old Testament.*

6.

When the Curses Kick In

How Israel Nearly Lost the Family Farm

As the book of Judges opens, Israel is well into the process of possessing and settling the land of promise. The nation is living at the crossroads of its world as a missional community of witness for the Creator, known by this people as Yahweh, the God of Egyptian deliverance and the Sinai Covenant. But time has moved on: Joshua, the last direct link with Moses, has died. So have all the Elders who worked with Joshua to shape the nation in ways defined by the suzerain-vassal treaty.

Meanwhile, there still remain pockets of non-Israelite identity and culture within the boundaries of the tribal allotments. That note of unfinished business ignites the strange saga recorded in this book, which rides the pendulum between marvelous tales of heroism and depressing dirges about toxic moral decay. There is only the slightest hint of all this, however, as the story begins. In fact, all we see at the start are continuing anticipations that the Israelites will fulfill their destiny, and create an uncompromised covenant community for their national identity (Judges 1:1–26). But the tale turns sour suddenly, when the tone shifts at Judges 1:27. In quick succession, a half-dozen headlines are linked together, declaring the lapses of various tribes in either conquest or occupation (Judges 1:27–36).

The Book of Judges at a Glance

Introduction (promises of success, failure, and judgment) (1:1–3:6)

- **The Cycles of the Judges** (3:7–16:31)
  - * 6 "Major" Judges:
  - * Othniel (paradigm)
  - * Ehud (loner, folk hero, from Benjamin, eastern enemy)
  - * Deborah (the woman)
  - * Gideon (Baal versus Yahweh is the critical issue)
  - * Jephthah (the social outcast)
  - * Samson (loner, folk hero, from Dan, western enemy)
- 6 "Minor" Judges: Shamgar, Tolah, Jair, Ibzan, Elon, Abdan
- 1 "Anti-" Judge: Abimelech

Appendices (a nation fallen from Covenant faithfulness) (17–21)

- * Religious Confusion and Removal of Dan (600 warriors) (17–18)
- * Moral Decay and Removal of Benjamin (600 warriors) (19–21)

The Sinai Covenant looms large as Judges 2 opens, for "the angel of Yahweh" travels through the land and makes a pronouncement that says, in effect, "You have failed to live in obedience to the covenant stipulations. Therefore the curses of the covenant will kick in rather than its blessings." Although this prophetic warning causes a brief moment of grief and repentance (Judges 2:4–5), the rest of the book is a litany of chaotic maneuvers in which the Israelites not only neglect the designs of their covenant missional identity as a city on the hill to the nations of their world, but they seem, in effect, actively to pursue religious and cultural transformation back toward realignment with those around them. The darkness deepens as Israel's apparent attempt to blend back into the world at odds with its Creator unfolds.

But the stories are carefully collected and preserved in Judges. There is a subtle symmetry that pervades this book and gives evidence that it is more than a mere chronology of certain decades. In fact, the incidents recorded in Judges are hard to date because most of the narratives appear to describe local matters that did not affect the entire population of Israel as a nation. It is likely, in other words, that some of these incidents actually overlap. Or, actually, there may well be years of gap and miles of geography separating some of them, so that they do not necessarily line up end to end. This is made clear by the literary flow from the story of Ehud (3:12–30) to that of Deborah (4:2–5:31), which is interrupted by the brief note about Shamgar (3:31), who is also identified as a successor to Ehud.

The "history" books of the Old Testament were never considered by Israel to be mere journalistic reports that would link seamlessly together, forming a complete account of their national or cultural past. These writings were always acknowledged as part of "the Prophets" (*nabi'im* in Hebrew, the second section of the Bible), and as such were more sermonic than simply a compilation of historical data. For that reason, it is important to acknowledge the literary cues which help shape both the materials of the book and its meaning. Note these things:

- In the very first story, the Israelites ask Yahweh which tribe should lead the fight against the Canaanites (Judges 1:1–2); in the last story told, the Israelites ask Yahweh which tribe should lead the fight against its own tribe of Benjamin (Judges 20:18). Each time, the answer is "Judah," giving special prominence to the tribe which will later produce the royal dynasty. But underlying this parallelism is the dark message that what began in confidence and obedience to Yahweh's great plans for the nation has ended up becoming an internal conflict which pits units or tribes within the covenant family against one another.

- Twelve judges are named in the book, analogous to the twelve tribes of Israel. There is no indication that at least one judge emerged from each tribe, but the number is significant. Furthermore, in the symmetry of storytelling, six of the judges receive considerably more than a passing glance, while the other six are only named and dispensed with in a verse or two.

- The paradigm for processing the stories of each judge is set by the initial tale of Othniel in Judges 3:7–11. Although the narrative is concise and economical, it contains all the elements that will recur in each of the following stories:

  * Israel sins by forgetting Yahweh and its covenant identity
  * Yahweh sends an enemy against them
  * They fall into oppressive subjugation for a number of years
  * Coming to their senses, the people cry to Yahweh for deliverance
  * Yahweh raises a leader of commanding significance, who defeats the enemy and restores appropriate worship and cultural lifestyle
  * The land has rest or peace for a certain number of years
  * In this way, the Othniel tale serves as a paradigm template for the series that emerges in its wake

- There is a social and geographical symmetry between Ehud, the first major judge, and Samson, the last major judge. Both are loners and folk heroes from tribes which form a kind of belt across the mid-section of the nation with Benjamin (Ehud's tribe) on the east and Dan (Samson's tribe) on the west.

- [1]Interestingly, this Benjamin-Dan geographical belt seems to play out in further ways in the appendix to the book (Judges 17–21), where there are two stories in which a Levite passes between Judah and Ephraim (the two domi-

The Story of Ehud Told Chiastically

The tale of Ehud in Judges 3:12–30 is a great example of chiastic narrative:

Israel is subjected by Moab (12–14)

- *Ehud is raised up as deliverer (15–18)*
- *Ehud meets privately with King Eglon (19)*
- *Ehud declares a message from Yahweh and*
- *plunges a dagger into Eglon's belly (20–22)*
- *Ehud leaves privately from King Eglon (23–25)*
- *Ehud is raised up as deliverer (26–29)*

Israel subjects Moab and has peace (30)

The "message from Yahweh," at the very heart of the story, is delivered as a lethal dagger into Eglon's belly.

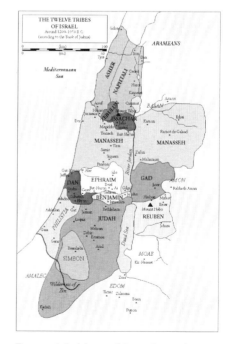

Figure 6.1 Map of Israelite tribes; notice the central belt formed by Dan and Benjamin.[1]

---

1 Copyright © Richardprins (CC by 3.0) at http://commons.wikimedia.org/wiki/File:12_Tribes_of_Israel_Map.svg

The Midianites

The Midianites are a furtive people, both within the Bible and beyond. Genealogical records in Genesis 25:1–2 tie the tribe to Abraham (fourth son of his third wife), and thus a sibling nation to Israel herself. Other notes identify Midianites as coinhabitants of Canaan, which makes sense, if they are descendants of Abraham. But they are always connected with the nations of the land that oppose Yahweh and Israel, and at odds with the covenantal mission. Biblical references include these:

- Midianite traders bought Joseph from his brothers and sold him as a slave in Egypt (Genesis 37:28, 36)
- Moses spent the middle third of his life among the Midianites as a shepherd (Exodus 2:15–21; 3:1; 18:1–27)
- The Midianites are identified as a subgroup of the Moabites (in Numbers 22:4-7) that oppose Yahweh and Israel, and thus are later singled out for extermination as a devious people, after tempting the Israelites to forget Yahweh (Numbers 25 and 31.):
- Here, in Judges 6-8, the Midianites appear to be a tribe cohabiting Canaan with the Israelites, but clearly superior in military might
- Isaiah will later make reference to the "camels of Midian" (60:6) in a passage predicting the restored and elevated glory of Israel among the nations

There are also ten references to the Midianites in the *Qur'an*, identifying this group (Arabic *Madyan*) as one of the tribes descended from Abraham, but also as an example of wickedness that was punished by *Allah*.

nant tribes on the central ridge of the country) crossing this Benjamin-Dan corridor. Each time, the Levite is manipulated in some way, sparking conflict between communities, and the outcome is that both these tribes (Benjamin and Dan) essentially lose their inheritance in the land.

- There is a social symmetry between Deborah and Jephthah, who are both community outcasts (she is a woman in a man's world; he is the illegitimate bastard in a nation where only the recognized male descendants are awarded an inheritance), and yet are each called upon by "civilized" society to win battles and restore social order.
- There is religious symmetry between Gideon and his son, Abimelech. Gideon is a legitimate judge, called to that office or role by Yahweh in order to free the Israelites from both the worship of Baal and also from political servitude to the Midianites. Abimelech reverses everything Gideon gains, restoring Baal worship while rejecting Yahweh, and turning the nation of Israel into a feuding mass of intertribal fighting.

The literary development of the book of Judges is very clear. Chapters 1:1–3:6 are the introduction: Here, the stage is set for the conflict to follow, first with promises of both success and failure on the part of Israel, and then moving directly into harbingers of coming judgment that are clearly tied to the Sinai Covenant curses on disobedience. Next comes the main body of the book, the stories of the twelve judges themselves (3:7–16:31), with six given significant review, and six merely listed briefly. Finally, there is a gloomy appendix (17–21), in which two sordid stories are told, each of which recounts how one of the tribes (first Dan, then Benjamin) is essentially removed from its God-given inheritance.

Two Significant Judges

All of the judges deliver the people from neighbors who are fairly close at hand, with the exception of Gideon. Gideon is more of a national deliverer, and his primary political foe is the Midianite nation, which is stealing Israelite grain and disrupting its social order. Yet, while Gideon is a reluctant military commander, his first priority is to rid Israel of Baal worship. This reformation must begin in Gideon's own family, because his father is the sponsor of a major shrine and altar for Baal worship.

Gideon's dual role as political deliverer and religious reformer highlights the continual intertwining of the religion of Israel with its political fortunes. Yahweh is and must be the Suzerain of the nation. Whenever this allegiance slips among the people, political disaster is close at hand. Precisely for this reason, the twinned stories of Gideon and his son, Abimelech, stand at the heart of the book of Judges. Gideon reluctantly steps into the role of a typical judge—called by Yahweh in a time of social crisis to serve as deliverer, and to restore the peace (or "rest") of the nation through religious revival as much as military command. Abimelech (whose name means "My Father is King!"), on the other hand, is a self-appointed ruler who defies the religion of Yahweh, restores Baal worship, and ultimately sends the nation into a tailspin of social, moral, and religious chaos.

The Judges

Name	Reference	Opponent	Length of rule
OTHNIEL	3:7–11	Aram	40 years
EHUD	3:12–30	Moab	80 years
SHAMGAR	3:31	Philistines	
DEBORAH	4–5	Cannaities	40
GIDEON	6–8	Midianities	40
TOLAH	10:1–2		23
JAIR	10:3–5		22
JEPHTHAH	10:6–12.7	Ammonites	6
IBZAN	12.8–10		7
ELON	12.11–12		10
ABDON	12.13–15		8
SAMSON	13–16	Philistines	20

Sandwiched in the middle of this series is Abimelech, son of Gideon (Judges 9). He is the epitome of an anti-Judge, opposite in every way to the true deliverers of Israel raised up by Yahweh. Abimelech calls himself to a leadership role, replaces worship of Yahweh with devotion to Baal, causes internal fighting within Israel, and brings chaos instead of peace.

While the central tales of Gideon and Abimelech are like doppelgangers, mirroring the dominant contradictory paths Israel might take, the greatest reflection of the national identity in its entirety comes at the end of the episodic series, and is found in the person of Samson. Here, the parallels between the nation and the man are striking and obvious:

- Both are miraculously born
- Both are dedicated to Yahweh from birth
- Both are unusually strong
- Both are supernaturally sustained by miraculous water flows
- Both are constantly lured by the enticements of surrounding nations
- Both call out to Yahweh only when in distress
- Both are willing to compromise their commitments and defile their religious purity
- Both continue to be agents of divine deliverance in spite of their failures

- Both experience times of subjection to the cruel dictates of others.

When the story of Samson was recounted among the Israelites in its day, it was like an illustrated sermon mirroring the nation back to itself. Samson was Israel in miniature, called by Yahweh to do great things, but constantly losing strength and identity because of the enticements of other nations. As Samson told his quirky riddles (Judges 14:14, 18) during the wedding celebrations he should not have been having, Israel would see itself as the truly great puzzle of divine grace: endowed with superior qualities, yet inevitably drawn away from Yahweh, and being weakened in the process. She was the "strong" who ate the forbidden "sweet(s)" of other nations (just as Samson continued to do in his inappropriate courtships), and in the end became weak.

Through this climactic story in the book of Judges, the whole of the divine mission is reiterated in summary form. Israel is Yahweh's special partner, an unlikely lion killer in the jungles of a creation gone awry, but constantly unfaithful, seeking more to be like the great evil beasts she is supposed to slay rather than remaining the example of human glory that Yahweh has intended for her. Rather than give witness of the wonderful Creator to the nations from her perch on her crossroads stage before the world, instead, Israel, like Samson, constantly sneaked off into the crowds for a little beer and bawdiness. In the end, although Yahweh graciously intervened time and again, Israel became a habitually unfaithful Covenant partner and was in danger of losing its very life.

A Strange Appendix

This impending demise is portrayed powerfully in the two main stories of the appendix (Judges 17–21). In the first (chapters 17–18), a Levite from Judah crosses the central belt-like corridor formed by the tribal allotments of Dan and Benjamin, and moves north into the hills of Ephraim. There, he becomes a cultic priest for a wealthy man, and gives advice to warriors from the tribe of Dan, who are dissatisfied with their landed inheritance in the conquest distributions. They return later as a band of six hundred warriors to steal away the Levite to become their private religious adviser and priest, along with all the silver and the idols of the shrine. Forsaking their assigned homeland, they resettle their tribe far to the north, beyond the national boundaries established by Yahweh. They cruelly massacre another civilization there in order to take what does not belong to them. In this way, the tribe of Dan (part of that central corridor of the nation of Israel) is displaced from the inheritance it received by divine allotment.

Similarly, in the second story of the appendix (Judges 19–21), a Levite travels across the Dan-Benjamin belt, this time from north to south. His goal is to recover his unfaithful wife from her family in Bethlehem. After some delays, they set out to return to Ephraim, and along the way receive hospitality in the home of a Jebusite family in a village that was later to become the great Davidic capital city of Jerusalem. Men from the tribe of Benjamin learn about these travelers, mob the house, and eventually brutalize and kill the Levite's wife. He then cuts her body into twelve parts, and sends these fleshly pieces, along with an angry message, to each of the tribal centers. Incited to vindictive rage, warriors from the other Israelite tribes wage a battle of retribution against Benjamin, and slay twenty-five thousand Benjamite soldiers. Only six hundred remain, and they flee into the desert. The result is that the tribe of Benjamin no longer has men to link its women and children to the landed inheritance (which was given only to the males of each tribe), nor husbands who can mate and provide a next generation to carry on as inhabitants of the promised land. In effect, Benjamin (like Dan) is being removed from its inheritance by its own shenanigans.

The tale of Judges closes with a mournful repeated refrain: "In those days Israel had no king; everyone did as he saw fit" (Judges 21:25). While these words anticipate the better times ahead under the leadership of David and Solomon, the coming great kings of Israel, they also have a condemnatory religious edge. The true king of Israel was Yahweh. There was no peace in the land because the nation had forgotten its covenant tie with the great Suzerain who delivered it from slavery in Egypt, and made it a powerful lion killer in the jungles of its world. The land of Canaan was given to Yahweh's people, in order to place them on the stage of their world as a model community, expressing what life could be like when people returned to their Creator. But as the narrative of Judges whimpers out, Israel is fast becoming a has-been and wilting leftover.

In the book of Joshua, a clearly appointed and prepared leader brings Israel into its "rest," as provided by the unique location and provisions of the Promised Land, so that she can live out her covenant destiny as the divine missional community of witness to the nations of the world. In the book of Judges, however, Israel becomes alienated from her "rest" through covenant breaking, and nearly loses her place in the land because of failure to posses what has been given. The people of God are seemingly about to forfeit their honored relationship with Yahweh and the missional identity it brings.

But there is light on the horizon. "In the days when the Judges ruled" (Ruth 1:1), another story was developing. To this we turn next.

Discussion Points

- What is the nature of a "Judge," and how does it fit into the overall picture of Israelite leadership during its Old Testament history?
- Compare and contrast the moods and messages of the books of Joshua and Judges, particularly as they relate to Israel's connection with the land of promise and the idea of shalom.
- Identify and explain the dealings of at least four Judges according to the record in that book.
- Compare and contrast the activities of Gideon and Abimelech, identifying through their stories how the one fulfills the role of "Judge" and the other turns it on its head.
- How do the tribes of Benjamin and Dan figure prominently in the various stories of the book of Judges?
- What does it mean for Samson's life to be a mirror of Israel's existence during the time of the "Judges?" Give specific elements of comparison.

For Further Investigation

Block, Daniel I. (Nashville: Holman, 1999). Judges, Ruth: *An Exegetical and Theological Exposition of Holy Scripture*.

7.

In the Mirror

Rendezvous with Ruth

When walking through the midway of a county fair, a man met a couple he knew and stopped to chat. Between the husband and wife tripped their five-year-old daughter, carrying a beehive of cotton candy almost as large as herself.

"My!" said the man, stooping to find her eyes behind the whirls of spun sugar, "How can you eat all of that? It looks twice your size!"

"Oh," she replied, "I'm bigger on the inside than I am on the outside!"

That might be a fitting reflection on the tiny drama of Ruth as well. The story is quickly told in only a few economical paragraphs. During the time of the Judges, unsettled by a nasty famine, Elimelech removes his family from the hill country of Judah to find food and work. They settle in Moab long enough for the two sons, Machlon and Kilion, to marry. Then, in short order, all the men of the family die, and Naomi is left a widow. Destitute, Naomi can only think of returning to Bethlehem, where she might find old friends who could give her a few handouts until she dies. Her daughters-in-law try to travel along, but Naomi resists their pity. She has nothing to offer them, not even future sons, if the unlikely should happen and she would marry again.

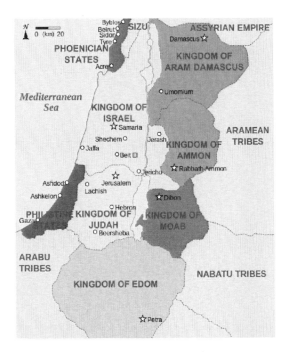

Figure 7.1 Israel and its neighbors. Notice the location of Moab.[1]

The Book of Ruth: A Literary Gem

Introduction: Succinct report of conditions (1:1–5; *71 words*)

Act 1 (two scenes: private/public): **The Condition** (1:6–22; *253 words*)

Act 2 (two scenes: private/public): **The Care** (2:1–23; *368 words*)

Act 3 (two scenes: public/private): **The Consecration** (3:1–15; *204 words*)

Act 4 (two scenes: public/private): **The Conclusion** (3:16–4:12; *263 words*)

Conclusion: Succinct report of conditions (4:13–17; *71 words*)

Epilogue: Link to King David (4:18–21; *30 words*)

Orpah is wise, and goes back to her Moabite community to start over. Ruth, however, is stubborn, and doggedly determined to accompany Naomi, in order to share the burden of her desperate situation.

On arriving in Bethlehem, Naomi is barely recognized, but warmly welcomed. She tells her woeful story and claims a new name, "Mara" (which means "bitter"), as an indication of her sorry state.

Ruth joins the other poor people who glean the barley fields for leftover corner patches, fallen stalks, and loose kernels after the reapers have taken in the bulk of the crop (see Leviticus 19:9 and 23:22 about reaping and gleaning practices). She catches the eye of Boaz, a wealthy landowner of some of the fields where she labors. He gets friendly, and Naomi sees a good prospect looming on the horizon. She urges Ruth to return Boaz's kind intentions, and before long, the gentleman makes public his courtship intentions. Quickly, he cuts through community red tape, and the two are wed. Already on their honeymoon, a child is conceived, and when little Obed is born, Naomi claims him as a sign of Yahweh's renewed blessing on her life. Of course, everybody lives happily ever after, and the closing credits show that this is the origin of the great family of David, who later restores glory and honor to Israel.

Brilliant Writing

The tale is as clean and crisp and delightful as any ever written. But like an iceberg, there is much more going on beneath the surface than first catches the eye. For one thing, the book of Ruth is a literary gem. Written with tremendous economy, it conveys a major story in only 1,260 Hebrew words. Moreover, within that brief venture, it manages to encapsulate an introduction and a conclusion (each of which has exactly seventy-one words) and four dramatic acts containing two scenes apiece. Furthermore, of the two scenes in each act, one

---

1   Copyright © BokicaK (CC by 3.0) at http://commons.wikimedia.org/wiki/File:Kingdoms_around_Israel_830_map_sh.svg

takes place in a private location and the other in a public location, and the order of these is reversed between the first and second halves of the drama. When analyzed from purely a grammatical and literary perspective, this is an incredible work of art, symmetry, and balance.

But there is more. A character study reveals that nearly every dramatic persona in the book is doubled and paralleled. Ruth and Boaz are the twinned lead characters. She is female, young, single (widowed), poor, and an alien in Israel; he, on the other hand, is male, older, single (unmarried), wealthy, and a leading citizen in Israel. Their interaction continually highlights both their similarities and their differences, making them a truly engaging couple.

Next to them stand their dramatic counterparts, lesser figures in the story, to be sure, but foils, in whose reflection these lead characters are further defined. Ruth's "other" is Orpah, another young Moabite woman who also married a son of Elimelech and Naomi. While Ruth becomes noble as the whole of the drama progresses, Orpah becomes ordinary, taking the typical human path at the beginning of the tale. Orpah reminds us of ourselves, acting with modest self-interest to make it through life. Meanwhile, Ruth soars in an impressive arc of witness, a triumph of the humble spirit focused relentlessly on things that really matter.

Similarly, there is a counterpart to Boaz. He shows up near the end of the tale as the "kinsman-redeemer," or nearer relative, who can follow through on the levirate customs that would allow Naomi and Ruth to regain title to the land evacuated by Elimelech. Once again, this man is very much like Boaz. He would also like to help Naomi and Ruth, but practical matters of family get in the way, and none among the elders of the community reproaches him for stepping back. Boaz, however, stretches beyond what circumstances require, and gives himself to pledges that define a new future for others, even when Boaz himself is not under obligation to them.

A third pair of dramatic characters is found in the background collectives that provide color commentary to the story. There is a group of women who congregate around Naomi and Ruth early in the tale (when these two enter Bethlehem after Naomi's exile) and again late in the story (in order to pronounce blessings on the household after Obed is born), announcing Naomi's situation and reflecting her changing fortunes. Likewise, a group of men gloms on to Boaz, first in the fields of harvest, where they act as his confidants and advisers, and then for a second time in the final gate scene, where they adjudicate the decisions that are being made.

Character Pairings in the Book of Ruth

Concise Character Parallelism:

Lead Characters:

Ruth—(female, young, widowed, alien)

Boaz—(male, older, wealthy, Israelite)

Dramatic Counterpoint Minor Characters:

Orpah—female, foil to Ruth

Other Kinsman—male, foil to Boaz

Background Support Choruses:

The women who surround Naomi

The men who surround Boaz

Note: The Role of Naomi is **_not_** paralleled!

Naomi is the main character!

Her changing situation is the point of the drama.

Notes on Two Customs

Ruth and Boaz at the threshing floor (Chapter 3)
- Why did Naomi make this happen? Only through a male child born to her or Ruth by way of a close relative could the family name and its patrimony be restored (cf. Deuteronomy 25:5–10).

Boaz and the "kinsman-redeemer" (Chapter 4)
- Why did Boaz force the other, closer relative of Elimelech and Naomi to decide whether he would marry Ruth? Only in this way would Naomi and Ruth be restored to a place in the community (cf. Leviticus 25:23–28).

What becomes strangely clear when reviewing these pairings is that Naomi stands alone. Elimelech, her husband, vanishes within the first few verses. Ruth may be a companion to Naomi, but she is never an equal. The women who chant are always in the background, even as Naomi lives at center stage. While the title of the book may focus our attention on Ruth, it is actually the figure of Naomi that emerges in the drama as the main character. She has no counterpart. She is the focus of the story. Although we delight in snuggling up to Ruth and Boaz, it is the fortunes of Naomi that become the prime concern of everyone else in the tale.

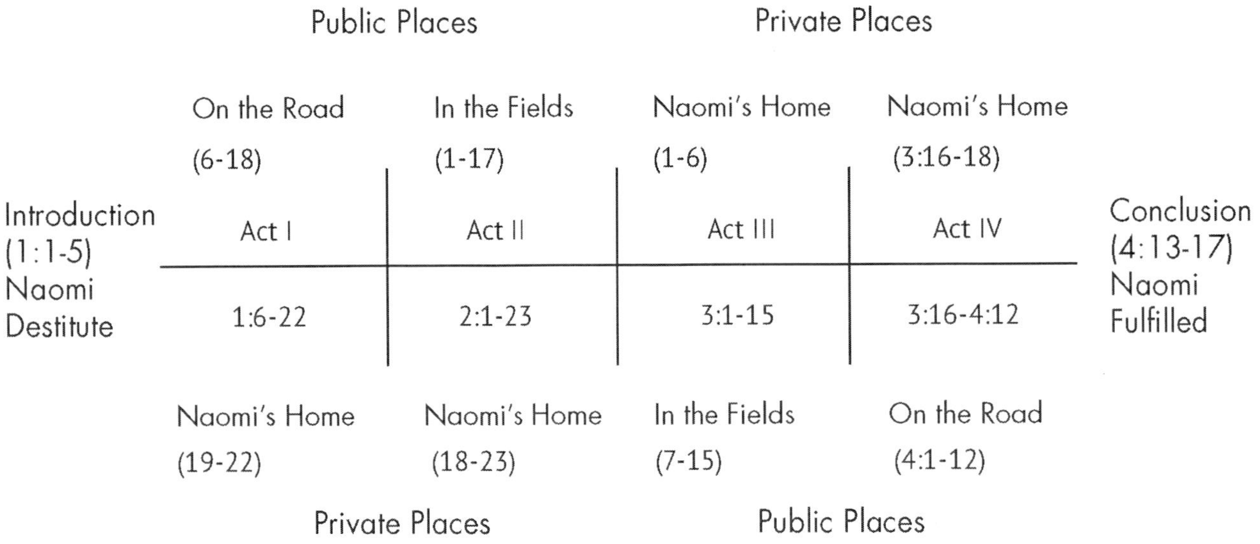

	Public Places		Private Places		
	On the Road (6-18)	In the Fields (1-17)	Naomi's Home (1-6)	Naomi's Home (3:16-18)	
Introduction (1:1-5) Naomi Destitute	Act I	Act II	Act III	Act IV	Conclusion (4:13-17) Naomi Fulfilled
	1:6-22	2:1-23	3:1-15	3:16-4:12	
	Naomi's Home (19-22)	Naomi's Home (18-23)	In the Fields (7-15)	On the Road (4:1-12)	
	Private Places		Public Places		

Figure 7.2 Graphic overview of the book of Ruth.

A Moral Mirror

In this light, we begin to understand the theological significance of the drama. While it is a story well told and beautifully staged, it is also a clearly moral and religious homily. Like Samson in the book of Judges, Naomi is the mirror reflection of Israel as a nation. The very fact that she has no parallel character within the tale makes her stand out as a type of something larger, something more significant.

This theological significance is highlighted by the striking use of setting and names throughout. The story begins in the time of the Judges, when the dominant motif, echoed particularly in the sordid appendix to the book of that name, is: "in those days there was no king in the land and everyone did what was right in his own eyes." The book of Ruth commences with a man consciously removing his family from their divinely granted inheritance, to seek fortune and security among Israel's enemies. This is the displacement warned about in the curses of the Sinai Covenant, and modeled in the failures of both the tribes of Dan and Benjamin.

> **Names in Ruth** 🔍⊕
>
> *Bethlehem*—"House of Bread"
> *Elimelech*—"My God is King"
> *Naomi*—"My Sweetness/Pleasant"
> *Machlon*—"Sickly"
> *Kilion*—"Weakling"
> *Ruth*—"Friend"
> *Mara*—"Bitter"
> *Boaz*—"In him is strength"
> *Obed*—"Servant"

At the same time, the book of Ruth ends with a clear and unambiguous link to the time of the kings, in its epilogue that lists the family succession directly to David. In this way, the story of Naomi bridges the awful destitution of life under the judges with the Camelot sparkle of Israel's grand existence during the reigns of David and Solomon. It is thus, coded in the weavings of Naomi's life, that the key to Israel's success is found. How does Naomi go from rags to riches? How will Israel claw its way back from destitution to restitution? The answer lies in the symbolism of this story.

Bethlehem, the home town of Elimelech and Naomi, means "house of bread." Yet, it is precisely here that there is famine "in the days of the judges" because of the failure of the Israelites to live as Yahweh's covenant community of witness. This becomes even clearer when Elimelech ("My God is King") leaves his inheritance to become, in effect, a Moabite man. The Moabites were cursed by Yahweh for having led Israel to lose its religious identity in Numbers 22–25. Though unstated, Elimelech's faithlessness prompts an underlying current of judgment against his family. This is why his sons are so frail (Machlon means "sickly," Kilion means "weakling") and die along with their father, leaving the one vision of hope in the family, wife and mother Naomi ("sweet" or "pleasant"—"Sweetie-pie," you might say!), turned sour (Mara means "bitter").

It is only through a faithful Israelite who did not leave his inheritance (Boaz means "in him is strength"), coupled with a despised Moabite woman who actually caught the vision of Yahweh's missional covenant community in spite of the failures of so many of Israel's citizens—that Israel/Naomi is restored. So the drama, which began when the "House of Bread" was empty, ends with a bountiful harvest in the same breadbasket community. Moreover, the family that gave up its inheritance, only to have its future obliterated under the curses of the Covenant (all of the males—who carry the inheritance links—die, leaving the women worse than dead), finds a new fulfillment that brings harvest, safety, home, wealth, and above all, a male child to restore a claim in the inheritance of the covenant people in the promised land. And what is the name of the boy? Obed. "Servant." Exactly! Only when personal self-interest (so Orpah and the kinsman-redeemer) is given up for faithful covenant service (so Ruth and Boaz) does life begin again to shimmer with significance. The book of Ruth is very fine drama indeed, but it is exceptionally great theology besides!

The book of Ruth is all about Naomi, and Naomi is all about Israel. It begins during the time of the Judges, when Israel was turning away from Yahweh and experiencing the curses of the Covenant, including losing its place in the Promised Land. It points to the need to return "home" to the Covenant inheritance if life is going to recover its significance. It shows how the problem of "Mara" (bitter destitution) is resolved through covenant obedience. And it ends with a direct link to King David, who will be given a royal grant (2 Samuel 7) that will keep his family on the throne of Israel forever, ensuring the success of Yahweh's missional enterprise.

The book of Ruth is much more than a good love story; it is a tale of covenant-breaking, judgment, faithfulness, and restoration. Both Ruth and Boaz lay their own selves on the line to meet the needs of Naomi's destitution. They embody the Sinai Covenant. Those who live in this way enter the true *shalom* (rest) that Yahweh intended for Israel. More than that, they bring others (Naomi/the nation of Israel) with them. Leave the land, the Covenant, the mission of Yahweh, as Elimelech did, and you only find death and destitution. Return home, and even the nations (cf. Ruth) are blessed, just as Yahweh promised Abram back in Genesis 12. It is for this purpose that Israel exists, and why she is to live in Canaan, the platform from which the whole redemptive drama of Yahweh will be visible to the nations, and draw them also into covenant blessing.

Discussion Points

- Is "Ruth" a good title for this book of the Bible, or should it perhaps be called "Naomi?" Why?
- How does the book of Ruth function as a bridge between the times of the Judges and the times of the Kings? What is its dominant message when viewing each of these eras?
- When looking at the character of Naomi, how might the nation of Israel experience a sensation that she is looking in a mirror?
- In what multiple ways is the book of Ruth finely and economically crafted as a literary document?

8.

Backing into Greatness

The Reluctant Monarchy—1 and 2 Samuel

I f the book of Joshua outlined the possession of Canaan by Israel (entering into its covenant mission as community of witness to the world), Judges showed how the nation nearly lost its place and identity through covenant disobedience, and Ruth beautifully hinted at the road back to covenant greatness, it is in 1 and 2 Samuel that the journey of restoration actually takes place. The Hebrew Bible has the books of Samuel and Kings forming a single literary unit. The divisions into separate sections happened out of necessity, since parchment scrolls could only be made large enough to accommodate about a quarter of the entire historical work on each. Since we have become attached to the more recent literary devices of chapters and verses in order to locate sections of text, it is almost impossible for us to recover the full story line that is woven in unbroken advancement through these books, taken together as a whole. Yet it is very important to try to step back a bit, and view the larger message that emerges from the total expanse of the four when regrouped as one.

After all, these writings are not mere histories. The narrator's perspective is from the time of the later kings, looking backward. Israel's "history" is being interpreted as a lengthy sermon, documenting the success or failure of the people to live obediently in their covenant relationship with Yahweh. For that reason, the Hebrew Bible includes these chronologies among the literature identified as the Prophets. While some divinely appointed spokespersons got that title by preaching on the street corners and in the Temple square, others were referenced as such because they communicated the same message of covenant judgment or blessing through a rehearsal of the religious and moral trek of the nation as a whole. Using the terminology of the Hebrew Bible, we might call the books designated "Former Prophets" (Joshua, Judges, 1 and 2 Samuel, and 1 and 2 Kings) as "narrative sermons," and those identified "Latter Prophets" (Isaiah, Jeremiah, Ezekiel, the Twelve) as "didactic sermons."

Although the Tabernacle does not play prominently in 1 and 2 Samuel, the Sinai Covenant continues to do so. There is a critical covenant renewal ceremony in 1 Samuel 11:14–12:25 that stands at the heart of the message. Just as the Israelites begin clamoring for a visible human king, like those found among the other nations around, Samuel crystallizes the deeper issue of identity by calling the people back to covenant faithfulness with Yahweh, their only true sovereign. When a human monarchy is finally allowed by Yahweh, it begins in tragedy (the story of Saul), and only blossoms into greatness (the story of David and Solomon) after the people become willing to enter this new era of their existence on Yahweh's terms. David, in this setting, will be known as "a man after God's own heart."

Early on in the story, a pair of contrasting characters is developed. Eli ("My God"), the aged high priest, fails to rally the nation into covenant obedience, while Samuel ("God hears") champions the cause of Yahweh in such a way that Israel is restored to honor and dignity among its neighbors. Similarly, Saul, the first king, is readily acknowledged as a leader, yet fails to follow through, while David, the second king, is only an ignored runt, who ultimately becomes a great leader because he stays true to his relationship with Yahweh. These two polarizing tales form the literary backbone of 1 and 2 Samuel. In summary, the books unfold in this manner:

- **Historical Setting** (1 Samuel 1–7):
  * Unique and miraculous birth of Samuel (note Hannah's song)
  * Demise of Eli and of Israel:
    ◊ Note that the sons of Eli attempt to use the Ark of Yahweh as a power tool
    ◊ "Ichabod" ("Glory departed") symbolizes the loss of both the Ark of Yahweh as well as Israel's covenant faithfulness
  * Yahweh wins battles over the Philistines and their gods without human aid, and returns home miraculously
  * A new voice of Yahweh emerges through Samuel
- **Transition from Samuel (Judges) to Saul (Kings)** (1 Samuel 8–15):
  * Consolidating the kingdom under Samuel
    ◊ Note the covenant renewal ceremony in 11:14–12:25
  * Acquiescing to the Israelite request for a king
    ◊ Saul starts like a prophet, ends like a demon
    ◊ Samuel remains in charge throughout, as primary human leader
  * Establishing the rise and fall of Saul
    ◊ Early victories (Ammonites, Philistines, Amalekites)
    ◊ Rash decisions (officiating as priest, stupid battlefield rules, sparing Agag)

- **Transition from Saul to David** (1 Samuel 16–2 Samuel 5:5):
  * David enters:
    ◊ Identified, anointed, early exploits (Goliath)
    ◊ Moves into Saul's house (Michal, Jonathan)
  * David the fugitive:
    ◊ Leader of the wilderness gang
    ◊ Spending time with the Philistines (Note: David never fights either *with* Saul or *against* Saul in the national struggles with this close neighbor)
  * Saul the declining king:
    ◊ Seeking Samuel through the witch of En Dor
    ◊ Death by suicide in battle with the Philistines
- **The Successes of David** (2 Samuel 5:6–9:13)
  * Over Israel and Saul's house
  * Over enemies
  * The covenant with David (2 Samuel 7):
    ◊ David wishes to build a house for Yahweh
    ◊ Yahweh instead pledges to build a house for David
    ◊ This plays a critical role in both the rest of the Old Testament and in all of the New Testament, making the house of David the key factor in tracing the next moves of Yahweh with Israel and beyond
- **The Decline and Troubles of David** (2 Samuel 10–20):
  * David's sin with Bathsheba
  * David's troubles with Amnon and Absalom (and all of Israel)
- **Appendix: Reflections on David** (2 Samuel 21–24):
  * His song
  * His Mighty Men and their exploits
  * His sin and punishment (and reprieve) in counting Israel's military strength

Samuel's Transitional Leadership

There are a number of key issues which emerge through the first half of 1 Samuel, as this new figure takes center stage. For one thing, the covenant theocracy with Yahweh as Israel's unseen King begins to seem inadequate to the people. This is so for at least two reasons: On the one hand, Yahweh's voice is hard to hear, unlike the days of Moses and Joshua, when it was quickly apparent what God desired or decreed. On the other hand, the urgent military threats from neighboring nations seem to demand a readily visible and immediate leadership that is not dependent on lengthy rituals of ceremony and sacrifice before Yahweh might or might not put in an appearance. Precisely because of these concerns, Samuel stands as the transition figure between the judges (who gave quick military leadership and then faded away without establishing ongoing royal courts or dynasties) and the monarchy, as it will emerge in part through Saul and to its full extent by way of David and his family. Samuel, as his name indicates, was a new communication link between the people and their God, and also a mighty general in battle. But his appearance on the scene was too brief to nurture public confidence in long-range national stability without a clearly identified temporal rule and an expectation of solid succession plans.

The clues to Samuel's special gifts and leadership role are scattered throughout the initial seven chapters of 1 Samuel. First, there seem to be injustice and lack of divine blessing in the land. Elkanah's first wife, Hannah, is barren, a typical sign of divine displeasure or even curse. His second wife, Peninnah, bears a number of children, but acts rudely toward Hannah about their contrasting situations. In short, the good wife is punished, and the bad wife is blessed. Things are definitely wrong in this upside-down world!

Second, the official representative for Yahweh, a priest named Eli ("My God"), neither recognizes true need and absolute devotion in Hannah's silent praying, nor is able to intercede on her behalf with Yahweh. At first, he rudely accosts Hannah, calling her a drunkard. Then, when she pours out her deep frustrations, all he can do is wish her well. He does not have Yahweh's ear, and Yahweh's voice does not speak through him, even though he is a priest.

Third, Eli's sons, who are priests in their own right, are wicked men. They fail to mediate between Israel and Yahweh. They rob the people to feed their own gluttony. They mishandle the sacrifices, although the rituals are clearly spelled out. They have sexual relations with women at the Tabernacle, just like the priest and prostitutes at the fertility shrines of other nations and gods. They fail to heed their father's admonitions. And then, to top it off, they presume leadership of the armies of Israel, and brazenly take the Ark of the Covenant into battle as a weapon of war!

Fourth, the writer uses one telling event during Samuel's childhood as the defining image of both the times and the man. "In those days the word of the Lord was rare," he tells us (1 Samuel 3:1). Then, simply, the story of Samuel hearing his name called in the night is told. Samuel does not know who is calling him, and at first, Eli does not either. But soon it becomes apparent to the older man that, while he has neither the ear nor the voice of Yahweh, this young child certainly does. The nation quickly learns the same, as the writer notes in his closing comments on this episode: "The Lord was with Samuel as he grew up, and he let none of his words fall to the ground. And all Israel from Dan to Beersheba recognized that Samuel was attested as a prophet of the Lord. The Lord continue to appear at Shiloh, and there he revealed himself to Samuel through his word. And Samuel's word came to all Israel" (1 Samuel 3:19-4:1)

Fifth, in battles against the neighboring Philistines, the Israelites are impotent. Not only do they lose the war, but the throne of their God—the Ark of the Covenant—is captured by the enemy through the foolishness of Eli's sons. Still, Yahweh personally battles the Philistines and their god Dagon, until the Philistines recognize defeat and send the Ark home. In the end, it is Samuel alone (1 Samuel 7) who can reconcile Israel back to Yahweh, and turn the page on this horrible chapter, with a clear divine deliverance from the Philistines.

When the Israelites finally grow bold enough to demand a human king, Samuel is the one who must mediate between Yahweh and the people until each party understands the consequences. Then, Samuel anoints both of the first kings of Israel, the obvious leader who turns out bad, and the overlooked runt who turns out great.

Saul's Flawed Reign

Saul is also a transitional figure. He expresses both what the monarchy can be and what it should not be. In this sense, he is flawed and expendable. David, on the other hand, becomes the paradigmatic king against whom all other rulers will be assessed. This is why an everlasting covenant (royal grant) places his family on the throne forever (2 Samuel 7). Throughout the Old Testament, this covenant is a source of hope for Israel (and later Judah), particularly during times of foreign oppression and alien occupation of the land. With the dawning of the New Testament era, the promised Davidic kingship feeds apocalyptic fervor and shapes messianic prophecy. When Yahweh fulfills the promises made to Israel, according to all religious and national expectations, it will take place through a descendant of this royal family.

The public transition from Saul's rule to that of David's actually begins on a battlefield, with the famous narrative of the shepherd boy who brought down the giant, Goliath. The story of David and Goliath stands in the ongoing tradition of tales that informed ancient Israel of its

> ### Dating It All
>
> *(The earlier dates are very approximate; the latter dates more accurate, though still inexact.)*
>
> 2000 Abraham
>
> 1445(?)/1250(?) The Exodus
>
> 1400–1350(?)/1200(?) Conquest of Canaan
>
> 1300–1100 Time of the Judges
>
> 1105 Birth of Samuel
>
> 1080 Birth of Saul
>
> 1050 Saul anointed as king
>
> 1040 Birth of David
>
> 1025 David anointed to become king
>
> 1010 Death of Saul, beginning of David's reign in Judah
>
> 1003 Beginning of David's reign over all Israel, capture of Jerusalem
>
> 991 Birth of Solomon
>
> 980 David's infamous census
>
> 970 Death of David, Solomon's reign begins

identity within its world. The younger son (Isaac, Jacob, Joseph) is preferred over the older brother (Ishmael, Esau, the sons of Leah) as the carrier of covenant promise, blessing, and initiative. The weaker (enslaved Israel, wandering Israel, Israel at Jericho, Israel among the powerful city-states of Canaan) proves to be the stronger in international clashes (over Egypt, Amalek, Moab, Ammon, Jericho, etc.). Even in the fairly recent (within David's context) remembered history, Samson became the agent of Israelite deliverance from the Philistines after he had been weakened through divine penalties on his corrupted Nazirite vows.

Now the morality play is acted out once more, with timid Israel no match for the Philistine mean machine. The Philistines controlled metallurgy in the whole region (see 1 Samuel 13:19–21), dramatically unbalancing the stockpiles and effectiveness of weapons between the competitors. Israel was out of the Philistines' league entirely, a weakling child being bullied on the wrestling floor of the WWF, a primitive nation bringing crude sticks against armor-clad swordsmen.

Moreover, the early campaign promises of King Saul have evaporated. In recent times, he had become less than a caricature of his old self. No longer the tall warrior heading a battle charge, he slumps now in his tent with no inspirational retort to Goliath's taunts. Israel's army was demoralized and insulted; Israel's God had become a joke among the priests of Dagon.

Into the tale skips a young lad. His parents couldn't remember him on the day of Samuel's subversive visit to Bethlehem to crown a replacement king (1 Samuel 16). Even now, after all of the secretive hoopla that identified him as future custodian of the realm, he remains only an overlooked messenger boy, bringing cheese sandwiches to his soldier brothers who are supposed to be the real men of the story.

David is a character of less-than-refined politeness. He hears Goliath's mighty screams, blaspheming Yahweh and shattering Israelite confidence. Rather than query diplomatically into what strategy might be developing as the generals huddle around Saul, David boldly asks about the rewards for the expected Israelite champion who must necessarily silence this audacity.

While David's brothers try to quiet his insolence, word reaches Saul that a newcomer is willing to take on the giant. The king is ever so ready to throw this young one to the enemy lion, for at least such action will detract attention from his own inaction. When David loses the contest (as obviously he will), Saul can shake his head at the tragedy, protest his own innocence in the matter, and use the boy's mangled body to rally indignation into a popular uprising. David is a key player in Saul's next move.

Even the enemy knows the obvious outcome to this silliness. Philistine soldiers who stand like a picket fence on the southern rim of the Elah valley laugh in derision at the comedy about to be played out. Goliath, their champion, is almost tenderhearted in his good-natured joshing with David, hoping to keep the wee one from obvious harm.

But the miracles of God's designs continue to shape history against its own flow. David's shepherding skills, honed in years of isolated vigilance, provide the underdog with guerilla tactics that reduce the favored combatant's skills to ineffective preponderance. Goliath falls, both the Philistines and the Israelites gasp, David claims the toys of the vanquished, and all craziness breaks loose. Where one minute there had been the interminable stalemate on the western front, now a torrent of repressed anger erupts from the Israelite camp, and quite literally the fear of God disrupts Philistine discipline into save-your-own-skin rabbit runs.

But what is the point? With regard to the development of the David arc in the annals of Samuel, this is the crucial corner at which David becomes king. From this moment forward, David is on the rise, and Saul is a lame-duck, brooding has-been. The message of this tale, at least in part, is to show the heart-commitment of David, from his earliest public disclosures, as a true through-and-through worshipper of Yahweh. David's first thought, when reaching the stalemated battleground camp, is that Yahweh's honor is being besmirched, and there is no one in Israel who ought to ignore this or let it slide. David is not concerned with winning or losing battles; he is completely sold on rallying to God's cause. Moreover, this is the whole reason for Israel's existence, according to David. In the end, David becomes king—not because he is so clever or capable—rather, he is raised to leadership precisely because he knows that he is not in charge. The true king in Israel is Yahweh. This is a lesson that Saul never fully learned.

Saul is savvy enough to recognize David's trajectory, and the fact that Yahweh is with him. So, Saul competes with both, seeking to destroy David, and trying to usurp Yahweh's place as Israel's rightful king. He fails miserably in both attempts. When Saul brings David into the royal palace to claim David's reputation and prowess as his own, David's goodness steals the hearts of Saul's son, Jonathan, and daughter, Michal (1 Samuel 18). When Israel's armies

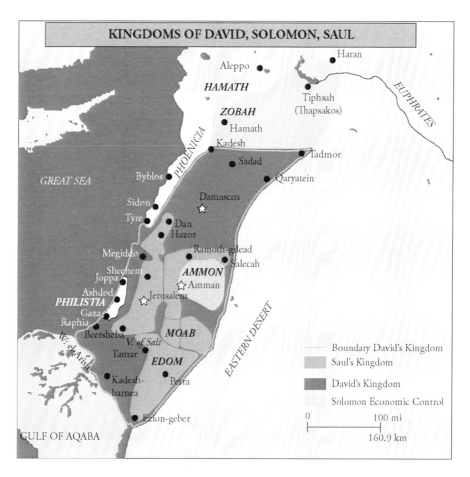

Figure 8.1 The Kingdoms of Saul, David and Solomon.[1]

continue their winning streak against the Philistines, all praise shifts from Saul to David. When Saul tries to kill David, David not only escapes numerous times, but actually turns the tables and refuses to harm Saul twice when the opportunities present themselves When Saul tries to marginalize David, David builds a new community of misfits and cast-offs who will eventually become the leadership team in his new administration. And when Saul finds himself spiritually bereft, he turns to witchcraft rather than Yahweh, and finds himself rejected by both.

One of the last stories in the transitional narrative of Saul's downward spiral is that of David defeating and destroying the Amalekites (1 Samuel 30), the nasty enemies of Israel whom Saul had earlier spared (1 Samuel 15). Saul failed, David succeeded. Saul's big-bang beginning whimpers into a battlefield suicide. David's obscure origins rise quickly into shining salvation for Israel, clearly tied to complete devotion to Yahweh, the nation's true and only Sovereign.

---

1   Copyright in the Public Domain.

Did David Actually Exist?

As with many of the earlier Old Testament stories, the tales told in 1 and 2 Samuel are significantly disputed by both biblical theologians and historians of the ancient Near East. Some say David never existed, and that he was only a heroic creation of later generations (like King Arthur of England), conjured up to provide political validation to a particular group in Israelite society. Others see in the stories of David hints of the *Habiru* identified by Egyptian sources as rebellious former slave gangs terrorizing the ancient Near East. Still others think David was a non-Israelite (son of a Moabite mother and a Jebusite father) warrior, who created a strong clan in Judah (over Saul's Benjamite clan), and then consolidated political influence over the whole of Israel in the chaotic vacuum after Saul was defeated by the Philistines.

A stone tablet (dated to about 835 B.C.) in Aramaic was found at Tel Dan in 1993, however, and appears to be an authentic historical conquest record of Hazael, king of Syria. It identifies the kings of Judah as "the House of David." So most agree today that David actually existed. Under dispute is whether the biblical record provides valid testimony for all the events listed, and in what manner the religious character of Israel actually developed. As stated in the Introduction, choices of interpretation must be made, and these reflect confessional standpoints.

David's Bold Leadership Moves

It is for this reason that David ties his reign to the restoration of the centrality of Yahweh and the visible indications provided by the Tabernacle and the Ark of the Covenant (2 Samuel 5–6). David is playing the political game with rules not appreciated by everyone, even in his own society. Within remembered history, the nation had emerged from its own "Dark Ages." Grandparents (and even some parents) could remember well the times during the Judges. Israel was, at best, a loose confederation of bickering tribes, each handicapped by inconsequential leadership. Now and again internal threats or neighboring nations would stir the political blood long enough for a savior to be identified (and sometimes martyred). These "judges" brought a bit of regional stability, but national unity and direction were more distant than the patchwork of a gaudy quilt.

More recently, David's predecessor, a Benjamite named Saul, rose to prominence and had welded the squabbling communities into a bit of an imperial hegemony. "Israel" now begins to take precedence over the clannish tribal names, especially in the face of Amalek and Philistine aggressions. But Saul's star has fallen by the time his body collapses in battle. The confederation is compromised, and not everybody wants young David to be on the throne; many even regret the establishment of a royal chair in the first place.

As David consolidates his rule, he makes a singular move on the national chessboard, which defines the character of his administration. In a stroke of genius which arose from the unswerving commitments of his heart, David brings the Ark of the Covenant up to Jerusalem from its forgotten and tattered site at Shiloh. Prophets and press would quickly point out to the people the remarkable history of this portable throne of the Creator, who had become Israel's chief resident at Mount Sinai. David's design was to restore national unity, but clearly mark it as solidarity under Yahweh, rather than under himself.

Who could deny that Israel's glory days were those of Moses and Joshua, when Yahweh was openly proclaimed as national King, and the Ark of the Covenant paraded through the deserts of the Sinai and the battlegrounds of Canaan as the visible symbol of the unconquerable power of the great God, who had claimed Israel as a divine possession? This is the theological and

 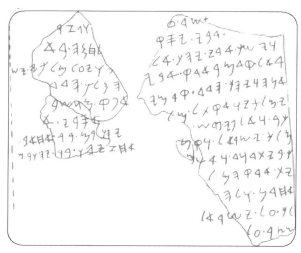

Figure 8.2 A stone tablet (dated to about 835 B.C.) in Aramaic was found at Tel Dan in 1993.[2]

historical background that David claims as he brings the Ark up to Jerusalem. Rather than quibble about whether he is a suitable replacement on a weak and challenged throne, David portrays himself as the servant of the One who rules beyond question among the tribes. Even if the religion of Yahweh has fallen onto hard times, it carries the great myth by which every Israelite stands tall and proud.

The brief setback experienced in David's plans (2 Samuel 6:1-1), when proper protocol for transporting the Ark is not followed, only serves to reinforce all of these themes. At first, David tries to haul the Ark up the rugged paths to his new and somewhat inaccessible capital city as if it is a piece of furniture. A little object lesson from Yahweh is enough to put the fear of God in everyone. After a decent period of mourning and waiting, David's tactic changes. He is no longer the new potentate, waiting for the moving company to finish furnishing his royal quarters. Instead, he becomes a shepherd boy again, dancing in humility around the throne of his Master, carried in solemn procession by its bearers through the countryside until it can take a commanding position over all from the heights of the Judaean mountains.

Of course, this disturbs some who think David's character is maligned in the process, and the dignity of his office quashed. Michal, in particular, spits on his exuberance (2 Samuel 6:20-23). She is, after all, King Saul's daughter, and she knows how regents ought to conduct themselves in aristocratic separation from the *hoi polloi*. David, her husband, has displayed himself like a cheap commoner, a public entertainer.

But Michal does not understand. Her husband is not like her father. For David, at least at this stage of his life (and throughout his reign, according to his deepest desires), the ultimate goal is not to be king, but rather to be first minister to Emperor Yahweh. In this, David's politics

---

2   Source: http://commons.wikimedia.org/wiki/File:Tel_dan_inscription.JPG

David's "Peace"-ful Children

David was not permitted by Yahweh to build the Temple as a permanent structure to replace the portable Tabernacle of Israel's wilderness wanderings because he was a "man of war." His son, a "man of peace," would be given the mandate to oversee the construction.

David probably pegged his hopes on Absalom, the son he loved very much. After all, the lad's given name meant "Father of Peace." Unfortunately, Absalom tried to rip the kingdom away from David by political maneuvering and military conquest, and actually became more bellicose than his father.
Solomon, on the other hand, whose name simply meant "Peace," was a child-king guided by David's advisers to establish both domestic tranquillity and national pride centering around the magnificent Temple in Jerusalem.

---

are of a completely different strain than that of his predecessor. Saul played the politics of man quite well. David plays the politics of heaven superbly.

David's Demise

The demise of David's reign is tied to a fascinating story that seems to be constantly repeated in political annals: an extramarital affair. Why would David do such a thing? Not just the romantic encounter itself, but the deliberately planned murder (engaging others of his trusted subordinates as willing or unwilling accomplices), the massive deceptions, the elaborate cover-ups, and even the personal delusions that kept him from seeing his own guilt.

Part of the answer has to be found in the very first verse of 2 Samuel 11: "In the spring, at the time when kings go off to war, David sent Joab out with the king's men and the whole Israelite army ... But David stayed in Jerusalem." This hints at several things. First, the time of the year lent itself to surging hormones and amorous thoughts. After the months of terrestrial hibernation, the world around David was beginning to bloom, the days were getting warmer (Jerusalem sometimes gets snow in winter), both animals and plants were exercising their mating rituals, and along with them the human crowd in the palace and the capital city were showing signs of frisky behavior. There is good reason to celebrate Valentine's Day in the spring, and David himself was a muscular male whose own body welcomed the virus of libido.

Second, David's life was a runaway success. His early contestants to the throne of Israel had all been killed, defeated, or swept aside. David was at the top of the corporate ladder, with no immediate challengers in sight. His kingdom was consolidated, his enemies vanquished, his market share a supreme monopoly, his income substantial and rising, his palatial mansion finished, and his goals achieved. David was at the place in his career where "can't" and "defeat" were no longer part of the vocabulary. What he wanted, he got. What he desired, he took. What he planned, happened. No questions asked. Winning a new territory or another heart were essentially the same: Get the idea and make it so.

Third, David had begun to isolate himself from the masses. He had the disease of wealthy insulation, where immediate consequences of actions cannot, and need not, be felt. The armies went off to war, but David stayed in Jerusalem. The workers buzzed about in their daily rituals, but he sat on the roof of his palace and surveyed the scene. Regular folks had to labor for a wage, but there was no schedule David had to keep. He could sleep or sneak or sulk or skulk or sidle or stroll at will. Adultery was at one time mainly the prerogative of the rich, simply because only they had the time and means. Mass transportation, suburban domestic isolation, and a culture of leisure dispense it liberally to all classes of society. But David lived in one of those eras when "fooling around" was a natural correlation to being rich and powerful.

These things come through in Nathan's ingenious invective against his friend and lord. Telling a story of the difference in lifestyle between the uncaring and presumptive rich man and the tenderhearted poor fellow aggravated David, as it should have. But his self-deception was so great that he did not see himself in the mirror until Nathan bashed it against his psyche.

The outcome of David's devious treachery would be family squabbles and the disruption of the monarchy for the rest of David's life. David and Bathsheba's first child would die, followed by the tragic demise of several other children. David himself would limp from the throne in his old age, barely keeping the restive kingdom alive.

Singing David's Song

The book of Psalms may well have had its origins as a small collection of songs written by David. Seventy-two of the Psalms are attributed to David, and most of these occur early in the volume. Among those naming David as author, some include specific references to events taking place in David's life at the time he wrote them. Many of these talk about the years of David's outlaw exile described in 1 Samuel 19–27, while others highlight critical junctures during David's reign. Most poignant is Psalm 51, written after David's adulterous affair with Bathsheba. Here are the clear connections linking a number of Psalms to David's biography:

- 59 (1 Samuel 19)
- 52 (1 Samuel 21:1–9; 22:6–23)
- 34 (1 Samuel 21:10–14)
- 63 (1 Samuel 22–26)
- 54 (1 Samuel 23:14–29)
- 57 (1 Samuel 24)
- 60 (2 Samuel 8)
- 51 (2 Samuel 11–12)
- 3 (2 Samuel 15)
- 18 (2 Samuel 22)

If one poetic verse were to summarize the heart of David, it would likely be Psalm 139, aptly titled "To the Leader."

With the establishment of the monarchy, the history of Israel angles in a new and decisive direction. From this time forward, the national identity will be bound up, once again, in a regenerating cycle of point-person human leaders, who will coalesce the religious, moral, and political vision of the nation. While Solomon will take that mandate to the expansive heights expected by Yahweh in the world-changing mission imparted originally to Abraham, the journey of jubilation will soon turn into a trail of tears, as subsequent kings mostly make mockery of the whole business. Only when David's last kingly scion, Jesus of Nazareth, appears, will the divine mission and the royal line converge again in a new and unprecedented way.

Discussion Points

- Describe Samuel's place in ancient Israel through some of the major stories of his life.
- Compare and contrast the lives, spirituality, and political fortunes of Saul and David.
- Why is it so important for David that the Ark of the Covenant be brought into his new capital city at the beginning of his reign?
- Explain the significance of God's covenant with David in 2 Samuel 7. Why is it fashioned as a royal grant, rather than a suzerain-vassal covenant? How does it play into the identity of Jesus in the New Testament?
- Compare and contrast the lives and fortunes of Absalom and Solomon.

For Further Investigation

Auld, A. Graeme. (Louisville: Westminster John Knox, 2011). *I & II Samuel: A Commentary*.

9.

Lessons in Self-Destruction

Failure of the First Covenant Experiment—Kings and Chronicles

1 and 2 Kings are a literary continuation of 1 and 2 Samuel. The current divisions are based upon the length of a text that could be written on a single roll of parchment. Because of this, the whole of "Kings" was subdivided into four manageable sections.

A huge focus of 1 Kings is on Solomon and the building of the Temple. It is clear from various notes and references that the Temple was to be considered the palace of Israel's true king, Yahweh. For one thing, the Temple was located at the top of the slope on which Jerusalem was built, geographically elevated above Solomon's own lavish residence. Topography was important for the kings of nations and city-states in the ancient Near East; like children pushing and shoving in playground games, there could only be one positional "king of the hill."

Who Is Israel's True King?

More significant still is the prayer of Solomon at the dedication of the Temple in 1 Kings 8. Although Solomon is clearly in charge of the political realm he inherited from his father, his address to Yahweh leaves no one guessing as to who is really the supreme ruler of the land and its people. In this, scriptural theology from Genesis through the time of the monarchy is consistent: Yahweh is the Creator of all, and has entered into a special relationship with Israel, in order that this community might be a witness of the divine presence and favor from its strategic position on the bridge-land between the nations.

Quite remarkable is the note in 2 Chronicles 3:1 that the location of the Temple is not only at the top of Jerusalem, the capital city, but also on the site where Abraham had been willing to sacrifice Isaac, the miraculous child born of divine promise to him and Sarah (2 Chronicles 3:1). Here, several strands of the great mission of Yahweh come together. First, by way of a suzerain-vassal covenant, Yahweh had claimed Abraham and his family as divine partners in the great redemption plan for the whole of the human race, and sealed the deal through Isaac ("Laughter"), who brought pleasure to his parents and hope for the world. On this very site, Abraham's faith and commitments were affirmed, Isaac was spared to carry on the promise and mission, and the hint of a substitutionary solution for meeting the needs of the human race was put in motion. Little did Abraham realize that two thousand years later, on this very spot, his later, greater son, the One who was more fully the Son of Man and the Son of God than any knew at the time, would become that substitutionary sacrifice. In Jesus, Abraham's prophetic words to his son Isaac ("God himself will provide the lamb for the burnt offering, my son." Genesis 22:8) would actually be witnessed on this same spot as the mission of God culminated in the coming of Jesus, and then shifted its focus to the international witness of the Church.

Second, because this was also the place where old King David pleaded for mercy after he had sinned in the pride of counting to see how great his military might really was (2 Samuel 24, 1 Chronicles 21), the site had intercessory significance. Here, the power of heaven was checked by a human plea for divine mercy. Here, Yahweh remembered and recommitted himself to the joint relationship of the Sinai Covenant. Here, an altar was erected for the burnt offering that knit eternity to time in communion and cooperation. Thus, for the Altar of Burnt Offering to be built in the grand and permanent Temple that would replace the tattered and traveling Tabernacle on this piece of real estate was extremely symbolic. It was right for the Ark of the Covenant, topped by the Mercy Seat of Yahweh's throne, to be situated in the royal palace of the Temple ("My house ...") exactly where mercy had stalled judgment, and grace had shone so brightly.

In this manner, the great *Shekinah* glory light of Yahweh's presence fills the new Temple and spills through the streets of Jerusalem, gushing and tumbling out through all of Israel to impact and change a darkened world that has forgotten its Creator. This is later pictured clearly by Isaiah and Micah, among others of the prophets:

> *In the last days the mountain of the Lord's temple will be established as chief among the mountains;*
> *It will be raised above the hills, and all nations will stream to it.*
> *Many peoples will come and say, "Come, let us go up to the mountain of the Lord,*
> *to the house of the God of Jacob.*
> *He will teach us his ways, so that we may walk in his paths."*
> *The law will go out from Zion, the word of the Lord from Jerusalem.*
> *He will judge between the nations and will settle disputes for many peoples.*

*They will beat their swords into plowshares and
their spears into pruning hooks.
Nation will not take up sword against nation,
nor will they train for war anymore.
Come, O house of Jacob, let us walk in the light
of the Lord* (Isaiah 2:2–5; Micah 4:1–5).

For forty years, Solomon built the nation into
an international superpower that could not be
ignored anywhere in the ancient Near East. It is
clear from the trade and commerce mentioned
during Solomon's reign that people on three
continents—Africa, Asia, and Europe—not only
knew about Israel, but wanted to enter into
her sphere of influence. This was the outcome
envisioned by Yahweh a thousand years earlier
when conversing with Abram about the divine
intention to bless all the nations of the earth
through his descendants.

Fractured and Disintegrating

The Temple itself stood as a visible reminder
of how the nation of Israel became great. For
that reason, the story of Jeroboam takes on
special significance. Jeroboam was obviously a
gifted man. He was chosen by Solomon
to head the national building projects
(1 Kings 11:28), then recognized as
a political threat by the king (1 Kings
11:40), and eventually identified as the
spokesperson for the general population after Solomon died (1 Kings 12:2).
When Rehoboam, Solomon's spoiled
brat of a son, publicly flouted his disdain of both the people and leadership
wisdom, Jeroboam was poised to wrest
away a portion of the kingdom.

One of the first things Jeroboam
did was to consolidate his territory by

> **The Literary Development
> of 1 and 2 Kings** 📖
>
> - **Solomon's Big Beginnings** (1 Kings 1–11)
>   * Seeking Wisdom
>   * Consolidating the Kingdom
>   * Spreading Fame
>   * Building Projects, Especially the Temple
>   * Folly and Demise
> - **Negotiating a Divided Kingdom** (1 Kings 12–16)
>   * Rehoboam's Folly
>   * Jeroboam's Strategies
>   * Dances of War and Divine Initiatives toward Consensus
> - **Shifting Leadership: The Times of Elijah** ("My God Is Yahweh") **and Elisha** ("My God Is Salvation") (1 Kings 17–2 Kings 8)
>   * Elijah versus Ahab and Jezebel (showdown at Carmel; depression at Horeb)
>   * Elisha's Many Miracles
> - **The Demise of Israel and Revival in Judah** (2 Kings 9–17)
> - **Renewal under Hezekiah and Josiah, but a Nasty End to It All** (2 Kings 18–25)]

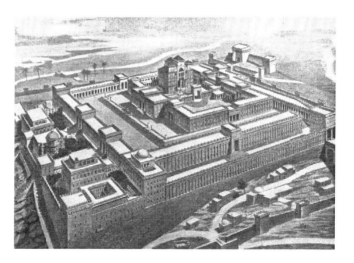

Figure 9.1 Artist's conception of Solomon's Temple at the heights of Jerusalem.[1]

---

1 Copyright in the Public Domain.

The Chain of Leadership

Point leadership for the covenant community moved from person/group to group, depending on faithfulness and calling:

- **Moses**—Original leader, mediator of Sinai Covenant
- **Joshua**—Moses's clear successor, conquest and settlement leader
- **Elders**—Heads of clans who had served under Joshua
- **Judges**—Unique and divinely appointed deliverers in Israel's dark period
- **Kings**—Monarchs who were to serve as visible regents on behalf of Yahweh
- **Prophets**—Divinely appointed spokespersons communicating covenant values in changing times

fortifying its borders. But then he also built new cultic shrines for worship at both the northern (Dan) and southern (Bethel) limits of his realm. As the text indicates (1 Kings 12:25-33), it is not likely that Jeroboam intended to change the religion of his portion of the nation of Israel; at the same time, he needed to replace the grand Temple of Jerusalem with other centers for worship so that his subjects would not be tempted to realign with Rehoboam, as might happen if they continued to journey to Jerusalem for sacrifices and festivals.

Thus, the grand kingdom of David and Solomon became divided, and its theological mission compromised. Yet, the perspective of Kings is that the northern tribes (now "Israel") and the southern portion (now "Judah") were never truly separated. Throughout the rest of these narratives, the political fortunes of both territories were equally considered. Furthermore, the kings of both realms were similarly judged by the prophetic author as either following in the ways of David and Solomon (and so seeking to fulfill the destiny intended by Yahweh), or compounding the covenant-breaking of those who caused the nation to stray from its divine calling and mission. This is most obvious in the harsh assessments given at the time of the northern kingdom's destruction by the Assyrians (2 Kings 17).

While the rulers of the divided kingdom are mostly (in the north) and often (in the south) forgetting and going contrary to the ways and wishes of Israel's true monarch, Yahweh, there comes a new development in the idea of who is in charge as God's anointed and appointed. Note, as 1 and 2 Kings unfold, the emerging and changing role of the public "prophets." Moses and Joshua each had a unique and ongoing relational interchange with Yahweh, which made their leadership positions virtually unassailable (cf. Numbers 12, 16–17). After the nation was settled in Canaan, such clear, regular and unequivocal communication with Yahweh appears to have been muted. During the times of Eli, we are told, "the word of the Lord was

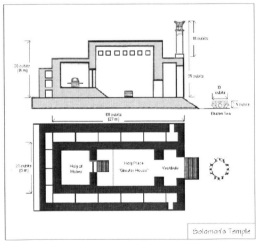

Figure 9.2 Artist's conception of Solomon's Temple side and top views.[2]

---

2   Copyright © Deror avi (CC by 3.0) at http://commons.wikimedia.org/wiki/File:Solomon%27sTemple.jpg

rare; there were not many visions" (1 Samuel 3:1). That is why, when Yahweh began speaking directly with Samuel, the Israelites were ready to follow him (1 Samuel 3:19–21). This seems to be the beginning of a national recognition of the status of prophets as part of the necessary social fabric.

When Samuel's leadership was challenged because the people wanted a king (1 Samuel 8), it caused the first subtle separation of church and state. Samuel was a priest by adoption, and worked within the parameters of the cultic shrine. But the kings were clearly outside of the Levitical priesthood or its extended family. Prophets at first began to bridge the connection, and then later sparred with the kings as the sovereignty role of Yahweh was increasingly forgotten.

This tension is clearly seen in the dominant stories of Elijah and Elisha, who battled with

The Prophets: A Changing Role

10th–9th Centuries: Royal Advisers
    Samuel, Nathan, Ahijah
8th Century: Loyal Opposition
    Amos, Jonah, Hosea, Jonah, Micah, Isaiah
7th Century: Doomsayers
    Jeremiah, Nahum, Habakkuk, Zephaniah
6th Century (Exilic): Theodicy and Restoration Eschatologists
    Ezekiel, Obadiah, Daniel
5th Century (Postexilic): Apocalyptic Moralists and Cheerleaders
    Haggai, Zechariah, Malachi, Joel

the rulers of the northern kingdom in 1 Kings 17–2 Kings 8. Elijah was given the weapons of the curses of the Sinai Covenant to bring Ahab and Jezebel to their knees (1 Kings 17:1). He wielded divine power in public displays of combat (1 Kings 18). He was authorized to determine and appoint the leaders of nations (1 Kings 19). And when Ahab and Jezebel presumed that

Figure 9.3 The divided kingdom.[3]

they could displace God-fearing Israelites from their divinely determined inheritance in the land (1 Kings 21), Elijah confronted the pair with stern prophecies that they instead would be removed.

Throughout the rest of the Old Testament history of Israel, the prophets would take on a changing and growing role as the legitimate and authorized spokespersons for Yahweh and the Sinai Covenant. Most of their speeches are not new revelations, but rather interpretations of the covenant stipulations for current situations. Ultimately, the prophets became the interpreters of Israel's history, and their writings were collected as a unique section of Hebrew scripture.

While the Israelites were able to live in somewhat sheltered isolation during their early years in Canaan, Solomon's reign vaulted them into the political fray of

3   Copyright © Kordas (CC by 3.0) at http://commons.wikimedia.org/wiki/File:Kingdoms_of_Israel_and_Judah_map_830-es.svg

The Nations of Israel's World

Egypt

—Oldest continuous civilization in the ancient Near East

—Former slave masters over the Israelites

—The only significant power to the south of Canaan

—Not overly aggressive militarily, but wished to control Canaan as a buffer zone against Mesopotamian expansionist nations

—Sometimes viewed by Judah as an ally

—Prophetic message: a "splintered" rod (lean on it like a walking stick and it will cut your hand)

Syria (also known as **Aram**)

—Small nation north of Israel

—Capital city: Damascus

—Tended to be a restless neighbor, sometimes harassing Israel, but later, when Assyria threatened, seeking an alliance with Israel against the larger power

—Destroyed (along with Israel) by Assyria in its expansionist campaigns

Assyria

—Major power of northern Mesopotamia

—Capital city: first Asshur, then Nineveh

—Grandly expansionist

—Fiercely aggressive and often cruel in battle

—Conquering policy: Destroy, then deport and mix up leftovers to ensure no possibility of rebellion

—Responsible for the demise of Israel in 722 B.C.

—Defeated by its eastern province, Babylon, in 612 B.C. in that country's own expansionist campaigns

Babylon

—Major power of eastern Mesopotamia

—Capital city: Babylon (built in great splendor by Nebuchadnezzar as an act of devotion to Marduk)

—Proud of its culture, which it sought to export

—Strategically successful in battle

new and increasingly powerful emerging nations. The Philistine threat, which had seemed so overwhelming during the days of Samuel and Saul, evaporated as an insignificant petty turf war before the successive onslaughts of first the Assyrians, and then the Babylonians. The expansive interests of these early superpowers were inseparably intertwined with the lives and preoccupations of four centuries of Israel's kings and prophets.

To the south of Israel lay Egypt, the oldest continuous civilization in the ancient Near East. Because of the Nile's regular pulsations, Egypt had a stable economy and a constant supply of food. Other nations (especially in Mesopotamia), whose agricultural fortunes were more tied to cycles of rain and drought, coveted Egypt's treasury of staples, and knew that control of these resources would enhance their abilities to supply their armies. So, first Assyria, and then Babylon sought to make Egypt a subservient province. Of course, on the way, they needed to deal with the old—but still significant—kingdom made great by Solomon.

Israel among the Nations

The written messages of the prophets make it clear that there were a number of challenges and options for the people of Yahweh. First, it was understood that these invaders were the scourge of God in response to the covenant unfaithfulness of the Israelites. Yahweh's people ought not to miss the point that they were no pawns caught on the scrimmage line of an international football game. As Yahweh proved to Hezekiah during the days of Isaiah and the Assyrian threat, no military incursion was either outside of Yahweh's intended influence or superior to Yahweh's mighty control. Things happened by divine plan, not whimsical fate, and the sooner the people learned this lesson, the more quickly they would return to covenant fidelity with their true Sovereign.

Second, international political alliances would not save the people; only Yahweh could do that. Many in Judah were tempted to connect with Egypt, hoping that its stable greatness would shield the tiny hill country from either Assyria or Babylon. Israel, on the other hand, was forever forming pacts with Syria (either willingly or under coercion) against Assyria, and wanted to take Judah into that coalition in order to strengthen it. Meanwhile, King Ahaz of Judah did an end run around Israel and Syria, appealing directly to Assyria for help. A generation later, King Hezekiah would do something of the same, this time cozying up to Babylonian ambassadors as a secret weapon against Assyrian assault. On each occasion, the prophets delivered a word from Yahweh, reminding the people that Israel was supposed to be a light to the nations, and not a mere ally among them. Moreover, Yahweh was not a small territorial god thumped about on the chessboard of international politics; Yahweh was the Master of nations, and the people must respect their Sovereign as such.

Third, the changing lead nations in this multinational strife shaped the history of bifurcated Israel in quite astounding ways. The northern kingdom was destroyed by Assyria in 722 B.C. (2 Kings 17). The Assyrians were fierce in battle and politics, and dispersed any local survivors of conquest in a grand Near Eastern mixer bowl of population displacement. For that reason, the remnants of the old kingdom of Jeroboam and Ahab became lost among the other peoples of the Assyrian empire, and eventually merged with the Arabic civilizations that would follow centuries later. By the narrowest of margins, the southern kingdom of Judah escaped this fate (2 Kings 18–19), only to be struck down by Babylonia just over a century

–Conquering policy: Retool conquered peoples as vassal provinces; if prone to rebellion, destroy homeland and resettle the rest into its cultural mosaic

–Responsible for the conquest and deportation/exile of Judah (606/597/586 B.C.)

–Defeated by its eastern neighbor, Medo-Persia, in 529 B.C. in that country's expansionist campaigns

Medo-Persia

–Major power north of India

–Culture shaped by Zoroastrian religion, which it sought to export

–Strategically successful in battle

–Conquering policy: Treat conquered groups with mercy and return displaced peoples to their homelands, assimilating all into the larger empire

–Responsible for the restoration of Judah (538 B.C.)

–Carried on an extensive assault on Greece, primarily over farmlands of western Asia Minor. Two major unsuccessful campaigns (490 and 480 B.C.) resulted ultimately in Greek retaliation under Alexander the Great

The Origin of the Samaritans

The "Samaritans" figure prominently in postexilic literature (Ezra) and also in the New Testament (e.g., Luke 10, John 4, Acts 8). Who were these people, and where did they come from?

The story begins in 2 Kings 17, where, after the northern kingdom of Israel had been conquered and displaced, the Assyrians relocated other tribes into the area. Following a series of local mishaps that fed their superstitions, these settlers begged for someone from among the former inhabitants who might teach them about the gods of this region. An Israelite priest was found. Since the northern kingdom of Israel had cut itself off from Jerusalem and the Temple, the only sourcebook of ancient Israelite religion was the Pentateuch, Genesis through Deuteronomy.

In that collection, Moses laid great emphasis on the covenant renewal ceremony that was to take place near Shechem from Mounts Gerizim and Ebal. Since the blessings of the Covenant were to be shouted from Mt. Gerizim, this high spot became associated with holiness. Instructions related to the Tabernacle (Exodus 25–40) were used to create a worship shrine on that mountain, and the minimalist religious identity of the Samaritans began.

Since the Jews (people of Judah) considered these Samaritans deficient in religious understanding, and ethnically outsiders to the original Israelite nation, they treated the Samaritans with disdain and scorn. This led to several incidents of military violence and terrorist activities as each community grew in resentment toward the other.

later (2 Kings 24–25). The Babylonians considered themselves much more civilized than the Assyrians, however, and employed both provincial politics and deportation as tools of conquest. First, the Babylonians would try to amalgamate a newly overrun people into the burgeoning Babylonian empire by retraining leaders to become loyal to their new overlord (so the stories of Daniel and Ezekiel, who were taken to Babylon to be trained, with the goal of ultimately being sent back as ambassadors of their new master). If that did not work, the Babylonians destroyed the centers of political and religious life, and resettled a captured community near the city of Babylon as a way of forming a new mosaic of cultures. This was done to Judah, and it saved the tiny nation from extinction. Finally, the Persians, who conquered Babylon, built an even larger empire by restoring displaced peoples to their homelands, placing them in this way in the debt of Susa.

That is how the "Jews" (i.e., the people of Judah) eventually returned from Babylonian captivity to make a new start.

But before we look at that next chapter in biblical history, there are three ideas to reflect on further. First, from the viewpoint of Kings and Chronicles, the success of Israel was tied to covenant faithfulness. Israel was not an emerging nation trying to build a new religion; it was the ancient people of Abraham settling in Canaan as a fulfillment of divine promises, and shaped as a community of witness by the Sinai suzerain-vassal covenant. This is made uncompromisingly apparent in the narrative commentary found in 2 Kings 17, and also in the records of the great "Reformer Kings" of Judah. Usually cited in this context are Asa, Jehoshaphat, Joash, Hezekiah, and Josiah. The last two of these, in particular, are evaluated openly with regard to the manner in which they revived or renewed covenant identity and practices among the people. This is most obviously seen in the actions of Josiah in 2 Kings 22–23, where, during the cleaning of the Temple after a period of disuse, the "Book of the Law" was discovered. Was this Deuteronomy? Was it the original text of the Sinai Covenant, Exodus 20–24? Was it the whole set of Torah, Genesis through Deuteronomy? We don't know. But what is

Judah's "Reformer" Kings

Dates approximate
Asa—910–870
Jehoshaphat—870–848
Joash—835–796
Hezekiah—715–686
Josiah—640–609

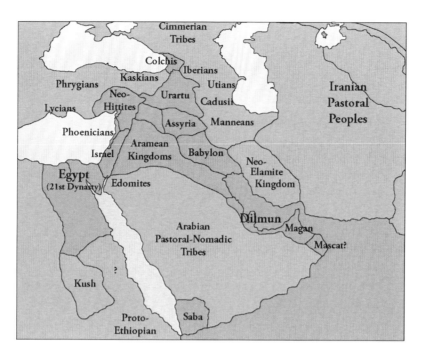

Figure 9.4 Israel's strategic location among the nations.[4]

beyond dispute is that the book contained both the covenant stipulations and its curses and blessings because the king and the people were scared into reformative actions, knowing that they were leaning over the precipice of divine judgment against them. In this light, the history of Israel, from a biblical point of view, cannot be interpreted as a growing desire for, or lately created, monotheistic religion which was then projected into the past by way of fabricated myths. Instead, it must be read forward from the critical and transforming events of the exodus and the covenant-making ceremony of Mt. Sinai. Otherwise, it makes no religious sense.

Second, the materials found in Kings and Chronicles overlap extensively, though there are notable differences between them. The interpreted history recounted in Kings emphasizes the affairs of the nation of Israel as a whole,

> ### Chronicles in Summary 📖
>
> **Prologue:** Genealogies (*1 Chronicles 1–9*)
>
> **David's Mighty Reign** (*1 Chronicles 10–29*)
>
> **Solomon's Splendid Reign** (*2 Chronicles 1–9*)
>
> **Rehoboam to Asa** (*2 Chronicles 10–16*)
>
> > Focus on Asa as Reformer King
>
> **Jehoshaphat to Ahaz** (*2 Chronicles 17–28*)
>
> > Focus on Jehoshaphat as Reformer King
>
> **Hezekiah to Amon** (*2 Chronicles 29–33*)
>
> > Focus on Hezekiah as Reformer King
>
> **Josiah to the Fall of Jerusalem** (*2 Chronicles 34–36*)
>
> > Focus on Josiah as Reformer King

A World in Religious Crisis While Israel Loses Its Missional Sense

- 1050 King Saul   604 Lao Tzu born (*Taoism*)
- 1010 King David   599 Mahariva born (*Jainism*)
- 970 King Solomon   590–550 *Upanishads* written (*Hinduism*)
- 958 The Temple   565 Zarathustra born (*Zoroastrianism*)
- 930 Split Kingdom   563 Siddhartha born (*Buddhism*)
- 722 Israel Destroyed   551 Confucius born (*Confucianism*)
- 586 Captivity of Judah   470 Socrates born (*Greek Philosophies*)

---

even though it was divided following Solomon's reign; Chronicles, on the other hand, focuses its attention primarily on the events that took place in Judah, including a glowing history of David and Solomon as they established the dynasty that would rule there. Kings explains the role of the monarchs, who were largely to blame for bringing the nation down through disobedience and covenant failure; although Chronicles does not mince words about these things, it also pays special attention to the role of the priests who were central in renewing and restoring faithfulness time and again. It is likely that Kings was written around the time of the exile of Judah as a prophetic indictment against the people; Chronicles, on the other hand, was probably penned a little later, most likely by priests who wished to encourage a restoration of covenant faithfulness among the remnant that survived. For these reasons, the books of Kings are included in the Hebrew Bible's section called "the Prophets," while the Chronicles are found in the mixed section known as "the Writings."

Third, the grand divine missional experiment of ancient Israel is judged at the close of Kings to be a failure. Israel was created by Yahweh to bring blessing to the nations of the world. That blessing would flow through these people who were intentionally situated on the crossroads of the nations as actors on the stage of life, revealing the character of human existence, as recovered and restored in fellowship with its Creator by way of the Sinai suzerain-vassal covenant. Unfortunately, like Samson, the Israelites ultimately became more enamored with the lifestyle and values of their neighbors than they did in giving witness to the unique treasure of religious insight they had received. During the sixth and fifth centuries B.C., just at the time that Israel was losing its faith and covenant distinctiveness, seven of the world's other great religions were being formed. One cannot help but wonder what our world would have looked like if these international seekers of transcendent meaning had found Yahweh through the witness of Israel.

Discussion Points

- How does the building of the Temple in Jerusalem by Solomon provide visible synthesis between the political and religious dimensions of Israelite society?
- In what way does the expansion of Solomon's fame and political influence serve as a fulfillment of the promise to Abraham in Genesis 12:1–3?

- Why does the Kingdom of Israel divide after Solomon's great reign? What is Jeroboam's role in Solomon's government that earned him national trust? How is he instrumental to this separation of the realm into two political divisions? What specific acts did Jeroboam take to consolidate his kingdom and religiously isolate it from the Temple in Jerusalem?
- Who were some of the "reformer" kings of Judah, and what significant events transpired under their leadership?
- Describe the conflict between Ahab and Elijah, and explain its implications for Israel.
- Identify the given titles for the participants in and explain the character of the chain of divinely appointed leadership in Israel from Moses on.
- What nations surrounding Israel and Judah were the major players in the larger political activities taking place in the ancient Near East? How did the changing fortunes of these nations, along with the political policies they established, impact the books of Kings and Chronicles?

10.

Restoring the Covenant Community

Redefining National Identity—Ezra and Nehemiah

The biblical writings identified as "Ezra" and "Nehemiah" actually form a single literary work, but one which is made up of a number of source materials loosely woven together. Included in the contents are pages from personal journals, organizational lists, government pronouncements, and historical records from both eyewitnesses and royal archives. Together, these have been crafted into four major sections:

- Zerubbabel and the Restoration of the Temple (Ezra 1-6)
- Ezra and the Restoration of the Covenant Practices (Ezra 7-10)
- Nehemiah and the Restoration of the City (Nehemiah 1-6)
- Ezra and Nehemiah Together and the Restoration of the Covenant People (Nehemiah 7-13)

From beginning to end, the stories told in Ezra and Nehemiah span nearly a century. They start with the decree of the Persian king, Cyrus, in 538 B.C. to allow and encourage the Jewish exiles in Babylon back to their homeland. A short narrative (Ezra 1-6) is devoted to the return under Sheshbazzar, Zerubbabel, and Joshua, and the rebuilding of a small Temple. Then there is a gap of nearly sixty years before Ezra (a "scribe"—someone who spent his time copying scripture, and teaching

Chronology of Ezra and Nehemiah

539—Capture of Babylon by Medo-Persia (Daniel 5:30)

538—Cyrus's first year, "Homelands" edict (Ezra 1:1–4)

537—Return under Sheshbazzar and Zerubbabel (altar rebuilt) (Ezra 2:1–3:7)

536—Work on Temple begun (Ezra 3:8)

536–530—Opposition during Cyrus's reign (Ezra 4:1–5)

530–520—Work on Temple ceased (Ezra 4:24)

520—Work on Temple renewed under Darius (Ezra 5:2; Haggai 1:14)

516—Temple completed (Ezra 6:15)

515–458—Huge gap: no records!

458 (April 8–August 4)—Ezra travels to Jerusalem (Ezra 7:8–9)

458 (December)–457 (March)—Ezra calls an assembly and organizes a community assessment (Ezra 10:9–17)

457–445—Big gap again: no records!

445—Nehemiah travels to Jerusalem (Nehemiah 1–2)

445—City wall completed (52 days! Nehemiah 6), Assemblies (Nehemiah 7), Feast of Tabernacles celebrated (Nehemiah 8), Fast (Nehemiah 9)

432—Nehemiah goes back to Persia and returns (Nehemiah 13:6)

and explaining it to others) makes the trip to Jerusalem (458 B.C.) and finds a demoralized people badly in need of religious and social renewal. A dozen years later (445 B.C.), Nehemiah (cupbearer to the king of Persia!) sneaks into town quietly (Nehemiah 1–2), and subsequently announces his presence with commanding respect that quickly remakes the community shipshape. After intensive building (52 days!), the walls of Jerusalem are restored, and the city becomes a viable commercial and domestic center again—for the first time since the Babylonian occupation and destruction one hundred fifty years before. Moreover, under Ezra's prodding, the covenant codes are read publicly, and the covenant institutions and moral behaviors are reinstituted. The book whimpers to an end with Nehemiah making trips back and forth to Persia, instituting further social reforms, and journaling prayers, asking that he be remembered for his faithful service.

While it is not laid out in organized detail, there is a clear theology of the Sinai Covenant pervading these recollections. First, there is absolute certainty throughout these writings that Yahweh is Sovereign over all the nations. This is why Cyrus sent the Jews back to Jerusalem, even though he may not have fully understood the divine leading. Nehemiah also regularly journals that Yahweh is in total control of peoples and nations.

Second, within Yahweh's overall international dominion, Yahweh continues to have a special relationship with Israel. Because of this, however small the remnant might be, it is to consider itself both privileged and responsible. It will not be destroyed, since Yahweh is faithful to the covenant promises made generations before. At the same time, Yahweh's faithfulness must not be misconstrued by the people as a free ride through life or as some automatic dispenser of blessings, regardless of their behaviors or activities. They are to model what it means to live before Yahweh, and as Yahweh's people, and in Yahweh's neighborhood. They are people of the Sinai Covenant, who share the mission of Yahweh to restake a claim of influence in the human arena, and who must give witness to the divine character and intentions.

Third, the recent exile to Babylon was a result of Israel's covenant-breaking. When the people failed in their obedience to the stipulations of the Sinai Covenant and lost their fidelity with their Suzerain, the curses of the Covenant were activated, and they were removed from the Promised Land as punishment. Thus, the exile was a chastening and cleansing event. Even the land itself had to recover the Sabbath years which had been neglected earlier.

Fourth, this recent restoration to the land of promise demands deeper covenant response and faithfulness. The nation must learn from its mistakes; next time, Yahweh may not be as gracious in redeeming them from foreign deportation or renewing their place of stability in the land of promise. For this reason, Ezra and Nehemiah lead a massive and comprehensive covenant renewal ceremony (Nehemiah 8–10), designed to inaugurate a new era of covenant obedience and divine blessing.

While the restored community considered itself to be the continuation of the entire nation of Israel, it was at this point that those who returned to Jerusalem became known as the "Jews," since they were mostly from the tribe of Judah. The other tribes (except for the Levites as priests and caretakers of the Temple, and a small clan that fiercely remembered its Benjamite family tree—see Philippians 3:5—but remained true to David's family and Temple worship in Jerusalem) had virtually disappeared, swept into the irreversible resettlement mixer of the Assyrians in the eighth century B.C.

Something changed, however, as this postexilic group searched for its new identity. As becomes clear from the interchanges with the Samaritans in Nehemiah 4 and the strict ethnic guidelines imposed on marriage by Ezra (Ezra 9), issues of covenant holiness and racial purity become intermingled. Earlier generations had no problem incorporating people of other nations into the growing family of Israel. The Gibeonites were received into Israel as an entire clan (Joshua 9). Rahab (Joshua 2) and Ruth

---

People of Significance

Leaders:

First Return:

> *Sheshbazzar* ("Prince of Judah")—return organizer and principal leader

> *Zerubbabel* ("Governor of Judah")—on-site leader

> *Joshua* ("High Priest")—cultic leader

Second Return:

> *Ezra* ("Scribe")

Third Return:

> *Nehemiah* (Persian royal cupbearer; "Governor of Judah")

Opposition:

First Return:

> *Tattenai* ("Governor of Beyond-the-River Province") and *Shethar-bozenai*

Second Return:

> *Sanballat* (Samaritan), *Tobiah*, "the Arabs," "the Ammonites"

Prophets: *Haggai* and *Zechariah*

Note Regarding Historical Periods

Hebrew/Jewish history is generally divided into at least four major eras:

- **First Temple Period** (960–586 B.C.)
- **Second Temple Period** (516 B.C.–70 A.D.)
- **Diaspora** (70–1947 A.D.)
- **Modern Israel** (1947–present)

From "Israelites" to "Jews"

While there is continuity between the Israelite nation that stands at the center of most of the Old Testament and the Jews, who are the people of God during postexilic times and into the New Testament age, something significant changes. The Jews are heirs to the scriptures, history, and land of Israel, but they are not entirely identical to the earlier nation, for several reasons:

- **Culture**: Although the tribes of Judah, Benjamin, and Levi (who become the Jews) carry forward the history and heritage of the nation of Israel, once the northern kingdom is annihilated by the Assyrians (722 B.C.), these remaining tribes embark on a new identity formation. In Jewish rabbinic traditions, Ezra is the founder of "Judaism" as a distinct social culture in its own right.

- **Politics**: For nearly a thousand years, from the exodus until the exile, the Israelites functioned as an independent nation. Even when other powers like the Assyrians and Babylonians had annexed the region into their larger kingdoms, the Israelites had maintained local sovereignty. From the time of the Babylonian exile forward, however—except for the brief and tenuous Maccabean monarchy—the Jews were a subject and minority people. Rabbinic literature credits Ezra with creating the "Great Assembly" (see Ezra 10) as the forerunner of the "Sanhedrin," which would become the new Jewish means of local rule throughout the Second Temple period.

- **Language**: Prior to the destruction of Solomon's Temple in 586 B.C., the official language of the Israelites had been Hebrew. During the Babylonian exile, the dominant Aramaic speech of their captors and other leading groups took over. While Jewish scribes maintained familiarity with Hebrew in their scroll copying and religious instructions, the people themselves switched to Aramaic, and lived in a world where Hebrew was relegated to the private language of ritualized ceremonies, but no longer shaped public discourse or cultural formation.

- **Scriptures**: While the covenant documents and related materials that formed the Torah (Genesis through Deuteronomy) were "Scripture" for all of Israel, the southern kingdom increasingly relied also on prophetic declarations as authentic revelation from Yahweh. By the time of Ezra, the "Prophets" were becoming an equal partner to the "Law" as authoritative scripture. At the same time, other documents were being read widely, and some would become a third section of the Hebrew Bible, the "Writings." This expansion of scripture marked a new era, in which Judaism became distinct from the older Israelite identity.

- **Worship Center**: For Israel, the Temple of Solomon was the center of worship life and national identity. The Temple was the royal palace of Israel's true Sovereign, Yahweh, and the natural successor of Yahweh's wilderness wanderings portable house, the Tabernacle. Even when the kingdom was divided into North and South after Solomon's death, King Jeroboam set up subsidiary shrines in Bethel and Dan, not as competing religious foundations, but rather as localized extensions of the Temple for his particular administrative district. The destruction of Solomon's Temple, however, and the lengthy time the people of Judah spent in exile, precipitated a new tradition of "synagogues," neighborhood gathering places for ritualized worship activities and cultural identity transmission. Even when the Second Temple was completed in 516 B.C., the Jews retained their new synagogue tradition as essential to Jewish identity.

- **Population**: Although Canaan was the absolute homeland for Israel, the Jewish population, in contrast, was scattered throughout the Mediterranean and Persian worlds. The idea of a territorial connection, essential for Israelite identity, was only symbolic for Judaism.

> The net result of these changes was to form a new Jewish world into which the later expressions of Christianity adapted more easily. Identity was no longer tied either to language or location; scripture became a fluid collection of authoritative literature; worship practices commonly took place in local gatherings; and religious orientation was disconnected from citizenship. These alterations accelerated the rapid expansion of the Christian church from its beginnings as a Jewish subgroup into a transnational religion.

were easily integrated into the community of faith. Even Psalm 87 anticipates the amalgamation of all Israel's neighboring nations into a large covenant family as Yahweh assumed rightful global sovereignty.

Yet, in the stress on purification under the leadership of Ezra and Nehemiah, new questions would emerge that continued to plague the Jews for centuries to follow. Are we defined by our religion? If so, can those from other ethnic groups become fully Jewish through proper religious observances, even if they do not become assimilated into our ethnic communities?

Or are we defined by our history? If that is the case, do we really need a "homeland" to survive?

Or are we in fact defined by our ethnicity? But if that be so, is it so necessary that we keep our bloodlines pure?

These issues will surface again in the New Testament as the early Christian Church begins fully within the Jewish community, but then quickly spreads beyond it. Jews will challenge Christ-believers that they are no longer Jewish (e.g., Galatians 2), while Paul will argue that gentile Christ-believers are, in fact, grafted onto the family tree of Judaism (e.g., Romans 9–11).

The restoration of the Jews seems to have begun as a manifestation of a sociological "centered set," in which the focus was on reactivating the religious practices of the Covenant to provide expressions of identity, in which all could join and participate. But along the way, it appears that the restoration became more of a sociological "bounded set," where the obsession with ethnic purity emerged as normative in shaping the community, to the exclusion of others who did not share a common racial background. Something of this shift might have been stimulated by the fascinating events told in the book of Esther.

Discussion Points

- How do the changing political fortunes of Assyria, Babylonia, and Persia affect the destinies of Israel and Judah? Why would the Jews of Ezra's time believe that Cyrus of Persia was an agent of Yahweh?
- Why is it significant that among the very first acts of the returning community under Zerubbabel was the rebuilding of the Altar of Burnt Offering as it once stood in the courtyard of Solomon's Temple?
- Who are the leading figures in the successive waves of returning Jewish populations? What are the emphases of each leader and group in the restoration of the covenant community?

- How is the Jewish self-identity being shaped and changed during the return to Jerusalem and the reestablishment of the community? What differing options for public self-awareness are available, and how do the books of Ezra and Nehemiah portray some of these?

For Further Investigation

McCready, Wayne O. and Adele Reinhartz, editors. (Minneapolis: Fortress, 2008). *Common Judaism: Explorations in Second-Temple Judaism.*

11.

Why Is This Story in the Bible?

Rereading Esther in Its Historical Context

The book of Esther is one of the most fascinating tales ever written. The Persian king Ahasuerus (otherwise known in extra-biblical literature as Xerxes, the son of Darius I and son-in-law of Cyrus the Great), who ruled from 485–465 B.C., throws a kingdom-wide party. During the drunken carousing, he demands that Queen Vashti appear at the party to be ogled. Vashti refuses, is deposed, and a replacement "Miss

Figure 11.1 The Persian Empire.[1]

---

1   Copyright in the Public Domain.

Figure 11. 2 King Xerxes.[2]

Ahasuerus's Reputation

Much of what we know about Ahasuerus comes from his younger contemporary, the Greek historian Herodotus (c. 484–425 B.C.). Since the Persians were the Greeks' greatest enemies during this time, the views of Herodotus are probably harsher than entirely accurate. Still, there is sufficient evidence, particularly in the specific details of Herodotus's stories, to warrant a somewhat negative view of Xerxes' character. One-third of *The Histories* by Herodotus is devoted to recounting Xerxes' exploits, including these incidents:

- He was influenced by bad advisers (7.5-6)
- He was blinded by pride (7.11-12)
- When his pontoon bridge at the Hellespont was destroyed by a storm, Xerxes had the waves whipped and chained until they were sunk, and then capriciously assassinated his own engineers–for their fault in the matter (7.34-35)
- When Xerxes' friend, Pythius, asked that Pythius's son be exempted from military duty, Xerxes had the young man hacked in

Universe" beauty pageant ensues with Esther, a Jew, crowned as winner.

Esther's cousin and guardian, Mordecai, discovers a plot to kill the king, and passes the information along to Esther. Haman is made vice ruler of the realm, and grows angry with Mordecai, who will not bow to him. Haman maneuvers to get the king to sign an edict which will destroy Mordecai and his people.

Mordecai brings the matter to Esther, asking her to act on behalf of her people. Esther reluctantly begins the process of petition by holding a special banquet for Ahasuerus and Haman. Haman's antagonism with Mordecai grows, leading him to build a gallows on which to hang Mordecai.

In an ingenious plot twist, Ahasuerus finds out that Mordecai has never been rewarded for uncovering and revealing the assassination plot, so the king gets Haman to publicly honor Mordecai on his behalf. When Haman and Ahasuerus gather for Esther's second banquet, she reveals Haman's genocidal plan. In desperation, Haman pleads physically with Esther for his life, for which he is accused by Ahasuerus of attacking the queen. He is sentenced to die on his own gallows, built originally to wring the life out of Mordecai.

Haman's family is destroyed, his property given to Esther, and Mordecai is honored. Ahasuerus cannot revoke his previous edict, but he signs a new one allowing the Jews to fight back and to take the property of any who are their enemies. The Jews kill multitudes (75,800) on Adar 13-14, and celebrate the great victory on Adar 14-15. These festivities become an annual event known as *Purim* because Haman cast a *pur* ("lot") to find the right date for their planned annihilation. Mordecai becomes chief officer of the realm, and does much good for his people.

A story this good needs to be told and retold, and ought even to be put on stage and screen. But should it find its way into the Bible? Theologians are quite divided.

Why the book of Esther *should not* be in the Bible

Some say it has no place in sacred literature. After all, there is no mention of God in it. Furthermore, its "heroes" are really "villains." Take Ahasuerus, for instance. According to historical records, he was temperamental, unstable, cruel, and childish. When he led a massive, yet unsuccessful, campaign against the Greeks in 480 B.C., he lost, and "celebrated" by throwing this obscene half-year-long orgy that further depleted his treasuries.

And Mordecai is no saint. His very name means "Marduk's man!" Marduk was the chief among Babylonian gods, and the one to whom Nebuchadnezzar dedicated the whole magnificent city of Babylon, imprinting his name on every brick in the place. Why is a Jew wearing with pride a name that honors the god of Judah's enemy?

Even Esther must not escape similar notice.

two, and forced the Persian army to march between the halves as a warning to any who might shirk their responsibilities (7:38–40.1)

- In the town of Ennea Hodoi, Xerxes ordered the live burial of nine boys and girls to show Persian dominance over local resistance (7.114)
- After the battle of Thermopylae, in which 300 Spartans bravely, but fatally, held back the Persian forces, Xerxes unnecessarily mutilated and displayed Spartan leader Leonidas's body as a kind of sinister sneer (7.238)
- Xerxes commands the total destruction and burning of twelve Greek cities, along with the rape of Greek women (8:31–33)
- Xerxes first presented his ship helmsman with a golden wreath, but then decapitated him because of the loss of sailors and soldiers in the campaign (8.118)

Her name seems far too close to the appellation of the eastern fertility goddess Istar to be mere coincidence. These correspondences to ancient Persian names even hint that the entire story is a work of fiction. No historical records have been found to place either a "Vashti" or an "Esther" on the throne of Persia, or tell of a "Mordecai" who was elevated to high government position. Nor is there any evidence that the threat against the Jews and its retaliatory massacre ever happened.

For such reasons, the book has been disputed by devout biblical scholars for centuries. The rabbis at Javneh, who formulated the final section ("Writings") of the Hebrew scriptural canon in the late first century A.D., very nearly excluded Esther. Christian theologians were often of the same mind. As late as the sixteenth century, Martin Luther believed Esther did not belong in the Bible. After all, it had no worthy purpose: It glorifies the slaughter of thousands in an act of sheer genocide, it affirms the right of revenge, and it establishes a yearly feast which is little more than a drunken party. How can such a book be a divine revelation?

Why the book of Esther *should* be in the Bible

Of course, there is another side to the argument. For one thing, even if the name of God is never mentioned, it is obvious throughout that there is divine leading and providential care orchestrating all that happens. Esther prays and asks Mordecai to rally the Jews to fasting and prayer as well. Certainly, the outcome is as miraculous as that of any story found in Exodus or Joshua.

Furthermore, the story's principal characters show how God can use anyone to accomplish divine purposes. Maybe Ahasuerus was pagan and childish and brutish, but it is God who guides international politics, just as the Jews believed about the edict of restoration issued by Ahasuerus's father-in-law, Cyrus, in 538 B.C. Along with that, why should Mordecai be judged for the name his parents gave to him? Perhaps they were only trying to survive in exile. To be sure, his actions show him to be a man of faith, a man of God. And who wants to tarnish Esther? She never does anything wrong in the story. She shows herself to be a devout woman, exuding graces that all girls should emulate. Perhaps, even, she had no choice in the matter of the beauty pageant, and was forced, along with thousands of others, to participate against her will. Even her name is more closely related to "Ister," which means "star," than it is to "Istar." Her Hebrew name is Hadassah, and that means "myrtle," a plant used in Temple cleansing rituals. One might even say that Esther prefigures Jesus, for they both save their peoples through personal sacrifice.

Again, if one wishes to call out the theologians of the centuries, it is important to remember that even though the rabbis at Javneh discussed and debated whether Esther was among the books that "dirtied the hands" (their phrase for judging whether a writing was divinely inspired, and thus showed us our human errors and frailties), ultimately they resolved that it did, in fact, belong in the collection of scripture. And even Martin Luther did not have the power to eradicate this book from among the pages of the Bible.

Moreover, the historical details noted in the book, and even its use of language, make it very accurate to its times. Xerxes did indeed throw a huge party following his ignoble retreat from the battlefields of Greece. He had a harem of royal women, and both Vashti and Esther might well have been among the unnamed companions of his bed and table. So, too, with Mordecai: not all government officials made their way into the court records. Even so, it is also true that the name Mordecai has been found among the archaeological relics of that time and place. Again, the details about the music and food at the party, and the locales about Susa, are precisely on target as representations of the times, as is the use of wording and terminology in the writing of the book itself.

Finally, the tale should not be quickly dismissed as having no worthy religious moral. Could it not focus attention on God's providential care which supersedes and trumps all human plans, especially when there is a threat to the community of faith? Might not the marvelous descriptions of Esther's character and actions motivate others to develop similar wonderful values and behaviors? Isn't it possible that Esther does, in fact, stand as a type of Christ, showing what it takes and what it means to give up personal security and high position for the sake of others? Even in a larger context, does not the entire drama restate the eternal struggle of good versus evil, and affirm the ultimate victory of that which is right? In this regard, the book of Esther may well serve as an allegory on the nature of divine-human love, just as Paul would later talk about the symbolic relationship between Christ and the Church (Ephesians 5:22–32).

A Second Look at the History Behind Esther

In addition, there might also be another way to look at the drama of Esther and suggest an alternative reason for its inclusion in the literature of the Bible shaped by the Covenant. This requires revisiting the chronology of the books of Ezra and Nehemiah:

- 539—Capture of Babylon by Medo-Persia (Daniel 5:30)
- 538—Cyrus's first year, "Homelands" edict (Ezra 1:1-4)
- 537—Return under Sheshbazzar and Zerubbabel (altar rebuilt) (Ezra 2:1-3:7)
- 536—Work on Temple begins (Ezra 3:8)
- 536-530—Opposition during Cyrus's reign (Ezra 4:1-5)
- 530-520—Work on Temple ceases (Ezra 4:24)
- 520—Work on Temple renewed under Darius (Ezra 5:2; Haggai 1:14)
- 516—Temple completed (Ezra 6:15)
- 515-458—Huge gap: no records!
- 458 (April 8-August 4)—Ezra travels to Jerusalem (Ezra 7:8-9)
- 458 (December)-457 (March)—Ezra calls an assembly and organizes a community assessment (Ezra 10:9-17)
- 457-445—Big gap again: no records!
- 445—Nehemiah travels to Jerusalem (Nehemiah 1-2)
- 445—City wall completed (52 days! Nehemiah 6), Assemblies (Nehemiah 7), Feast of Tabernacles celebrated (Nehemiah 8), Fast (Nehemiah 9)
- 432—Nehemiah goes back to Persia and returns (Nehemiah 13:6)

When does the story of Esther take place? Surprisingly, exactly in the huge historical gap between Ezra 6 and 7! Ezra 1-6 relates the initial modest return of a small number of Jewish exiles under the leadership of Zerubbabel and the rebuilding of a rather embarrassing Temple. Ezra 7 picks up the recitation fifty-seven years later, after the Jerusalem community has almost lost its way and will. Suddenly, out of nowhere and with no warning, Ezra and Nehemiah and a whole host of other Jews show up in Jerusalem, and get the community back on track. Why? Was it perhaps that the events explored in the book of Esther prodded the people back into action?

In reality, during the times of Esther, Yahweh's people were in the wrong place. The decree to return to Palestine had been issued half a century before, but many Jews remained in Babylon and Persia because life was easier there. Even Mordecai's name may indicate that he and his family have capitulated to Babylonian and Persian cultural influences.

Esther and Mordecai are themselves in the wrong place at the wrong time. Why would Mordecai, as guardian of his cousin, put her into a beauty pageant for a cruel and despotic ruler?

Through Mordecai's irritations of Haman, all Jews (including those who have returned to Palestine under Persian protection) are in danger of being destroyed. It is very likely that the sudden returns of Ezra and Nehemiah to Jerusalem to help rebuild the failing community may well have been precipitated by the crisis of near slaughter that shocked the Jewish community into action, and challenged it to recover its roots, its homeland, its identity, and its religious commitments.

Perhaps the theological meaning of the book of Esther includes these ideas:

A word of warning to God's people who forget their identity and live in the wrong places at the wrong times for the wrong reasons.

A word of comfort to God's people that the God of the Covenant is still in control and still cares.

A word of encouragement that no matter where we find ourselves in life, we can make a difference.

Discussion Points

- Summarize the reasons given for either rejecting or admitting the book of Esther to the literary collection of the Bible.
- Explain the possible theological messages of the book of Esther for both Jews and Christians.

For Further Investigation

Herodotus. The Histories.

Bible "Big Picture"

Covenant Making: God establishes a covenant relationship with a missional community by way of a redemptive act

Old Testament: The Exodus and Sinai Covenant

  Genesis—Why?

  Exodus—What?

  Leviticus—How?

  Numbers—Who?

  Deuteronomy—How Long?

New Testament: The Person and Work of Jesus

Covenant Living: God guides the covenant relationship with the missional community by way of authorized spokespersons

Old Testament: The Prophets, with Their Interpreted History and Sermons

  Stories: The Interpreted History of Israel

- *Joshua*—Possessing the Land with Missional Significance
- *Judges*—Nearly Losing the Land through Covenant Failure
- *Ruth*—The Model of Covenant Obedience That Restores
- *1 & 2 Samuel*—Establishing the Monarchy That Might Fulfill the Covenant Mission
- *1 & 2 Kings, 1 & 2 Chronicles*—Failure of the Old Testament Covenant Community Mission Experiment
- *Ezra and Nehemiah*—Restoring the Covenant Community in Anticipation of Yahweh's Next Major Act
- *Esther*—Responding to the Warning That Yahweh's People Have a Covenant Identity and Purpose

New Testament: The Apostles, with Their Ecclesiastical History and Letters

Covenant Questions: God nurtures the covenant relationship with a missional community by way of spiritual wisdom and insight

Old Testament: The Poetry and Wisdom Literature

New Testament: The Comparison of Covenants and the Apocalypse

---

Covenant Questions (1)

The Creator nurtures the covenant relationship with a missional community by way of spiritual wisdom and insight

12.

Covenant Language (1)

Finding Fundamental Human Identity—The Drama of Job

In the Bible's current configuration, the books of poetry intrude between the prophetical histories (typically called the "Former Prophets") and the prophetical discourses (the "Latter Prophets"). This is different from the Hebrew Bible arrangement, where the "Prophets" are collected together as the second section, prior to the gathering of later and diverse works simply known as the "Writings." The benefits of the Hebrew Bible arrangement are in keeping the sermonic writings of the prophets close to the prophetic interpretations of Israel's history, and also in visually segregating the documents of scripture by way of their importance. The "Torah" (or "Pentateuch" or "Books of Moses" or "Law") is always primary in authority, for it is the direct revelation of God that created and defined the nation of Israel as the unique people of God. The *Nabi'im*, or "Prophets," are second only to the "Torah" in theological importance and revelatory significance. Their authority is derived from the Sinai Covenant, in that the prophets were called and commissioned by God to help the people live in faithfulness to that earlier, normative defining moment and its revelatory documents. In the Hebrew Bible, the *K'tuvim* ("Writings") are a catch-all collection of various documents, mostly written later in Israel's history, that have been recognized as communicating the divine will,

---

Hebrew Bible: TaNaK

The Hebrew Bible, though containing the same documents as the Christian Bible Old Testament, is arranged in a slightly different manner. Sometimes, the Hebrew Bible is known as the "TaNaK," a name derived from the first sounds of the Hebrew terms identifying each of its subdivisions.

"Torah" ("Law/Covenant"):

Genesis, Exodus, Leviticus, Numbers, Deuteronomy

"Nabi'im" ("Prophets"):

"Former Prophets": Joshua, Judges, Kings

"Latter/Writing Prophets": Isaiah, Jeremiah, Ezekiel, "The Twelve"

"K'tuvim" ("Writings"):

Ruth, Chronicles, Ezra-Nehemiah, Esther, Job, Psalms, Proverbs, Ecclesiastes, Lamentations, Song of Songs, Daniel

---

but which do not have the foundational revelatory significance of the other two sections. A detriment of the Hebrew Bible arrangement is that some documents among the "Writings," such as Ruth, Chronicles, Ezra-Nehemiah, and Esther are essentially the same kind of literature as the "Former Prophets" and probably ought to be considered with them, and Daniel, though it contains both historical narratives and apocalyptic visions, is usually understood to be similar to other works in the collection of the "Latter Prophets."

While the other six "books" among the "Writings" are dissimilar in many ways, they share at least three things in common: (1) they are composed mostly in poetry rather than prose; (2) they are a-historical in message, not depending on specific chronological contexts to understand or enhance their meanings; and (3) they presume the cultural context of a worldview shaped by the principles of the Sinai Covenant relationship. Since they are positioned after Esther in our Bibles, we will spend some time looking at them before returning to the prophetic literature of the Old Testament.

The Tools of Hebrew Poetry

Parallelism:

Usually two lines that either restate the same idea in differing words (Synonymous) or in opposite terms that ultimately mean the same thing (Antithetic)

Sometimes a longer combination of lines that build upon each other for a compounding effect (stair-like)

Meter:

Rhythm in repetitive stress patterns

Widely used poetic literary techniques:

Acrostics, Alliteration, Assonance, Enveloping, Chiasm

Introductory Notes on Wisdom Literature

What is often called the "Wisdom Literature" of the Bible is a collection of documents, mostly penned in poetry, that probe human issues, problems, needs, and values. These writings are usually anonymous; even though many of the Psalms have titles that identify authors, these relationships are neither necessary in order to use or interpret those texts, nor do they enhance the importance of the Psalms to which they are attached. Invariably, though, these verses, dramas, and pithy proverbs assume that there is a divinely initiated moral matrix, of the kind outlined in the Sinai Covenant, between Yahweh and Israel. Actions matter, precisely because there are values that shape the world and culture. When people respond to one another in harmony with the mores and norms established by God, they will generally see and expect certain outcomes that enhance life. Doing the opposite, of course, brings ends that are much less desirable.

For such reasons, gaining wisdom ought to be a key goal of any life. Moreover, this wisdom is not mere intelligence, education, or even street smarts; rather it is linked directly to the religiously oriented outlook of the community that knows the Creator, and is bound to this God in intentional partnership. As both the Psalms (111:10) and Proverbs (1:7) put it, "The fear of the Lord is the beginning of wisdom."

Implied in this perspective are a combination of human sin and responsibility. If there are moral choices to make in life, it is possible to choose badly, and many do. But since God is revealing the divine will in a variety of ways, no person can be excused for doing what is not right, or for neglecting those things that impinge upon us as ethical obligations. Therefore education is the responsibility of parents, first of all, and also the confessional community as a whole. These documents of "Wisdom Literature" are resources and tools to use in that corporate training process. They include Job, Proverbs, Ecclesiastes, Song of Songs, and some of the Psalms. The rest of the Psalms and the five Lamentations also have "wisdom" dimensions, and therefore are included in our consideration here.

Hebrew poetry, which is the primary literary device employed to convey these wisdom truths, has one major element that translates quite well into other languages, one significant element which does not, and several lesser techniques that transfer only according to the skills of the translator. The dominant feature of Hebrew

---

Examples of Parallelism in Hebrew Poetry

Synonymous:

> *Hear my words, you wise men;*
> *listen to me, you men of learning.* (Job 34:2)
> *The heavens declare the glory of God;*
> *the skies proclaim the work of his hands*
> (Psalm 19:1)

Antithetic:

> *For his anger lasts only a moment,*
> *but his favor lasts a lifetime* (Psalm 30:5)
> *Wicked men are overthrown and are no more,*
> *But the house of the righteous stands firm*
> (Proverbs 12:7)

Stair-like:

> *The voice of the Lord shakes the desert;*
> *the Lord shakes the Desert of Kadesh.*
> *The voice of the Lord twists the oaks*
> *and strips the forests bare.*
> *And in his temple all cry, "Glory!"*
> (Psalm 29:8–9)

The Drama of Job in Outline

Opening Setting (*prose*): A Dispute in Heaven (1:1–2:10)

First Dramatic Dialogue (*mostly poetry*): Condemnation and Confusion (2:11–31:40)

Introduction: (2:11–3:26)
    Job's Friends Attend Him (2:11–13)
    Job's Lament (3)
Round #1: (4:1–14:22)
Eliphaz's Testimony: (4–5)
    God is pure and just! (4)

Humans bring trouble on themselves! (5)

Job's Response: (6–7)

Show me where I've sinned! (6)

God, forgive me if I've sinned! (7)

Bildad's Challenge: (8)

Only the ungodly suffer! (8:1–19)

If the shoe fits, wear it! (8:20–22)

Job's Response: (9–10)

God is wise and powerful! (9)

God, why do you punish me?! (10)

Zophar's Plea: (11)

God is in control! (11:1–12)

Turn back to him! (11:13–20)

Job's Response: (12–14)

I've never left him! (12)

You're no help to me! (13)

God, will you help me?! (14)

Round #2: (15–21)

Eliphaz's Attack: (15)

Humans are wicked! (15:1–16)

The fate of the wicked is sure! (15:17–35)

Job's Response: (16–17)

You're no help to me! (16)

God, I plead my case before you! (17)

Bildad's Harshness: (18)

Who do you think you are?! (18:1–4)

The end of the wicked is sure! (18:5–21)

Job's Response: (19)

Have pity on me! (19:1–12)

God, vindicate me! (19:13–29)

Zophar's Condemnation: (20)

You make me angry! (20:1–3)

The wicked will be cut short! (20:4–29)

Job's Response: (21)

But many wicked people prosper! (21:1–33)

So all your arguments are false! (21:34)]

poetry is parallelism. This means that usually two lines of roughly equal length are written together to help convey a thought. When the sentiments expressed by both halves of this "couplet" are nearly the same, the parallelism is called "synonymous." When the lines make the same point, but do so by using contrasting opposite ideas, the parallelism is known as "antithetic." Together, these two expressions of Hebrew poetry make up the vast majority of lines found in the Hebrew Bible. There are a number of other forms of parallelism identified by Hebrew literary scholars, but their occurrences are minimal compared to synonymous and antithetic.

If more than two lines are used to convey an idea or sentiment in Hebrew poetry, most often this is perceived as "stair-like" parallelism. Here, the concept stated in the first line provides material to be expanded upon in the second line; that line, in turn, is mined to develop a thought or perspective further in the next line, and so on, for as long as the linkage is maintained.

A significant element of Hebrew poetry that cannot easily be conveyed in other languages is meter. There is a clear pattern of syllabic stresses in the reading of Hebrew poetry that is lost when the terms are translated.

Finally, Hebrew poets use a lot of the techniques of lyrical style and emotional heightening that are found in similar literature throughout the world. Personification, alliteration, assonance, enveloping, chiasm, acrostics, metaphor, and simile are tools of the trade, and may come through in translations of Hebrew poetry insofar as the translator has the ability to find dynamic equivalents in the target medium.

The Drama of Job

With these things in mind, it is possible to appreciate more fully the language used to convey the powerful message found in the drama of Job. According to the prose prologue of Job 1, the story is set somewhere in Mesopotamia because of references to "the land of Uz" (Job 1:1) and "the people of the East" (Job 1:3). When the lifestyle of Job is described, it has the same qualities and feel about it as do the conditions expressed regarding the patriarch of Genesis, Abraham, Isaac, and Jacob. So the cultural context of Job's misfortunes is an agrarian society around the year 2000 B.C., somewhere in the eastern half of the Fertile Crescent.

While it is likely that the drama of Job is based upon actual incidents and historical characters, this is neither necessary nor important for giving the book a place among the Wisdom Literature of the Old Testament. Obviously, no one recorded the exact words that were recited among the caregivers of a terribly pained man. Even if they had, it is apparent that the current poetic dialogues have been refined, shaped, and staged in such a way that their importance is not found in careful accuracy to the original speeches, but rather in clearly enunciating certain theological points of view.

What makes this book inherently a part of biblical literature is that it was written in Hebrew, and there are no other copies or portions of the drama found in any other ancient Near Eastern culture. Moreover, it assumes a worldview like that found in the rest of the Bible. There is a creator deity (named "Yahweh"), who retains final control in all terrestrial matters. Evil is seen to be an intrusion into God's good world, rather than an original or necessary harmonic force intrinsic to the creation itself. There is a collection of spiritual creatures who share oversight of the physical world, and hints that "Satan" (which means "accuser," the role

---

The Drama of Job in Outline (continued)

First Dramatic Dialogue (*continued*):

Round #3: (22–31)

Eliphaz's Accusation: (22)

　Submit to God!

Job's Response: (23–24)

　But I can't find God!

Bildad's Rebuke: (25)

　You can't be righteous—nothing is righteous before God!

Job's Response: (26–31)

　God is great and just and wise! (26–28)

　Remember how good life used to be?! (29)

　But look at me now! (30)

　Still, I maintain that I am innocent! (31)

Second Dramatic Dialogue (*mostly poetry*): A New Voice (32–37)

Introduction: (32)

　Job's three friends reach an impasse (32:1)

　Elihu enters the picture (32:2–5)

　Elihu's summary of the situation (32:6–22)

Four Speeches: (33–37)

　Speech #1 (to Job): God speaks through pain! (34)

　Speech #2 (to the three friends): God is just! (35)

　Speech #3 (to Job): It pays to serve God! (36)

　Speech #4 (to Job): God is just, kind and sovereign! (37)

Third Dramatic Dialogue (*mostly poetry*): The Voice of God Thunders (38:1–42:6)

Introduction: (38–39)

　God appears (38:1)

　God displays divine glory (38:2–39:30)

　Ten object lessons from the physical realm (38:2–38)

　Ten object lessons from the animal realm (38:39–39:30)

Round #1: (40:1–5)

> God's Demand: Who accuses me?! (40:1–2)
>
> Job's Reply: I'm sorry! (40:3–5)
>
> **Round #2:** (40:6–42:6)
>
> God's Challenge: Can you rule in my place?! (40:6–41:34)
>
> Job's Reply: I'm sorry for doubting you! (42:1–6)
>
> **Closing Setting** (*prose*): Peace on Earth (42:7–17)

played by Yahweh's sparring partner in the opening chapters) may have originally been a good spiritual being who lost his way.

Although there is a brief prose narrative which sets up the drama at the beginning (Job 1–2), a tiny prose interruption to explain a change of scenes in 32:1–5, and a short narrative concluding note (Job 42:7–17), the essence of the book of Job is found in the dramatic dialogues which make up its bulk. These are rhythmically arranged and contain nuances of theodicy, which attempt to answer the question of why Job is suffering. After Job makes his initial lament (Job 3), there are three rounds of dialogue, in which Job's primary friends, Eliphaz, Bildad, and Zophar, explain their views. Each time, Job responds in an attempt to refute their harsh judgments about him. The friends focus on some secret, heinous sins that must recently have been uncovered by God, resulting in Job's horrible current condition as divine payback in a tit-for-tat mechanistic moral world. Job continually protests his innocence and decries their poor bedside manners.

The third round of these dialogues seems to be cut short. As usual, Eliphaz (Job 22) and Bildad (Job 25) rush in to challenge Job, but Zophar is not included this time, and Job's final response is more extended (Job 26–31). The apparent incompleteness of this round of disputations may be a literary device hinting that Job's three friends have not been able adequately to respond. At precisely this moment, a new voice enters (Job 32–37), bringing the younger—yet more complex and profound—insights of Elihu. While the earlier interactions muddied down into almost tedious

Job in the Rest of the Bible

There are two references to the person Job in the Bible outside of the drama itself (Ezekiel 14:14; James 5:11). Each of these holds up the character of Job as something to be emulated.

In the New Testament, Paul twice quotes passages from the book of Job (5:13 in 1 Corinthians 3:19, and 41:11 in Romans 11:35), without naming his source.

In Revelation 12, there appears to be a direct literary allusion to the tormenter of Job, for the enemy of God is called "Satan," and his manner of antagonism is that of "accusation."

accusation and defense, Elihu adds the dimensions of divine chastisement and education as possible causes for pain. Although suffering is usually a sign of divine judgment for identifiable nasty deeds, Elihu notes, sometimes it comes merely because it is part of our lot as human beings living in a compromised world. Moreover, even where there are no specific sins on our part to merit punishment, God often uses pain as a means to keep us aware of our limitations and remind us of our need for divine help.

We are not given an indication as to how Job responds to Elihu's assessment, for before Job can answer, Yahweh suddenly thunders in (Job 38:1–42:6). We do not know why God chooses to make a speech at this time, nor are we party to what conversations might have happened in the heavens of the opening scenes as the rest of the earthly exchanges unfolded. Also, to our frustration, Yahweh does not answer the assertions made by either the friends or Job. Instead, Yahweh gives ten object lessons from the physical realm (Job 38:2–38) and another ten object lessons from the animal realm (Job 38:39–39:30), which apparently are meant to remind the participants in the drama (and also those who read it) that Yahweh's power vastly supersedes human exploration or co-engagement. Because of this, according to the brief encounters which Yahweh then has with Job (Job 40:1–42:6), we ought not presume too much about why things happen as they do, nor pride ourselves about any normative or comprehensive insights we might think we have.

In the end, although Satan is never mentioned again, nor are we taken back to the transcendent perch granted at the beginning, Job is vindicated. His suffering, which was not specifically brought on because of grievous sins in his life, is ended, and his world is restored to its former prosperity.

Lingering Lessons

What are we to make of this drama? In answering that question, it is probably helpful first to sketch out the specific responses that are given in the book of Job to three questions: (1) who causes Job's suffering; (2) what is the immediate cause for that suffering; and (3) what is the ultimate outcome expected as a result of that suffering?

When the drama is taken as a whole, it becomes apparent that Job's message is not entirely about suffering. Instead, the book seems to be at least as much about what might be termed the fundamental values that make humanity human. Suffering merely provides a context in which the critical issues of meaning rise quickly to the surface.

Dramatis Personae	From whom?	Why?	Toward what end?
Narrator	Satan	Spiritual test	Show faithfulness
Job's Wife	Satan	Job's god was bettered	"Curse God and die!" (2:4)
Three Friends	God (4:9)	Job has sinned	Repentance
Job	God (6:4; 12:9; 16:11–14)	"I don't know!"	"I don't know!"
Elihu	God (33:29)	Sometimes sin (34:11); humanity's lot (33:19–34)	Guidance (33:29); dependence
God	(not answered)	Confirm relationship with God	Surrender
Conclusion	God	Punishment (friends); chastisement (Job)	Surrender

---

How Do We Respond to Pain and Suffering?

- *Option 1—accuse and placate* (Job's friends: strident religious cause-and-effect)
- *Option 2—change "gods"* (Satan: find another higher power when yours fails you)
- *Option 3—give up in the face of the absurd* (Job's wife: fatalism)
- *Option 4—live with existential boldness* (Job: I don't know, but I won't give in)
- *Option 5—wrestle and worship* (Narrator: Ultimate to our existence is the Creator/ creature relationship; it is the only norming value that endorses our truest human identity, no matter what happens

---

Do we live in a world where we are masters to ourselves? No, this is a moral universe, and there are laws that have to be obeyed if we are to survive.

But is it then a mechanistic cosmos, in which cause and effect are the only determiners of outcome? Not at all, for above and around and beyond our typical powers of perception swirls a spiritual realm, in which God, angels, and demons take a vital interest into our habits and activities of life.

So what can we learn about our existence from this drama? Mechanistic worldviews belittle and reduce life, either by claiming that physical possessions and prosperity are the end product of right living, or that pain and suffering will automatically drive one away from God. The former forgets that God desires to have meaningful relationships with humans, even when they are flawed and sinful. The latter believes that atheism is a viable option in a world where things no longer make any sense.

This is a moral universe, according to the drama of Job, though not all pain and problems are the direct result of our sinfulness. The normal or natural human identity involves acknowledging and worshipping God, but this worship cannot be coerced. The fundamental challenge to human living is that of continuing to be our truest God-worshipping selves—even when the limited evidence of daily experience sometimes seems to speak to the contrary. Job neither gives in to his friends' reductionist worldview nor gives up in the face of insufficient evidence to confirm God's care or presence. In this, Job remains truly human at its most fundamental level: He believes in God, not for the sake of trinkets he might gain by that relationship, but because to lose that transcendent connection would be to deny his very self and its reason for existence.

Discussion Points

- Explain and give examples of the major characteristics of Hebrew poetry.
- What is the cosmology of the world that informs the book of Job? Who is Yahweh among the other spiritual creatures at the beginning? What role does "Satan" play? How are the affairs that take place on earth viewed from the reference point of the narrator?
- How does the structure of the speeches in the book of Job heighten its forward thrust?
- What are the differing answers given in the book of Job to the question of why Job is suffering?

13.

Covenant Language (2)

Learning to Talk with God—The Prayers of Psalms

The one hundred fifty poems found in the Psalter were originally meant to be chanted or sung. This is obvious from performance notes attached to many of the psalms (e.g., Psalms 4–"For the director of music. With stringed instruments."), as well as the internal cues that often indicate how the words are to be used (e.g., Psalm 9:2–"I will be glad and rejoice in you; I will sing praise to your name, O Most High."). The current collection has been stable since at least the first century A.D., when the final form of the "Writings" section of the Hebrew Bible was determined by rabbis who gave shape to Judaism after the destruction of Jerusalem and the Temple. Other "Psalms" have since been found in ancient Hebrew and Jewish literature, including at least another ten in the Qumran collections, but there has been no attempt to expand the biblical psalter or keep it open to ongoing additions.

In their current expression, the psalms are divided into five "books," each of which ends with a short doxology (song of praise to God) that is not to be considered an essential part of the psalm to which it is attached (see, for instance the incongruity of Psalm 89:52 with what precedes it). It is not clear why these "books" have been used to organize the psalms, or

---

The Five "Books" of the Psalms

Book 1—Psalms 1–41
      Doxology: Psalm 41:13
Book 2—Psalms 42–72
      Doxology: Psalm 72:18–19
Book 3—Psalms 73–89
      Doxology: Psalm 89:52
Book 4—Psalms 90–106
      Doxology: Psalm 106:48
Book 5—Psalms 107–150
      Doxology: Psalm 150

Why Are the Psalms Numbered Differently?

Although all Bibles are printed with 150 psalms, the numbering varies from one translation to the next. This is because there are two versions of the Psalter, one in the Hebrew language ("Masoretic Text") and the other in the Greek translation ("The Septuagint," or "LXX") widely used by both Jews (from the second century B.C. on) and early Christians. Hebrew Psalms 9 and 10 are the same as Greek Psalm 9 (thus slowing the numbering momentum in that translation). Similarly, Hebrew Psalms 114 and 115 are together, the same as Greek Psalm 113, stalling the advance a bit once again. But then, Hebrew Psalm 116 is equivalent to Greek Psalms 114 and 115, and Hebrew Psalm 147 becomes Greek Psalms 146 and 147, bringing both collections to the same conclusion of 150 psalms.

---

when the divisions might have taken place. One idea is that the successive "books" are evidence of the development of psalmody over the centuries, and that later "books" are more recent collections of songs that either were not available before, or gave testimony to the changing musical or liturgical styles of the community. There might be some internal confirmation for this, since most of the Psalms of David occur in the first "book," and he is usually identified with the origin of the psalms. Along with that, groups of psalms attributed to Asaph and "the Sons of Korah" are found in the middle of the collection, and these figures were a key part of the grand Temple worship developments during David's later years and on into Solomon's reign. Furthermore, a song reflecting the time of the exile (Psalm 137) is posted very late among the psalms.

Prayer and poetry are the hallmarks of the psalms. The prayers come in a variety of types:

- **Individual Laments**: Cries of the individual in times of distress (5, 6, 10, 13, 22, 26, 35, 38, 39, 40, 42, 43, 51, 54, 55, 56, 57, 59, 64, 69, 70, 86, 88, 102, 109, 120, 130, 142, 143)
- **Communal Laments**: Cries of the community in times of distress (60, 74, 79, 80, 90, 108, 123, 137)
- **Hymns of Praise**: Celebrations of Yahweh's goodness and character (8, 9, 19, 29, 30, 33, 34, 65, 66, 67, 68, 76, 95, 96, 97, 98, 99, 100, 103, 104, 111, 113, 116, 117, 134, 135, 138, 144, 145, 146, 147, 148, 149, 150)
- **Songs of Confidence**: Declarations of trust in Yahweh (3, 4, 7, 11, 12, 16, 17, 18, 20, 23, 27, 28, 31, 36, 41, 46, 50, 58, 62, 63, 71, 77, 82, 83, 85, 89, 91, 92, 93, 94, 114, 115, 121, 124, 125, 126, 129, 139, 140, 141)
- **Royal Psalms**: Song in praise of Yahweh as Israel's true King, and honoring the monarch who rules well on Yahweh's behalf (2, 21, 24, 45, 47, 61, 72, 110, 132)

- **Psalms of Zion**: "National anthems" that extol the earthly residence of Yahweh (14, 48, 53, 84, 87, 122)
- **"Thanking" Psalms**: Expressions of appreciation for Yahweh's deliverance (75, 118, 136)
- **Wisdom or Priestly Instruction**: Poems that contain condensed teachings that are designed to be passed along to others by way of memorization (1, 15, 25, 32, 37, 44, 49, 52, 73, 78, 81, 101, 105, 106, 107, 112, 119, 127)

While the prayers are shaped in various ways, there is a common theology that runs through them. It is a worldview that sees life through the lens of Israel's covenant relationship with Yahweh. Every good thing that happens is a gift from Israel's great Sovereign. Every difficulty emerges because people (either the psalm singer, his friends, the larger community of Israel, or the nations around) fail to understand their responsive and responsible relationship with Yahweh.

Prayer itself is rooted in the covenant relationship by implication. Since Yahweh has connected the divine enterprise to Israel as a nation, one can expect Yahweh's presence in the Temple and its surroundings (code-named "Zion"). More than that, it is right to assume that the fate of Israel ought to be one of blessing and prosperity where faithfulness to the covenant stipulations are held in honor. Conversely, if the people sin, the curses of the Sinai covenant kick in, and repentance and renewal are expected to follow, both on the social and individual levels. Yet, even where there is pain and frustration and disease and alienation, the psalms are raised in supplication, because the Covenant binds Yahweh to Israel. Prayer is the essential language of lovers (even when they are quarreling) or marriage partners (who might well seem to be divorcing). Yahweh cannot walk out of this relationship, any more than can Israel. Therefore, both parties have a right and a privilege—even a duty—to demand things from the other. Yahweh constantly calls for the people to remain true to the lifestyle and stipulations of the covenant; but Israel, too, can require that Yahweh not walk away or fail to restore the covenant relationship and its blessings.

Hebrew Poetry Parallelism in the Psalms

Synonymous—two (or more) lines that say the same thing using different words

"My soul is full of troubles,
  my life draws near to Sheol." (88:3)

"He established a decree in Jacob,
  and appointed a law in Israel." (78:5)

Antithetic—two lines that declare opposite ideas in order to support the same conclusion

"I hate the double-minded,
  but I love your law." (119:113)

"He did not spare them from death,
  but gave their lives over to the plague." (78:50)

Stair-like—three or more lines that build up an idea by expanding on terms used in the previous lines

"Bless the Lord, O my soul,
  and do not forget all his benefits—
  who forgives all your iniquity,
  who heals all your diseases,
  who redeems your life from the Pit,
  who crowns you with steadfast love and mercy,
  who satisfies you with good things as long as you live
  so that your youth is renewed like the eagle's."

(103:2–5)

Common themes pervasive throughout the psalms include:

- Yahweh is always acknowledged as the true King of Israel (e.g., 24, 93)
- "Zion" is Yahweh's capital city (e.g., 48, 76, 84)
- The Covenant with David authenticates the right of this family to rule (e.g., 89, 110)
- Yahweh is also understood to be Ruler over all nations (e.g., 2, 60, 87, 96, 97)
- Israel's purpose is to be witness to the nations (e.g., 67, 87)
- Divine blessing is linked to covenant faithfulness, and punishment to covenant curses (e.g., 15, 78, 79, 80, 81, 85, 101, 106, 107)
- Laments are based upon the right to plead for God's Covenant faithfulness, even when the people have sinned (e.g., 80, 109)
- Praise is an extension of the witness intended to be communicated through Israel (e.g., 113, 115, 117, 135, 145)

In all of this, it is poetry and music that serves as the vehicle for communication. Poetry provides a language that heightens emotions, condenses ideas, summarizes thoughts that are more easily memorized, and gives rhythm that allows choirs and congregations to recite these testimonies in unison.

A Perfect Pair!—Reflections on Psalm 19

The heavens declare the glory of God. …
The law of the Lord is perfect, reviving the soul.
—Psalm 19:1, 7

"You can't stand on one leg!" A hostess says that to her mealtime guests, urging second helpings on them. It seems that only the pink flamingos at the zoo know it's not true.

Some things come naturally in pairs: salt and pepper, hammer and nails, sackcloth and ashes. We never use a scissor; only a pair of scissors will do the job. Children in school learn quickly about "show and tell"; you can't do one without the other. And the way we're made demands a pair of pants, a pair of glasses, and a pair of gloves.

An old song says that one is the loneliest number that you've ever heard. It's true in marriage. It's true in friendship. It's true in conversation. Some things have to come in twos in order to exist.

Hand in Hand

Psalm 19 praises the perfect pair: the shout of God's glory in creation and the testimony of his goodness in the Bible. They walk hand in hand. They stand side by side. They know each other face to face.

You can't have the one without the other. Creation is the splash of splendor, and the Bible is its interpretive handbook. Nature speaks of God's power, and the Scriptures define that power in the shape of love. The star-spangled heavens exalt a transcendent deity, while the pages of the Book bring God as close as a good friend.

Bible scholars have tried for centuries to plunge in a knife at verse 7 and divorce the two parts that "obviously" stood separate long ago. But with grudging admiration, all of them finally agree that the balance is perfect, the partnership fits, and the whole is greater than its halves. As C. S. Lewis says, "I take this to be the greatest poem in the Psalter and one of the greatest lyrics in the world!"

Double-Talk

Sometimes, double-talk can be deceitful. The ancient Roman god, Janus, was always depicted with two faces: one facing forward, the other facing to the rear. He was worshipped originally as the all-seeing one, knowing both the future and the past. But later he became the epitome of contempt, speaking from two mouths at the same time. Today, his name describes the liar, the hypocrite, the charlatan. A "Janus" is a deceitful, double-dealing person.

George Orwell's powerful novel, 1984, portrays a society in which the official language was Newspeak. But Newspeak is really doubletalk; nothing actually means what it was supposed to. And in a world of double-talk, nobody trusts anybody else.

Two Witnesses

But the delightful thing about God's "double-talk" is that each testimony confirms the other. What creation proclaims in bold patterns is matched by scripture's poetic narrative. What thunders from the heavens above is validated by the whisper from the page. God is good. God is glorious. God is gracious.

When the famous soprano Jenny Lind was on her way to her first concert tour of North America, she told Captain West of her desire to see sunrise across the expanse of the ocean. One cloudless morning he had her called at early dawn.

Silent and motionless, she stood by his side on the rear deck, watching every change of shade and tint in the sky and the reflections on the water below. As the rays of the sun leaped from the horizon, she spontaneously broke out in song. Her message was Job's testimony, set to the magnificent melody of Handel: "I know that my Redeemer liveth!"

In that moment of exaltation, Captain West later wrote, the Word of God was complete. The pair of God's speeches had become one. And the only response possible was the awe-struck prayer of David: "May the words of my mouth and the meditation of my heart be pleasing in your sight, O LORD, my Rock and my Redeemer" (v. 14).

The most obvious literary device used by Hebrew poets is parallelism, placing two or more lines next to one another for emphasis and effect. Synonymous parallelism is most common, adding weight to ideas by repeating them, using similar words and phrases. Occurring less frequently, but still often enough to be a dominant form of expression, is antithetic parallelism, where two lines express opposite ideas, which ultimately confirm a single truth. Stair-like parallelism is the third most widely used form of the craft, much less in evidence than either of the others, but scattered throughout the psalms; here, each successive line builds on an idea expressed in the previous line, so that the end product is like a mushrooming exploration of a concept.

The Great Acrostic Testimony

While a number of Psalms are simple acrostics (e.g., 9, 34, 37), none is as marvelously and extensively crafted as Psalm 119, which is built in groupings of eight parallel couplets, having each section begin with successive letters of the Hebrew alphabet ($22 \times 8 = 176$ verses). Through this literary device, the completeness ("A to Z") of Yahweh's Word/Law/Precepts is portrayed.

Headings or "Titles" of the Psalms

There are a number of psalms that have "titles." These are not part of the actual psalms, and may or may not reflect original circumstances.

Some "titles" purport to give the original historical context for the creation of the psalm:

- Psalm 3: "A Psalm of David, when he fled from his son Absalom"
- Psalm 18: "A Psalm of David the servant of the Lord, who addressed the words of this song to the Lord on the day when the Lord delivered him from the hand of all his enemies, and from the hand of Saul"
- Psalm 34: "Of David, when he feigned madness before Abimelech, so that he drove him out, and he went away"
- Psalm 51: "A Psalm of David, when the prophet Nathan came to him, after he had gone in to Bathsheba"
- Psalm 52 "A Maskil of David, when Doeg the Edomite came to Saul and said to him, 'David has come to the house of Ahimelech'"

Some "titles" appear to be dedications:
- "To the Leader" (5, 6, 8, 9, 11, 12, 13, etc.)
- "To Jeduthun" (39)

Some "titles" appear to give instructions about tunes or performance cues:
- "Psalm"–with instrumental accompaniment (e.g., 64)
- "Song"–without instrumental accompaniment (e.g., 65)
- "According to 'The Deer of the Dawn'" (22)

While parallelism is fairly easy to bring across in translations, there are other poetic literary devices which cannot be duplicated well in other languages. Rhythm and meter are at the top of this list. Hebrew poetry bounces along with great attention to syllabic stresses. Unfortunately, these are lost, for the most part, because of the significant difference between biblical Hebrew and most modern languages. Assonance (the repetition of certain vowel sounds), consonance (the repetition of certain consonant sounds), alliteration (the repetition of word-beginning letters), and acrostics (beginning successive poetic lines with the letters of the Hebrew alphabet in serial order) also all drop out when the poetry of the Psalms is brought into other languages.

Other subtle or complex literary devices can be seen even in the translated poetry if the reader is observant. For instance, "enveloping" is the technique of surrounding an inner verse with a repeated chant or refrain, like that in Psalm 118:1, 29: "O give thanks to the Lord, for he is good; his steadfast love endures forever!" Another structural pattern sometimes built into the poetry is chiasm, where lines mirror one another in general content or phrases across a midpoint. One of the most obvious examples is Psalm 114, where the outer pairs of poetic couplets reflect one another, and the two inner pairs of poetic couplets form a second mirror image. The result is a concise history of Israel's early redemption that becomes a living testimony of Yahweh's faithfulness:

When Israel went out from Egypt,
the house of Jacob from a people of strange language,
   Judah became God's sanctuary,
   Israel his dominion.
      The sea looked and fled;
      Jordan turned back.
         The mountains skipped like rams,
         the hills like lambs.

Why is it, O sea, that you flee?
O Jordan, that you turn back?
　　O mountains, that you skip like rams?
　　O hills, like lambs?
Tremble, O earth, at the presence of the Lord,
at the presence of the God of Jacob,
　　who turns the rock into a pool of water,
　　the flint into a spring of water.

One grouping of Psalms fairly late in the collection is often regarded as a type of traveling hymnbook. Psalms 120–134 all share the title "Song of Ascent," and traditions put these songs in the hands of the Hebrew pilgrims wending their way up to Jerusalem for the three annual feasts that required attendance by all Israelites (Passover, Firstfruits, and Tabernacles). While we cannot be certain that this subset of the psalms functioned in this manner, it is interesting to note how, taken together, Psalms 120–134 begin in distress and at a distance from Jerusalem (120), anticipate seeing Jerusalem (122, 125, 134), speak about traveling (121, 126), and end in worship at the Temple (134).

- "According to 'Lilies'" (45, 69)
- "According to 'Alamoth'" (46)
- "According to 'The Lilies of the Covenant'" (60, 80?)
- "A Maskil" (42, 44, 45, 52, 53, 77, 78, 88, 89, etc.)
- "A Miktam" (56, 57, 58, 59, 60, etc.)
- "With stringed instruments" (61, 67, 76, etc.)
- "For the memorial offering" (70)
- "According to 'The Gittith'" (81, 84)

Some "titles" identify the author:
- David (on 73 Psalms, mostly near the beginning)
- Solomon (72 and 127)
- Sons of Korah (42–49, 84–85, 87–88)
- Asaph (50, 73–83)
- Heman the Ezrahite (88)
- Ethan the Ezrahite (89)
- Moses (90)

Rejected!—Reflections on Psalm 60

You have rejected us, O God, and burst forth upon us.

—Psalm 60:1

A retired man tells of his "experiment" with the little birds that flock each morning in his backyard. He loves to scatter seeds and other treats for them and watch their "humanlike" manners. The doves are more aggressive than the others, probably because of their voracious appetites. He's found that if he waits quietly long enough, they will be the first to eat from his hand.

One morning, he tried to play a little game with a certain dove that had become a regular at these feedings. He held out his hand with birdseed in it, and silently coaxed the bird to come. Just as the dove reached for the offered grain, the man closed his hand abruptly. The bird stopped, cocked its head in disbelief and uncertainty, and then hopped back a few paces.

The hand opened again. The bird began another bold approach. And once more, the hand clamped shut just before the dove could reach the food. Several more times the pair repeated the little ritual, the man playing "god" and the dove growing in frustration and impatience. Then the bird flew off. It never returned.

Pain

Rejection hurts. Professional writers know only too well the pain of another rejected article or book. English romance novelist Elinor Glyn's first full-length manuscript was rejected by so many publishers that she tried a bolder approach. She sent it to yet another publishing house with this note attached: "Would you please publish the enclosed manuscript or return it without delay, as I have other irons in the fire."

The editor's reply was firm and quick. He returned the pages with this scribbled message: "Put this with your other irons."

Flamboyant British statesman and one-time prime minister of England, Benjamin Disraeli, had a similarly witty standard acknowledgment for people who sent him unsolicited manuscripts for his opinion. They received this reply: "Thank you for the manuscript; I shall lose no time in reading it."

Growth

Rejection is a tough business. But when it helps us grow in character, it can be a very good thing. Gaston Palewski, aide to former French president Charles DeGaulle, was well-known for his sexual come-ons to the women he encountered. One night after a party, he offered to drive a young woman home. She had the firmness of spirit to step on his toes, as hundreds of others had only wished to do. She coldly but very politely responded, "Thank you, but I'm too tired; I think I'll walk."

That kind of rejection was what he needed most to grow up. Diogenes, who founded the ancient Greek philosophic school of the Cynics, knew that rejection could bring strength. Someone once caught him trying to beg for food from a statue. He explained: "I am exercising the art of being rejected." He was preparing himself to cope with life.

Alienation

The midnight hours of history have been dampened by the tears of those whose heartache grows deeper because of rejection. "Sticks and stones may break my bones, but words can never hurt me," we say with bold face in the morning sun. But loneliness returns in the darkness, and every nasty name or spurious glance becomes a taunting reminder that we're not wanted.

That's the pain of David in Psalm 60. He's been well-schooled in rejection. King Saul was a master teacher. So were the Philistines, and so were members of his own family. But one thing always gave him hope: God would never leave him; God would never forsake him.

Now he's not so sure. Even God seems a silent and foreboding foe. Even God seems an enemy warrior. The rejection of the nations is a strain on Israel's resources; the anger of God, for whatever reason, shatters them.

The title notes of the psalm seem to indicate that it was written after the tide had turned, after General Joab had won a decisive battle over the Edomites, after faith and hope glimmered again in David's heart. But the pain of once being rejected, especially by God, is not something from which he can easily retreat.

It would be another thousand years before the world would hear a cry of alienation so bitter that it alone could bring peace to others who felt rejection. For not far from David's palace, one day in the future, a son of his would be rejected by society, condemned by the governing authorities, and displayed in death on a hideous cross, at odds even with God above.

His lips would cry, "My God, my God! Why have you forsaken me?" The answer is the mystery of salvation: "So that we might never again be forsaken by him."

The ideas expressed in this small grouping of psalms may well serve to indicate the manner in which the whole collection may profitably be used:

- Enjoy the poetic images: 19, 29, 104
- Rest in the gracious comfort of Yahweh: 23, 139
- Marvel in the compact simplicity of finely stated ideas: 1, 131
- Vocalize sorrow for sinfulness: 32, 51
- Express spiritual longing: 42–43, 73
- Ponder great evil and pain: 22, 88
- Gain a moral compass: 15, 107
- Learn the language of praise: 100, 145, 150

The psalms continue to function as the songbook of biblical faith. They shape the language of prayer, petition, and praise for those who believe that they are still bound to Yahweh, the God of creation and covenant.

Discussion Points

- Find examples of the different forms of Hebrew poetic parallelism, and explain how these groupings uniquely communicate the author's ideas or intentions.
- Create a modern psalm in one or more of the categorical types listed above, using as much parallelism as possible, and explain to others how and why you crafted it. Compare and critique one another's psalms for their fidelity to the biblical literary traditions.
- Why might some psalms praise a location (Psalms of Zion) or a ruler (Royal Psalms)? How do these fit into the theology of the Sinai Covenant, which informed Israel's history and identity?
- Does Psalm 87 imply Israelite racial and ethnic superiority over other nations, or does it indicate equality with them in a larger divine purpose? Why?

For Further Investigation

Brouwer, Wayne. (Muskegon, Voventure: 2013). *Hear Me, O God.*

14.

Covenant Language (3)

Living in Wisdom's House—The Proverbs

I magine a scene in a farmhouse kitchen. It is early September. Crops are still in the fields, and the smell of freshly cut hay mixes with the odors of manure and the pungent staleness of last year's silage. Flies buzz everywhere, leaving their small black dots of contamination. The air hangs heavy with choking humidity, begging for a late afternoon shower to wash clean the atmosphere.

A ticking wall clock rivets the silence of three who sit around a kitchen table with its plastic red and white covering. Cups of tea, hardly touched, idle in front of each, an older husband and wife, and their strapping teenage son, nearly a grown man in his own right.

Suddenly, the young fellow stands and says, "Well ..." Mom and Dad jump up quickly, and walk him to the door. Outside is a battered compact car crammed with the stuff a first-year student takes off to college, deluded into thinking his mother knows what he will need there.

There are too many important things to say, so nobody uses words. Mom grabs her son around the waist and clenches the air out of his lungs in surprising ferocity as she weeps into his chest. When he finally pats her away and turns toward Dad, there is a glistening of almost-tears in the older fellow's eyes that the son hasn't seen before. They shake hands, man to man, in a grip no

149

> ### Proverbs in Overview 📖
>
> **Prologue:** The purpose of Proverbs (1:1–7)
>
> **Lectures on Wisdom and Folly** (1:8–9:18)
>
> **Collections of Proverbs:** (10:1–31:9)
>
> "The Proverbs of Solomon" (10:1–22:16)
>
> "Sayings of the Wise" (22:17–24:22)
>
> "More Sayings of the Wise" (24:23–34)
>
> "More Proverbs of Solomon" (25:1–29:27)
>
> "The Sayings of Agur" (30:1–23)
>
> "The Sayings of King Lemuel" (31:1–9)
>
> **Epilogue:** "The Wife of Noble Character" (31:10–31)

bear could pull out of. Finally, Dad manages a few expressions. "Son," he says, "remember what we've taught you! When you get to the big city, and you find your place at the university, there will be all sorts of women who come after you. Pick wisely, or it will be the ruin of you. Remember who you are!"

And with that, the son escapes to find his fame and fortune. What will he be like in a year or four? What will he do with his opportunities? How will he face the challenges that cultured life has to offer him, once the protective structures of rural society no longer define how he is to live? Most importantly, who will he date, and why, and will he find a mate with whom he can thrive? Or will he get caught in the lure of enticements that steal his soul as well as his heart?

This is the way we need to enter the book of Proverbs. It is built upon a love story. In fact, the book of Proverbs starts out as an allegory on a love triangle, with a voice of parental reason whispering from offstage.

An Important Prologue

While it may seem at first glance to be a tedious collection of rather dry one-liners, Proverbs is much more than that. It is our doorway into the educational system of the Israelite community. Our word "proverb" is derived from a Latin term which means "for a verb." So these are "words" which take the place of "more words," or concise distillations of wisdom compacted into a few carefully conceived phrases. The wisdom presumed by the proverbs is the worldview of the Sinai Covenant, as the prologue (Proverbs 1:1–7) indicates. The message of the book derives its direction from Solomon, who was enormously wise because of the special gift of God (1 Kings 3). Solomon is the father of Proverbs in several ways. First, he created Yahweh's Temple in Jerusalem, which gave a permanent home to Israel's covenant marriage partner. Second, the wisdom of Yahweh spoke powerfully through Solomon, so the whole world came to hear his proverbs and pithy sayings (1 Kings 3–4). Third, the greatest bulk of this book called "Proverbs" is attributed directly to Solomon (1:1, 10:1, 25:1). Fourth, Solomon was also known for his wide-ranging—and ultimately catastrophic—flirtations, courtships and marriages, which may well be reflected in the pointed moral sermons of the first nine chapters of Proverbs. In truth, both Solomon's early expressions of pithy wisdom (which drew the attention and the attraction of the world; 1 Kings 4:29–34, 10:1–13) and his disastrous sexual alliances (which caused his downfall; 1 Kings 11:1–13), served to shape the collection of Proverbs in its final form.

Lectures on Wisdom and Folly

This is seen in the "Lectures on Wisdom and Folly" that stand at the head of the book. In the Hebrew language, both "wisdom" and "folly" are feminine nouns. Thus the use of the repeated literary device "my son" in Proverbs 1:8–9:18 is intentional. All readers or hearers of these lectures become the "son" who is courted by two women, "Wisdom" and "Folly." By the end of these carefully crafted lectures, in which each woman is given ample opportunity to present her case, all of us must choose which woman to wed. The choice is real, personal, and life-changing. Wisdom brings stability and well-being; Folly offers quick experiences and tragic ends.

Dating often seems to be a trivial pastime and sexuality sometimes merely the arena for power plays and sporting events. But in Proverbs, the high calling of courtship is held out as the definer of human identity. None of us remains single. All of us are swept up into the drama. It is forever a triangle: Whether female or male, in this affair, we are the young man pursuing and being pursued by two women, Folly and Wisdom. Each parades her virtues. Each calls for a choice and a commitment. But there the similarities end. For Folly brings us into an endless addiction to one-night stands, in which we lose ourselves in the delirium of mere titillation, and ultimately lose all substance and self-respect. Wisdom, however, wants to take things slowly, and seeks as much to get to know us as we her. Wisdom desires a relationship where respect deepens and both parties are enriched.

If, at the close of these lectures, one should choose Folly, the rest of the proverbs have no meaning. That person should slam shut the book and get on with other destructive behaviors, for she or he cannot understand the language that is used in the house of Wisdom.

If, however, one hears and understands these lectures, and responds with an appropriate desire to court and marry Wisdom, the rest of the book of Proverbs becomes the stuff of which her house is made. When one is bound to Wisdom, the proverbs are the furnishings of her home, the decorations on her walls, the conversation pieces in her rooms, and the lifestyle that organizes her economy. The many, many proverbs are not to be read together as an unbroken narrative, but are supposed to be savored and tasted like the multitude of meals taken in the marriage house of Wisdom, and breathed as if they were the life-sustaining rhythms of respiration itself.

Lectures on Wisdom and Folly

Proverbs 1:8–9:18
Enticement to Perverse Ways (1:8–19)
Wisdom's Call (1:20–33)

Benefits of Wisdom (2:1–22) [22 poetic lines]
Benefits and Specific Instructions (3:1–20) [20]
Benefits and Specific Instructions (3:21–35) [15]
Benefits of Wisdom (4:1–27) [27]
Warning against Adultery (5:1–23) [23]
Warning against Perverse Ways (6:1–19) [20]
Warning against Adultery (6:20–35) [16]
Warning against Adultery (7:1–27) [27]

Wisdom's Call (8:1–36)
Wisdom's Invitation and Folly's Enticement (9:1–18)

Dominant Themes in Proverbs

God's Character—2:5–6, 3:6, 3:32, 16:6, 19:21, 20:12, 21:3, 29:25

Wisdom:

- *As Instruction or Training*—1:2, 1:3, 3:11, 4:1, 23:13, 24:32
- *As Understanding*—1:2, 2:2, 6:32; 10:13
- *As Wise Dealing*—1:3, 2:7, 8:14, 10:5, 12:8,
- *As Shrewdness*—1:4, 1:5, 12:2, 22:3
- *As Knowledge and Learning*—1:5, 2:5, 3:6

The Fool—1:32, 10:1, 12:15, 15:15, 14:15, 17:16, 17:21, 17:24, 19:25, 22:23, 26:11

The Lazy—6:6, 6:9-10, 12:27, 13:4, 19:24, 20:4, 21:25-26, 22:13, 26:15, 26:16

Friends and Friendship—2:17, 3:29, 11:12, 14:21, 16:28, 17:9, 17:17, 18:17, 19:4, 19:6, 19:7, 21:10, 22:24–25, 25:8–9, 27:6

Words as Power or Poverty—6:14, 10:11, 10:21, 11:9, 12:18, 14:23, 15:1, 15:4, 15:30, 16:13, 16:24, 16:27, 18:21, 24:12, 25:11, 26:23–28, 28:24, 29:5

Family—12:4, 10:5, 13:1, 13:24, 14:1, 15:20, 17:17, 18:22, 19:7, 19:14, 20:20, 22:15, 23:14, 29:15, 30:11, 30:17

Life and Death—10:16, 11:7, 13:12, 14:27, 14:30, 15:4, 15:11, 15:24, 16:15, 16:22, 23:14, 27:20, 28:17, 30:16

The Collections of Proverbs

Most of the proverbs are formed as antithetic parallelism couplets: two pithy lines of general truth are bound together, each stating the converse of the other:

> *A wise son brings joy to his father,*
> *but a foolish son grief to his mother.* (10:1)

> *Lazy hands make a man poor,*
> *but diligent hands bring wealth.* (10:4)
> *The memory of the righteous will be a blessing,*
> *but the name of the wicked will rot.* (10:7)

Taken together, these doublets are like the twin sides of a single coin. Neither statement is superior to the other, but only when they are held in tandem is a larger truth revealed.

Proverbs of Solomon

The "Proverbs of Solomon" (10:1–22:16) forms the largest group among the various collections in the book as a whole. Here, there is a subtle subtext which is only apparent when the proverbs are counted and found to number 375. There are no numerals in the Hebrew language, so numbers are indicated by the use of the letters of the alphabet in ways that represent certain values. The letters in Solomon's name have a combined numerical value that would be recognized as 375. Hence, the collection of "Proverbs of Solomon" is complete when 375 have been listed together.

It is possible that these proverbs were created by Solomon for entertainment at state banquets or common meals. Some could also have been recorded first as official statements of Solomon in the context of his executive decisions. They might also have been published for training the young among the many royal families created by Solomon's excessive marriages, or to guide the preparation of those on government leadership tracks for assuming their official duties.

In any case, this collection of 375 proverbs probably dates from the forty years of Solomon's official reign, 970–930 B.C. Virtually all of the first 180 proverbs in this collection are shaped in antithetic parallelism, while the remaining 195 have more varied parallelism forms.

The Sayings of the Wise

Immediately following the "Proverbs of Solomon" is a collection called "The Sayings of the Wise" (Proverbs 22:17–24:22). After a brief introduction (Proverbs 22:17–21) which echoes the prologue (Proverbs 1:1–7), thirty "wise sayings" describe appropriate behavior in a variety of social settings. Interestingly, an Egyptian book of proverbs called "The Wisdom of Amenemopet," dated to around 1000 B.C. (very close to the time of Solomon), is nearly parallel in structure and content. It also has thirty brief "wise sayings," of which ten are virtually identical to ten of these in the collection of the proverbs. Scholars differ as to which came first, but there seems to be some interaction between the sources behind both collections.

The fragment of five "More Sayings of the Wise" (Proverbs 24:23–34) seems related to the preceding collection in style, character, and substance, but little else is known about these. Together, the "Sayings of the Wise" and "More Sayings of the Wise" have the feel of published pamphlets which might have been distributed as handbooks for government officials. Perhaps Solomon used these to shape the culture of his courts. It may well be that either he adapted a similar collection ("The Wisdom of Amenemopet"), which he came to appreciate through his interactions with the royal house of Egypt, or the Egyptians, bound to Solomon and Israel by a royal marriage (1 Kings 3:1–3), found this administrative tool of Solomon's too good to not plagiarize for their own use.

More Sayings of Solomon

A second packet of Solomon's proverbs follows (Proverbs 25:1–29:27). These are identified as having been gathered and published by "the men of Hezekiah." This would locate the publication event in Israel's history at a time just over two hundred years after Solomon, during a period of reform and strong religious resurgence in Judah. It is likely that Hezekiah, in consolidating and strengthening his realm after the miraculous deliverance from Assyria (2 Kings 18–19), would have reached back to the literature of Israel's golden age to find language and values that would buttress his efforts. Scouring the pages of official court records, the pithy wisdom of Solomon was served up nicely.

Though similar to the first, larger collection of Solomon proverbs, there is more diversity of subject matter and literary form among these later offerings. Most, again, are shaped as antithetic parallelism independent couplets, but there are also more multiple-line proverbs among them.

Sayings of Agur and King Lemuel

Two very interesting collections of wisdom instruction appear next. "Sayings of Agur" (Proverbs 30:1–23) and "Sayings of King Lemuel" (Proverbs 31:1–9) are the product of people not otherwise mentioned anywhere in the Bible. They were not kings of Israel or Judah. Some speculate that they might have been from the Ishmaelite tribe of Massa (Genesis 25:14), and that their words entered Israelite culture by way of traders coming from Edom. This, however, remains only one speculation among a host of unprovable theories.

The form of these sayings is strikingly different from others in the Proverbs collection, particularly in the use of numbers for identifying extremes or adding emphasis:

One More Note on "Wisdom"

In its personification of Wisdom, Proverbs 8 includes a section that makes "Wisdom" the creative partner of Yahweh (verses 22–31). Correlating this to the prologue of John (1:1–18), where "the Word" is the creative agent of God, some Christian theologians have interpreted the "Wisdom" of Proverbs 8 as a pre-incarnate manifestation of the second person of the Trinity. This seems to violate the good sense and theological intentions of each passage, and lingers as an unhelpful theological speculation that detracts from beneficial interpretation for either text.

There are three things that are never satisfied,
Four that never say, "Enough!" (Proverbs 30:15)

There are three things that are too amazing for me,
Four that I do not understand: (Proverbs 30:18)

The "Agur" reflections focus mostly on general life situations, while the brief "King Lemuel" notes probe more specifically the necessary character of good rulers. Together, they add additional wisdom to the collection of proverbs, even if their origin is uncertain.

Epilogue: the Wife of Noble Character

Finally, Proverbs ends with a short description often called "The Wife of Noble Character" (Proverbs 31:10–31). Shaped as an acrostic poem, the twenty-two couplets each begin with a successive letter of the Hebrew alphabet. In this way, the very literary technique communicates the completeness of the idea explored: Here is everything you need to know about the noble wife, A to Z.

But what is the purpose of this culminating articulation? Does it describe the ideal woman every young man should seek when dating? Is it the catalog of traits to be found in the most respectable of Israelite wives? Can it be used to identify the appropriate tasks of a homemaker in ancient Israel?

Perhaps any or all of these are possibilities, and that is why so many Christian preachers use this passage as a text for the homily on Mother's Day. But if the book of Proverbs is taken as a whole, and careful attention is paid to its development, there is a wonderful completeness brought about by this acrostic poem.

The opening lectures of the book place before the reader the requirement to choose between two women, Wisdom and Folly, each of whom presents her attractions and enticements. If we choose to marry Wisdom, chapters 10–31 of Proverbs describe the furnishings and lifestyle in the home created by our new spouse. This acrostic poem then forms a concluding testimony of the good life created by Wisdom. In that sense, it is more than a sociological description; it is a theological culmination of the life-engagement processes found in the covenant community.

Wisdom, according to Proverbs, is not merely intelligence, for people with big brains can do very foolish things. Nor is wisdom simply street smarts or hardscrabble experience, though both of these can help us figure out what really matters in life. At its root, true wisdom is the process of entering and appreciating the worldview developed out of the Sinai Covenant community. When one learns to live with Yahweh in holy awe, the contours of the world begin to be defined by the resurgence of the Creator's design. Living in this universe, one becomes married to Wisdom, because Wisdom is the human expression of Yahweh's presence at the heart of the society. And in Wisdom's house, conversations of daily simplicity, as well as the intimacies of family relationships and the governing principles of kings and courts, are formed by the language of these Proverbs.

Discussion Points

- Trace the expressions about Wisdom and Folly through the "Lectures" of the first nine chapters of Proverbs. What are the key benefits of Wisdom over Folly as a life partner? What are the principal distractions from opting for Folly over Wisdom as a spouse or lover? Why might these be selected as the most important aspects of each?
- Create a topical index of themes addressed among Proverbs 10–31, and attempt to categorize them in general or completely. What are the dominant concerns addressed by the writers of the proverbs? Why might that be? What themes or categories would you use if you were to create a new collection of proverbs for your current society? Why?
- Using the experiences of your daily life, create ten proverbs in the antithetic parallelism style most favored by Solomon. Explain to others how these proverbs function from a literary standpoint, and then describe the moral basis for the content of your proverbs.
- Besides the notations of the prologue to the book of Proverbs, what other evidence is there in the text that the world of ancient Israel and the Sinai Covenant are presupposed as points of reference?
- How does the "Wife of Noble Character" acrostic poem in Proverbs 31:10–31 provide a fitting conclusion to the book as a whole?

For Further Investigation

Kidner, Derek. (Downers Grove: InterVarsity Press, 1964). *The Proverbs*.
Kidner, Derek. (Downers Grove: InterVarsity Press, 1985). *The Wisdom of Proverbs, Job & Ecclesiastes*.

15.

Covenant Language (4)

The Worldview of Biblical Religion—Ecclesiastes

When I was in high school, a spiritual revival swept our area, and many of us pondered together the big questions of life and meaning. A friend and I formed a Bible study group (that was actually more of a social club), in which we tried to wrestle with faith and angst, while sheltered in the home of some trusted adults who were not yet over the horrible age of thirty. We would meet together on Sunday evenings, often deciding only when we arrived what we were going to "study" that night. Invariably, Jeff, hidden back in a corner between sofas and stuffed chairs, would murmur that we should read Ecclesiastes because he was depressed, and it was depressing, and maybe these two woeful laments would find each other and somehow make the world right.

Jeff was on to something, of course. Ecclesiastes is indeed a rather dark and depressing diatribe. "All is meaningless!" is the cry, both in the beginning (Ecclesiastes 1:2) and again at the end

A Great Wedding Text

While many couples planning to get married are attracted quickly by passages like 1 Corinthians 13, which speak overtly about love, Ecclesiastes 4:9–12 is at least as fitting:

Two are better than one, because they have a good return for their work. If one falls down, his friend can help him up. But pity the man who falls and has no one to help him up! Also, if two lie down together, they will keep warm. But how can one keep warm alone? Though one may be overpowered, two can defend themselves. A cord of three strands is not quickly broken.

(Ecclesiastes 12:8). In between there are lists after lists of things that only prove the "Teacher's" dark and troubling point of view:

- A king builds a massive empire and his successor wastes it to nothing (2:12).
- A man wrestles out an education that makes him incredibly perceptive, but he dies the same death as a fool and is forgotten (2:13–14).
- A man works all his life to create a marvelous and productive estate, but there is no one to leave it to, and he dies alone (4:7–8)
- A wealthy man amasses greater fortunes, but dies consumed by greed (5:10–12).

The litany is incessant, and drums its way into our brains like a leaky faucet chasing away sleep on a muggy and worrisome night. Wisdom, pleasure, folly, toil—they all come to nothing (1:12–2:26). Time itself is a cruel taskmaster that binds and breaks down (3). Other dimensions of life leave us hopeless: oppression, hard work, friendlessness, political advancement, unfulfilled vows to God, amassing wealth (4:1–6:12).

How do we stay sane in such an existence? The Teacher suggests that we ought to try at least to get a bit of practical working wisdom, for this seems in some way to take the cynical edge off the meaninglessness of life. As a push in that direction, he offers a variety of proverbs which sound very similar to those in the more famous book known by that name (7:1–8:6).

But the full impact of the Teacher's observations is left for some concluding reflections (8:7–12:7). Since we cannot find certain or standardized meaning in the whimsical affairs of our lives, we must look beyond. In chapter 3, there was already a hint of this: "[God] has made everything beautiful in its time. He has also set eternity in the hearts of men" (verse 11). The Teacher even suggested a way to make it through life with some degree of sanity: "I know that there is nothing better for men than to be happy and do good while they live" (verse 13). Again, in chapter 5, the Teacher nods in this same direction (verses 18–20).

Yet the deepest insights of the book are to be found in the last chapters. Here, there is a reminder that all of life is progressing toward a common end, and one which we are powerless to control. So we might as well enjoy life while we have it, and go *with* the flow rather than *against* it, by gaining some

Ecclesiastes in Outline

Prologue: Theme ("Meaninglessness") and Brief Explanation (1:1–11)

Meaningless Things: Wisdom, Pleasures, Folly, Toil (1:12–2:26)

Interlude: The Bondage of Time (3)

Other Meaningless Things: Oppression, Toil, Friendlessness, Political Advancement, practical wisdom. But in the end, it is our relationship with our Creator that puts the rest of life into focus.

So the final reflections of the Teacher might be summarized in this manner:

- If this world we live in is a closed system, then all is tragedy and meaningless.
- But if there is a God, life may be brief and seem random, yet it is ultimately very meaningful.
- We may not be able to understand the ultimate meaning of all things and experiences from our vantage point; nevertheless, we sense it as we connect with transcendent realities.
- If we truly believe there is a God, then the three most important things for us to use as core values for life are these:
  * Live boldly, for it is better to engage life than to fear it.
  * Live joyfully, for laughter melts the sorrows of our sometimes meaningless existence.
  * Live godly, for though we are not always able to understand meaning and purpose in life, the Creator's ways are still the best, even if we know them only in part.

> Unfulfilled Vows to God, Amassing Wealth (4:1–6:12)
>
> **Practical Wisdom That Brings Sanity to Life** (7:1–8:6)
>
> **Reflections on All of the Teacher's Observations:** (8:7–2:7)
>
> The meaning of life must be found beyond life—in God alone
>
> All of life is progressing toward a common end
>
> So enjoy life while you have it
>
> And be wise
>
> In summary—Live Boldly! Live Joyfully! Live Godly!
>
> **Epilogue:** The Theme and Its Value, Plus Final Reminders (12:8–14)

Who is this cruel and winsome Teacher? The internal hints (1:1, 12, 16; 12:9–10) suggest it might have been Solomon, mainly because of the links to the royal family, the quest for wisdom, and the greatness of the kingdom touted as having been gained by the writer. Since the tone of the reflections is like that of an elderly man looking back at a life both lived to the full and also wasted in many dimensions, it is not impossible to see these as the journalings of Solomon in his later years, perhaps to be left as a legacy for his son, Rehoboam, who would ascend next to the throne in Jerusalem. That would give Ecclesiastes a date of around 935 B.C.

> Literary Forms in Ecclesiastes 📖
>
> **Personal Reflections**—e.g., chapter 2
>
> **Rhetorical Questions**—e.g., 1:3, 10; 2:2, 12
>
> **Proverbs**—e.g., 1:4–9, 15, 18; 3:1–8; 4:5–6; 7:1–13; 9:17–11:4
>
> **Allegory**—e.g., 12:1–7

If someone else wrote these pages, it could have happened sometime during or after the exile of Judah to Babylon. In this scenario, some of Solomon's own proverbs and pithy reflections might have been turned against him as a later judgment about the king who led Israel to unbelievable heights of greatness, and yet rotted away his own life and that of the nation into a horrible and decadent mess that ultimately ripped apart the realm when he died.

Names for the Book:
"Qoheleth" and
"Ecclesiastes"

Hebrew—"*Qoheleth*" ("convener of an assembly for instruction")

Greek – "*Ecclesiastes*" ("teacher/preacher")

My friend Jeff was right. Ecclesiastes is depressing. But that is only the beginning of the story. On its surface, and especially at its beginning, the screaming message is this: *All we do and everything that happens to us is ultimately meaningless and has no lasting value!* But if we take the time to hear the notes of hopeful optimism that begin to leak through, starting already in chapter 3, a more moderate message speaks out: *Yet life goes on, so let's make the best of it and be more wise about it than foolish.* And if we attune our ears to the religious confidence that forms a bedrock foundation underlying all of the Teacher's reflections, a subtle but profound message whispers as well: *Life can only mean something if there is a God who sets the values (e.g., time and morality), and gives us a link to eternity which confirms our right to exist.*

For this reason, Ecclesiastes is in the Bible. It expresses powerfully the worldview of the Sinai Covenant. This is the message that Israel could portray to the nations of her world. Indeed, this is, at its best, the true wisdom of Solomon that should have been the evangelistic beacon of his great kingdom. After all, Israel had been strategically poised to preach these things in a social and political arena where the Creator had come to be largely forgotten, and because of that, life itself often had burdened down into meaningless tedium and recurring cycles of incessant depressing failure. But only if people stopped their depressing busyness long enough to think might these woeful thoughts drive them desperately to look for a religious perspective that was never meaningless.

Discussion Points

- Taken as a whole, is the message of Ecclesiastes more depressing or uplifting? Why?
- How do the writings in Ecclesiastes explore and express the worldview of ancient Israel and the Sinai Covenant with Yahweh?
- Who might the "Preacher" of Ecclesiastes be? What status could he have in the ancient Israelite community that would allow and encourage him to use his platform to put forward these views? Why would he do so?

For Further Investigation

Kidner, Derek. (Downers Grove: Intervarsity Press, 1976). *A Time to Mourn, and a Time to Dance.*

16.

Covenant Language (5)

Love Song's Theme and Variations

Everyone falls in love. A high school romance, a workplace attraction, an online conversation partner, a springtime passion, a neighborly friendship, an old-age companion ... *Everyone* falls in love.

But what is love? Feelings? Obsessions? Friendship? Physical intimacy? Companionship? Domestic partnering? Choices? Commitments? All of us ask at some point, "Is this love?"

So there is in the Bible an engaging, titillating, and maddeningly difficult-to-interpret little volume of love poetry known as the "Song of Songs," or "The Greatest Song," or sometimes, "The Song of Solomon." While the verses flow around each another in a complex maze, it is obvious that there are clearly several literary genres hidden within the whole. For instance, some collections of verse seem to be refined love songs meant to be staged like opera arias (e.g., 4:1–7). At other points, there are autobiographical reflections (e.g., 1:5–7). Then, now and again, a chorus will break in with a communal assessment of the current passionate dealings (e.g., 6:10, 13). Along with these, there are search narratives that seem to move the storyline along (e.g., 5:2–7).

If it were not for the constant notations of action behind these passionate songs and robust dialogue, it would be possible merely to receive the verses as some form of love poetry. But the hints of background narrative, along with the changing voices of the poems themselves (sometimes solo masculine, sometimes solo feminine, and sometimes chorus collectives), require at least an attempt at charting out a storyline. Yet, this again brings up a key interpretive question: How many main characters are there in the drama?

Interpretive Choices

It is clear from the gender and voice forms of the Hebrew verbs that there are at least two dominant solo voices in the song, one male and one female. Yet, when reading the dramatic musical through in its entirety, interpreters wrestle with whether the leading man parts are all from just one person, or perhaps two. If there is only one romantic male lead, the drama as a whole seems to be a dialogue between King Solomon and a beautiful, but hesitant, country girl, whom he seeks to woo and wed. But if there are *two* primary masculine voices in the story line, everything changes. In that case, a love triangle is set up in which a pair of young country friends-who-have-become-lovers are suddenly ripped apart, because the lustful and powerful lecherous King Solomon has decided to add this young thing to his harem, regardless of her protests or her lover's opposition.

Both options fit with the text and its interpretive possibilities. The outcomes for the meaning of the book, however, change dramatically, depending on which path is followed.

Within its interpretive history, several directions have been taken. Many have been embarrassed by the blatant sexuality of the book, and have tried to sanctify things by transforming it into an allegory on the mystical love between God and Israel (like that described in the prophecies of Hosea), or Christ and the Church (as Paul suggests in Ephesians 5:25–33). Others have left the drama stand as a morality play intended to be staged, one which either gives a bawdy encouragement to stuffy members of the Judeo-Christian faith community to let loose a little and enjoy the God-given gift of sexuality, or more conservatively directs its actors to moralize judgment against Solomon's wicked ways.

Whether it was created originally as some element of the wedding ceremony or reception entertainment used at one of Solomon's many marriages, or came to life as the passionate pennings of a mystic in search of union with God, the drama was included in Hebrew scripture, and now requires theological interpretation. If there is some narrative sequencing behind the poetry that expresses an original story line, and if a measure of the subtle negative aspersions pointed in Solomon's direction (cf. 8:12) are to be taken at face value, it seems likely that the love triangle understanding of the drama is reasonably valid. Such a view would certainly be consistent with

---

Schools of "Song of Songs" Interpretation

Divine/Human Allegory:
Yahweh and Israel (cf. Hosea)
Christ and the Church (cf. Ephesians 5:25–33)

Morality Play: "Don't do what Solomon did!"

Royal Nuptials: Elaborate wedding drama developed for entertainment at Solomon's many weddings

Liturgical Ecstasy: Language of spiritual union between the soul (feminine) and God (masculine)

"Sanctified" Pornography: God created sex, so enjoy it!

the repeated refrain: "... do not stir up or awaken love until it is ready!" (2:7, 3:5, 8:4; compare 5:8). Also, this approach is in harmony with the testimony of the prophetical histories, which declare that Solomon was led astray by his over-infatuation with wives and marriages and concubines, and that in this part of his personal world, at least, he got it wrong. If there is a love triangle behind the scenes of the Song of Songs, one which speaks negatively about Solomon's corrupting harem and the psychological downside of polygamist marriages, the plotline might flow something like this:

- King Solomon has brought the Shulamite maid into his palace harem and tries to overwhelm her with power and poetry (1:2–2:7).
- The maid's true lover comes seeking her at night and is chased, but the two escape to their country community (2:8–3:5).
- Solomon mounts a royal procession to reclaim his current infatuation (3:6–4:8).
- Once again, the maid's lover comes, trying to get her free. She misses him, runs into the streets after him when he is chased away, and is beaten until rescued by the harem guard (4:9–6:3).
- Solomon continues his wooing with more sensual love songs (6:4–7:9).
- But the Shulamite maid spurns Solomon's advances and returns to her rural community, and to the lover who waits for her there (7:10–8:14).

The message emerging from the drama, understood in this manner, would be that true human love thrives best in monogamous relationships which take their time in building solid commitments, and are

Song of Solomon and Christian Mysticism

Christian mystics have, for centuries, adopted the language of the Song of Solomon as the vocabulary of faith, prayer and meditation. There are several reason for this. First, it allows the amorous language to become religious without embarrassment. Second, it deepens the communication of intimacy with God. Third, it provides an allegorical interpretation of the book which parallels the mystical assent.

As Evelyn Underhill famously described it (Mysticism, 1911), there are five stages to a person's deepening connectedness with God:

- Awakening of Self—growing restlessness with my current situation and a recognition that there must be a higher purpose for life

- Purification of Self—cleansing thoughts and heart in order to be ready for and worthy of a transcendent Lover

- Illumination—contact with the divine Lover, in which chatter forms the prelude to intimacy, and the partners glow in proximity to one another

- Dark Night of the Soul—an attack of the remorse of inadequacy threatening to sabotage the relationship, since the Lover is so much grander than the Beloved

- Unification—the climax of intimacy between the Lover and the Beloved, often expressed in sexual terms, with the human soul (always feminine) being ravished by Jesus (the masculine Lover and Lord and Husband)

These are often mapped to the presumed story of Solomon's affair with the Shulamite maiden in the Song of Solomon. While this allegorical interpretation of the book (akin to the messages of the prophet Hosea, and the representations of Paul regarding Jesus and the Church in Ephesians 5:21-33) has lit the fires of spiritual passion in many private hearts, it does not seem to take seriously either the original purposes of the Song of Solomon as literature, or the communal nature of faith.

not excessively focused on external physical aspects. Solomon got it wrong; the country friends-become-lovers (and all who hear the truth of God through this drama) got it right.

There are, of course, other interpretations given to this book. Often, it is viewed as allegorical love talk which seeks a mystical union between the soul and God. But the historical notes in the Song of Songs plead with us to find some historical grounding for the work, and not spiritualize it too quickly.

Solomon and the Wisdom Literature

A final reflection is in order here. While the connections with Solomon in Proverbs, Ecclesiastes, and Song of Songs are mostly indirect, his name and circumstances are clearly present in each. What might this indicate? One possibility is that each of these three literary creations expresses Solomon's wisdom—or his lack of it—from a differing vantage point. The bulk of the **Proverbs**, for instance, may well emerge from the young Solomon, who displayed much wisdom and who colored Israel's international character because of it, precisely in line with the divine missional intent. **Ecclesiastes**, in turn, might well have been the reminiscences of an old Solomon, who finally came to his senses about much of his mid- and later-life folly, and was trying to recover perspective and wisdom in his dying days, particularly as he saw his spoiled son Rehoboam about to repeat many of Solomon's own stupid mistakes. **Song of Songs**, on the other hand, could be the creation of a thoughtful dramatist living some time after Solomon died, who created a morality play about love based upon the failings of the great king.

We are not likely to find a clear and unambiguous answer to such conundrums. Yet, we would be poorer, including spiritually, if these writings, emerging from the wisdom of reflection on the character of life shaped by the Sinai Covenant, were not still traveling with us.

Discussion Points

- How might the poetry of Song of Songs best be used in a synagogue or church? Does it need to be chaperoned or censored, or can it stand on its own alongside other biblical literature? Why?
- What differences emerge in the interpretation of the Song of Songs if the drama underlying it is viewed as a love triangle rather than a simple love duet? How do these differences affect the moral and ethical issues addressed by the literary work?
- Jewish and Christian mystics have long been drawn to Song of Songs as a primary text for spiritual nourishment. Why might that be? What would be the manner of interpretation they might typically adopt? Why?

For Further Investigation

Seerveld, Calvin. (Palos Heights: Trinity, 1967). *The Greatest Song: In Critique of Solomon*.

17.

Covenant Language (6)

Lamentations about the Mystery of Election

The five dirges of Lamentations are typically ascribed to Jeremiah. Consequently, they have found a canonical home following the prophecies of that discouraged, but faithful, figure of the seventh century B.C. Yet these laments often get lost in their usual location, tacked on as a mournful appendix to the prophet's cries. Our energies generally have been sapped by Jeremiah's tribulations from his last years in Jerusalem, and the lamentations weigh us down as an exercise in emotional excess.

In truth, these lamentations would better be considered along with the other poetry of the Wisdom Literature. In literary form, the lamentations are quite similar to one another. Each of the first four laments is an acrostic poem. This means that the beginning word of each short stanza (in groupings of mostly synonymous parallelism couplets) starts with a successive letter of the Hebrew alphabet. Since there are twenty-two letters in this language, the opening words in each new couplet progress sequentially from *aleph* to *taw* when claiming beginning letters. For laments one and two, there are three couplets in each stanza grouping (only the first word of which begins with the next Hebrew letter in acrostic pattern), producing grieving songs that each consist of twenty-two short verses (22 Hebrew letters times 3 synonymous parallelism couplets).

The third lament is very similar, but adds the additional creative touch of having each couplet within a threesome begin with the same Hebrew letter (deepening the acrostic expression threefold). The fourth lament seems somewhat abbreviated, since each short stanza, while still acrostically developed by way of its initial letter, is formed from only two synonymous parallelism couplets rather than three. Finally, in the fifth lament, there are twenty-two couplets of synonymous parallelism, but their initial letters do not form an acrostic.

This careful attention to the shape of the poetry gives evidence that the laments were crafted by someone who felt deeply about the fall of Jerusalem and wanted to preserve memorial dirges that would testify to the complete collapse of confidence it produced. These funeral songs are designed to tell that dark story from *aleph* to *taw* ("A to Z").

But how do they tell that tale of woe? In theme and variations, the main thrust of the five laments is something like this:

Lament One—Jerusalem is like a lonely widow suffering from many oppressions, brought on by her great sins.

> How deserted lies the city,
>   once so full of people!
> How like a widow is she,
>   who once was great among the nations!
> She who was queen among the provinces
>   has now become a slave.
> Bitterly she weeps at night,
>   tears are upon her cheeks.
> Among all her lovers
>   there is none to comfort her.
> All her friends have betrayed her;
>   they have become her enemies. (1:1–2)

Visualizing the Five Lamentations

Laments #1 & #2

A
_____
_____
_____
_____
_____
_____

B
_____
_____
_____
_____
_____

C
_____
_____
_____
_____
_____

(and so on)

Lament Two—Yahweh's covenant anger has erupted, resulting in the judgments now experienced.

> The Lord has rejected his altar
>   and abandoned his sanctuary.
> He has handed over to the enemy
>   the walls of her palaces;

> they have raised a shout in the house of the Lord
>   as on the day of an appointed feast.
>
> The Lord determined to tear down
>   the wall around the Daughter of Zion
> He stretched out a measuring line
>   and did not withhold his hand from destroying.
> He made ramparts and walls lament,
>   together they wasted away. (2:7–8)

Lament Three—The pain of destruction and exile is personalized, asserting Yahweh's propriety in raining down judgment, but nuancing this difficult message with expectations of restoration and words of hope.

> I remember my affliction and my wandering,
>   the bitterness and the gall.
> I well remember them,
>   and my soul is downcast within me.
> Yet this I call to mind
>   and therefore I have hope:
>
> Because of the Lord's great love we are not consumed,
>   for his compassions never fail.
> They are new every morning;
>   great is your faithfulness.
> I say to myself, "The Lord is my portion;
>   therefore I will wait for him." (3:19–24)

Lament Four—The torment of Jerusalem's ruin becomes personalized in horrifying description.

> But now they are blacker than soot;
>   they are not recognized in the streets.
> Their skin has shriveled on their bones;
>   it has become as dry as a stick.
>
> Those killed by the sword are better off
>   than those who die of famine;
> racked with hunger, they waste away
>   for lack of food from the field.
> With their own hands compassionate women

Visualizing the Five
Lamentations

Lament #3

A

_____

A

_____

A

_____

B

_____

B

_____

B

_____

C

_____

C

_____

C

_____

(and so on)

> *have cooked their own children,*
> *who became their food*
> *when my people were destroyed.* (4:8–10)

Lament Five—A prayer of repentance, seeking Yahweh's deliverance predicated upon the inviolable strength of divine covenant commitments and promises.

> *Remember, O Lord, what has happened to us;*
> *look, and see our disgrace.*
>
> *You, O Lord, reign forever;*
> *your throne endures from generation to generation.*
> *Why do you always forget us?*
> *Why do you forsake us so long?*
> *Restore us to yourself, O Lord, that we may return;*
> *renew our days as of old*
> *unless you have utterly rejected us*
> *and are angry with us beyond measure.* (5:1, 19–22)

Visualizing the Five
Lamentations

Lament #4

A

_____

_____

_____

B

_____

_____

_____

C

_____

_____

_____

(and so on)

What emerges within this collection is a profound reflection on the nature of covenant election. There is absolute affirmation that the judgments of Yahweh against Jerusalem and the people of Judah were appropriate. Such is the logical outcome of the curses of the Sinai Covenant, which clearly expressed the intended divine response to covenant unfaithfulness. The Israelites failed to remain true to the lifestyle of a community shaped by Yahweh-in-residence, and there had to be consequences. But attached to these notes of near-deterministic theology is also a strong and lingering question. How can Yahweh carry out the divine mission if Yahweh's human partner is annihilated? What sense does it make for Israel to be utterly destroyed? What kind of testimony is left if Jerusalem and the earthly dwelling of Yahweh become nothing more than a stinking, rotting wasteland? How will the nations reflect on the values Yahweh sought to display on the billboard of the world, if Yahweh's own marriage to Israel ends in divorce?

These are serious questions of faith. If the Creator is forgotten by the creatures who are made in the divine image, things are seriously askew on planet Earth, and the entire cosmos is tilting toward ruin. Judgment and destruction are legitimate and logical outcomes, whether or not the Creator wishes to start over with Plan B. But once the Creator stepped into human history and wed a bride named Israel, everything changed. Can Yahweh be trusted if Israel is punished beyond recovery? Is the mission of God possible if the human partner in the enterprise consistently wimps out? Where do we go from here?

The conundrums of divine election, and the relationship between God and a community that is sealed by such a deal, continue to intrigue and plague religious people generally, and theologians specifically. Why would God make these kinds of covenant commitments? How certain can we be about the strength of those commitments? What are the possible outcomes to promises made of both blessing for faithfulness and curses for infidelity? Can God ever fulfill the divine missiological designs pledged by the Covenant? Is it possible for a marriage of such unequal partners to endure?

Visualizing the Five Lamentations

Lament #5

M

_____

_____

_____

J

_____

_____

_____

X

_____

_____

_____

(and so on)

The New Testament apostle Paul will probe these issues again in his great letter to the Roman congregation. There, in chapters 9–11, he will pick up the themes of Lamentations. If God made such strong promises to Israel—and those promises seem to have been voided by the nation's unfaithfulness, resulting in Yahweh's legitimate covenant curses upon it—how can anyone claim confidence in the God of Jesus? What does election mean? How true is the divine pledge to us if we are unable, because of inbred sinfulness, to maintain our part in the spiritual marriage?

While the five lamentations give voice to our concerns, they also hint at the amazing promises of grace, which always overcome the bad news of current affairs:

> Because of the Lord's great love we are not consumed,
>   for his compassions never fail.
> They are new every morning:
>   great is your faithfulness.
> I say to myself, "The Lord is my portion;
>   therefore I will wait for him." (Lamentations 3:22–24)

Bible "Big Picture"

Covenant Making: God establishes a covenant relationship with a missional community by way of a redemptive act.

Old Testament: The Exodus and Sinai Covenant

  Genesis—Why is the Covenant necessary?

  Exodus—What is the Covenant all about?

  Leviticus—How does it affect daily living?

  Numbers—Who is in the covenant community, and why?

  Deuteronomy—How long will the Covenant be in force?

New Testament: The Person and Work of Jesus

Covenant Living: God guides the covenant relationship with the missional community by way of authorized spokespersons.

Old Testament: The Prophets, with Their Interpreted History and Sermons

Stories: The interpreted history of Israel

  Joshua—Possessing the land with missional significance

  Judges—Nearly losing the land through covenant failure

  Ruth—The model of covenant obedience that restores

  1 & 2 Samuel—Establishing the monarchy that might fulfill the covenant mission

  1 & 2 Kings, 1 & 2 Chronicles—Failure of the Old Testament covenant community mission experiment

  Ezra and Nehemiah—Restoring the covenant community in anticipation of Yahweh's next major act

  Esther—Responding to the warning that Yahweh's people have a covenant identity and purpose

New Testament: The Apostles, with Their Ecclesiastical History and Letters

Covenant Questions: God nurtures the covenant relationship with a missional community by way of spiritual wisdom and insight.

Old Testament: The Poetry and Wisdom Literature; Questions of Fundamental Human Identity as Illuminated by the Theology of the Covenant

  Job—"Why do I suffer?"

  Psalms—"How do I pray?"

  Proverbs—"What is true wisdom?"

  Ecclesiastes—"What is the meaning of life?"

  Song of Songs—"What is the meaning of love?"

  Lamentations—"What is the meaning of divine election?"

New Testament: The Comparison of the Two Covenant Expressions

Discussion Points

- What does the literary device of "acrostic" indicate about the writer's views regarding the content of his or her poem? Why?
- Is there any sequential significance to the five lamentations? How would you know if there was?
- How is the doctrine of divine election under critical scrutiny in the lamentations? What outcomes or interpretations might be suggested to the writer's religious dilemmas?

Covenant Living (1B)

The Creator guides the covenant relationship with a missional community by way of authorized spokespersons

18.

Surfing the Transcendent

Isaiah as the Master Prophet

The poetry and wisdom literature of the Old Testament have taken us on a brief side journey away from the historical flow of Israel's covenant history. Turning to the prophets, we jump immediately into a boiling cauldron of international politics.

While the Hebrew prophets address many social issues, they cannot be understood if isolated from the political turmoil of their times. The prophets are social and political critics, constantly analyzing the actions of their own people, along with the affairs of the nations surrounding Israel, and making judgments about leaders and policies.

Isaiah stands at the head of the collection of Old Testament prophets for good reason. While he is not the earliest among them (Samuel was already considered a prophet three centuries before, and many of the first prophets noted in the Bible—e.g., Nathan and Ahijah—were evidently not "writing prophets"; they have bequeathed to us no documents to peruse), Isaiah is chief over them. He gave the prophetic message lyrical power, and addressed every theme that others would pursue only in part. Isaiah is the grand master of covenant prophecy.

According to the list of kings that Isaiah identifies, during whose reigns he received and

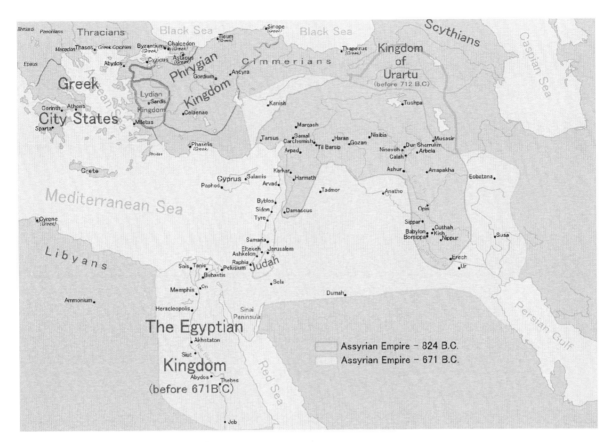

Figure 18.1 The Assyrian Empire.[1]

Growth of the Assyrian Threat

Ashurnasirpal II (885–860) stabilized Assyrian power and created a strong central state.

Shalmaneser III (859–824) spent his 31-year-rule expanding the Assyrian empire in all directions, but Syria (*Hadadezer/"Ben-hadad"* of 1 Kings 20) headed a "Twelve Kings of the Seacoast" coalition of 62,000 soldiers, including 10,000 plus 2,000 chariots from *Ahab* of Israel, which kept Assyria out of Palestine. *Hadadezer* of Syria was assassinated in 842, and his successor, *Hazael* (see 1 Kings 19:15 for *Elijah*'s commission to anoint him and 2 Kings 8:7–13 for his dastardly transition to power), in a brief respite from Assyrian domination, turned his attention to Israel and Judah, and almost continuously raided them during the reigns of *Jehoram* (852–841), *Jehu* (who assassinated Jehoram, 841–813), and *Jehoahaz* (813–798) of Israel; and *Ahaziah* (842), his mother *Athaliah* (daughter of *Ahab and Jezebel*, 842–835), and his son *Joash/Jehoash* (the great reformer, 835–796) of Judah.

Adadnirari III (810–783) came to the assistance of *Jehu* (Israel) and *Joash* (Judah), helping them find relief from *Hazael*'s (Syria) incessant raids and tribute demands. This placed all of Palestine under Assyrian domination. Adadnirari's early death led to internal Assyrian intrigues until his youngest brother came roaring to the throne.

Tiglath-pileser III (745–727) was a strong Assyrian king who put down an early Babylonian revolt in the east, and twice forced his way through Palestine (in 738 and 734), creating a vassal state out of Israel (under *Menahem*), and forming an imbalanced alliance with *Ahaz* of Judah. This is the point at which Isaiah enters.

Shalmaneser V (727–722), *Tiglath-pileser's* son, is likely the Assyrian ruler who obliterated Israel (2 Kings 17) in 722. His Palestinian march was continued by his more famous successor, *Sargon II*.

Sargon II (722–705) was busy with the Egyptians and the Babylonians. While he was fighting with Egypt, *Ahaz* of Judah pretended to call him an ally (see Isaiah 20).

Sennacherib (705–681) put down a revolt in Palestine with brutal violence (701), including the destruction of nearly all of the cities and towns of Judah (46; see 2 Kings 18–19, Isaiah 36–37). By a miracle, *Hezekiah* and Jerusalem were spared (this unusual incident is found in *Herodotus*, ii.141; also, the Assyrian Taylor prism, 691, records *Sennacherib's* attempts to take *Hezekiah*, and his wall carvings describe the fall of Lachish, and how he made his field headquarters there as he besieged Jerusalem.

declared messages from Yahweh, this prophet's work spanned about fifty years (740–690 B.C.). For all of that time, Assyria was the constant superpower threat in his contemporary world. "Israel" (the northern portion of David and Solomon's kingdom) had been split off from "Judah" for nearly three hundred years (since 922 B.C.). Because of the tenacious advance of the Assyrian war machine, Israel was desperately seeking ways in which to form alliances that might hold it back for a time. Syria and Israel became partners throughout most of the eighth century, often as much by the sheer dominance of Syria's military might coercing Israel into defensive pacts as by the choice of the Samaria-based government. This temperamental twosome made many overtures, both friendly and threatening, toward Judah, seeking to draw the smaller kingdom into their anti-Assyria alliances either by compliance or force. Throughout a succession of kings, Judah tried to retain its own identity in several ways:[1]

- Uzziah chose to come under the protectorate of Israel, and thus allowed Judah to become a vassal province of the Israel-Syria alliance.
- Ahaz made an end run around his northern neighbors and appealed directly to Tiglath-

What Was So Important about King Uzziah's Death?

Isaiah's commissioning happened, he tells us, "in the year that King Uzziah died" (6:1). Why was that date so auspicious?

King Uzziah grew proud of his expansive rule, and presumed to take charge of the ritual ceremonies in the Temple because of his growing self-importance. The offering of sacrifices on the Altar of Burnt Offering was, however, the clear mandate of the Levitical priests. Uzziah's pride was divinely punished—he suddenly contracted leprosy (a sign of heaven's judgment), and was driven from the palaces in disgrace. He lived out his remaining years as a rejected beggar.

Anyone who presumed to be worthy of officiating at religious rituals was quickly made aware of the holiness of Yahweh, which was not to be taken lightly. For that reason, in a time when all were already quaking as they entered the Temple, Isaiah's unique encounter with Yahweh was doubly frightening.

---

1   Copyright in the Public Domain.

Isaiah's sons

During the tense political times while Ahaz ruled, Isaiah and his wife bore two sons. Their arrivals (one as the original sign of Isaiah 7:14) would stand as testimonies of both Yahweh's grace and judgment:

Shear-Jashub (Isaiah 7:3): "A Remnant Will Return"

Maher-Shallal-Hash-Baz (Isaiah 8:3): "The Spoil Speeds, the Prey Hastens"

---

pileser of Assyria for protection against Israel and Syria, hoping that in their destruction, Judah would regain some of the old territory as its administrative district.

- Hezekiah first formed a tentative alliance with ambassadors from Babylon, as that eastern province of Assyria was beginning to stir in rebellion. Later, he joined Egypt in a stop-payment of tribute to Assyria, which roused their ire against him until he was forced into reasserting submissive ties to Nineveh. Later, after a miraculous escape from what seemed an imminent crushing defeat by Assyrian forces, Hezekiah renewed his subversive contacts with Babylon.

All of these international political policies (and several more beside) were possible choices for tiny Judah. The prophets probed them all, assessing each according to the evaluation of Yahweh, and then asserting what they believed was the only political option true to the theology of the ancient Sinai Covenant. In summary, these were the options:

- Join Egypt, the only nearby strong nation, in opposing Assyria.
- Join the Israel-Syria confederation in opposing Assyria.
- Declare allegiance to Assyria, and become a vassal province of that empire, in hopes of reaping enlarged borders when the fighting was finished, and northern neighbors Israel and Syria were destroyed.
- Ally with Babylon, the restless eastern province of Assyria, in hopes of an overthrow of Assyria, which would net independence in their remote mountainous locale.
- Stay neutral from all international alliances, relying solely on Yahweh for protection and deliverance.

Only this final piece of political and religious advice was put forward consistently by Isaiah and the other prophets. This was the single viable path open to those who truly believed that Yahweh was Sovereign over all nations, and that Israel's (Judah's) mandate was to continue as a witness to the surrounding nations, rather than becoming a subservient vassal to their gods and cultures.

A Man of His Times

Who was Isaiah? His name means "Salvation is of Yahweh," and this truly typifies his words and prophecies. He was married (Isaiah 8:3) and had at least two children (Isaiah 7:3, 8:3), who were themselves illustrations of Isaiah's prophetic declarations. The commissioning scene of Isaiah 6, with its Temple location, along with all of the liturgical language surrounding Isaiah's call, suggests that Isaiah might have been a priest, or at least a member of a Levite family. At the same time, his easy and constant access to successive kings (cf. Isaiah 7:3, 38:1, 39:1) might imply that he was an employee of the royal court, although his statement in 37:6 ("Say to your master ...") could be interpreted as setting him outside of the political system, at least at some point. Nevertheless, with the narratives of chapters 36–39 incorporated directly into the book, Isaiah obviously was, at minimum, a court recorder, scribe, or historian of some kind (see also 2 Chronicles 26:22). Most likely, he was the chief historian in the royal house, and possibly even a member of the extended royal family. In his duties he appears to have functioned as the official scribe or court recorder. Using that platform as a pulpit, he expressed magnificently worded prophetic analyses and judgments about the religious and political actions of the kings.

Although the elements of Isaiah's prophecy, in their current literary form, have been pieced together from a variety of independent oracles, there is a logical flow to the whole of the book:

1–12 Messages for Judah and Jerusalem:

- There is crisis in the land because of sin
- Remember what Yahweh intended for Israel
- Isaiah's call and commissioning
- In the context of threatened judgments, a Deliverer will come

13–23 Prophecies against the nations around

- Babylon: the haughty hunter will become the prey
- Assyria: the crusher will be crushed
- Philistines: the viper will be bitten and beaten
- Moab: a divine lament for a boaster who will be bested
- Damascus: fading glory because of fading faith in Yahweh
- Cush: the tall people will wilt as the crops fail
- Egypt: the Nile will dry up until death brings the nation to its senses and all will seek blessing from Yahweh

Frequently Cited Isaiah Passages

- 2:1-5—The great "Mountain of Yahweh"
- 5:1-10—The Vineyard analogy
- 6—Isaiah commissioned by a direct vision of God
- 7:14—"The Lord himself will give you a sign ..."
- 9:1-7—The people who walked in darkness ...; for to us a child has been born ...
- 11—"A shoot shall come out of the stump of Jesse ..."
- 12—The great Song of Salvation
- 14:12-21—The fall of "Lucifer" (king of Babylon)
- 31—"Alas for those who go down to Egypt for help ..."
- 35—Joy of the redeemed who travel the highway of return
- 36-39—Stories of Hezekiah and divine deliverance
- 40—"Comfort, O comfort my people ..." "Those who wait on the Lord ..."
- 42-53—The Suffering Servant songs
- 54—Lengthened cords, strengthened stakes
- 55—Come, thirsty and hungry! Seek the Lord while he may be found!
- 60:1-3—"Arise, shine; for your light has come!"
- 61—"The Spirit of the Lord is upon me ..."
- 64:1—"O that you would tear open the heavens and come down ..."
- 66—New heavens and earth]

Isaiah's "Servant Songs"

The four "Servant Songs" in Isaiah were first identified in a commentary on the prophecy by Bernhard Duhm in 1892:

- **Isaiah 42:1–9**—Yahweh identifies and commissions his special envoy, who will bring justice among the nations through quiet ministry to the marginalized and the disenfranchised. His work will be successful because the great Creator has chosen this one to be the agent of divine renewal.

- **Isaiah 49:1–13**—The Suffering Servant testifies of his unique call and commissioning. His voice and message are then confirmed by successive oracles in which Yahweh speaks, announcing that his servant was ordained for this ministry from before his birth, and that both kings and outcasts will experience divine favor through the work of this one. The outcome will be a restoration of joy to the entire world, which has too long suffered under the consequences of evil.

- **Isaiah 50:4–9**—Now the voice of the chosen one is heard even more clearly. The entire poem is in the first person, and is a reflection on both divine anointing for the tasks at hand and also the early backlash of those who do not want Yahweh to disturb their evil machinations. The confrontation thickens between good and evil, and the Suffering Servant stands at its vortex.

- **Isaiah 52:13–53:12**—The last and longest of the poems personifies the Suffering Servant most clearly. Here,

- Arabia: your caravans will become furtive fugitives
- Israel: Yahweh will become a warrior against you
- Tyre: your ships and security are shattered

24–27 News of Yahweh's impending worldwide judgment, the outcome of which will be the restoration of Israel

28–35 A cycle of judgments and woes, especially if an alliance is made with Egypt

36–39 The historical events during Hezekiah's reign that shaped a revival, and brought renewed confidence in Yahweh (note that this section is virtually identical to 2 Kings 18:13–20:19, with the addition of Hezekiah's prayer in Isaiah 38:9–20)

40–55 Prophecies of future restoration through a "Suffering Servant"

- Great Comfort (40–41)
- Servant Songs (interspersed with calls to Covenant faithfulness):
  * *Isaiah 42:1–9*—Yahweh identifies and commissions his special envoy.
  * *Isaiah 49:1–13*—The Suffering Servant testifies of his unique call and commissioning.
  * *Isaiah 50:4–9*—The confrontation thickens between good and evil, and the Suffering Servant stands at its vortex.
  * *Isaiah 52:1353:12*—What began as a shout of confidence and joy in the first song has now turned dark and almost defeatist here. Only the final lines of this song serve to remind us that Yahweh is still in control, and that these things do matter for eternal purposes.
- Future Glories (54–55)

56–66 This coming restoration expanded into a global, creational renewal

- All are invited to repent and participate (56–59)
- Glorious visions of a world reborn (60–66)

Most biblical scholars acknowledge that there are at least two major sections in the current book of Isaiah. These may or may not indicate different authors; the language and theological content affirms their close relationship:

Chapters 1–39—The judgmental prophet caught up in the intrigues of political challenges, and finding only Hezekiah to be a like-minded reformer.

Chapters 40–66 (sometimes called "Deutero-Isaiah")—The visionary poet who sees a bright future, after God has led the way through a painful recovery by means of a "Suffering Servant."

Many students of these prophecies further split chapters 40–66 to form three major sections in the book as a whole. Again, this might possibly suggest multiple authorship to the collection of prophecies in their final version:

1–39 —The judgmental prophet caught up in the intrigues of political challenges, and finding only Hezekiah to be a like-minded reformer.

40–55 ("Deutero-Isaiah")—The empathetic visionary who sees that the only way to a new future is through a cleansing period of repentance and renewal led by the "Suffering Servant."

56–66 ("Trito-Isaiah")—The visionary poet who sees a bright future in which God restores Israel, and in so doing renews all of creation, including the nations that have formerly been viewed as enemies and national threats.

the focus is less on the grand justice that will result from his ministry, and more on the agony that he will endure to accomplish his assigned task. What began as a shout of confidence and joy in the first song has now turned dark and almost defeatist here. Only the final lines of this song serve to remind us that Yahweh is still in control, and that these things do matter for eternal purposes.

Jews believe that it is the people of God themselves who function in the role as the arbiter of God's justice among the nations, a task which ultimately crushes its vocalizer in the evil machines of human depravity. This is why the Jews remain the prophetic voice of God to the nations, and why they also mark their history with the awful pogroms and bloody reprisals that have been unleashed against them.

Christians, on the other hand, quickly found in these passages a kind of messianic blueprint describing the coming, anointing, teaching, ministry, suffering, and death of Jesus. There is no question but that the hints at divine initiative, personal character, and contextual backlash all fit hand-in-glove with the events of Jesus' career. Both interpretations are likely intertwined.

Regardless of whether one person, or several from a community that was shaped by a larger-than-life teacher, wrote the various and combined oracles of Isaiah, the message is consistent throughout. Isaiah was overwhelmed by a divine commissioning (6) that took place in the Temple during the year that King Uzziah died. Isaiah was guided by the theology of the Sinai Covenant (2–5), which mandated that Israel was supposed to have a unique lifestyle among the nations, a set of behaviors which would serve as a missional call for others to join this holy community in a global return to the ways of their Creator. He was confident that Yahweh could resolve all political problems (7–11), no matter how daunting they might seem. Isaiah believed Israel/Judah needed to repent (12), and recover their original identity and purpose as Yahweh's covenant partners and witnesses. He was certain that Yahweh was Sovereign over all nations (13–35), even if Yahweh's primary focus was attached to Israel/Judah. He heard the heartbeat of divine love and compassion, wrestling for the soul and destiny of Israel/Judah as a loved companion and partner (36-41). He saw Yahweh transforming Israel/Judah's identity and fortunes through a "Suffering Servant" leader (42-53). He envisioned a future age in which all the world and every society—and even the universe itself—would be restored to harmony with its Creator, and would resonate with magnificent glory (56-66).

Among the prophets of ancient Israel, Isaiah was truly a prince, and his writings shaped the language of theological reflection among his peers and on into the age of the New Testament Church.

Discussion Points

- What clues to Isaiah's identity are found in his prophecies, and what bearing do these have on his understanding of Israel's political, social, and moral situation?
- In what manner do the lengthy prophecies of Isaiah against the surrounding nations fit into the missional covenant theology of Genesis 12 and Mt. Sinai?
- Why do you think that portions of 2 Kings and Isaiah, containing the Assyrian threats against Judah during the times of Hezekiah, are virtually identical? What might this say about the authorship of these documents?
- How do the "Suffering Servant" passages function in Isaiah's prophecies? Why have these become particularly intriguing for Christian theologians?
- Explain the general message of Isaiah with reference to Israel's present and future, in the context of the political intrigues of its age.
- What were the primary political options for Judah during the periods of Assyrian and Babylonian expansion? How did the prophets address these?

For Further Investigation

Childs, Brevard. (Downers Grove: InterVarsity, 2000). *Isaiah.*

19.

Miserable Ecstasy

The Melancholy Hopefulness of Jeremiah

Jeremiah lived almost a century after Isaiah. By his time, Assyria had long ago destroyed Judah's northern brother neighbor, Israel (722 B.C.). Judah was itself only a tiny community now, limping along with diminishing resources, and constantly tossed around by the bigger nations of its world.

But things were changing rapidly on the international scene. Assyria was being beaten down in 612 B.C. by its eastern bully province, called Babylon. After snapping the backbone of Assyrian forces at Carchemish and wrestling the capital city of Nineveh to the ground, Babylon immediately took over Palestine, the newer name for the old region of Canaan.

Judah was experiencing a rapid turnover of kings, many of whom were puppets of Babylon. For decades already, the country had been paying yearly tribute or security bribes to Babylon. Since 606 B.C., Judah had been forced to turn over some of its promising young men for propaganda retraining exile in the capital of the superpower, in anticipation that they would return to rule the nation as regents of Babylon.

For reasons like these, Egypt began to loom large in many minds as the only possible ally strong enough to withstand Babylon's domination of the region. Even though Israel's identity had been forged through a divine exit strategy from oppressive Egyptian mastery several centuries before, now a good number of voices were publicly suggesting that the remaining citizens of Jerusalem get out of town before a final Babylonian occupation, and find refuge in the safer haven of Egypt.

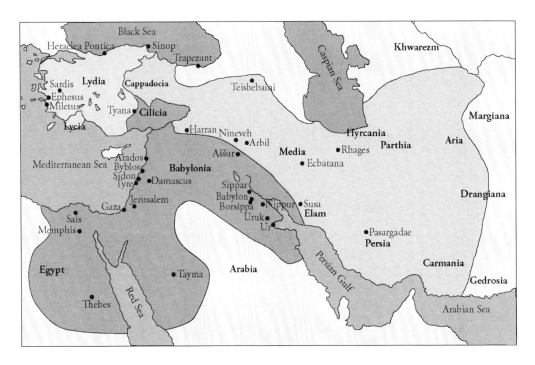

Figure 19.1 The Babylonian Empire.[1]

"Jeremiad"

Jeremiah's name and the often haranguing tone of his prophecies came into the English language as a unique word in the late 18th century. A "jeremiad" is a diatribe, rant, or tirade against sin or social ills or some undesired social group. While the term unfortunately stereotypes the good prophet's larger identity and message, it is hard to deny that this portion of the Bible is one of the most caustic and condemning. Jeremiah's times were politically, socially, economically, and religiously challenging, and the general character of life in Jerusalem was in great disharmony with the Covenant lifestyle espoused in the Torah.

Into these times and circumstances Jeremiah was born. From his earliest thoughts, he was aware of Yahweh's special call on his life (1:4–10). This knowledge only made his prophetic ministry even gloomier, for it gave him no out in a game where the deck was stacked against him (chapters 12, 16). So he brooded through his life, deeply introspective. He fulfilled his role as gadfly to most of the kings who reigned during his adult years, even though it took eminent courage to do so. Although he lived an exemplary personal lifestyle, political officials constantly took offense at his theologically charged political commentaries, and regularly arrested him, treating him very badly. Jeremiah was passionately moral, never allowing compromise as a suitable temporary alternative in the shady waters of international relations, or amid the roiling quicksand of fading religious devotion. He remained pastorally sensitive, especially to the poor and oppressed in

---

1   Copyright in the Public Domain.

Jerusalem, weeping in anguish as families boiled sandals and old leather to find a few nutrients during Babylonian sieges, and especially when he saw mothers willing to cannibalize their dying babies in order to keep their other children alive. Above all, Jeremiah found the grace to be unshakably hopeful. He truly believed, to the very close of his life, that though Babylonian forces would raze Jerusalem and the Temple, Yahweh would keep covenant promises, and one day soon restore the fortunes of this wayward partner in the divine missional enterprise.

Toward the end of his ministry, Jeremiah was aided by his good friend, Baruch, whose very name meant "blessing." It was Baruch who made sure Jeremiah got at least a little food, even when the prophet was thrown to the slimy bottom of a dry cistern as punishment for his opposition to the current government and its practices. And Baruch salvaged Jeremiah's writings when kings were systematically burning them as treasonous. Baruch patiently wrote and rewrote the messages of Yahweh that were delivered through the mouth of Jeremiah (chapter 36).

Jeremiah's prophecies are not collected in a chronological order. When tracked against the reigns and events of various kings, the following challenges, indictments, and promises can be chronicled:

- **King Josiah** (640–609): the indictments of chapters 3–6 and the support for reforms as spelled out in chapters 30–31.
- **King Johoahaz** (609–608): the brief lament found in chapter 20:10–12.
- **King Jehoiakim** (608–597): in 607–606, the Babylonians made their first official incursion into Jerusalem, confirming Jehoiakim as king only if he would declare his small country a vassal territory of Babylon. The invaders were allowed to retrain some of the maturing sons among the noble families (including Daniel and his friends) in Babylon, so that they could return one day as proper Babylonian regents. Jeremiah gave his famous "Potter's House" sermon at this time (chapter 18), and later wrote about the battle of wills taking place, which would ultimately result in Judah's captivity by Babylon for seventy years (chapters 25–26).
- **King Jehoiakim** (597): after Jehoiakim grew reckless with false bravado and thought he could declare independence from Babylon, Nebuchadnezzar sent his troops again, and re-

---

The Jeremiah Collection:
Contents

Call, commissioning, and early visions (1)

Various oracles of divine judgment against Judah, especially its kings (2–28)

A letter to the exiles: "Settle in, for the exile will be seventy years long." (29)

Promises of Restoration (30–33):
- The "New Covenant" (31:31–34)
- The wartime land purchase (32)
- The reiteration of the Davidic Covenant (33:14–26)

Prophecies of Zedekiah's final days (34)

A social example: the Rechabites (35)

Writing a scroll for King Jehoiakim, who burns it (36)

The last days of Jerusalem and the flight to Egypt (37–43)

Two letters:
- To the Judaeans who fled to Egypt: Judgment! (44)
- To Baruch: You have been a faithful friend and helper! (45)

Oracles of Judgment on the nations (46–51)

Summary of the events of the Babylonian conquest of Jerusalem, plus fortunes of King Jehoiakin in Babylon (52)]

"Seventy Years" of Exile

While most of the prophet utterances are somewhat vague and general, with promises of future judgment or blessing, Jeremiah expresses a number of very specific messages from Yahweh. None are more exact, however, than the promise of exactly thirty years of captivity forecast in chapter 25:1–14. How this precise number figures into the larger dimensions of Old Testament chronology is quite astounding.

First, in Leviticus 25, the practice of "sabbatical" years and the "Year of Jubilee" are mandated for Israel, once the nation is established in the Promised Land. Every seventh year, the farmland was to remain untilled, giving it rest. And each fiftieth ("Jubilee") year, a second-in-a-row annual noncultivation was supposed to happen. Yet, no records of Israel's history indicate that these times of fallow recovery for the farmland and orchards ever took place. It would be a great test for an agricultural nation simply to shut down its primary industry every seven years.

Second, the span of time from Israel's settlement into Canaan (around 1200 B.C.) until this prophecy of Jeremiah (606 B.C.) is just over five hundred years. During that span of time, the Israelites should have observed approximately seventy year-long farming sabbaticals. But they had not.

Third, it was in 607–606 that the Babylonian armies came for the first time to claim political ownership of Judah, and to assert tribute payments. Part of the process included having sons of royal and priestly families taken away to Babylon to be schooled in the overlord's culture, religion, and politics, in order that these retrained subjects might later be sent back to Jerusalem as puppet rulers. Daniel and his friends were part of this first group (Daniel 1). A similar event took place in 597 B.C., during which time Ezekiel was taken away. These reeducated locals never came back, however, because the Babylonians tired of rebellions in Judah, and destroyed the city in 586 B.C. A final remnant was deported to Babylon at that time.

Fourth, the Temple's Altar of Burnt Offering was rebuilt in 536 B.C., and the Second Temple actually completed, after a number of serious delays, in 516 B.C. Thus, from the first deportation to the rebuilding of the main Temple altar, seventy years elapsed. And from the final deportation to the dedication of the Second Temple, seventy years passed, during which the land had its rest.

This prophecy of the seventy years of exile stayed fresh in many Jewish minds, as Daniel 9:2 indicates. There was a clear understanding that at least one reason for the Babylonian captivity and deportation was a failure on Israel's part to heed the Sinai Covenant commands for providing the Promised Land with its agricultural sabbatical rests.

placed him with his son, Jehoiakin. The eighteen-year-old lasted less than a year before the Babylonians took him away to exile (along with Ezekiel and others), and installed his uncle Zedekiah as the final ruler of Judah. Jeremiah's messages were warnings for the people to prepare themselves for deportation, the only outcome they could expect after so many years of flouting Yahweh's ways (chapters 24, 35–36).

- **King Zedekiah** (597–586): the last king of Judah apparently was spineless, placating all in sight, and making secret deals with everyone. In the end, he tried secretly to flee Jerusalem in order to save his own skin (chapters 21–22, 27–28). During these dark times, Jeremiah wrote a letter to the people of Judah who had already been deported to Babylon (chapter 29), urging them to settle in. Although Yahweh would surely restore the nation in the future, said Jeremiah, the current generation had to suffer punishment for its sinfulness. At the same time, during the final siege of Jerusalem, when the entire economy and real estate market had collapsed, Jeremiah bought a field deemed worthless as a token of good faith that Yahweh would call the people back from exile to prosperity (chapter 32). But when Zedekiah got overly confident about his valued position as Babylon's local appointee, Jeremiah warned him that the judgment of Yahweh was irreversible, and days of destruction were just around the corner (chapter 34).

- **Governor Gedaliah** (586): the Babylonians were willing to take Jeremiah to join the other exiles in deportation, or to leave him with the small and impoverished remnant left to scrounge in the rubble of Jerusalem. Jeremiah chose the latter, soon witnessing the assassination of Governor Gedaliah, who was left in charge, and the complete collapse of whatever social organization might have been left (chapters 40–41).
- **Remnant Leader Johanan** (586–585): another person loosely connected with the royal family took over after Gedaliah's assassination, and then feared Babylonian reprisals because of the anarchy in Jerusalem. Johanan decided to take the remaining people down to Egypt to find safety. Jeremiah refused to go along, reminding the remnant that Judah was their homeland, and that Yahweh had promised peace following the deportation of the rest to Babylon (chapters 41–42). Johanan and his thugs played bully politics, however, and bound Jeremiah, taking him along with them to Egypt against his will.

The theme of the Sinai Covenant is very prominent in Jeremiah's prophecies. Most striking is his recognition that it governs both Israel's success and its demise, and that one day soon Yahweh will have to find a way to renew that covenant in a manner which will keep the restored nation more faithful to its identity and true to its mission. As Jeremiah put it:

> "The time is coming," declares the Lord,
>   "when I will make a new covenant
> with the house of Israel
>   and with the house of Judah.
> It will not be like the covenant
>   I made with their forefathers
> When I took them by the hand
>   to lead them out of Egypt,
> Because they broke my covenant,
>   though I was a husband to them," declares the Lord.
> "This is the covenant I will make with the house of Israel
>   after that time," declares the Lord.
> "I will put my law in their minds
>   and write it on their hearts.
> I will be their God,
>   and they will be my people.
> No longer will a man teach his neighbor,

> or a man his brother, saying, 'Know the Lord,'
> Because they will all know me,
>   from the least of them to the greatest," declares the Lord.
> "For I will forgive their wickedness
>   and will remember their sins no more." (Jeremiah 31:31–34)

Discussion Points

- Compare and contrast the prophecies of Isaiah and Jeremiah in terms of focus, content, style, and dominant issues.
- How is the political world of Jeremiah different from that of Isaiah? What unique issues does this present to him and to the people of Judah, in terms of their relationship with Yahweh and their sense of the future?
- Why were the last kings of Judah generally so antagonistic to Jeremiah? What was it about his message from Yahweh that they did not like? Why?
- What message is being conveyed to those already in exile in Babylon by the letter sent in Jeremiah 29? How do you suppose they responded?
- What would Jeremiah and those around him have in mind when they heard the message of Yahweh concerning the "New Covenant" in Jeremiah 31:31–34? How have Christians interpreted this passage?
- Imagine yourself as the real estate agent who helps Jeremiah transact his purchase of the field in chapter 32. What would you think about this particular purchase under the political and social circumstances of the day? What would it declare about Jeremiah's understanding of the future? Why?

For Further Investigation

Thompson, John A. (Grand Rapids: Eerdmans, 1980). *The Book of Jeremiah.*

20.

The View from Exile

Ezekiel's Reconstruction of the Kingdom Vision

Ezekiel was an "almost priest" who became a prophet. This, in and of itself, is not so unusual, since prophets were generally invested in other occupations before the call and urging of Yahweh drew them into the public fray as social critics. In Ezekiel's case, however, his background in a family of priests clearly colored the manner in which he understood the dealings of Yahweh:

When Ezekiel sees Yahweh approaching him, the descriptions he gives sound like the Shekinah glory that fell from heaven, first into the Tabernacle and later upon the Temple, and resided over the Ark of the Covenant (Ezekiel 1).

His physical features include the typical priestly beard (Ezekiel 5).

The worst form of sin among the people of God, as reported by Ezekiel, is the desecration of the Temple (Ezekiel 8).

When reporting Yahweh's coming judgment against the people, Ezekiel describes how it will commence with Yahweh's departure from the Temple, visibly expressed by the removal of the Shekinah glory cloud from that facility (Ezekiel 9–10).

Symbols of judgment against Jerusalem are portrayed using scenes from the Altar of Burnt Offering that stood in the courtyard of the Temple (Ezekiel 24).

The future restoration of the people of Yahweh, according to Ezekiel, will take place using ceremonial cleansing rituals from the Temple worship times (Ezekiel 36).

In the messianic age to come, as Ezekiel sees it, the rebuilt Temple will be so massive that it will take in most of the land area of Judah, and all the people will be employed in its services and rituals (Ezekiel 40–48).

The sign of restoration will be the return of the *Shekinah* glory cloud to the new Temple (Ezekiel 43).

All life on planet Earth is essentially derived from the power of Yahweh that flows out of the Temple from the Ark of the Covenant (Ezekiel 47).

More of Ezekiel's priestly background emerges from his careful documentation of the times and circumstances, in which he receives visions from Yahweh. Thus, we know that Ezekiel was born into a family of priests in Jerusalem in 622 B.C., just as the Babylonians were ramping up their revolt against the Assyrians. In 597 B.C., when Ezekiel was twenty-five (the age at which sons of priests began their five-year apprenticeship in the Temple), he was taken to Babylon by that invading army. The Babylonians wanted to leave conquered peoples in their homelands, but made provisions to retrain their potential leaders in Babylon so that they could be returned as representatives of the Babylonian government. This was to be Ezekiel's fate, according to the eastern occupiers.

But Yahweh had another plan. For five years, Ezekiel lived in Babylon, probably studying religion, culture, and politics at the schools set up to be retooling stations for the brightest and best of Babylonia's foreign captives. When he turned thirty, the age at which he should have graduated from apprenticeship into fully vested service as a Temple priest, Ezekiel must have thought nostalgically of what would have been his lot, had he not been removed from Jerusalem. But his career advancement suddenly takes a major shift when Yahweh blazes out of a thunderstorm that year, and begins revealing ideas and scenes and words of both judgment and blessing. Ezekiel suddenly becomes a prophet, a mouthpiece of God, and begins passing along messages from the people's true Sovereign, who had not forgotten them, even in exile.

Ezekiel dates his visions at fifteen specific points, which can be plotted along a twenty-year time line (593–573 B.C.). Most of the visions have remained in chronological order in the book named after him.

Dates Mentioned among Ezekiel's Visions

1:1: July 593

1:2: July 593

3:16: July 593

8:1: August/September 593

20:1: July/August 591

24:1: January 588

26:1: March 587 to March 586

29:1: January 587

29:17: March–April 571

30:20: March–April 587

31:1: May–June 587

32:1: February-March 585

32:17: February–March 585

33:21: December 586–January 585

40:1: March–April 573

The strange vision in chapter 1—though sometimes called an ancient UFO sighting—is, in reality, Ezekiel's first perception of the glory of Yahweh on the move. Yahweh rides the Ark of the Covenant, just as in the times of Moses and Joshua. But now, in Ezekiel's vision, it is propelled by angels rather than Levites. These heavenly beings have the capacity to lift and move the Ark through the air, making Yahweh's portable throne even more mobile than usual. There are two implications to this vision. First, because the vision comes to Ezekiel in the land of Babylon, those who have already gone into exile have not been forgotten or abandoned by Yahweh. Just because they are no longer living in Jerusalem or Palestine does not mean they have ceased being the people of Yahweh. Yahweh comes looking for them.

Second, the same vision has a darker side for those still remaining in Jerusalem. Those still hanging on in Palestine must understand that they are not safe simply because they have the Temple nearby. Yahweh will not be confined to a box or a building, even if it is the grand Temple erected by Solomon. Nor will Yahweh be tied down like a magical servant, or a slave who has to do the bidding of those performing ritual incantations. Yahweh is free to move and use divine power wherever Yahweh chooses.

Thus, from the start of Ezekiel's prophetic ministry, these themes are reported and often recur:

- Yahweh is Sovereign, and will neither be held in bondage by those who claim to be his people, nor those who try to subdue his covenant community.
- Yahweh is on the move, bringing hope and comfort to the exiles who are despairing, and removing the Divine Presence from those who are abusing the Jerusalem rituals and Temple precincts.
- Yahweh is powerful over all nations, including the Babylonians, and will bring about outcomes in international politics that benefit the plans and purposes of the divine mission, entrusted originally to Israel through the Sinai Covenant.

An Outline of Ezekiel's Visions

Ezekiel's Call and Commissioning (1–3)

The Glory of Yahweh comes to Babylon (1)

Ezekiel's Call (2:1–3:15)

Ezekiel's Commission and Message (3:16–27)

Judgment on Jerusalem and Its People (4–24)

Graphic Prophecies of Jerusalem's Destruction (4–7)

Sins of the People and Their Leaders (8–9)

God's Glory Leaves the Temple (10–11)

Prophecies of the Captivity/Exile (12–24)

Judgment on the Nations around Judah (25–32)

Ammon, Moab, Edom, Philistia, Tyre, Sidon, Egypt

Visions of Renewal and Restoration (33–48)

Taking Responsibilities and the Fall of Jerusalem (33)

The Spiritual Revival (34)

The Destruction of Edom (35)

The Restoration of Israel (36–37)

The Final Battle between Good and Evil (38–39)

Symbolic Pictures of the Age of Restoration (40–48)

The Temple and Return of God's Glory (40–46)

Blessings of the Land and the City of God (47–48)

- The Temple will be a critical piece in all that takes place: its demise will be the final declaration of Yahweh's judgment against his people, according to the curses of the covenant; its restoration will be the sign of the coming messianic age, in which Yahweh's missional purposes will be fulfilled.

When reading Ezekiel's early prophecies, it is hard not to imagine him as a marvelous Sunday school teacher or an incredibly gifted elementary school teacher. He communicates as much through "Show and Tell" as he does with mere words. In the first half of the book, as it has come to us, Ezekiel eats a scroll (3), plays war games with a clay brick (4), lies on his side for over a year in full public view (4), eats junk food cooked over manure (4), shaves his beard and destroys the clipped hairs in three ways (5), does a round of hand-clapping and foot-stomping exercises (6), digs through a wall at night and leaves with only a backpack (12), tells soap opera tales (23), and watches his wife die without mourning her (24). Each of these actions is meant to portray how the people should respond to Yahweh's coming judgments.

But the divine warnings are not limited to Judah and Jerusalem. Collected into chapters 25–32 are prophecies of destruction directed at seven of Judah's neighbors. Whether or not Ezekiel was supposed to send these diatribes to the representative capitals is neither apparent nor important. Through these messages, Yahweh communicates two clear ideas to the exiles. First, Yahweh is not a tribal or national god who is now defeated by the Babylonians; Yahweh remains Sovereign over all nations and can be trusted, even though it seems right now like other gods and nations are dominating the scene. Second, although these other nations have had a part to play in the divine plan to punish Judah, they will themselves be held accountable for their actions; every act of political violence or public evil will be redressed. Both ideas would provide strength to the exiles, and keep them religiously focused.

The covenant theology that pervades the Old Testament is clearly visible throughout Ezekiel's prophecies, but jumps out in bold form in chapters 33–37. Here, Yahweh speaks of a "covenant of peace" that will guide the restored people in the future. All the images used to describe that covenant, however, are taken from critical events related to the Sinai Covenant, including Abraham (33), David (34, 37), and Israel (as if the kingdom had never been split) (36, 37). Earlier covenant promises are reiterated in terms of a renewed relationship between God and the people that would not be different, but would be stronger because of Yahweh's energized presence. So, according to these prophecies, the future community will be known as "Israel" and not merely Judah, since the survivors of the exile would be the foundation of a restored national covenantal people, with all the meaning that was originally attributed to the full community that stood at Mt. Sinai. In fact, the valley of dry bones vision (37) is essentially a resurrection image, as if this judgment and exile experience is a death which wipes the slate clean for a restart:

"My servant David will be king over them, and they will all have one shepherd. They will follow my laws and be careful to keep my decrees. They will live in the land I gave to my servant Jacob, the land where your fathers lived. They and their children and their children's children will live there forever, and David my servant will be their prince forever. I will make a covenant of peace with them; it will be an everlasting covenant. I will establish them and increase their numbers, and I will put my sanctuary among them forever. My dwelling place will be with them; I will be their God, and they will be my people. Then the nations will know that I the Lord make Israel holy, when my sanctuary is among them forever" (Ezekiel 37:24–27).

The cataclysmic battles of Ezekiel 38–39 are hard to pin down or easily interpret. They seem to be a symbolic confrontation between good and evil that will precede the ultimate restoration of Yahweh's spreading kingdom (40–48). It is important to note in this light, that many of the images painted by John in the book of Revelation are taken directly from Ezekiel's visions:

- The vision of Yahweh's glory (Ezekiel 1; Revelation 4)
- The scroll eaten (Ezekiel 3; Revelation 10)
- The judgment on the nations (Ezekiel 25–32; Revelation 14)
- The great battle (Ezekiel 38–39; Revelation 20)
- The restored city of Jerusalem (Ezekiel 40–46; Revelation 21)
- The river of life and the renewal of creation (Ezekiel 47–48; Revelation 22)

The closing scenes of Ezekiel's prophecy portray a time when all the tribes of Israel will return from their various exiles, and the one nation reborn will have at its center a Temple even more magnificent than Solomon's. In fact, this new version of the Temple will be so huge that its courts will spread throughout most of the hill country of Judah, and virtually everyone will live within its shadow or sphere of influence. These ideas portray an age when the presence of Yahweh will be felt so strongly that no one will be able to toss it aside flippantly. Everything in the territory of Israel will experience the pervasive influence of Yahweh and the covenant relationship. From Ezekiel's vantage point in Babylonian exile, these prophetic messages would precipitate a longing for the future age, which would nurture the best kind of homesickness among the people. It would keep the deported community focused on its unique identity, stoke their passions for renewed covenant faithfulness, and engender survival optimism in the face of very trying times.

Discussion Points

- How does Ezekiel's priestly heritage impact his prophetic messages?
- Why do Ezekiel's prophecies take a turn from negative forebodings about judgment in the first half to positive promises of a coming messianic age in the second? How would these messages have been received by the Jewish exiles in Babylon?
- Why do most of the prophets of Israel and Judah include sections that speak of Yahweh's judgment against the surrounding nations? How would the covenant community interpret these strongly worded sermons?
- Why might there be such a strong correlation between many of the prophetic scenes in Ezekiel and those in the book of Revelation? How do these graphic pictures function to communicate divine actions to the faith community?

For Further Investigation

Block, Daniel I. (Grand Rapids: Eerdmans, 1997). *The Book of Ezekiel.*
Duguid, Iain M. (Grand Rapids: Zondervan, 1999). *Ezekiel.*

21.

Apocalyptic Countercultural Revolution

Daniel and the Redefining and Expansion of God's Mission

According to the note that opens the stories and visions of the book of Daniel, this famous young man and his friends were removed from Jerusalem to Babylon in the first deportation (607/606 B.C.). The fact of their relocation implies that Daniel and his friends were sons of royalty or priestly families. It was Babylonian policy to take promising candidates from the ruling families of conquered nations, and train them to become Babylonian officials for the next phase of local government.

The stories of Daniel 1–6 are great tales of courage and honor, showing how Daniel and his friends remained true to their religious heritage, even in completely overwhelming circumstances. As a collection, these narratives convey at least two messages. First, they show how the later deportees could sustain their covenant heritage and identity, even while living in societies shaped by other gods and values. Second, they give testimony that Yahweh is the global Divine Power, speaking through kings and dreams in lands far away from Palestine, and announcing, even in these unlikely places, the growing influence and ultimate victory of heaven's true kingdom.

The visions of Daniel 7–12 are harder to interpret. For one thing, they are clearly apocalyptic in character. This genre of literature, deriving its name from the Greek word for "uncover" or

---

The Book of Daniel in Summary

Six Stories of Survival and Success:
- Daniel and Friends remain pure (1)
- Nebuchadnezzar's Great Dream (2)
- Friends survive fiery furnace (3)
- Nebuchadnezzar's pride (4)
- Ominous divine handwriting (5)
- Daniel in the lions' den (6)

Three Visions of Kingdoms in Conflict:
- Vision #1—Four Beasts (7)
- Vision #2—Ram and Goat (8–9)
- Vision #3—Warring Nations (10–12)

Names and References

Daniel's Hebrew name means "God is my judge." The strength and testimony of this name may be a reason why he never seems to use the Babylonian name given him in exile, Belteshazzar ("prince of Bel" or "Bel protects the king").

Daniel's friends' names are equally impressive in meaning, although they are invariably referred to by their Babylonian ascriptions:

- Hananiah ("Yahweh is gracious") becomes Shadrach ("Command of the moon god")
- Misha'el ("Who is like God?" or "God provides") is called Meshach ("Who is what Aku is?")
- Azariah ("Yahweh has helped") is renamed Abednego ("Servant of Nebo")

Ezekiel arrived in Babylonian exile almost a decade after Daniel had become established there, and refers to Daniel three times, with great honor (14:14, 20; 28:3).

"reveal," emerged during the stressful decades just prior to Jerusalem's destruction, and continued to appear on into the Babylonian captivity of Judah and the times of postexilic uncertainty. All expressions of apocalyptic literature have a number of common characteristics, including:

- A cosmic dualism, declaring that the forces of good and evil are engaged in a final, winner-take-all desperate struggle.
- An angelic messenger who guides a particular human being, chosen for unknown reasons to be the agent for communicating this secret—but necessary—divine revelation, through the visions and their interpretations.
- Mysterious revelatory images that involve cryptically portrayed creatures, symbols, and dates, all of which are supposed to add up to a certain victory on the part of God's forces and kingdom, but only after periods of intense crisis.
- Language that is vivid, action-oriented, and involves colorful descriptions of things and scenes which are very different from daily human experience.
- Secret messages and coded communications which may or may not be explained fully enough for the human agent to understand and pass along.
- Urgent calls for reader awareness that the whole human race is caught up in this spiritual struggle, even though most people are completely oblivious of these things.
- Hints that sinister forces are controlling government, business and commerce, and that leaders among these have been taken over by evil influences.
- A massive and critical ultimate battle, in which the full weight of conflict will be unleashed in an all-out engagement that will bring final and total resolution to the friction between competing worldviews and value systems, and the annihilation of the key leaders of the losing side.

- Concluding scenes of cosmic resolution when victory is won by the side of God and the good; all is restored or redeemed or made better than ever; and a kingdom of peace and prosperity is ushered in.

Apocalyptic literature as a distinct genre in the late Jewish and early Christian communities seems to have been initiated by several things. First, there were the initial apocalyptic visions of Daniel (Daniel 7–12), Jesus (Mark 13, Matthew 24, Luke 21) and John (Revelation), which were received as authentic and important by their respective faith communities. These served as the foundational representations for this type of language and message, after which others would be created, and upon which many would be built. Second, there was the seeming failure (or at least uncertain outcome) of some future-oriented prophecies issued through Isaiah, Jeremiah, and their kin. Because the actual outcomes of history did not always mesh with those predicted, people attempted to find alternative or secret explanations about the exact nature of God's intended future within their times or shortly to come. Third, there were the great political and social crises of the first centuries B.C. and A.D., in which the remnant people of God found themselves. Their small stature among the enormous dominant governing powers of the Mediterranean world caused them to feel as if they were losing ground under a crushing press of persecution. Together, these promptings inspired many other writers to imitate the accepted apocalyptic visions, in order to suggest other ways of looking at their contemporary history and its possible outcomes.

While interpretations within the general groupings of apocalyptic literature invite comparisons of themes, symbols, purported divine plans, and projected cosmic outcomes, it is important to remember that very little Jewish and Christian apocalyptic literature was recognized as truly revelatory. Daniel was the only book written primarily in apocalyptic format to gain Old Testament access,

---

Apocalyptic Literature 📖

In the Old Testament/Hebrew Bible:
- Ezekiel 38–39
- Zechariah 12–14
- Joel 3:9–17
- Daniel 7–12

In Jewish Postexilic Literature:
- Book of Noah
- Enoch (Ethiopic Book of Enoch)
- Testaments of the Twelve Patriarchs
- Psalms of Solomon
- The Assumption of Moses
- Syriac Apocalypse of Baruch
  - Greek Apocalypse of Baruch
- Apocalypse of Abraham
- Lost Apocalypses: Prayer of Joseph
- Book of Eldad and Modad
- Apocalypse of Elijah
- Apocalypse of Zephaniah
- 2 Enoch (Slavonic Enoch)
- Oracles of Hystaspes
- Testament of Job
- Testament of the Three Patriarchs
- Sibylline Oracles

In the New Testament:
- Jesus' Temple Destruction Speech (Mark 13; Matthew 24; Luke 21)
- End Times Teaching in 2 Thessalonians 2, 2 Peter 3
- Revelation

In Early Christian Literature:
- Greek Apocalypse of Peter
- Testament of Hezekiah
- Testament of Abraham
- Oracles of Hystaspes
- Vision of Isaiah
- Shepherd of Hermas

5 Ezra

6 Ezra

Apocalypses of Paul, Thomas, and Stephen

Apocalypse of Paul

Apocalypse of John

Arabic Apocalypse of Peter

Apocalypse of the Virgin

Apocalypse of Sedrach

Apocalypse of Daniel

The Revelations of Bartholomew

Questions of St. Bartholomew

and Revelation had a similar New Testament fate. These canonical books were viewed as more authoritative than the others, and their visions were not considered to be mere products of overactive imaginations or coercive religious propaganda.

Although we may be as troubled as Daniel was regarding the visions he had been given (Daniel 7:15), the interpretations put forward within the book are fairly simple. Later visions of the collection build upon Nebuchadnezzar's great dream about a series of world-dominating empires (Daniel 2). In the subsequent visions (Daniel 7, 8, 10–11), the implications of that earlier dream were broadened and deepened, so that more information about its message of successive kingdoms was revealed. The imminent overthrow of the Babylonian government by its restless eastern provinces, Media and Persia, seems to set the stage for Daniel's initial disturbing vision (Daniel 7–8). When the Persians actually take over a short while later, and the Jewish exiles are granted permission to return to their homeland, Daniel offers his prayer of chapter 9. This, in turn, precipitates the next vision

The Visions of Daniel and the Kingdoms of History

Most scholars find a correlation among the visions of this book and the kingdoms that took successive control over the ancient Near East:

Vision in Daniel 2	Vision in Daniel 7	Vision in Daniel 8	Empire	Period of Domination
Head of Gold	Lion		Babylon	626–539 B.C.
Chest and Arms of Silver	Bear	Ram	Medo-Persia	539–330 B.C.
Belly and Thighs of Bronze	Leopard	Goat	Greece	330–146 B.C.
Legs of Iron; Feet of Mixed Iron and Clay	Terrifying and Frightening Beast		Rome	146 B.C.–476 A.D.

of what was still to come, as the changing powers foretold in Nebuchadnezzar's dream vie for dominance. While the outcome of these latter visionary events remains uninterpreted (note that there is no final word of explanation for the scenes of chapters 10–11 in Daniel 12:9, as there had been for the other visions) and somewhat mystical, there is no ambiguity about the implications: the God of covenant partnership with Israel is also the Sovereign of all nations.

The book of Daniel is found among the prophets of the Christian Bible for good reason. Although it was written too late to be included among the "Prophets" (*Nabi'im*) of the Hebrew Bible (that collection seems to have been "closed" during Judah's exile to Babylon, with the exception of three short prophecies, all of which emerged early in postexilic Jerusalem; hence, Daniel is found there among the "Writings"–*K'tuvim*), this document breathes with the covenant confidence that undergirds the messages expressed by all of the other divinely authorized prophetic spokespersons. Yahweh alone is Lord over every human kingdom; Israel has a unique role to play in the destinies of nations; and the ultimate goal of history is the return of all peoples to participation in the one true transcendent Kingdom of God. Nebuchadnezzar's dream already pointed in that direction (Daniel 2). The latter visions found in the book only served to reaffirm the same themes (Daniel 7–8, 10–11). In fact, first-century Jewish historian Josephus records that in 329 B.C., as the Greek armies were moving into Palestine, Jewish high priest Jaddua uses the book of Daniel to show Alexander the Great his future. Because of this, he did not destroy Jerusalem, and instead offered sacrifices in the Temple to the God of the Jews, who had provided this clear revelation.

Discussion Points

- Why were Daniel and his friends taken to Babylon for further education? What outcome was expected? What did this indicate about the Babylonian intentions for Judah at the start of their occupation of that country?
- How would the stories of faithfulness, as expressed in the lives of Daniel and his friends, be viewed and used by later deportees to Babylon? What message would these tales convey?
- What cultural circumstances are likely to give rise to "Apocalyptic Literature?" What examples of this genre can you find in other historical settings or recent times? How do you know when writings (or visual media–paintings, sculptures, stage plays, films) are part of this type of literary and artistic expression?

For Further Investigation

Baldwin, Joyce. (Downers Grove: InterVarsity, 1981). Daniel.

22.

The "Day of the Lord" According to the Twelve

The Minor Prophets and Yahweh's Impending Judgment

I srael's prophets often appear, at first glance, to be strange creatures. A number of them harangue with incessant tirades (e.g., Amos), making us uncomfortable to spend too much time with such grumpy old men. Some are constant political gadflies (e.g., Jeremiah), always taking positions opposite of those in power. Others veer off into strange visions that are worlds removed from our everyday life (e.g., Zechariah), chafing readers with their oddness. There are even a few who have very compromised personal lives (e.g., Hosea), leading us to suspect more than a little psychologizing in their soap opera–ish theology.

Still, there is an inherent consistency of message and focus among all of these diverse religious ruminations and rantings. First of all, the prophetic sermons are invariably rooted in the web of relationships created by the Sinai Covenant. Israel belongs to Yahweh, and her lifestyle must be shaped by the stipulations of that suzerain-vassal treaty. Obedience to Yahweh triggers the blessings of the Sinai Covenant, while disobedience is the first reason for Israel's experiences of its curses: drought, war, famine, enemy occupation, destruction of cities and fields, deportation, etc. For this reason, the prophetic writings are laced with moral diatribes that carry a strong emphasis on social ethics.

Why "the Twelve?"

While the writings of the Major Prophets (Isaiah, Jeremiah, Ezekiel, Daniel) each took up a large scroll when copied out as a collection, the short prophecies of the rest could be bundled together on a single scroll of their own. That is why they are often titled the Minor Prophets, and known in the Hebrew scriptures as "the Twelve."

This is not to say that Israel was held to a different behavioral standard than would otherwise be expected among the nations of the earth. Rather, through Israel's lifestyle there was supposed to flow a witness toward its neighbors, revealing the unique splendor of her God. By looking at the people of Yahweh, living in Canaan, other tribes and nations were to gain a sense of the true character of life when it was experienced in harmony with the forgotten Creator of all. As such, the public actions of Israel were crucial to its covenant existence. Both Isaiah and Micah succinctly summarized it in this way:

In the last days the mountain of the Lord's temple will be established as chief among the mountains; it will be raised above the hills, and all nations will stream to it. Many peoples will come and say, "Come, let us go up to the mountain of the Lord, to the house of the God of Jacob. He will teach us his ways, so that we may walk in his paths." The law will go out from Zion, the word of the Lord from Jerusalem. He will judge between the nations and will settle disputes for many peoples. They will beat their swords into plowshares and their spears into pruning hooks. Nation will not take up sword against nation, nor will they train for war anymore. Come, O house of Jacob, let us walk in the light of the Lord (Isaiah 2:2–5; nearly identical is Micah 4:1–5).

Who Were the Prophets?

Unlike royal dynasties and the inherited professions of priests, the prophets were not a single career group within Israelite society. Instead, the term prophet was applied to all who were acknowledged as having a unique calling from Yahweh to address social, moral, and political issues in light of the Sinai Covenant. Some who were identified as prophets apparently functioned in that role for virtually a lifetime (e.g., Isaiah), probably because other vocational roles they played in society placed them at the center of cultural assessment. Most, however, seem to have been raised and equipped to prophesy for only a limited period. Among the other occupations identified among these prophets of Israel were farmer (Amos), priest (Ezekiel), and possibly court historian (Isaiah).

Second, the function and message of prophecy were very political. Since Yahweh alone was Israel's Sovereign, for the nation to come under the domination of other political powers was always seen as a divine scourge which resulted from the application of the covenant curses due to Israel's disobedience. How Israel handled its international relations showed plainly whether she trusted Yahweh, or if she had otherwise become enamored with power and politics rooted in lesser gods. Constantly, the prophets asked whether Israel was Yahweh's witnessing people, or if she was merely another nation with no particular mission or divine purpose. Israel's self-understanding was thus always very religious, and at the same time invariably political.

It is in this light that the typical prophetic litany against the nations surrounding Israel must be read. These other social and political entities were assessed for public moral behavior by Yahweh alongside Israel because Yahweh was the Creator of all, and continued to be Lord of the nations. All countries are chided for their own internal social sins, as well as for their inappropriate aggressions toward one another, including—and especially for—their treatment of Israel. While they may be used by Yahweh as a temporary tool of chastisement, punishing Israel according to the covenant curses, they might never presume to hold dominance over either Israel or her God. This typical hubris of nations was regularly condemned as idolatrous by the prophets, and any society afflicted by it would receive divine retribution in its own turn.

Third, as the epochs of Israel's political fortunes unfolded, the message of the prophets became increasingly apocalyptic. There was a growing sense that because things had not gone the way they should have, producing heartfelt and ongoing national repentance and covenant restoration, Yahweh will have to intervene directly again, in a manner similar to that during the time of Moses. When Yahweh interrupts human history the next time, however, along with judgments on the wickedness of the nations of the world, Israel will also fall heavily under divine punishment. But because Yahweh is on a mission to restore the fallen world, this next major divine intervention will be paired with a focus on establishing a new world order as well, even while the old is falling away under the conflagration. In this coming messianic age, everything in both society and the natural realm will finally function in the manner the Creator had intended in the beginning. Furthermore, because Yahweh is faithful to promises made, Israel will not be forgotten, and a remnant of God's servant-nation will be at the center of all this renewal, restoration, and great joy.

This increasingly forward-looking thrust of prophecy leads some to think of it as primarily foretelling, a kind of crystal ball gaze into the future. In reality, however, the nature of prophecy in ancient Israel is more forth-telling: declaring again the meaning of the ancient Sinai Covenant, explaining the mission of Yahweh (and thus Israel also) as witness to the world, and describing the implications of the morality envisioned by the suzerain-vassal treaty stipulations. Included in this forth-telling is the anticipation of how things will look when everything is renewed. This becomes the basis for the "new covenant" of Jeremiah and Ezekiel. This forms the background to the prophecies about the "new heavens and new earth" in Isaiah. This shapes the contours of the messianic age described by Isaiah, Ezekiel, Joel, Micah, and Zechariah.

The growing clarity of the prophetic message is best seen when these divinely called and authorized covenant spokespersons are reviewed in historical sequence. While not all aspects of each prophetic experience is fully known, a great amount can be learned from the information provided within most of the prophecies. In large outline, the biblical prophets can be grouped in eras spanning about a century each.

Tenth-to-Ninth-Century Prophetic Beginnings: Royal Advisers

The earliest prophets have several things in common. First, they are closely attached to the royal dynasties and function significantly as political, moral, and religious advisers. Second, few of their words are written down for posterity. Third, they seem to have close connections vocationally with either the extended royal household or the priestly families who cared for the Tabernacle and later the Temple. **Samuel** is the archetype of these prophets, according to 1 Samuel 3, and appears to have given name and status to the role of prophecy in the nation as a whole (see 1 Samuel 9).

Others in this group include **Nathan**, who has direct and easy access to King David (2 Samuel 7, 12); **Ahijah**, who seems to have been significantly responsible for the partition of the nation of Israel after the death of King Solomon (1 Kings 11:29–39), and later spoke a strong word of judgment against the king he had ensconced (1 Kings 14); and the nameless prophets of 1 Kings 13, who talk with the kings and advise them. Each plays a direct role in the political life of the nation, but does so as an acknowledged representative for Israel's true King, Yahweh. For them, there is no distinction between the religious and political dimensions of society.

Eighth-Century Prophets: Loyal Opposition

Things appear to have changed significantly for prophets in the eighth century. While **Isaiah** was expressing the passion and purposes of Yahweh with lyric eloquence in the south, prophecy took on a decidedly angry character in the north. The powerful team of **Elijah** and **Elisha** railed against the royal pair of Ahab and Jezebel (1 Kings 17–2 Kings 9) for their anti-Yahweh religious stance and their anti–Sinai Covenant betrayal of people like Naboth (1 Kings 21). **Micaiah** joined their entourage for one brief incident (1 Kings 22), lending credence to their pronouncements of judgment, even while having direct access to the royal council room.

The most enduring voices from this era belong, however, to those members of "the Twelve" minor prophets, whose words were recorded in blunt detail. **Amos** left his large estate near Tekoa in Judah to travel northward into the territory of its sibling rival, Israel, around the year 760 B.C. He explored the expansive prevalence of social sins in that realm which, he made clear, would soon result in divine judgment upon these people. According to Amos:

- There was a growing economic gap between very rich and very poor, accentuated by the callousness of the wealthy (6:4–6).
- Public worship had become repetitions of superficial liturgical acts (4:4–5; 5:21–23).
- The rich were stealing the lands of the poor through criminal lending practices, coupled with repossessions when impossible borrowing terms caused inevitable loan repayment defaults (2:6; 8:4, 6).
- Law courts were routinely denying justice to the helpless, simply because they could not pay bribes and had no social standing (2:7; 5:10, 12).
- In the marketplace, the poor were constantly cheated (8:5).
- Throughout the nation, there was overt conspicuous consumption (4:1).
- Added to these were blatant debauchery and other forms of an immoral lifestyle (6:5–6).

All in all, the word from Yahweh through Amos was dark, gloomy, and pointedly judgmental. Because of his pithy precision, coupled with verbal economy, Amos has become the model of street-corner prophets who rail against their societies in epigrammatic diatribes.

The same message is communicated in a very different tone and manner by **Hosea**, a contemporary of Amos. Hosea also spoke in the northern kingdom of Israel, but probably as a resident of that community. His oral and written communications are dated to the years 750-723 B.C. because of the rulers identified within the prophecy's pages.

Hosea has a very bad marriage. His wife, Gomer, was a prostitute before they wed, and bore at least two sons during their time together. It is uncertain, though, whether these children were biologically related to Hosea, since Gomer was not one to stay in her marriage bed at night. Her escapades and his faithful pleadings, which sound more like a soap opera than a biblical drama, become the analogy for Yahweh's relationship with Israel. Through the voice of Hosea, Yahweh poignantly reviews the past, detailing the amazing story of love that had brought young Israel into a very privileged and powerful position among the nations of the world. But this reminiscence grows bitter as both Hosea and Yahweh mourn their scorned loves, and weep for their respective wives, who are each destroying themselves and their families.

Although more polished and less dramatic, the message of another contemporary is much the same. **Micah** orated his prophecies over a period of about five decades, from 740-690 B.C. He begins this ministry in the north, but after Israel was destroyed by the Assyrians in 722 B.C., he heads south and uses the terrifying international political threat as a warning to Judah. God is faithful, Micah intones, but Israel (and also Judah) has been unfaithful to the Sinai Covenant. Therefore, judgment is surely coming. Indeed, precisely during Micah's prophecies, it arrives in vengeful force against the northern kingdom, wiping it out of existence.

A truly strange incident was also unfolding on another front, during the years of these prophets. **Jonah** was commissioned by Yahweh to travel all the way to Nineveh, capital of the dreaded Assyrians, and speak a message of divine judgment against this aggressive civilization. One might think that any loyal Israelite would gladly rise to such a task. After all, Assyria was the great political enemy of the day, constantly threatening life in Canaan. Jonah, however, is wise enough to understand the heart of Yahweh. It is not God's desire to destroy the Assyrians, he knew, but rather to bring them, along with all the other nations of the world, into a larger

---

Meanings of the Prophets' Names

Names usually carried more weight and significance in the world of the ancient Near East than is true today. Although not every prophet's name is necessarily indicative of his character, many of these men carried profoundly meaningful names:

- Isaiah—"Yahweh is salvation"
- Jeremiah—"Yahweh raises up"
- Ezekiel—"God will strengthen"
- Daniel—"God is my judge"
- Hosea—"Salvation"
- Joel—"Yahweh is God"
- Amos—"carry (?)"
- Obadiah—"Servant of Yahweh"
- Jonah—"dove"
- Micah—"Who is like Yahweh?"
- Nahum—"comforter (?)"
- Habakkuk—"embrace (?) or "wrestler (?)"
- Zephaniah—"Yahweh has concealed" or "Yahweh is hidden"
- Haggai—"make pilgrimage" or "festive (?)"
- Zechariah—"Yahweh has remembered"
- Malachi—"My messenger"

family of peoples who were returning to their Creator in worship and submission and the recovery of full human joy.

So Jonah tries to evade his task by getting as far away from Nineveh as possible. In the famous story told in Jonah 1–2, Yahweh pursues Jonah on the high seas, causes a storm that nearly swamps his ship, and preserves the prophet from suicide-by-drowning in the belly of a large fish. Yet, when Jonah finally resumes his unwelcome mission to Nineveh, his suspicions come true, as the people of that great city actually repent for a time. God's promised judgment is put on hold, and Jonah cries like a spoiled brat.

The meaning of the tale is clear, however, and genuinely prophetic: Although the Creator's world has turned against its maker, Yahweh has prepared Israel as a special missionary people; through it, as promised to Abram in Genesis 12, all the nations of the earth will be blessed. The tiny book of Jonah is one of the greatest affirmations of the missional nature of the redemptive covenant established by Yahweh with Israel at Mt. Sinai.

Seventh-Century Prophets: Doomsayers

By the time the seventh century B.C. rolls around, the prophets are rarely welcome in the royal palaces, even though all that is left of once-proud and expansive Israel is the tiny mountainous territory of Judah. During the 600s, although Assyria keeps threatening Jerusalem, it is increasingly occupied in defending itself against its rebellious eastern province of Babylon. During these years, while **Jeremiah** develops his gloomy diatribes in the heart of the capital city, several among "the Twelve" also make brief statements about coming judgment. **Zephaniah** (630–610 B.C.) provides a few paragraphs against Judah and the nations that surround it (chapters 1–2), couching the imminent intervention of Yahweh in the increasingly common term, "the Day of the Lord." In a final, somewhat lengthier chapter, Zephaniah turns his attention toward restoration and renewal, pointing to a future time when the fortunes of Yahweh's people would be made full once again.

Also, for just a brief moment (probably around 615 B.C.), **Nahum** renews the mission of Jonah against Nineveh and the Assyrians. This time, however, there is no outcome of repentance and restoration. Instead, the short-lived turnabout that had followed Jonah's challenge evaporated entirely, and Nahum declares irreversible divine judgment against this fierce kingdom, which had wreaked so much havoc on its neighbors in the Fertile Crescent. Yahweh's word through Nahum would come true a few years later when the Assyrians are trounced by the Babylonians, first in the destruction of the capital city of Nineveh (612 B.C.), then at their secondary administrative center, Harran (610 B.C.), and decisively in the battle of Carchemish (605 B.C.), where even the allied armies of Egypt prove insufficient to turn the Chaldean tide.

Finally, during this era as well, comes the disconcerting dialogue between **Habakkuk** and Yahweh. Formulated around the year 600 B.C., just as Babylon is rapidly overwhelming the whimpering remnants of the old Assyrian regime, Habakkuk asks Yahweh a series of questions that are answered in ways that almost bring more pain than the situations they are supposed to resolve. If summarized, the conversation would sound something like this:

- **Habakkuk**: "Why do you ignore the social evils that plague our land (Judah)?" (1:1–4)
- **Yahweh**: "I'm working on it. Very soon now, I will bring punishment through my dreaded scourge, the growing Babylonian conquest machine that is rolling through the area." (1:5–11)
- **Habakkuk**: "O God, no! You can't do that! They are even worse than the most evil among us! How can you talk about balancing the scales of justice with such an unfair sentence?!" (1:12–2:1)
- **Yahweh**: "I understand your frustration. That's why I'm giving you a message for all to hear. The sins of my people are terrible, and require drastic measures. For this reason, I am bringing the Babylonians against them. But the Babylonians, too, are my people, and will come under my judgment for the wickedness they perform. In the end, all will bow to me, as is appropriate when nations come to know that I am the only true God." (2:2–20)

At this point, Habakkuk breaks into a song of confidence and trust (chapter 3) that rivals anything found in the Psalms. Habakkuk charts the terrifying movements of Yahweh on Earth, bringing death and destruction as the divine judgments swirl. But in the end, Habakkuk raises a marvelous testimony of faith:

"Though the fig tree does not bud and there are no grapes on the vines, though the olive crop fails and the fields produce no food, though there are no sheep in the pen and no cattle in the stalls, yet I will rejoice in the Lord, I will be joyful in God my Savior. The Sovereign Lord is my strength; he makes my feet like the feet of a deer, he enables me to go on the heights" (Habakkuk 3:17–19).

A Long and Nasty Rivalry

Though Obadiah's prophetic tirade is very short, it embodies an ongoing tension between the families of Jacob and Esau. Besides the sibling rivalry that eventually brought the covenant blessing to the younger twin, the nations of Edom and Israel came to blows at various times throughout their empire-building years. Even during the time of the prophets, at the demise of Judah by the Babylonians, this sinister clash was only heating up for the final big event. Almost six centuries later, when the remnant of Judah had reestablished itself in Palestine, and when Edom had recovered from defeats at the hands of several nations, it would be an Edomite who would usurp the Jewish throne. Herod the Great, an "Idumaean," personified a last-ditch attempt against the redemptive purposes of Yahweh by slaughtering the babies of Bethlehem in a futile plan to annihilate Jesus before he could become a rival king (Matthew 2).

Sixth-Century (Exilic) Prophets: Messianic Optimists

The prophets of the sixth century B.C. were mostly engulfed by the occupation of Judah and its quick demise (Jerusalem was destroyed in 586 B.C.), along with the subsequent Babylonian exile, in which the bulk of the remaining population was deported. During these years, as we saw in the prophecies of **Ezekiel** and **Daniel**, the center of action shifts from Jerusalem to

Babylon. There is only one tiny prophetic reflection from back in the homeland. **Obadiah**, whose name means "Servant of Yahweh," tosses off a brief—but strident—condemnation of Edom. This nation, which emerged from the same family as Israel by way of Jacob's fraternal twin Esau, had played gadfly to Yahweh's covenant nation for many centuries. Now, through the prophet's voice, Yahweh berates it for the pride and willful cunning that leveraged Judah's demise for its own gain. When the Babylonians marshaled the deportees out of Jerusalem in 586 B.C., the looters of Edom raided and scavenged that troubled city. Moreover, as the stragglers were being shepherded down the road to exile, sharpshooters among Edom's bowmen sat on the hillsides and picked them off in an unholy target practice. For these reasons, according to Obadiah, divine judgment will soon destroy Edom's red-rock strongholds.

While Obadiah's vision is too short to encompass the many dimensions of messianic optimism found in other prophets of his age, there is contained within it a firm confidence that Yahweh is still active among the nations. Once again, the "Day of the Lord" (verses 15–21) emerges as the catchall phrase for Yahweh's looming intervention that will redress injustice with divine punishment, and will usher in the renewed covenant order, spreading out from its epicenter in Jerusalem to the ends of the earth.

Fifth-Century (PostExilic) Prophets: Cheerleaders and Apocalyptic Moralists

Four among "the Twelve" remained after the first five centuries of Israelite prophecy were swallowed up into the Babylonian exile. Haggai and Zechariah appear on the scene at exactly the same time (summer and fall of 520 B.C.); the former issues four brief messages from Yahweh on three separate days that year, while the latter continues to have visions for another two calendar cycles. Malachi shows up a generation or two later, and Joel's prophecy marks the conclusion of Old Testament revelations some time after.

Haggai is a cheerleader. He returns from Babylon to Palestine with the first wave of freed exiles under the leadership of Zerubbabel in 536 B.C. Although it took a while for the community to get its bearings, eventually there was a push to sift among the stones still left at the site of Solomon's Temple, and rebuild a house for Yahweh there. In 520 B.C., Haggai urges the workers on with divine encouragement. No obstacle can stand in the way of this central task, neither disobedient lifestyles (1:2–11), fainthearted leadership (1:12–14), poverty (2:1–9), ritual defilement (2:10–19), or the rattling sabers of bellicose nations (2:20–23). Under Haggai's

---

Zechariah's Strange Visions

- Visions Calling for Repentance (1–8):
- Call to Repentance (1:1–6)
- Night Visions (1:7–6:8):
    * Four horsemen promising restoration (1:7–17)
    * Four horns, four smiths, calling judgment on the nations (1:18–21)
    * Man with measuring line, urging rebuilding of Jerusalem (2:1–13)
    * New clothes for Joshua/Jeshua the high priest (3:1–10)

promptings and Zerubbabel's governing, the Temple is rebuilt in the next four years. By 516 B.C., it stands again, only a mean miniature compared to the glorious structure created generations before by Solomon in his seven-year building project. Nevertheless, with Haggai's oratorical help, Yahweh's house is reborn.

The visions of **Zechariah** begin in exactly the same year as Haggai's brief prophecies (520 B.C.). But Zechariah's temperament is more like a combination of Jeremiah and Ezekiel; his graphic descriptions of Yahweh's revelations involve strange creatures, heavenly scenes, and amazingly cartoonish episodes, in which Yahweh's kingdom is confirmed as chief among the nations. Because of a change in literary style after chapter 8, Zechariah 9–14 is sometimes viewed as emerging from a second voice.

While Haggai's messages were quick, pointed, and easily understood in their references to the work of the day, Zechariah's allegorical pronouncements seem only obliquely connected to his contemporary setting. They pick up on the problems experienced by the postexilic community, but then shimmer off into grand apocalyptic visions, with no fixed chronology or tidy resolutions. Still, Zechariah's lofty homilies serve well to remind the tiny and lackluster community that these people remain essential to Yahweh's original missionary purpose for Israel. Thus, the Sinai Covenant and its stipulations continue to be Israel's greatest treasure, and the source of its public identity (see Zechariah 8:18–23).

About sixty years after Haggai's and Zechariah's brief prophetic careers, **Malachi** comes on the scene. His name means "My Messenger," and may well have

* Gold lampstand and two olive trees affirming rebuilding of the Temple through Spirit-anointed Zerubbabel (4:1–14)
* Flying Scroll of Judgment (5:1–4)
* Woman in a measuring basket, wickedness being removed to Babylon (5:5–11)
* Four chariots patrolling earth (6:1–8)
* A crown for Joshua/Jeshua symbolizing divine authority (6:9–15)
* Appropriate fasting (7:1–14)
* Promises of Yahweh's return and blessing (8:1–23)
* Apocalyptic Oracles (9–14):
* Events leading to the end of this age (9–11):
  * Yahweh reclaiming all cities and nations (9:1–8)
  * Zion's King comes! (9:9–17)
  * The Great Shepherd gathers his flock (9:14–11:17)
* Events of the end times (12–14):
  * The siege of Jerusalem (12:1–3)
  * Divine deliverance through a pierced son of David (12:4–13:9)
  * Restoration of Jerusalem (14)

been a nickname either given to him by Yahweh or assumed by the man himself in the course of his activities as spokesperson for God. As was true in Habakkuk's situation, Malachi's prophetic utterances take on the form of a dialogue. Here, however, the parties in conversation are not the prophet and Yahweh, but rather Yahweh and the people. Yahweh instigates the interlocutions, interrupting daily life around Jerusalem with a series of searing questions:

- "Why have you people turned away from me?" (1:2–14)
- "Why have you priests failed to honor me?" (2:1–9)
- "Why do you divorce your wives?" (2:10–16)
- "Why do you think I'm not coming back to my Temple?" (2:17–3:5)
- "Why have you withheld tithes and offerings?" (3:6–15)

These issues match the problems Ezra and Nehemiah struggled with and affirm Malachi's dates as contemporary with those leaders. Even the covenant renewal ceremony of Nehemiah 8–10 may have been the occasion for the brief note in Malachi 3:16, which tells of a scroll of testimony being penned by repentant Jews, who wished to repossess their identity as the community of Yahweh.

It is likely that the short prophecy of Joel was written after Malachi's days, but the position of Malachi at the end of "the Twelve" is perfectly understandable. For Jews, it closed off the postexilic rebuilding of the Temple. Now the community waited with eager anticipation for Yahweh to return again in the Shekinah glory cloud that first descended on Mt. Sinai into the Tabernacle, and later came to dwell in Solomon's Temple. Malachi's final vocalization of Yahweh's speech promised a speedy arrival of the divine presence.

For Christians of the New Testament age, Malachi's prophecy was viewed directly in connection with the gospels. The messianic church community quickly interpreted Jesus as the embodiment of Yahweh's returning glory. In fact, the gospel according to Matthew, which stands at the head of the New Testament, makes a very deliberate effort to choreograph the travels of Jesus in such a way that his arrival at the Temple on the week of the final Passover is understood as the return of divine glory to the house of Yahweh, which has been left in the hands of clueless caretakers (see Matthew 21).

The prophecy of **Joel**, although given a position early in the collection of "the Twelve," was probably penned sometime in the last half of the fifth century B.C. Biblical scholars have moved it all over the map of prophetic chronology, precisely because it contains no other temporal referents than the terrible plague of locusts that shaped its contents. The sweeping devastation of successive waves of locusts devouring the entire crop in Palestine that year caused Joel to hear a higher word of judgment against the nation of Yahweh. Partly because it contains no mention of kings, and also because of some words and language forms that seem more in tune with nuances of later Hebrew and postexilic times (see, for instance, the note in Joel 3:4–6), many now believe it was written sometime after Malachi.

It is really not very important to place Joel in a historical setting. In fact, Joel's prophecy is a marvelous summary and distillation of all points of theology scattered throughout the rest of the prophets. After the strident tattoo of approaching judgment, still in rhythm with the grinding march of the locust plague, Joel sees a critical and decisive turn of history taking place when Yahweh breathes new life across the face of the Earth. Everything turns on the imminent "Day of the Lord" (Joel 2:11).

The "Day of the Lord": The Prophets in Summary

The prophets began to emerge on Israel's scene shortly after its settlement in Canaan. At first, they functioned as lingering echoes of Moses's booming voice, now fading in the historic distance. Although they continued in this role, seeking ways to translate the theology and social lifestyle of the Sinai Covenant into new and changing circumstances for Israel, the prophets also became a third national leadership team, standing somewhere between the cultic role of the priests and the political venue of the kings. There is little evidence that they considered themselves as providing new revelations for Israel. Rather, they were interpreters of the Sinai Covenant, subservient to Moses and the original suzerain-vassal documents. Their authority, while rooted in contemporary visions, was derived from the ancient standards, and never ran ahead of Exodus, Leviticus, or Deuteronomy.

What eventually coalesced from their common declarations, however, was the rallying point of the "Day of the Lord." Increasingly, the prophets heard Yahweh declaiming that things were getting so bad, both within Israel and among the nations of her world, that only a direct divine intrusion could set things right again. This impending divine visitation became known as the great and terrible "Day of the Lord."

While God's visible actions in this imminent momentous occasion would probably span a lengthy period of time, the outcomes would be so decisive that it could be termed a single event. Three major things would happen when Yahweh arrived on that "day":

- There would be a catastrophic judgment meted upon all the nations of earth, including Israel/Judah. It would fall as a divine judicial assessment that none were living appropriately to the lifestyle of the Sinai Covenant, or changing their behaviors toward that direction because of the missional influence of God's people.
- In spite of the conflagration, a remnant of Israel would be spared. This small group would be evidence that not all of the people had forgotten their God, and similarly, that God would never forget the divinely created community.
- After the cleansing of judgment and the restoration of the remnant, a new and vibrant messianic age would be ushered in. This would be a time in which all the implications of the Sinai Covenant would be lived out with fresh and natural devotion by the renewed people of Yahweh. Furthermore, throughout the world, every nation would actively seek to conform its moral behaviors to that same pattern of life. The creation itself would be reinvigorated with its Edenic glories, and the Creator and all creatures would find themselves enjoying the harmony and unlimited bounty intended by God at the beginning of time.

The "Day of the Lord," thus, was to be no less than re-creation itself. It might take a direct intervention of God into human history to bring about, but when it happened, everything would be set right.

On this note, the Old Testament closes. The Creator remains on a mission to recover the lost citizens of the kingdom of heaven, as well as renew the painfully twisted elements of nature. In order to make this restoration happen, the family of Abraham was enlisted as a witnessing partner. Unfortunately, the nation of Israel proved to be unequal to the task, and the divine redemptive enterprise limped toward an inglorious demise, even while the prophets were seeing and stating grander visions of the coming age. In the end, a muted—but stirring—prophetic voice charmed the hearts of all who waited in longing for the imminent "Day of the Lord."

What everyone in the covenant community anticipated actually was about to happen, but in a way that none had expected. Yahweh finally does show up, but appears as a weak child, rather than in the guise of a mighty warrior. Moreover, the "Day of the Lord" itself is split in two, so that the beginnings of the messianic age blessings arrive in whispers, long before the warning trumpets of judgment sounded.

Hebrew Understanding of the "Day of the Lord"

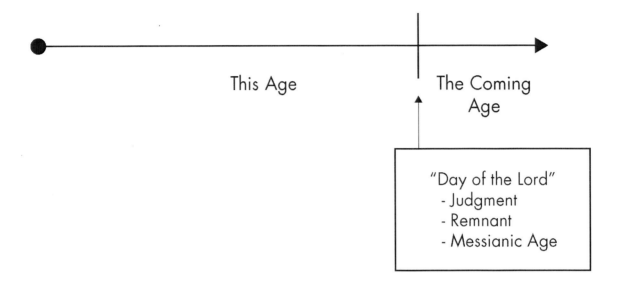

Figure 22.1 Hebrew understanding of the "Day of the Lord."

Discussion Points

- Explain what is meant by the "First Temple Period" and the "Second Temple Period." Review some of the major events that occurred during each.
- How does the prophetic role first emerge in Israelite society? How did people become "prophets?" In what ways did the public role of prophets change through the centuries? Why might that have happened?
- In what manner do the prophetic pronouncements presuppose the demands and social structures of the Sinai Covenant? How does this assist in understanding their messages?
- Why did the prophets often speak oracles of judgment on the nations surrounding Israel and Judah? How does this play into the larger purpose of prophecy as the voice of the Creator?
- What did the prophets mean by the term "the Day of the Lord?" How did it serve as a summary statement of what the prophets uniformly saw coming in the not-too-distant future? What were some of the major aspects of this impending "Day of the Lord?"
- Locate the various prophets of Israel and Judah along a time line, and try to summarize the distinctive message of each in a few lines that reflect their sociopolitical contexts and key prophetic themes.

Christian Understanding of the "Day of the Lord"

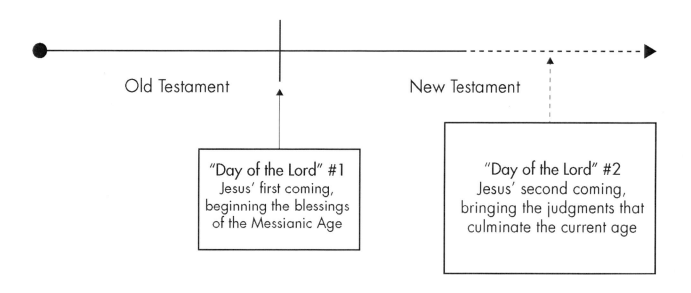

Figure 22.2 Christian understanding of the "Day of the Lord."

For Further Investigation

Achtemeir, Elizabeth. (Grand Rapids: Baker, 2009). *Minor Prophets 1*
Bright, John. (Minneapolis: Fortress, 1976). *Covenant and Promise.*
Goldingay, John. (Grand Rapids: Baker, 2009). *Minor Prophets II.*
Heschel, Abraham Joshua. (New York: Harper, 2001). *The Prophets.*

Bible "Big Picture"

Covenant Making: God establishes a covenant relationship with a missional community by way of a redemptive act.

Old Testament: The Exodus and Sinai Covenant

  Genesis—Why is the Covenant necessary?

  Exodus—What is the Covenant all about?

  Leviticus—How does it affect daily living?

  Numbers—Who is in the covenant community, and why?

  Deuteronomy—How long will the Covenant be in force?

New Testament: The Person and Work of Jesus

Covenant Living: God guides the covenant relationship with the missional community by way of authorized spokespersons.

Old Testament: The Prophets, with Their Interpreted History and Sermons

  Stories: The interpreted history of Israel

- *Joshua*—Possessing the Land with missional significance
- *Judges*—Nearly losing the Land through covenant failure
- *Ruth*—The model of covenant obedience that restores
- *1 & 2 Samuel*—Establishing the monarchy that might fulfill the covenant mission
- *1 & 2 Kings, 1 & 2 Chronicles*—Failure of the Old Testament covenant community mission experiment
- *Ezra and Nehemiah*—Restoring the covenant community in anticipation of Yahweh's next major act
- *Esther*—Responding to the warning that Yahweh's people have a covenant identity and purpose

  Sermons: The verbal declarations of Yahweh's designs and intents

- *Isaiah*—Divine deliverance from Assyria, coming global renewal
- *Jeremiah*—Doom and gloom in Judah's final years, promises of restoration
- *Ezekiel*—God on the move, bringing judgment and promises of a new age
- *Daniel*—Struggles of faithful exilic living, plus visions of God's growing kingdom
- *Hosea*—The divine/human soap opera
- *Joel*—Hints of "the Day of the Lord" found in a locust plague
- *Amos*—Imminent divine judgment because of social covenantal disobedience
- *Obadiah*—Edom condemned for harming Judah at the time of deportation
- *Jonah*—Missionary trek to Assyrian enemy capital showing global divine favor
- *Micah*—Yahweh's faithfulness, Israel's unfaithfulness, and imminent judgment
- *Nahum*—God will destroy Assyria because of its cruelty to other nations
- *Habakkuk*—Dialogue with Yahweh on the mysteries of social sins and divine judgment
- *Zephaniah*—Brief notes on impending divine judgment and future redemptive restoration
- *Haggai*—"Let's get that Temple rebuilt!" and "God bless Zerubbabel!"
- *Zechariah*—Visions of judgment on the nations and visions of glory on restored "Israel"

- *Malachi*—Dialogues between Yahweh and the people on failures and the future

New Testament: The Apostles, with Their Ecclesiastical History and Letters

Covenant Questions: God nurtures the covenant relationship with a missional community by way of spiritual wisdom and insight.

Old Testament: The Poetry and Wisdom Literature; Questions of Fundamental Human Identity as Illuminated by the Theology of the Covenant

Job—"Why do I suffer?"

Psalms—"How do I pray?"

Proverbs—"What is true wisdom?"

Ecclesiastes—"What is the meaning of life?"

Song of Songs—"What is the meaning of love?"

Lamentations—"What is the meaning of divine election?"

New Testament: The Comparison of the Two Covenant Expressions

23.

How Did Old Testament Israel Transition into New Testament Judaism?

The Story of Times between the Testaments

A lthough the Assyrians destroyed the northern kingdom of Israel in 722 B.C., they were unable to fulfill their conquering plans against Judah. A miraculous deliverance during the times of King Hezekiah and the prophet Isaiah brought a window of relief for those living in the mountains of southern Palestine.

But Babylon soon accomplished what Assyria could not, and, after several decades of imperialistic domination in the region, destroyed Jerusalem and the Temple in 586 B.C. The good news for Judah, however, was that the Babylonians followed a different international strategy from the total social deconstruction practiced by the Assyrians. The Babylonian practice of deportation and resettlement meant that a culturally intact community from Jerusalem was spared, and was given continued autonomy to develop itself religiously in a neighborhood set apart.

The importance of this policy became even more evident a short while later, when Cyrus of the Medes and Persians toppled Babylon in 539 B.C. In order to foster greater allegiance among the diverse communities his government amalgamated into one of the largest territorial kingdoms ever assembled, Cyrus issued decrees encouraging deported communities to return to their homelands. In response, a small band from the old nation of Judah wended its way back to

Palestine in 537 B.C. Among the changing languages around them, these people became known by a shortened form of their old tribal designation: Henceforth, the leftover people of "Judah" would be known as the "Jews."

The restored Jewish community in Jerusalem managed to rebuild a small Temple by 516 B.C., under the encouragement of prophets like Haggai and Zechariah. Nevertheless, times were not easy in Palestine, and the group drifted through decades of oppression by their neighbors, gouging and discrimination from some of the more crafty among their own people, and a great deal of religious lethargy. All of this was suddenly changed when a plot to annihilate their race was discovered in Susa, the Persian capital city. It had been precipitated by antagonisms meted toward Jews who had not returned to Palestine (the story is told in the book of Esther). Immediately after surviving this crisis, large waves of Jews, who had remained in the eastern regions of their exilic deportation, flooded back to Palestine. Under the leadership of Ezra and Nehemiah, the covenant community was reborn and renewed.

Important Dates

960 B.C.—King Solomon; First Temple Period begins

922 B.C.—Division of kingdom

722 B.C.—Assyrians destroy northern kingdom

606/597/586 B.C.—Babylonian occupation of Judah; First Temple Period ends

606–537 B.C.—Seventy years of Babylonian exile

537 B.C.—Persian King Cyrus's decree encouraging Jewish exiles to return home

520 B.C.—Temple rebuilding begins; Second Temple Period starts

470 B.C.—Esther and Mordecai

450 B.C.—Ezra and Nehemiah

336–323 B.C.—Alexander the Great

323–167 B.C.—Judaea on the border between the Ptolemys (Egypt) and the Seleucids (Syria)

165–63 B.C.—Jewish independence

63 B.C.—Roman rule begins

37–4 B.C.—Herod the Great rules

Under the Greeks

Judaea remained a province of Persia, however, until Alexander the Great strutted through in 329 B.C. He had recently won major victories over the Persian armies in Asia Minor, and was planning to strike at the heart of the Persian homeland after first winning Egypt. En route to that Nile-hugging nation, he marched through Palestine. There, according to Josephus (*Antiquities of the Jews*, 11.317–47), he was confronted by the Jewish high priest Jaddua, who showed him the prophecy of Daniel, and told Alexander that he was the one in its pages who was divinely destined to conquer the Persians.

Because of this, Alexander annexed Judaea to his growing empire without any battles against these people. In fact, Alexander granted the Jews significant freedom, since their religious documents espoused him as the legitimate ruler of the entire Near East.

But Alexander died in Babylon a few years later (323 B.C.), as he guided his increasingly homesick troops back toward Greece. With no ready successor, Alexander's generals divided his realm into four sections. After a period of internal fighting, these territories were soon reduced to three. Seleucus created the Antiochid dynasty and ruled out of Syria over the eastern regions.

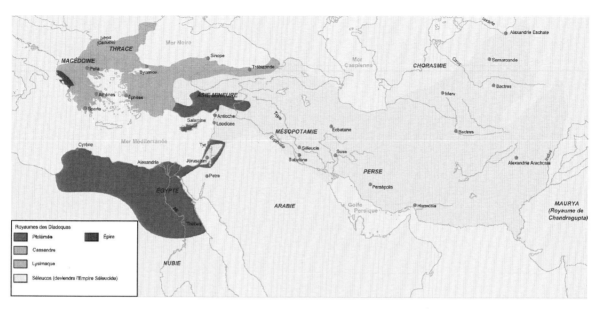

Figure 23.1 The Hellenistic World.[1]

To the south, Ptolemy fashioned a royal family that established its dominance over Egypt, reigning from the newly built Greek city of Alexandria.

Unfortunately, Judaea was on the borderland between these two great powers, and became a political football wrestled back and forth between them. For the first century of this arrangement (323–223 B.C.), Judaea remained mostly under Ptolemaic control, experiencing a great deal of continuing freedom. During this period, there was some pressure for the people of Jerusalem and other larger population centers of the Mediterranean to become more Hellenized, but in Palestine, this urging tended to be more cultural than either religious or political.

Then, in 223 B.C., Seleucid king Antiochus III began campaigns against Egypt that netted him control of Palestine. Now, the demand to become increasingly Hellenized was pushed up to coercion level. Two branches of the high priest family in Jerusalem emerged as leaders out of this boiling pot, with divergent views as to what the Jews should do. The Oniads tried to keep Judaism more orthodox and less Hellenized, while the Tobiads were fully in favor of Hellenizing—to the extent even of revising and rewriting the Jewish religion in the form of the Greek beliefs, gods, and cultic rites.

When Antiochus IV ("Epiphanes," as he liked to call himself—"God Revealed"; his opponents mumbled this nickname slightly differently: "Epimanes"—"Madman") came to power in 175 B.C., he exploited these differing Jewish perspectives by playing them off against each other in bids for his endorsement. First, Antiochus IV received bribe money from Menelaus of the Tobiads, who was seeking to have himself appointed as high priest (which, of course, was completely inappropriate by Jewish tradition; the office of high priest was an inherited position). This created enormous internal controversy among the Jews, with those wishing

---

1   Copyright © Fabienkhan (CC by 3.0) at http://commons.wikimedia.org/wiki/File:Map_Diadochs-fr.png

further Hellenization supportive of Menelaus, and those horrified by Hellenization grating at this tragic turn of affairs.

Orthodox Jews viewed Antiochus IV as a powerful and unwelcome foreign meddler. When reports circulated of his death in a military campaign against Egypt, a small revolt in Jerusalem put Menelaus's brother, Jason, into the role of high priest (171 B.C.). But Antiochus IV was not dead. Furthermore, the Romans (whom Antiochus admired) informed him that they controlled Egypt now, and that he had to get out. In double consternation, Antiochus IV turned his angry attention toward Jerusalem.

With great rage, he stormed the city, defiled the Temple (25 Kislev 168 B.C.), set up an image of himself in its courts, and forced the Jews to become overtly Hellenized. In order to coerce their fealty toward this new direction, Antiochus IV sent his soldiers throughout the land, requiring the sacrifice of pigs in every town and city (a sacrilege to the Jews).

Jewish Independence

In Modein, a small village northwest of Jerusalem, an old priest named Mattathias refused to officiate at the sacrilegious offering. A younger priest agreed to stand in, but Mattathias became enraged, and killed the man on the spot. Things escalated immediately, and Mattathias and his four sons then murdered the soldiers of Antiochus IV, precipitating what became the Jewish revolt for independence.

Although Judas was the second son of Mattathias, he was soon designated the military leader. People called him "the Hammerer" because of his lightning-quick, powerful raids that pummeled the Syrian forces. This is the origin of the name "Maccabees."

The Jewish Sociopolitical Spectrum in the First Centuries B.C. and A.D.

Herodians	Hellenists	Sadducees	Pharisees	Essenes	Zealots
Politically and culturally tied to Rome through the Herods. Mentioned in Matthew 22:16; Mark 3:6.	Wanted Jews to become part of the greater Hellenic culture and religion.	Priests ("Zadokites") and political leaders; led the fight for Jewish independence; rich, rulers, theologically liberal, keepers of the Temple.	Mainly laypeople; took Temple cleansings into daily life; theologically conservative; chafing to recover Jewish independence.	Latecomers from Babylon, seeking religious holiness after independence; strict and separate. Possibly the community of John the Baptist.	Socially and politically conservative; willing to fight to get rid of foreign domination. Jesus' disciple Simon is called a Zealot; Judas "Iscariot" may identify him among the assassins' group, the "Sicarii."

The revolution forces quickly took back Jerusalem, and managed to cleanse and rededicate the Temple (25 Kislev 165 B.C., exactly three years to the day from the sacrilegious defilement initiated by Antiochus IV). There was almost no oil for the Temple lamp, but what was left miraculously replenished itself until the dedication was complete, and a new quantity of holy oil could be created and sanctified. This event is the origin of Hanukkah, the "Festival of Lights."

Figure 23.2 The Temple as Herod reconstructed it[2]

Antiochus IV did not realize the tenacity of the orthodox Jewish will, and underestimated the strength of their guerrilla warfare. Beset with troubles back home, he could not long endure another battlefront, and his successor made peace with the Jews in 162 B.C., granting them virtual blanket freedom.

But Jewish independence opened the way for internal conflicts, particularly between the Hellenizing and the orthodoxy emphases. The Hasmonean family, descended from Mattathias and his sons, retained control of the high priest office, and later added to it the designation of "king." Social tensions escalated between the "separatist" party, increasingly called the "Pharisees," and the remnants of the Maccabean priestly clan, now known by the term "Sadducees" (priests, nobility, political leaders), who were much more in favor of Hellenistic trends. To the left of these were people who identified themselves proudly as "Hellenizers" and some even as "Herodians," groups who wished to blend Judaea and its people into the unified world order created by Alexander the Great. On the other end of the spectrum, to the right even of the Pharisees, were the "Essenes," eagerly anticipating divine judgment to fall down on this whole mess. While these waited in smoldering political quietude for God to act, others believed they must take matters into their own hands. The "Zealots" formed armed brigades and trained them to make guerrilla raids against the foreign occupiers. Some among them were hard-nosed terrorists and assassins, called the "Sicarii" after the short, curved knives they carried in hopes of drawing blood.

Roman Rule

When Hasmonean family feuds escalated, Antipater, governor of Idumaea (Edom), began a persistent campaign to bring in Roman rule. His grandson, Herod, married into the Hasmonean family, and in 63 B.C., Roman general Pompey was invited to bring peace to Jerusalem. In this way, Herod the Edomite became king of the Jews.

Herod set out on a vast construction campaign that rebuilt most of the major religious and political venues in Palestine. While the general Jewish population regretted Roman occupation, they resented even more Herod's background and power plays. Perhaps to offset this ill will, one of Herod's greatest architectural triumphs was the massive reconstruction of the Temple in Jerusalem, until it rivaled the earlier one created by Solomon. Even in Jesus' day, people begrudgingly acknowledged the size, scale, and grandeur of Herod's Temple (see Matthew 24:1; Mark 13:1; Luke 21:5; John 2:20).

So, the world into which Jesus was born—and out of which would emerge the Christian Church—was a society that had been bounced around for centuries like a plaything of greater powers, fought mightily to win independence when crushed too hard by oppressors, flirted with global Hellenization to the point of losing national and religious unity, and lived now in the uneasy recognition that the Romans were able to keep order better than they would be able to do on their own. Simmering beneath the surface of an enforced coexistence of philosophically and religiously divergent social groups was an apocalyptic hope that a new deliverer would soon rise to public attention, someone who would bring in a new world order. So, the message of John the Baptist, ranting out of the wilderness with a shout that "The Kingdom of God is near!" rarified the air in Palestine until it sparked with electric fever. When John pointed to Jesus and identified his cousin as the one to watch, the world held its breath in confused anticipation. Something huge was about to happen.

Discussion Points

- How does the history of the Jews under Greek and Roman rule help to explain the rise of the social groups which dominated the society into which Jesus was born? Where would Jesus and his disciples fall along the spectrum of social and political groups? Why?
- What are the pressures urging the Jews to Hellenize? What are the values resisting Hellenization? Which of these are winning the day when Jesus was teaching in Galilee and Judaea? Why?
- How does the political crisis of an Edomite king and Roman domination, following a period of Jewish independence, inform the consciousness of the nation in Jesus' day? How might this shape the response of the people to Jesus' teachings about the Kingdom of God, and their view of how this kingdom should come to power?

For Further Investigation

1 & 2 Maccabees

Bruce, F. F. (Grand Rapids: Eerdmans,1963). *Israel and the Nations.*

Josephus, Flavius. *The Antiquities of the Jews.*

VanderKam, James C. (Grand Rapids: Eerdmans, 2001). *An Introduction to Early Judaism.*

Covenant Making (2)

The Creator establishes a covenant relationship with a
missional community by way of a redemptive act

24.

Shifting Gears

The Same Message in a New Form

To define a theology of the New Testament is a modest enterprise, and a reasonably uncontroversial task. After all, the textual data is limited (twenty-seven manuscripts, most of them very short), and the nuances of interpretation rather narrow in scope. Although among New Testament theologians there are differences of emphasis or arguments about the significance of certain terms and ideas, they rarely find themselves in fundamentally different camps from one another.

Developing a theology of the Old Testament (or Hebrew Bible) is a much more daunting task. Not only is the literature of this collection considerably more extensive, but it varies extensively among multiple genres, topics, and provenance. Added to these challenges are questions of dating, inherent worldview, and the extent of influence from other ancient Near Eastern cultures. Old Testament theologians can square off from very different ideological points of view.

Most intimidating of all, however, is any attempt at a biblical theology that encompasses both Testaments, seeking to remain faithful to the origins and directions of each, while pursuing the historical, cultural, and religious bonds that have brought them together as the Christian Bible.

Fundamental to this challenge is the question of the relationship between the two collections. Choices made here are inherently theological, philosophical, and confessional. Five major options are most often posited:

Comparing the Literature

Old Testament
39 books
Written over 1000 years (1300–300 B.C.)
Understood to be both the "Hebrew Bible" of Judaism and the "Old Testament" of Christianity
Focuses on the Sinai Covenant and the Kingdom of Yahweh in and through Israel

New Testament
27 books
Written in 50 years (48–98 A.D.)
Understood as the primary sourcebook for Christianity
Focuses on the person, work, and teachings of Jesus

The Old Testament is essential Christian scripture, with the New Testament serving primarily as its explanatory footnote. Because Jesus and the first Christians were Jewish, and the preaching of the apostles was based upon the Hebrew Bible, there is a sense in which the Old Testament is sufficient when considering what revelation God might have given. The New Testament documents, in this view, do not alter or add to the theology of the Old Testament. Instead, they provide notes about the life and teachings of Jesus, and collect together the interpretive nuances about him that were put forward by the Church's first preachers.

The Old Testament is prophecy, and the New Testament describes its fulfillment. This is a significantly New Testament–centered approach. It views the Hebrew Bible and its context as an incomplete religious world, in which its leaders invariably point to meanings and future happenings that could not be apprehended immediately by their contemporaries. God's designs, accordingly, were focused on Jesus, and for that reason Israel's history and religion were inherently still evolving, forming at best a prelude or prologue to the real event.

The Old Testament is historical background, while the New Testament is essential scripture. In this overtly Church-centered analysis, all Christian theology is derived from the New Testament. It alone is the complete "Word of God." The Old Testament is, of course, beneficial and convenient, for it gives historical context to the life of Jesus, and helps explain some of the terms and ideas bandied about in New Testament writings which are shaped by certain ancient cultures. Clearly, however, the New Testament is the guidebook for the Church, and for that reason, it can be published separately from the Hebrew Bible and studied independently of that other collection, which belongs to a different religion.

The Old Testament is primarily an expression of Law, while the New Testament is truly Gospel, "good news." This approach believes that the God of the Judeo-Christian tradition acted in fundamentally different ways when nurturing the lives of these sibling faith communities. The "Law" of Old Testament covenant theology was a somewhat misguided attempt that viewed God as standing like a nanny or teacher over a spiritually immature people, until an appropriate time when they would hunger for freedom as believers come of age. The New

Testament breathes with grace and spiritual maturity that was not possible during Old Testament times. Jesus is the one who explains the new religious outlook, and takes care of the penal code associated with the Old Testament "Law," so that New Testament believers would not have to worry about it.

The Old Testament begins God's covenant mission to reclaim the wayward peoples of earth through a centripetal geographic strategy. The New Testament reaffirms this core design while retooling its missional thrust centrifugally outward to the far reaches of human settlement and expansion. In this perspective, there is a single unifying motif that binds the two Testaments together: the mission of God. This mission is largely channeled through Israel in Old Testament times, with a result that the nation needed to be located at a significant crossroad of international interaction, so that all peoples might eventually have an opportunity to connect with Israel's God. Furthermore, because the missional activities of God were expressed through a specific cultural context, many of the scriptural teachings were designed in and around and through Israelite culture and history. The New Testament does not alter this divine missional drive, but it renegotiates the parameters, so that it becomes more portable and transferable. The critical event that initiated the Old Testament era of the mission was the exodus of Israel from Egypt, and the formation of its identity through the Sinai Covenant. The critical event that initiated the New Testament era of the mission is the incarnation of the divine identity into human form (Jesus), so that the transition could be made quickly, and its redemptive transaction secured once and for all.

Dating the New Testament

Although there are many suggested chronologies (especially with regard to the appearance of the gospels), this is at least a reasonable ordering:

- 49 Galatians
- 49 James
- 50 Thessalonians
- 53 1 & 2 Corinthians
- 54 Romans
- 58 Philippians, Philemon, Colossians, Ephesians
- 59 Matthew, Luke, Acts
- 55 Mark
- 63 1 Timothy, Titus, 1 Peter, Jude
- 64 2 Peter, Jude
- 65 Hebrews
- 67 2 Timothy
- 81 1, 2, & 3 John
- 88 Revelation
- 97 John

This fifth perspective informs the approach taken in this study. The literature of the New Testament will be investigated in parallel forms to the three major types of Old Testament literature analyzed previously: Covenant Making, Covenant Living, and Covenant Questions. As with the Old Testament, covenant-making documents derive their authority directly from the intrusive divine redemptive event. This was the miraculous deliverance of Israel from Egypt in the first covenant setting, along with the establishment of a unique religious missional identity through the Sinai suzerain-vassal treaty. In the New Testament age, the intrusive divine redemptive event is the birth, life, teachings, death, and resurrection of Jesus.

Covenant Living documents in the New Testament age, like the prophetic histories and sermons of the Old, will be found in the apostolic writings about the unfolding story of the early Christian Church, and the hortatory letters by which the culture and character of these congregations was guided by the apostles. As with the Covenant Questions documents of the Old Testament, similar purposes are found in Hebrews and Revelation, which seek to nurture faith in a changing world environment.

The span of time over which these documents of the New Testament were written is very short—fifty years!—especially when compared to the millennium it took to produce the writings of the Old Testament. Although the letters are the earliest New Testament documents to emerge, at least a decade or more before the first gospels, these latter stand appropriately at the head of the collection in its final form, for they focus specifically on the redemptive event of Jesus' coming, life, death, and resurrection, from which the rest of the New Testament writings draw their meaning.

Obviously, there are more early Christian writings than the twenty-seven documents collected as the New Testament, just as there were more Hebrew and Jewish literary productions besides those that became part of the Old Testament. These additional and related writings are often termed "apocrypha" (from a Greek word meaning "hidden things"), and come in three major groupings:

> Old Testament "pseudepigripha": books in Hebrew related to Old Testament themes, but considered less authentic or authoritative than those which were canonized.

> Jewish "apocrypha": books in Greek mainly related to times and writings during the Second Temple period, but considered less authoritative.

> Christian "apocrypha," or "spiritual writings": books in Greek or Latin which purport to continue stories begun in New Testament writings, or to come from authors mentioned there.

The emergence of the apocryphal books as distinct from the canonical collection resulted from an interesting development that interweaves language changes, translations, political fortunes, and reforming movements. By the time of Jesus, there were two collections of Hebrew Bible writings that were received as divinely authoritative and unique: the Torah (the writings of Moses: the covenant documents of Genesis through Deuteronomy) and the Nabi'im (the prophets, both historical and sermonic). The Hebrew language, however, was no longer widely used, and most of the Jews outside of Palestine relied on the Septuagint, a Greek translation of the Torah and Nabi'im. Appended to these was a growing body of other literature, simply known as the K'tuvim ("Writings") that had also been translated into Greek, or were written in Greek. Because so many of the first Christians, both Jews and Gentiles, lived outside of Palestine, the Septuagint was their primary scripture collection.

After the destruction of Jerusalem and the Temple by the Romans in 70 A.D., rabbinic Judaism began to place a huge emphasis on the need for an authoritative scriptural text for synagogue readings and teachings. During the last decades of the first century A.D., the Hebrew Bible became standardized in its current form, with the complete Torah and Nabi'im, plus a selection drawn from among the K'tuvim, but pared down from the growing body of literature circulating with the Septuagint.

The Christian Church generally used the Septuagint as its authoritative scriptures for the first few centuries, including the many documents that had been part of the extended K'tuvim eventually found in the Septuagint. Most Christian leaders, though, began to distinguish between those books that had greater authority (usually because of their closer connection to direct apostolic teaching), and those that had less. At the time of the Reformation (sixteenth century), Protestant scholars sought to get back to early Church identity and practices, and in so doing, they adopted the Hebrew Bible as the normative Old Testament of the church. This meant that in Protestant circles, the Old Testament was somewhat shorter than that used in the Church until that date. The distinction between the Bible used by Protestants, and that servicing Roman Catholic and Eastern Orthodox communities, served to clarify the higher authority of the generally accepted "canonical" scriptures over the lower authority of the apocryphal additions.

Discussion Points

- How does one's view of the relationship between the Old Testament (or Hebrew Bible) and the New Testament relate to one's understanding of God, the purpose of biblical religion, the character of Israel's identity, and the significance of Jesus?
- How might the mission of God, as described in the Old Testament, be considered centripetal (pulling toward a center)? How might the mission of God, as described in the New Testament, be considered centrifugal (pushing out from a center)?
- What is your view of the relationship between Israelite/Jewish identity and Christian identity? Why?
- Why should certain writings be considered "biblical," while others from the same time periods and communities be deemed "apocryphal?" What standards of inclusion or exclusion might apply?
- How does the three-part assessment of the writings in each Testament inform their priority and authority in relation to one another? Where is the locus of authority found for each different section of writings? Why might this be the case?

For Further Investigation

Brouwer, Wayne. (1985). *Revelation and History: An analysis of approaches to the relationship between revelation and history in recent theological systems.* Hekman Library, Calvin College: Unpublished Master's Thesis.

Baker, David L. (Downers Grove: InterVarsity, 1991). *Two Testaments, One Bible: A Study of the Theological Relationship between the Old and New Testaments.*

25.

The Gospel Quartet (1)

Mark's Melody

Although the gospels of the New Testament are among the most widely recognized and read documents in the world, it remains difficult to explain their exact genre. The gospels have no clear parallel in any other religious or literary tradition.

Certainly, the gospels are not mere biographies. They do not offer enough data about the life of Jesus to construct a full story of his existence, or to offer a well-developed social portrait of his presence among his contemporaries. While Matthew (1:18–2:23) and Luke (1:5–2:40) each relate a few events surrounding Jesus' birth, their selections differ significantly from one another. Luke briefly tells of a single incident in Jesus' early adolescence (2:41–52), and then jumps quickly to Jesus' baptism by John, indicating that this took place when Jesus "was about thirty years old" (2:23). The bulk of all four gospels proceed from this inaugurating event, bypassing almost entirely Jesus' first three decades of life. Since John includes notes about Jesus participating in three Passover celebrations (2:13–25; 6:4; 13:1), the last of which became the occasion for his crucifixion, it is commonly assumed that Jesus was thirty-three years old when he died. But the gospels are certainly not clear, concise, or comprehensive biographies of Jesus' life.

Nor is it true that the gospels are a complete and systematic summary of Jesus' teachings. What has been preserved as the record of Jesus' sayings and speeches is too haphazardly gathered to form a codified compendium that would neatly explain his wisdom or theology. Indeed, while Jesus' parables, sermons, and dialogues are essential to the gospels, the activities of Jesus' life also remain important, even though they do not form a detailed biographical life history. One significant example of this is the Passion narrative found in all four gospels. There is a deliberate and extensive accounting of what happened during Jesus' last week in Jerusalem, to the extent that approximately one-third of each gospel is consumed by this brief and critical event. If the gospels were intended primarily as teachings of the master, they would not likely give so much place to these other dimensions of Jesus' life.

The most fitting designation for the gospels seems to be that of "proclamation." These documents are records of early Christian preaching about Jesus, describing the significance of his coming, the meaning of his personhood, the content of his teachings, the importance of his actions, the character of his death, and the miracle of his resurrection. Moreover, all of this material is communicated as a means to espouse a particular understanding of the divine mind and initiatives among the human race. The gospels are the Church's early homilies.

Although the designations that give name to each of the four canonical gospels are extremely familiar ("The Gospel According to Matthew," " ... Mark," " ... Luke," and " ... John"), these were added by the early church on the basis of traditions which emerged very early in the transcription process. Apart from the brief introduction in Luke's gospel (1:1–4), and the few words of personal reflection at the end of chapters 20 and 21 of John's gospel, those who originally penned these documents had no desire to claim the contents for themselves or call attention to their own part in the activities recounted. The purpose of these writings was to proclaim Jesus, and that they did.

Yet, the ascription of authorship ties each of the gospels to a particular provenance and purpose early in its existence, and this is important for those who try to probe the uniqueness of each document. Although New Testament scholars continue to debate whether these presumed writers actually penned the proclamations attributed to them, no widely affirmed, viable alternatives have ever been put forward. So the Gospel according to Mark is as well interpreted as any through the eyes of Papias, a second-century bishop, who declared (according to Eusebius in Book 33 of his *Church History*): "Mark, who was Peter's interpreter, wrote down accurately, though not in order, all that he remembered of what Christ had said or done."

Who Was Mark?

What do we know of this Mark about whom Papias wrote? Most of our data comes from the book of Acts in the New Testament, along with snippets from the "greetings" sections of Paul's and Peter's letters. The man had at least two names (Acts 12:12; 12:25; 15:37), which was not unusual in his world: *John* was probably used mostly in his Palestinian Jewish context, and *Mark* provided a Hellenized name for interaction with the larger Roman world. From the twelfth chapter of Acts, we glean a few interesting tidbits about Mark's early life, growing up in Jerusalem. He is called the "son of Mary," probably indicating that there had been no husband/father in the household for some time. Most likely, this meant that Mark's father had died while he was still relatively young.

Furthermore, it is clear from the same passage that Mary's house was the meeting place for the early Jerusalem Christian congregation. When Peter was imprisoned, the Christ-believers of the city gathered for an all-night prayer meeting at this location. Indeed, Peter himself was aware of it, so that when he came to his senses after his middle-of-the-night miraculous release, although he was not a native of the place, he quickly found his way to Mary's home, expecting help.

Furthermore, the description of the house itself indicates that Mary was a woman who lived in the more well-to-do part of Jerusalem. When Peter arrived at her home, he knocked for entrance on a gate that was separated from the living quarters by a courtyard. This arrangement was only true for those with some financial means, and was not common for most people whose domestic space abutted the street. Evidently, John Mark was from the wealthier part of town.

This information supports a strong probable connection between Mark and the priestly ruling class within first-century Palestinian Judaism. Mark's tribal background, after all, was Levite. His cousin, Barnabas (Colossians 4:10), was a wealthy Levite who had a second home on the island of Cyprus (Acts 4:36). It was probably because of this family link that Mark traveled with Barnabas and Paul to become part of the first Christian Church planted outside of Palestine, in the old Greek administrative city of Antioch (Acts 11:27–30; 12:25), and then joined the pair on their initial mission journey into Asia Minor (Acts 13:1–5). Something happened during those travels, which caused Mark to return home to Jerusalem (Acts 14:36) before the rest. Different speculations suggest that Mark might have been angered at the changing role between Barnabas and Paul (it seemed that Barnabas's younger protégé was actually becoming the leader of the group, since in his reporting of their travels it was always "Barnabas and Paul" until they had finished crossing Cyprus, after which the two were listed as "Paul and Barnabas"), or that the harsh experiences of the journey proved too much for Mark to endure. In any case, his failure to go the distance later caused a difficult rift between Barnabas and Paul, to the extent that they parted in anger (Acts 15:38-42).

Mark and Paul were eventually reconciled, as made clear when, a decade later, Paul would write that Mark was his faithful fellow worker (Colossians 4:10; Philemon 24). Near the end of Paul's life, he even called Mark a useful assistant whom Paul wanted to have with him as he faced martyrdom (2 Timothy 4:11). Peter also, just a few years earlier, had called Mark "my son" (2 Peter 5:13), indicating the close bond that had developed between Mark and the key leaders of the apostolic church.

Some rather strange and interesting glimpses of Mark have filtered through the pages of scripture and history. First, only in the gospel attributed to Mark does this very unusual note about someone who observed Jesus' arrest appear: "A young man, wearing nothing but a linen garment, was following Jesus. When they seized him he fled naked, leaving his garment behind" (Mark 14:51–52). Since this incident seems to add nothing to the theology of the gospel, it is often thought that here Mark made a single reference to his own experiences, growing up in Jerusalem during the years of controversy swirling about Jesus.

Second, there are several references to a nickname gained by Mark in the early church. Transliterated from Greek, the appellation would be *Kolobodaktulos*, a word that meant "stubby finger" (cf. Hippolytus, *Philosophumena*, VII, xxx). One story suggests that Mark gained this name because he was born into the home of a priest's family. At the age of twenty-five, he should have become an apprentice priest in the Temple, along with all other unblemished males from priestly families. But by this time, Mark had become a follower of Jesus, and no longer believed it would be proper to continue offering animal sacrifices. In order to mar his features physically, so that he would become disqualified from priestly duty, he cut off part of one of his fingers. Although this report cannot be confirmed, it is interesting to note that when Paul and Barnabas take young John Mark with them on their first mission journey, he is called an "assistant," using the same Greek term that also designated the apprentice priests in the Temple.

What Was Mark Trying to Communicate?

Papias knew that the Church of his day recognized this shortest of the gospels as consisting essentially of the preaching of Peter about Jesus, even though the words themselves were recorded by Mark. There are several internal hints to support this hypothesis: Peter's call to be a follower of Jesus is the first to be recorded (Mark 1:16), even though each of the gospels reports the various callings in different sequences; Peter is identified as "Simon" early in the gospel (Mark 1:16, 29, 36), which fits with the probable way Peter was addressed by his family and friends, before Jesus renamed him (Mark 3:16) "Rocky" (the essential meaning of the Greek name Peter); the story of Jesus healing Peter's mother-in-law is told with more personal detail (Mark 1:29–37) than is found in its other gospel recordings (Matthew 8:14–15; Luke 4:38–39). Together, these clues cement a close connection between Mark's gospel and the preaching of Peter. Like as not, the old apostle declared these remembrances to his congregation in Rome, and his younger assistant took down notes that eventually morphed into this earliest gospel.

The first glimpse of Jesus in the Gospel according to Mark is found immediately in the introductory heading or title of 1:1—"The beginning of the good news (gospel) about Jesus Christ, the Son of God." Several things are important in this short statement. First, the author presumes there is much more to declare about Jesus than what will be contained in these proclamations; this is only "the beginning." Second, whatever one might think about Jesus, even with the gruesome crucifixion story still ahead, the impact of his life and ministry is "good news." This colors how one should receive the message that follows. Third, Jesus is already understood at the beginning of this story to be the Messiah foretold by the prophets of the Old Testament. The term Christ, appended to Jesus, is a title, not a name (although it would come to be used as such). Jesus is "the Christ," meaning the one anointed to be the great deliverer of the Jews.

"Gospel" = "Good news"

While the term "gospel" has become a unique concept in its own right, its origin is tied very specifically to the Greek word *ευαγγελιον*, which means "good news." The English word "evangelism" is virtually a direct absorption of the Greek term, signifying that when one "evangelizes," one is merely declaring or sharing the good news about Jesus.

This is why the baptism and divine commissioning of Jesus are told first (Mark 1:9–11), and are clearly expressed as a divine anointing (verse 10). Fourth, an additional designation is given to Jesus; he is called "the Son of God." While Christianity has made this a common theological phrase, it was originally a very specific political term used to honor the Roman emperor. When Caesar Augustus died, the Roman Senate declared him to be divine. All of the rulers who came after him were, in turn, identified as the "Son of God" when they mounted the throne. For Mark to call Jesus the "Son of God" was a deliberate move to identify him as a rival to the Roman emperor of the day.

Our initial impressions about Jesus, as the narrative unfolds, are those showing him to be a man of action, healing, and power. In the first two chapters alone, Jesus is breathlessly busy, flitting all over Galilee, healing and teaching with such abandon that he is constantly followed (Mark 1:45), and always under urgent demand (Mark 3:7–8). While the gospel seems, at the start, to be merely a collection of stories about Jesus' healings and brief teachings, it soon begins to take linear shape. In fact, its literary form will be copied by Matthew and Luke, who depend extensively on Mark's record. This is why these three are together called the Synoptics (those who see similarly). In very broad outline, the gospel of Mark looks like this:

- 1–8 Jesus blasts the powers that harm human life by means of the greater power of the Kingdom of God
    - ◊ *Transitional Event*: Transfiguration in chapter 9
- 9–10 Jesus teaches his close companions about the cost and character of discipleship
    - ◊ *Transitional Event*: Entry into Jerusalem in chapter 11
- 11–16 Jesus moves to the cross and beyond in a fulfillment of the cost of discipleship upon himself, and a paradoxical expression of the power of the Kingdom of God

Among the many things that can be said about Mark's gospel, there are a number of interesting and critical features that are unique to it. First, no infancy story is recorded (in distinction from Matthew and Luke). This gospel about Jesus begins with his full-grown adult powers in place, and these are immediately confirmed and amplified by the commissioning endowment of the divine Spirit. In other words, according to Peter's preaching and Mark's penning, Jesus jumps out of the starting gate at full throttle—a man on a mission—with energy and purpose.

Second, the prophecy of Isaiah is recalled up front. That Old Testament spokesperson announced the coming of the great Day of the Lord, speaking of a time when Yahweh would break into human history to bring judgment against the nations of the world and the evil in Israel, save a remnant, and begin the new and transforming messianic age. In this way, Mark links the coming of Jesus directly to the Old Testament identity of God, and the actions of salvation history contained in it. This connection is further affirmed when Jesus opens his mouth to preach. His very first words are written by Mark as "the good news of God" (1:14), and commence as a staccato summary of the prophetic "Day of the Lord" theology: "The time has come. The kingdom of God is near. Repent and believe the good news!" (1:15).

Third, within the body of Mark's gospel, Jesus' first extended teaching is the parable of the Sower and Seeds (Mark 4:1–20). Its placing and expansive size, in comparison to the snippets of teaching that came earlier, highlight it as distinctive and important. As one reads these pages in continuous narrative, the pace suddenly slows, and Jesus demands that we reflect on what has happened so far. We have been watching the Jesus of power and action through the eyes of Peter and Mark. Now, we must respond to the person of Jesus. How will the sower's seed find purchase in our own lives? What kind of soil are we? Both for Jesus' initial audience and for those who encounter Jesus through this gospel, the multilayered metaphor serves as a call to self-assessment and belief. Reaching behind the literary origins of the gospel, it is clear to see that Peter was not preaching merely to communicate information, nor was Mark recording Peter's sermons as a nice collection of spiritual writings. This was a document intended for volitional reaction. One *must* respond to Jesus, and the outcome of that engagement would be seen in direct changes of lifestyle and behavior.

Fourth, the healings (particularly the raising of the dead girl) in chapter 5, appear to trigger public animosity which will eventually lead to Jesus' death. Chapter 6 opens with the first major negative reaction against Jesus; it is predicated on the idea that people like the "magic tricks" of Jesus' miracles, but they don't appreciate having a local boy regarded as special in a messianic sense. What is received as "good news" by the crowds becomes bad news for the social and religious leaders. Without credentials, this man is challenging their authority, since the presence and power of God seem to flow much more easily and immediately than it does through them.

Fifth, this divided outlook about Jesus' actions and character may well be the reason for the unique and somewhat odd emphasis in Mark's gospel toward what has come to be known as the "Messianic Secret." On a number of occasions, when Jesus heals someone, he gives orders for the miracle to be kept quiet (Mark 1:34; 1:43–44; 3:12; 5:43; 8:26; 8:30; 9:9). While there are a few instances in which Jesus encourages people to talk about what he has done (e.g., Mark 5:18–20), it seems that most of the time, Jesus does not want his mighty works widely publicized. Although it may seem contradictory for Jesus to expend the energy of heaven so dramatically and then wrap it up in a blanket of secrecy, there is probably good reason for the hushing. Crowds, titillated by these unusual events, might quickly develop into mobs which could short-circuit his full messianic task by trying to crown him as king too early, and

---

What about the Strange Ending to the Gospel?

All of the earliest manuscripts of Mark's gospel end after 16:8—"Trembling and bewildered, the women went out and fled from the tomb. They said nothing to anyone, because they were afraid."

Obviously, this seems to be a strange way for the gospel to conclude. For that reason, several different endings have been drafted and appended over the centuries, although none resonates with authentic connection to the rest of the gospel.

Some suggest that the original conclusion was lost, torn away from the rest of the manuscript early on. Perhaps this is true, but it would be difficult to know why the earliest copies would uniformly not include some note about it, or some means by which to understand its abrupt end.

For that reason, others have suggested that the gospel finishes exactly where Mark intended. The last, great, reality-changing miracle of Jesus' life was his death-overturning resurrection. If this event is indeed true, then everything of human experience is altered. That is a very frightening message, and much more powerful than any romantic notions of returning springtime seasonal greenery or flowers. If Jesus is truly the "Son of God," no one can afford to ignore him, and the fear of either terror or awe follows in his wake.

only in a temporal realm (see Mark 1:45). If that had happened, Jesus could have ended up becoming merely a temporary human teacher, bogged down with the care of an endless stream of clients looking for a quick fix to their perceived problems. As such, Mark records Jesus' urgent warnings, early in his career, for people not to tell what has happened. Later, as the crisis of his life and identity heats up, these warnings will no longer be necessary.

Sixth, while all of the evangelists report Jesus' entry into Jerusalem at the time of his final Passover in very similar manners, each offers nuances in the details in a way that hints at the larger themes intended through their writings. In the case of Mark, there is an immediate shadow of rejection reported in the events of the day. "Jesus entered Jerusalem and went to the temple," writes Mark in 11:11. But then he adds this peculiar assessment: "He looked around at everything, but since it was already late, he went out to Bethany with the Twelve."

Figure 25.1 Who is most powerful? Emperor Nero or King Jesus?[1]

While it is certainly possible to take this statement as a mere reference to the lengthened shadow on the sundial, Mark couples it immediately with the cleansing of the Temple and the cursing of the fig tree. Each of these actions is an overt judgment of Jesus imputed on the religious system of the day. The first rails against the leaders, who have allowed the Temple ceremonies to become something foreign from their original purposes, while the latter castigates the nation as a whole for not fulfilling its Sinai covenant mission. The image of the fig tree (or similar domesticated flora) was a recognized cipher in the Old Testament, used to refer to Israel as the unique partner with Yahweh for the blessing of the nations (see Psalm 80; Isaiah 5:1–7; Micah 7:1–6; Jeremiah 8:13). Although it may not have been the season of the annual cycle for this particular tree to bear figs, there was never a time when the planting of Yahweh was not to produce fruits as evidence of its unique mission in the divine global recovery plan. So when Jesus curses the tree, even though it is not the season for it to hang with ripe figs, he is using it as a metaphor or teaching tool for those who hear him.

Mark assures us that this is Jesus' meaning when cursing the tree, for he adds Jesus' teaching that through true belief "this mountain" (i.e., the place where Jerusalem and the Temple were built) could be tossed into the sea. In other words, there was a shift in the mission methods of God taking place through Jesus' ministry. This city and nation, which had been the political, temporal, and geographical vehicle for announcing Yahweh's presence to the world, was now relinquishing those ties. In its wake would come a new focus on the person and work of Jesus, portable in its delivery to all nations through the preaching of his followers.

---

1 Copyright © shakko (CC by 3.0) at http://commons.wikimedia.org/wiki/File:Nero_pushkin.jpg

This message is confirmed at the close of the gospel. As Mark narrates the story of Jesus' crucifixion, he appears to draw deliberate and specific parallels to the public ceremony of the Roman Triumph. The Roman Triumph was an often repeated celebration granted by the Senate to honor generals who had achieved striking or particularly significant victories in battle. On the day decreed by the Senate, the honoree was lauded by his entire regiment at his quarters, known as the praetorium, about mid-morning. He was dressed in a royal robe (purple dye was reserved for use only by the emperor and those of the highest ranks of nobility), and a garland was woven for his head as a crown. His face was painted red, reflecting the presumed color of Jupiter, chief of the Roman gods and protector of the great city. The soldiers declared their general's successes, and declared him to be king of the city of Rome for the day. Then they led him in public procession through the streets of Rome, while crowds of citizen cheered and gawked, released from work for celebration on this public holiday.

The honoree was accompanied by a bull for sacrifice, who was guided by a slave carrying the large axe used as the weapon of execution. The route of the procession moved toward the Capitolium, which literally meant the "Head Hill." Once there, the general was offered myrrhed wine (a scented drink generally reserved for the elite), but he was supposed to refuse it to show his desire to retain the full command of his senses throughout this event. The bull was then executed, around noon, and placards announcing the royal status of the honoree were held aloft to the cheering crowds. The general, or king for the day, turned to face the crowds, flanked by two of his comrades. The crowds would applaud and chant slogans of the man's successes. If everything was fully confirmed by the gods, it was hoped that they would miraculously express their approval by some supernatural sign. At some such triumphs, solar eclipses were recorded, obvious divine affirmations of the victory celebrated and the true honor of the one feted.

In the spare language of Mark's description of the events of Jesus' crucifixion, these steps are exactly paralleled. The entire Roman regiment gathers at the Pratorium (15:16) to adorn Jesus with a robe and woven crown (15:17). They regale him with shouts about his supposed triumphs (while turning their accolades into torture), and "worship" him as honored one among them (15:18-19), before leading him out to the crowds in public procession (15:20). A slave is commandeered to join the entourage, and carry the weapon of execution (15:21), as they move slowly toward "Head Hill" (Mark rarely translates any term in his gospel, but in 15:22 makes certain that his readers know that "Golgotha" means "The Place of the Skull" or "Head Hill") for the culminating event in the celebration.

Jesus is offered myrrhed wine, which he refuses (15:23), and the execution takes place (15:24). While Mark knows that Jesus is on the cross from around noon until three p.m. (15:33), he also notes that the whole crucifixion "triumph" is a full-day event, beginning already at mid-morning (15:25). Placards stating Jesus' triumphs are written and presented to the people (15:26), and others of Jesus' "peers" flank him, as he faces the crowds (15:27) which shout slogans of his "victories" (15:29-32). The "triumph" is divinely affirmed by way of a supernatural darkness (15:33)

It is hard to image how Mark, writing in Rome for Roman Christians who had all experienced other officially-declared "triumphs," could pen these lines without intending a direct correspondence between Jesus' crucifixion and these other public ceremonies. What the Romans accomplished in lauding their great generals, declaring them to be "king of the city" for the day, was ironically and sarcastically accomplished also for Jesus on the fateful occasion of his spectacular death in Jerusalem. While Roman generals and emperors received their momentary accolades and disappeared, Jesus endured the horrors of his mock ceremony to rise immediately into full and eternal victory. This is confirmed in the final scene of the crucifixion. The last person to make a declaration about Jesus in Mark's version of the gospel proclamation is the centurion at the cross (Mark 15:38-39). As the overwhelming impact of Jesus' crucifixion begins to shudder through the world, this soldier makes a powerful and overtly religious/political testimony. When he entered the ranks of the Roman military, he had to take an oath of loyalty to the emperor, the "son of god." Here, at Jesus' cross, however, he begins to understand that there is a ruler above the man in Rome. Although this person is dying in the ignominy of a social reject, there is something about him which announces a grander outlook on life and calls for a bigger allegiance, in order to make sense of his brief existence. The centurion, in a dramatic transferal of his military oath, publicly declares, "Surely *this* man was the Son of God!"

As a message first being preached by Peter in Rome during the days when Nero was coming to power, and then read by the Christians of Rome while official persecutions were mounted against them, the implication of the "good news" about Jesus was incredibly political. Nero demanded obedience through force; yet, even his own soldiers recognized that in Jesus was a higher power, a greater power, a more worthy power, that alone could overcome all of the other powers that enslaved people through demon possession, dehumanization, disease, or even death.

The Crucifixion as Roman "Triumph"

Elements of Roman "Triumph"
1. Specification of place and gathering of the whole guard
2. Ceremonial dress (robe & crown)
3. Accolades as ruler
4. Public procession
5. Slave commandeered to carry death weapon
6. Procession to the "Head Hill" (Capitolium)
7. Offering of myrrhed wine which is refused
8. Killing of a bull as sacrifice
9. All day long event
10. Announcement of ruler's triumphant identity
11. Ruler faces the crowds flanked by two others
12. The crowd applauds, chanting slogans of the ruler's successes.
13. Hopefully, the gods confirm this triumph with a solar eclipse

Mark's Description of the Crucifixion
1. Mark 15:16—"The soldiers led Jesus away into the palace (that is, the Praetorium) and called together the whole company of soldiers."
2. Mark 15:17—"They put a purple robe on him, then wove a crown of thorns and set it on him."
3. Mark 5:18-19—"And they began to call out to him, 'Hail, King of the Jews!' Again and again they struck him on the head with a staff and spit on him. Fall on their knees, they worshiped him."
4. Mark 15:20–"Then they led him out…"
5. Mark 15:21—"A certain man from Cyrene, Simon, the father of Alexander and Rufus, was passing by on his way in from the country, and they forced him to carry the cross."
6. Mark 15:22–"They brought Jesus to the place called Golgotha (which means The Place of the Skull).
7. Mark 15:23—"Then they offered him wine mixed with myrrh, but he did not take it."
8. Mark 15:24–"And they crucified him."
9. Mark 15:25–'It was the third hour when they crucified him."
10. Mark 15:26–'The written notice of the charge against him read: The King of the Jews."

> 11. Mark 15:27–'They crucified two robbers with him, one on his right and one on his left.
> 12. Mark 15:29-32–'Those who passed by hurled insults at him, shaking their heads and saying, 'So! You who are going to destroy the temple and build it again in three days, come down from the cross and save yourself!' In the same way the chief priest and the teachers of the law mocked him among themselves. 'He saved others,' they said, 'but he can't save himself! Let this Christ, this King of Israel, come down now from the cross, that we may see and believe.' Those crucified with him also heaped insults on him."
> 13. Mark 15:33–'At the sixth hour darkness came over the whole land until the ninth hour."

Taken as a whole, the "good news" about the "Son of God" in Mark's gospel is clear. Jesus is the heaven-sent Christ (Messiah, or "anointed one"), who arrives as the means by which the "Day of the Lord" will be accomplished in both judgment and blessing. Jesus tears into his world with action and power, overturning the many threats to human existence, and bringing the healing graces of restoration and hope. Because people might misinterpret his miracles and want to make him their trophy ruler too quickly, Jesus cautions recipients of his transforming power to keep quiet about these things. Finally, when the big confrontation between Jesus and those who seem to hold social authority is unavoidable, Jesus declares a new strategy in the divine redemptive mission that takes the old "promised land" out of the picture, commissions his close followers to begin a "good news" blitz to the nations, and changes all the rules of the game by dying in pain and shame—in order to be reborn in power and hope.

"The time has come. The kingdom of God is near. Repent and believe the good news!" (Mark 1:15)

Discussion Points

- Why do the literary categories of "teachings" and "biography" fail to fully account for the genre of the gospels? How is the designation "Christian proclamation" more fitting?
- What are the "Synoptic" gospels, and why are they called that? What is the basic outline of the teachings and life of Jesus as developed by the Synoptics?
- What was the origin of the Gospel of Mark, according to sources in the early Church? How does that background inform us about Mark's emphases when writing the gospel?
- What are the dominant themes found in the Gospel of Mark? How are these reiterated and emphasized?
- What might be the relevance of the title "Son of God," given by Mark to Jesus at the beginning of the gospel? How might this find correspondence to the testimony of the Roman centurion at the crucifixion of Jesus?
- Why does the ending of the gospel provoke questions about its adequacy? What explanations might be given to this apparent "problem?"

For Further Investigation

Edwards, James R. (Grand Rapids: Eerdmans, 2001). *The Gospel According to Mark*.

Lane, William. (Grand Rapids: Eerdmans, 1974). *The Gospel of Mark*.

26.

The Gospel Quartet (2)

Matthew's Jewish Harmony

When the gospels according to Mark and Matthew are placed side by side, it is very obvious that there is a strong literary dependence between them. Approximately 90 percent of the material in Mark's gospel shows up in Matthew's gospel. There are many good reasons to believe that Matthew used Mark's material in developing his own homiletic testimony about Jesus—editing a number of forms and expressions to make them come out more polished, altering terms (like the "Kingdom of God" to "Kingdom of Heaven") to fit a different audience, adding teachings and incidents that expand upon Mark's rudimentary offerings, regrouping certain materials to collect them into more memorably themed sections, and providing additional personal details in the conclusion.

A Gospel for the Jews

Whatever the reasons, the result expands the amount of teachings from Jesus that are made available to the Church. Also, a second gospel provides a fuller picture of who Jesus was, and

Figure 26.1 The Via Maris
(The Way by the Sea).

The "Synoptic Problem"

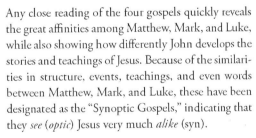

Any close reading of the four gospels quickly reveals the great affinities among Matthew, Mark, and Luke, while also showing how differently John develops the stories and teachings of Jesus. Because of the similarities in structure, events, teachings, and even words between Matthew, Mark, and Luke, these have been designated as the "Synoptic Gospels," indicating that they *see* (*optic*) Jesus very much *alike* (syn).

Of course, this awareness leads to speculations about what relationships of dependence or priority there might be among these three. The dominant theory holds that Mark's gospel came first, and was used significantly by both Matthew and Luke when they later penned their proclamations about Jesus for differing social communities. Often, a second major source, "Q" (from the German term *quelle*, meaning "source"), is posited, with the suggestion that Matthew and Luke may have drawn on this document for other materials which are not contained in Mark. No reference to this imaginary proto-gospel is found among early Church writings, and no manuscripts or fragments of it have been discovered.

what he did, simply because it highlights his activities and teachings from another angle. Most importantly, through Matthew's account, the specific needs of Jewish Christians were addressed. This was critical because the first century A.D. was a time in which the people of God were moving from the ethnic, geographic, and cultic parameters surrounding the mission of Yahweh through Israel, to becoming the expanding missionary enterprise of the New Testament Church. Matthew's gospel ties together both the past of Israel's Sinai Covenant identity and the Christian Church's Jesus identity. Both express the single divine mission which remains unchanged from Abraham's first encounters with God. What is now different is the new strategy by which the Creator will reengage the world.

By way of internal evidence alone, it is clear that the author of this gospel was Jewish: he was certainly well versed in customs and beliefs that were the cultural and religious rites of these heirs of Israel. Moreover, the author had a good education, for his use of the Greek language is more polished than that of Mark, and he quotes the Old Testament extensively, in both its Septuagint and Hebrew Bible versions.

Early Christian testimony declared that this gospel was written by Matthew, one of Jesus' disciples, and that it was produced during his pastoral work among the Jewish Christians of Syria. One small historical note, which certainly supports this theory, is that Matthew's gospel was first quoted by Ignatius of Antioch around 115 A.D. Antioch was the capital of Syria, and the place where Matthew based his ministry. It would make sense that if Matthew wrote this gospel in Antioch, it would be first noticed and quoted there.

As with John Mark, Matthew was known also by two names: *Levi*, probably reflecting his tribal background (Mark 2:14; Luke 5:27–28), and *Matthew*, a Greek transcription of the Hebrew name meaning "gift of Yahweh." (Matthew 9:9). Matthew is identified as a "tax collector," who sat at a booth in Capernaum (Luke 5:27–28). This seaside town was the regional customs center for trade passing along the *Via Maris* ("the Way of the Sea"), the major commercial route from India to Egypt. It is likely that Matthew was from a family of at least moderate means, particularly since he was able to host a large crowd for a banquet at his home (Luke 5:29).

While built upon Mark's earlier gospel manuscript, Matthew's expansion includes the birth narratives of chapters 1–2, extensive inserts of Jesus' teaching material ("the Sermon on the Mount" in chapters 5–7, missionary teachings in 10, kingdom parables in 13, instructions about the Church community in 18, and the eschatological discourses of chapters 24–25), and a more fully developed conclusion (chapter 28). Our first glimpse of Jesus through this gospel's lens clearly connects Jesus with the Jewish community (Matthew 1:1–17). Jesus

Various other theories of mutual influence have also been asserted:

- Some declare the priority of Matthew, with both Mark and Luke borrowing from its pages
- Others suggest that Mark came first, but both Matthew and Luke used independent sources (other than "Q") along with their dominant reliance on Mark
- There are also explanations that believe all three have had mutual impacts on one another

Still, the most prevalent explanation for the similarities among Matthew, Mark, and Luke begins with Mark as the lead gospel, with both Matthew and Luke making extensive use of it, even while they brought other materials into their amplified versions.

is identified as a son of David and a son of Abraham. The link with Abraham ties Jesus to the unique covenantal community of Old Testament Israel, and all of the religious and missional implications that it carries. The filial relationship with David identifies Jesus as royal stock, and forms the basis for the many references in the gospel to consider Jesus as the true king of Israel or the Jews, based upon the eternal promise of Yahweh in 2 Samuel 7. Both of these themes are more fully developed throughout the gospel as a whole.

Although it might seem strange to begin the story of Jesus in a cemetery, reviewing genealogical tables (Matthew 1:1–17), Matthew turns this unusual prologue into a fine homiletic art. Since there are no numerals in the Hebrew language, letters stand in for numbers when communicating quantities. When added together, the arithmetical values attributed to the characters found in David's name equal fourteen. Matthew uses fourteen as a reference when defining the movement of salvation history. He counts out fourteen generations from Abraham to David, fourteen more from David to the exile, and another fourteen from the exile to Jesus' birth. In so doing, even though he has to elide some generations together, Matthew declares that the very flow of Israel's existence gives evidence that God was about to do something extraordinary, and of great redemptive significance. In other words, Jesus' coming as Messiah was heralded by the very insistence of time itself. Furthermore, whatever God was doing on this anticipated occasion required double-dipping into the resources of heaven, for "Jesus" is actually the *thirteenth* name of the third set of fourteen generations, with the additional name "the Christ" completing the count for this category. Putting it all together, according to Matthew, history itself tells us that

God is going to act in powerful ways once again, and the double nature of Jesus-as-the-Christ explains the uniquely potent dimension of this next great revelation. In symbolic communication, Matthew insists that we know Jesus to be both human ("Jesus") and divine ("the Christ").

The Messiah King Who Relives Israel's Existence

Next, Matthew gets into the birth narrative itself. Immediately, he brings a further insight, declaring that Jesus, like Isaac, Samson and Samuel, is a divinely sent deliverer (Matthew 1:18–25). Each of these great figures in Israel's history was miraculously born to mothers who were barren, and all of them provided new hope for their families and also the whole of the people of Yahweh. As with those earlier stories, here an angelic messenger explains the matter to one of the soon-to-be parents (Joseph), and provides a name for the child. Even more significant, in this case, Jesus will be recognized as both a local *and* a global ruler from birth. "He will save his people," says the angel. But then, almost immediately, foreign dignitaries (the Magi of Matthew 2:1–12) follow an internationally available heavenly sign, seeking a king who is *of* the Jews, but who also serves as a beacon to the nations.

Matthew then does a quick-step through a variety of incidents in Jesus' early life to reveal even more about the essential character of this unique lad. Jesus, Matthew makes clear, is actually destined to replay or relive the life of Israel in a host of dimensions:

Jesus copies Israel's miraculous existence and purpose, born through divine intervention as savior of nations (1:18–25).

He is spared from the murderous intents of a scheming king (2:3-8), who goes on to slaughter the innocents (2:16–18), just as Moses was delivered in Exodus 2 while many Israelite boys were slaughtered.

Like the nation as a whole, Jesus is gathered out of Egypt (2:15).

From his earliest days, he is dedicated to a divine mission (thus the play on the words "Nazirite" and "Nazarene" in 2:23).

His ministry is set in motion by passing through waters (3), right at the same spot where Israel crossed the Jordan River in order to begin its witness to the nations from the Promised Land.

Jesus also wanders in the wilderness for forty days (4:1–11) before he can fully assume his adult responsibilities, mirroring Israel's traumatic forty years described in the book of Numbers.

As Matthew brings these quick comparisons to a close, he relates that Jesus goes up on a mountain (Matthew 5:1), and from that vantage point restates and reinterprets the Law or Covenant as it was previously mediated through Moses (note the content of Matthew 5–7, particularly as most major points of the original Sinai Covenant are reiterated, renewed, and reinterpreted). What has come to be known as the "Sermon on the Mount" is deliberately cast by Matthew in a manner which identifies Jesus as the new Moses for a new age.

Following Mark's pattern, Matthew's large outline for unfolding the life and teachings of Jesus has three significant parts:

- 1–16 Jesus teaches the crowds about the kingdom
  - ◊ 17 *Transitional Event*—the Transfiguration
- 17–20 Jesus teaches the disciples about discipleship
  - ◊ 21 *Transitional Event*—entry into Jerusalem
- 21–28 Jesus moves through the Passion to his coronation

A New Moses

But superimposed on this basic development is a second, more subtle arrangement of materials. Since Matthew wants us to know that Jesus is the new Moses who delivers the covenant documents for a new age, he presents the narratives and teachings of Jesus in what is sometimes called a "Five Books of the Law" structure:

Prologue: Jesus identifies with Israel and the world (1–3)
Book #1—**Narrative**: *Preaching and healing in Galilee* (4)—Look! Messiah has come!
       Discourse: *Sermon on the Mount* (5–7)—Listen! Messiah speaks a new world order!
Book #2—**Narrative**: *Mighty works, especially healings* (8–9:34)—Look! This is the one to follow!
       Discourse: *Mission of the Disciples* (9:35–10:42)—Listen! This is the message of hope for all!
Book #3—**Narrative**: *Rejection of Jesus* (11–12)—Look! People are becoming divided about Jesus!
       Discourse: *Parables about the Kingdom* (13)—Listen! The Kingdom brings division!
Book #4—**Narrative**: *Founding of the Church* (14–17)—Look! Here is what the Church is about!
       Discourse: *Teachings about the Church* (18)—Listen! This is how the Church functions!
Book #5—**Narrative**: *Travels from Galilee to Jerusalem* (19–22)—Look! We are on the way to the end!
       Discourse: *Eschatological Teachings* (23–25)—Listen! This is how we prepare for the end!
Epilogue: Jesus identified as global Messiah King (26–28)

Each of these "books" concludes with a similar declaration (7:28; 11:1; 13:53; 19:1; 26:1), noting that Jesus has finished teaching in a particular place or about a certain topic. The implication is simple and direct—Jesus has come to carry out the mission of Yahweh, first initiated with Israel, in a new way for a new, messianic age.

The Return of the King

The theme of Jesus' royal identity is consistently emphasized throughout Matthew's gospel, with a slightly different nuance than that found in Mark's gospel. For Mark, who was publishing the preaching of Peter in Rome during the crisis of Nero's persecution, Jesus was declared to be the mighty ruler who alone had the resources to defy and deny dehumanizing oppression in whatever form it challenged. In this way, Mark deliberately shows Jesus to be the only real alternative to the brutish power of the Roman Caesar. That is why even a Roman centurion could make the last and greatest testimony in the gospel, declaring Jesus' preferred rule over that of the might of Rome.

For Matthew, however, Jesus' kingship and kingdom are rooted directly in the Covenant Yahweh made with David in 2 Samuel 7. In that passage, the themes of God's house and David's house come together in powerful symmetry. David wished to build a house for God, since Israel was now settled in the Promised Land. While God appreciated this appropriate desire on David's part, through the prophet Nathan, God communicated that it would be David's son, a man of peace, who would take up that honor and responsibility. But because David's heart and desires were in the right place, God made a return commitment to him. God would build a royal house out of David's descendants, and there would always be one of his sons ruling as king over God's people.

This promise began well, with the amazingly successful reign of Solomon. The great Temple was built, the borders of the kingdom were expanded from Mesopotamia to Egypt, the economy soared, and people flooded to Jerusalem from all over the world to hear the wisdom of Solomon and experience the blessings of Yahweh. Then it all began to falter. Solomon's massive empire was split at his death (922 B.C.), and the family successors who ruled the truncated kingdom from Jerusalem were a mixed lot with varying degrees of success in both politics and religion. By the end of Matthew's second set of fourteen generations, only a remnant of the people remained to be deported in the cataclysmic Babylonian exile. Fewer still returned to Jerusalem later under Persian rule, and they were not permitted to reinstall David's descendants to a self-governing throne. Only recently, through the Maccabean revolt, had a measure of Jewish self-determination been regained. But David's family was not on the throne.

Now, however, Matthew makes it clear that this miraculously born deliverer, Jesus, is indeed the one who will fulfill—both at this time and forever—God's commitment to David. Matthew communicates powerfully in the opening chapters of the gospel, when he links Jesus to David, and in chapter 2, when the Magi question King Herod's authority as the "King of the Jews." But the biggest statement of Jesus' kingly status takes place a bit later in the gospel, when Matthew narrates Jesus' entry into Jerusalem (chapter 21).

Upon Jesus' arrival at the capital city of ancient Israel and modern Judaea, he is welcomed as king. The crowds immediately and publicly connect Jesus to David's royal family (21:9) and give him a royal salute. Furthermore, when Jesus enters the city, he moves directly to the Temple. This, of course, is "God's House," the dwelling of Yahweh on earth. It is the permanent replication of what the Tabernacle had been throughout Israel's wilderness wanderings. Just as when that portable structure had been dedicated by Moses, and the glory of God swooshed in as Yahweh took up residence (Exodus 40), so the same had happened while Solomon dedicated the first Temple (1 Kings 8). But a vision later recorded by the prophet Ezekiel announced the awful portent that the glory of God was leaving the Temple, and that God had gone back to heaven, moving out of Israel's neighborhood (Ezekiel 9–10).

It was Yahweh leaving "God's House" that precipitated the Babylonian destruction of Jerusalem and the Temple, and initiated the years of Jewish exile and captivity. When Cyrus of the Persians issued an edict sending the exiles back to Jerusalem, they rebuilt the Temple on a small scale with their modest resources. But the glory of God never returned to the rebuilt Temple. During the times of the prophet Malachi, around 400 B.C., the people were still pleading with God to return and take up residence with them again (Malachi 3-4).

It is this history that Matthew draws upon, as he marks the steps of Jesus entering Jerusalem. Jesus goes directly to the Temple, the house of God, and by implication, his own house *as* God. He cleans the place, a task that only the owner of the house can authorize (Matthew 21:12-13). There, Jesus receives his kingdom subjects who need royal favors—the blind and the lame (Matthew 21:14). While Jesus is holding royal court, he is also presented with an impromptu concert from the most trusting stakeholders in his realm: the children (Matthew 21:15). When the "chief priests" (i.e., those who have been left in charge of God's house), chide Jesus for inappropriately seeming to take over, Jesus quotes Psalm 8 as if it were his own, to verify the correctness of these happenings (Matthew 21:16). Jesus is king. Jesus is the eternal ruler who has a right to sit on the throne of David, fulfilling the covenant Yahweh made with him. Jesus is the obvious resident of Israel's royal palace.

But just as Mark ominously notes in his narrative, these tenants have no use for Jesus, and do not want him to disturb their hold on power and territory. A few verses later, Jesus' authority is directly questioned (Matthew 21:23-27), within the very Temple courts themselves. In response, Jesus tells two parables (Matthew 21:28-46), each of which declares the horrible things that are about to happen because the tenants reject the royal claims of the Creator's family. Jesus is king, but this rule will not be won easily. It will be gotten only through the horrible death that Jesus is about to endure.

Matthew never relents from this central message that Jesus is the last and greatest—and eternal—Son of David. Before the crucifixion, Jesus is identified openly as king at least four different times (Matthew 27:1-44). When Jesus dies, the curtain of the Temple, which marked Yahweh's hidden quarters and separated God from the people, is torn away, so that the place becomes ceremonially dysfunctional (Matthew 27:51); Israel's ruler must move out of this particular residence. Even the earth itself heaves and groans in the seismic religious shift that is taking place between the old and new forms of the covenant mission of Yahweh (Matthew 27:52).

As Matthew brings his preaching about Jesus to a close, he emphasizes Jesus' kingship one more time. The last words of Jesus in the gospel are a royal declaration and commission. Jesus, the risen king, addresses his key leaders, the ones who will take the mission of Yahweh to the world (Matthew 28:18-20), and says to them: "All authority in heaven and on earth has been given to me. Therefore go and make disciples of all nations, baptizing them in the name of the Father and of the Son and of the Holy Spirit, and teaching them to obey everything I have commanded you. And surely I am with you always, to the very end of the age."

History itself predicted that Yahweh, the God of Israel, was about to do something really big, says Matthew (1:1-17). As Yahweh has done in the past, now again he raises up a miraculously born and commissioned savior (1:18-25). This time, the deliverer is announced as King of God's people with global impact (2:1-23), and his own life circumstances parallel and replay Israel's own existence. When he rises up as leader (4), the old Covenant is confirmed and updated (5-7). Then, embarking on a deliberate campaign to reclaim his throne (7-21), this

Son of David is challenged on all fronts (22–27). By overcoming death itself, Jesus claims "all authority," and reinvigorates the divine mission begun with Abraham. "Go and make disciples of all nations ... "

The King has come! Long live the King!

Discussion Points

- How does Matthew use the opening chapters of his gospel to show the parallels between Jesus' life and Israel's history? What message would this convey to Jews living in Matthew's time?
- Find instances in Jesus' "Sermon on the Mount" (Matthew 5–7) where the Sinai Covenant is referenced. How does Jesus deal with the commandments and ordinances of the Mosaic Law, and what does this say about Jesus' self-identity, as Matthew portrays it?
- How is Jesus identified as "king" throughout Matthew's gospel? What impact might this have had on the Jewish community of Matthew's time?
- Why would Matthew consistently use the term "Kingdom of Heaven" instead of "Kingdom of God," as is typical in the other gospels?
- How does Matthew's recounting of Jesus' arrival in Jerusalem, on what has come to be known as Palm Sunday, show a slightly different emphasis from that given to the events by Mark? What is the important message Matthew is attempting to communicate?
- How does the additional layering of literary structure subtly reiterate the overt message regarding Jesus that Matthew puts forward?
- How is the uniquely Jewish-focused audience of Matthew's gospel clearly in mind when the story of Jesus' resurrection is told (Matthew 28)?

For Further Investigation

Blomberg, Craig L. (Nashville: Holman, 1992). *Matthew*.

France, R. T. (Downers Grove: InterVarsity, 2007). *The Gospel of Matthew*.

27.

The Gospel Quartet (3)

Luke's Gentile Counterpoint

I f the portrait of Jesus in Mark's gospel is that of the Son of God who arrives with great authority to overcome all other powers that demean, demoralize, demonize, dehumanize and diminish, and the portrait of Jesus in Matthew's gospel is that of the Messiah King who fulfills Old Testament prophecy, relives the life of Israel, teaches the life of discipleship, and rises to rule over all nations, the gospel of Luke expands these themes for a more specifically Gentile Christian audience. Luke indicates in his introduction (Luke 1:1–4) that he spent time with eyewitnesses of Jesus' life and ministry in order to gain additional knowledge beyond that which was otherwise available through the oral traditions of the apostles and the written proclamations of Mark's gospel.

Who Is Luke?

As with the other gospels, putting Luke's name to it as author is a bit of a detective search, coupled with a reliance on the testimony of early Christian sources. From the gospel itself, we

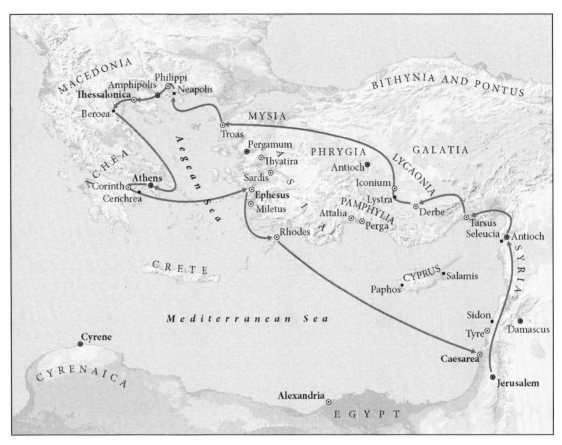

Figure 27.1 Paul's second mission journey

become aware that the author is certainly well educated. He uses excellent literary Greek style and vocabulary, he knows history and current affairs, he is aware of geography and distances in travel, and he understands social customs in various places. He is also curious, and pursues investigative research because he believes that knowledge is a source of wisdom and insight. More than that, the author of this gospel shows a special interest in the sick and the culturally marginalized. More than any of the other gospels, this one resonates with moments when Jesus sees those who have been turned out by polite society, and shows how they matter greatly to God.

The introductions to both this gospel (Luke 1:1–4) and the Acts of the Apostles (Acts 1:1–2) affirm their common authorship. Moreover, when probing who this writer was, and where he came from, there is a revealing testimony in Acts 16:6–12.

> Paul and *his* companions traveled throughout the region of Phrygia and Galatia, having been kept by the Holy Spirit from preaching the word in the province of Asia. When *they* came to the border of Mysia, *they* tried to enter Bithynia, but the Spirit of Jesus would not allow *them* to. So *they* passed by Mysia and went down to Troas. During the night Paul had a vision of a man of Macedonia standing and begging him, "Come over to Macedonia and help us."

> After Paul had seen the vision, *we* got ready at once to leave for Macedonia, concluding that God had called *us* to preach the gospel to them. From Troas *we* put out to sea and sailed straight for Samothrace, and the next day on to Neapolis. From there *we* traveled to Philippi, a Roman colony and the leading city of that district of Macedonia. And *we* stayed there several days. (Italics added)

From a literary standpoint, what is interesting about this paragraph, besides the actual details of the travel itinerary, is the change in person from third to first as the narrative moves from beginning to end. It starts with a description of what Paul and his companions were doing, and how they got to Troas. But when this missionary troupe leaves that city, suddenly the narrative becomes personal: "we" traveled on to Macedonia because God had called "us" to preach there.

This indicates that the author of the book of Acts (and thereby the gospel of Luke) was someone living in Troas, who joined Paul's missionary tour from that city. Other notes from Paul's letters and testimony from the early Church indicate that this "someone" was Luke, a doctor who may well have been called in to treat Paul for a recurrent malady. In Colossians 4:14, Paul called Luke "our dear friend … the doctor," and in the greetings of Philemon 24–25, Luke is listed as one of Paul's "fellow workers."

Because many doctors in that world started their professions as slaves who functioned as assistant apprentices to other doctors, some have speculated that this may also have been Luke's background. It might help explain his constant attention to the oppressed social outcasts encountered by Jesus. Some legends also tell of Luke's painting skills, but like other tidbits of information we might glean, this is at best speculation.

If we note the first-person testimony as it dips in and out of the narrative of the book of Acts, we find that Luke is with Paul when Paul makes his final visit to Jerusalem (Acts 21:17), around mid-54 A.D. Then, when Paul finally sets sail from Palestine to Rome, two years later, Luke again identifies himself as a member of the traveling group (Acts 27:1). These years, when Paul is in Palestine under arrest, would likely be the occasion during which Luke was able to interview those who knew Jesus personally.

How Is Luke's Gospel Shaped?

As with Matthew's gospel, Luke's is also clearly built upon Mark's gospel, and has the same broad outline of Jesus' activities and teachings. Luke's use of Mark is much more selective than was Matthew's, however. Only about 55 percent of the Markan text is incorporated into Luke's gospel, and it comes mainly in three sections:

- 3:1–6:1 (John the Baptist, temptations, call of disciples)
- 8:4–9:50 (teachings, healings, sending disciples out)
- 18:15–24:11 (teaching, Jerusalem entry, the Passion)

Interestingly, there are two sections of Mark's gospel that are not used by Luke:

- The "Big Omission": Mark 6:45–8:26 (teachings and healings)
- The "Little Omission": Mark 9:41–10:12 (teaching on causing others to sin, and on divorce)

While it would be interesting to know why Luke made these selections as he prepared his own version of the story and teachings of Jesus, such information is not available to us. At the same time, there are considerable portions of text that are unique to Luke's proclamation of Jesus, including these:

First, in a personal introductory note, Luke speaks to his specific intended audience, a man called Theophilus. While this is likely the official name of an actual individual, it is also possible that the term was a nickname or pseudonym for a person whom Luke wanted to protect, because he was in a position of government leadership that could be compromised if he was found to be associating with this suspiciously regarded branch of Judaism. "Theophilus" might also be a generic term used to indicate Christians generally, since it means "God's friend." In any case, this person appears to be a recent Gentile convert to Christian beliefs, possibly through Paul's preaching on one of the mission journeys where Luke was a partner. The designation "most excellent" (Luke 1:3) was often used as a formal manner of address for Roman officials, and this may indicate that Theophilus was a local or regional ruler.

As does Matthew, Luke also augments Mark's narrative with birth stories (Luke 1–2). Luke not only tells us about Jesus' miraculous appearance, but also shares the earlier events that precipitated his cousin John's divinely initiated conception. Together, these things focus on the preparation that took place to ensure Jesus' appropriate arrival and setting. Luke wants us to know that Jesus came into this world with a divine mandate and under heaven's clear planning and purpose. With great drama the stories unfold, accompanied by the marvelous songs of Mary, Zechariah, and Simeon, all of whom speak of the reversal of fortune that will be brought about by this wonderful act of God.

Luke ties the events of Jesus' life directly to historical circumstances in the greater Roman world. He reports that Jesus' birth occurred during the reign of Caesar Augustus and the governorship of Quirinius (Luke 2:1–2). Later, he mentions that the beginnings of Jesus' ministry took place in the fifteenth year of Tiberius Caesar's rule (Luke 3:1). The connection with Caesar Augustus is particularly striking, since Augustus was the great ruler who brought

> Storytellers: Jesus and Luke
>
> Luke loved the stories and parables of Jesus and was himself a great storyteller ... Our understanding of Jesus' life and ministry would be much impoverished if we did not have the gospel of Luke. Only in this gospel do we find these stories:
>
> - Two miraculous births (1–2)
> - Jesus in the Temple at the age of 13 (3)
> - Jesus' "Homecoming" in Nazareth at the start of his ministry career and fame (4)
> - The Good Samaritan (10)
> - The Rich Fool (12)
> - The Lost Sheep, Lost Coin, Lost Son (15)
> - The Clever Steward (16)
> - The Rich Man and Lazarus (16)
> - The Ten Lepers (17)
> - The Pharisee and the Tax Collector (18)
> - Zaccheus (19)

about the *Pax Romana*, the peace of Rome. Luke makes evident, particularly through the song of the angels to the shepherds, that even in those times of relative international calm, the greater gift of divine peace was needed by humankind, and could be brought only through Jesus.

Also unique to Luke's presentation is the strong emphasis on worship and song and prayer. The gospel itself begins and ends in the Temple, where people are gathered for times of public devotion. At the coming of Jesus, a number of songs are sung (by Mary, Zechariah, the angels, and Simeon). Prayer also forms a key element of Jesus' teachings, with an even greater emphasis brought to it than noted by Mark (see especially Luke 11:1–13).

Perhaps the most striking and clearly Lukan focus in conveying the message about Jesus is his recognition that God has special care for the poor (noted in Mary's song, identified in the offering brought by Joseph and Mary at Jesus' circumcision, asserted through the record of Jesus' pronouncements of woes on the rich and blessings on the poor, and insinuated in the story of Lazarus and the Rich Man), the sick (notably the number of demon-possessed who are healed by Jesus, and also the lepers who are cleansed and the paralyzed who are restored to mobility), the marginalized (shepherds, children, tax collectors, prostitutes, Samaritans, and the blind), and women (Mary, Elizabeth, widows, the hemorrhaging woman, Mary and Martha, and the crippled woman).

At the close of his gospel, Luke brings one more unique and representative story (Luke 24:13–35). Two people are walking away from Jerusalem after the terrible events of Jesus' crucifixion. Suddenly, they are joined by a man who seems familiar and yet remains a stranger. As they review the sad story of recent days, their fellow traveler, whom Luke has

The Songs of Jesus' Birth

Jesus' mother Mary sings:

My soul praises the Lord
and my spirit rejoices in God my Savior,
for he has been mindful of the humble state of his
servant.

From now on all generations will call me blessed,
for the Mighty One has done great things for me—
holy is his name.

His mercy extends to those who fear him,
From generation to generation.

He has performed mighty deeds with his arm;
he has scattered those who are proud in their inmost
thoughts.

He has brought down rulers from their thrones
but has lifted up the humble.

He has filled the hungry with good things
But has sent the rich away empty.

He has helped his servant Israel,
Remembering to be merciful to Abraham and his
descendants forever,

Even as he said to our father. (Luke 1:46–55)

Jesus' uncle Zechariah sings:

Praise be the Lord, the God of Israel,
because he has come and has redeemed his people.
He has raised up a horn of salvation for us in the
house of his servant David
(as he said through his holy prophets of long ago),
salvation from our enemies and from the hand of
all who hate us—

to show mercy to our fathers
and to remember his holy covenant,
the oath he swore to our father Abraham:
to rescue us from the hand of our enemies,
and enable us to serve him without fear
in holiness and righteousness before him all our days.

And you, my child, will be called a prophet of the
Most High;

for you will go on before the Lord to prepare the way for him,

to give his people the knowledge of salvation through the forgiveness of their sins,

because of the tender mercy of our God,

by which the rising sun will come to us from heaven

to shine on those living in darkness and in the shadow of death,

to guide our feet into the path of peace. (Luke 1:68–79)

The angels sing:

Glory to God in the highest,

and on earth peace to men on whom his favor rests. (Luke 2:14)

Old man Simeon sings:

Sovereign Lord, as you have promised, you now dismiss your servant in peace.

for my eyes have seen your salvation, which you have prepared in the sight of all people,

a light for revelation to the Gentiles and for glory to your people Israel. (Luke 2:29–32)

told us is actually the resurrected Jesus, begins to call their attention to the promises of the Old Testament, which somehow illumine both the life of their friend and the recent events that have troubled them. Then, when they enter their village of Emmaus, these two travelers urge Jesus to take a meal and hospitality with them. During time together, while Jesus blesses the bread, they suddenly recognize him, and he disappears. The two quickly retrace their steps to Jerusalem, scurrying to tell the news that they have seen the risen Jesus. Their message is heard with joy by the other disciples, of course.

Luke seems to have a particular reason for including this tale at the end of his gospel. How would those who were not privileged to live in Palestine during Jesus' days on earth (like Luke himself, or Luke's friend Theophilus, to whom this gospel was addressed), ever encounter Jesus? Luke could answer that question from his own experiences: he had found himself seeing Jesus in one special location—the Church and its ministries. When the congregation met together to reenact the Last Supper of Jesus with his disciples, Jesus himself was present among them in his postresurrection, spiritual form. If Luke or Theophilus or any other person wished to see Jesus these days, the place to find him was in the Church. So it was important for Luke to conclude his gospel with this memorable story. It is a clear indicator of the great truth needed in this new, messianic age: Jesus could still be found in the Church's breaking of the bread.

What Does Luke Want Us to Know About Jesus?

Our first glimpse of Jesus in Luke's gospel is the heaven-heralded Savior, born in a miraculous way to the poor, and announced to the poor (Luke 2). Our first impressions of Jesus reveal the common pedigree he shares with those around him, which makes him one of us in the whole human race (Luke 3:23–38; note the different way that Luke and Matthew handle Jesus' genealogies), his unusual gifts as a teacher (Luke 2:41–52), and his miraculous healing abilities (Luke 4–5). As with the other Synoptics, Mark and Matthew, Luke tells the big-picture story of Jesus' life in three major sections:

- 2–9 Jesus heals, as evidence of the Kingdom of God
  - ◊ 9 *Transitional Event*—the Transfiguration
- 9–19 Jesus teaches the meaning of discipleship
  - ◊ 19 *Transitional Event*—entry into Jerusalem
- 20–24 Jesus teaches through self-sacrifice, and heals even death

But just like Matthew overlaid this general movement with a more specific subtle paradigm, so Luke builds a traveling motif into both this volume and the book of Acts. Here, Jesus moves toward Jerusalem as the culmination of his ministry. In Acts, Paul makes a very similar journey toward the capital city in Palestine that serves to climax his missionary efforts. Luke's additional emphasis in the gospel looks something like this:

- 2–9 Jesus' northern ministry of healing
  - ◊ 9:51–62 *Transitional Event*—the road to Jerusalem and the cross
- 10–19 Jesus' journey and ministry of teaching
  - ◊ 19 *Transitional Event*—entry into Jerusalem
- 20–24 Teaching and healing come together in Jesus' own experience

> ### The Genealogy of Jesus
>
> Both Matthew (1:1–17) and Luke (3:23–38) provide genealogies tracing the family of Jesus back into the distant past. But their reasons for these ancestor trees are somewhat different. Matthew wishes to show his fellow Jews that Jesus is the Messiah promised as a fulfillment and culmination of the great covenants made by Yahweh with Abram (Genesis 12–17), and with David (2 Samuel 7). In this way, Matthew emphasizes Jesus' connectedness with the specially called people of God, Israel, and their survivors—the Jews.
>
> As a non-Jew writing to other gentiles, Luke wants to emphasize Jesus' participation in the life of all nations. So he brings the genealogical table backward even further, beyond the era of Abraham's family, all the way back to the beginning of biblical time, when God created humanity itself. Jesus emerges from recent Jewish stock, certainly, but like all people on earth, he belongs to the one great humanity which is ultimately born of the Creator, and not limited to the culture or religion of just one tribe or nationality.
>
> These are not contradictory interpretations of Jesus. Instead, they complement one another well as the same message is given through the gospels: Jesus, the Jew, is Savior of the nations.

If Jesus' entry into Jerusalem was rather sinister in Mark's gospel (Jesus has no place, so he goes out and curses the fig tree as a sign), and a grand—but temporary—homecoming of the glory of God in Matthew's gospel, for Luke, Jesus is the humble King who enters his capital city after the successful northern campaigns. This was a common theme in the Roman world, which had seen great generals leading the legions in northern Europe, and then coming home to Rome for a Senate-declared "triumph." In Jesus' case, however, it was the people who initiated the "triumph" of Palm Sunday (Luke 21), while the leaders whipped up opposition behind the scenes until the celebration was tragically overturned on Good Friday. But this gentle Teacher, loving Physician, and benevolent King had the last word on the matter. On Easter Sunday, he came back to rule with grace and beauty, and all who knew that began to pray and worship (Luke 21).

Strong Missionary Emphasis

Perhaps because he was brought to the Christian faith through Paul's evangelistic efforts, Luke continually identifies the missional character of the gospel:

- The shepherd's mission testimony (2)
- Levi's neighborhood mission party (5)
- "Disciples" called to be "Apostles" (6)
- The Twelve sent out as missionaries (9)
- The 72 sent out as missionaries (10)
- Pharisees chided for not having mission hearts (15)
- Witness to all nations before return of Jesus (21)

Discussion Points

• How do the opening chapters of each of the Synoptic gospels give clues about the unique emphases of each? What can be learned from Luke's beginning narratives?

• How do Luke and Matthew each use the genealogical material of Joseph and Mary to locate Jesus into the story of humanity in differing ways? What are the ideas they are seeking to communicate through these family tree lists?

• What does Luke's brief introduction to the gospel tell us about his purposes for writing it? Are there any additional aspects to Luke's designs that can be learned from the opening notes of the book of Acts?

• How does Luke consistently reveal Jesus' identification with the poor in the world of his day? How is the missionary emphasis of the gospel continually communicated?

• Why does Luke highlight the story of Jesus and the two men on the road to Emmaus near the conclusion of the gospel? What lingering implications does this have for Luke's understanding of the Church and its sacraments? How does Luke's love for the worship of the Church find additional expression in the gospel?

For Further Investigation

Bailey, Kenneth E. (Downers Grove: InterVarsity, 2008). *Jesus through Middle Eastern Eyes*.
Green, Joel B. (Grand Rapids: Eerdmans, 1997). *The Gospel of Luke*.

28.

The Gospel Quartet (4)

John's *Basso Profundo*

The gospel of John is unlike any other biblical or extra-biblical writing. Since it has most literary kinship with the Synoptic gospels, in that it rehearses elements from the life and teachings of Jesus, it forms part of the "gospel quartet" of the New Testament. But even a quick read will show significant differences from these other uniquely Christian writings. First, the fourth gospel has a global philosophic introduction that places the story of Jesus in a comprehensive cosmological frame of reference. Second, it is often more cryptic in its conversational narratives than are the other gospels, making it harder to understand how or why some of these dialogues could have taken place. Third, while it acknowledges that Jesus did many miracles, the gospel of John actually reports only seven (during his public ministry), and then elevates the significance of these few by calling them "miraculous signs," and attaching to them deeper and more complex secondary meanings. Fourth, in these pages, there are extended monologues by Jesus which are both mystical and doctrinal, and that have no clear parallel to the manner of Jesus' teachings or conversations as recorded by the Synoptics. In short, the fourth gospel is a wild ride in a theme park of its own.

Yet, at the same time, this gospel is also so homey and comfortable, that elements of it are like old jeans and shirts worn easily. The Greek language, through which the text is communicated, is basic and simple, so that even beginner students can quickly read it. Many of the teachings recorded here, from the lips of Jesus, have become the inextricable metaphors and motifs by which we know him and ourselves—the *Good Shepherd*, the *Light of the World*, the *Resurrection and the Life*, the *Vine*, etc. Some of the conversations Jesus has with others are conveyed in a manner that makes us feel as if we were the only ones they were penned for, and we are always sitting next to Jesus again when we read them. Even our Christian theology and worldview has been so shaped, over the centuries, by themes from this document, that we cannot separate it from us, or imagine Christianity apart from these twenty-one chapters. The gospel according to John is a key element of biblical faith.

>
>
> Remembering:
>
> **MARK'S PORTRAIT OF JESUS**—The Son of God who arrives with great authority to overcome all other powers that demean, demoralize, demonize, dehumanize, and diminish
>
> **MATTHEW'S PORTRAIT OF JESUS**—The Messiah King who fulfills Old Testament prophecy, relives the life of Israel, teaches the life of discipleship, and rises to rule over all nations
>
> **LUKE'S PORTRAIT OF JESUS**—The wise Teacher and Healer who cares for the sick and marginalized, and brings the world to worship through the witness of the church

Who Was John?

Perplexity about its complexity extends into debates about Johannine authorship. From early church sources comes testimony that it was penned by the beloved disciple and closest friend of Jesus (Irenaeus), and that the apostle (Tertullian) who wrote it in Ephesus (Origen, Clement) as the last among the gospels (Irenaeus, Eusebius), under the urging of others, was nearing the end of his life (Clement). From within the text of the gospel, other clues confirm these perceptions:

- It was written by a Jew:
- Someone who had clear knowledge of Jewish customs (e.g., the water ceremonies on the final day of the Feast of Tabernacles in 7:37–38)
- Someone who thought in the languages and linguistic patterns of Palestinian speech, giving evidence of this in his choice of words and phrases (e.g., the dialogue with the Samaritan woman in chapter 4, particular with reference to different interpretations of ancient Israelite customs and theology)
- It was written by a Jew of Palestine:
- Someone who knew Palestinian geography firsthand (e.g., the location of the "Sheep Gate" and pool of "Bethesda" with its "five covered colonnades in chapter 5:2)
- Someone with a knowledge of festival practices in Jerusalem (e.g., the Sabbath laws in chapter 5)

- It was written by an eyewitness:
- This person knew specific topography and incident details from the travels of Jesus (e.g., the location and geographical features of Aenon in 3:23)
- It was written by a disciple of Jesus:
- The writer knew intimate and minor details of travels and events that would not likely be reported by someone who had only later researched these matters as an investigative reporter (e.g., the conversations of specific people in 1:35–51, 2:3–10, 3:1–10, 4:7–38, 5:6–8, 6:60–71, 11:1–44)
- It was written by John the Apostle, the beloved disciple:
- So the text leads us to understand, from both the writer (John 13:23; 18:15–16; 19:25–27; 20:1–9, 30–31) and his own disciples (John 21:24)

At the same time, a good number of scholars do not believe this John wrote the gospel. There seems to be, they say, historical confusion about several different possible Johns (the apostle, the evangelist, the elder), and the variety of different ways in which the obviously edited text reached its final form. While these conversations continue with great energy, it is still widely recognized that there is a very close link between this gospel and Jesus' disciple, John; however issues of authorship might one day be resolved.

How Is the Gospel Shaped?

Although its development is markedly different from that of the Synoptic gospels, there is a very clear pattern to John's portrayal of Jesus' activities and teachings in this gospel. When reading straight through the document, one notices

---

A Possible Chronology of John's Life

–Raised in a moderately wealthy fish merchant home in Capernaum (5–30 A.D.)
–Called by Jesus to itinerant ministry (30–33 A.D.)
–Cared for Mary, Jesus' mother, in Jerusalem for eleven years (33–44 A.D.)
–Stayed on in Jerusalem sharing Church leadership (44–68 A.D.)
–Left for Ephesus when the Jerusalem Church spread (68 A.D.); possibly wrote the gospel there in the 70s
–Arrested by Domitian, tried in Rome and exiled to Patmos (82 A.D.), where he penned the book of Revelation
–Released from Patmos at Domitian's death (96 A.D.), returned to Ephesus and wrote the Epistles; most likely wrote the gospel in the late 90s
–Died sometime near 100 A.D. in Ephesus in his nineties

The Gospel of John in Broad Outline

Prologue: Re-Creation (1:1–18)
The "Book of Signs" (1:19–12:50)
  Sign #1 – Water into Wine
  Sign #2 – Nobleman's Son Raised
  Sign #3 – Man at Pool Healed
  Sign #4 – Crowds Fed
  Sign #5 – Waters Tamed
  Sign #6 – Blind Man's Eyes Opened
  Sign #7 – Lazarus Raised
The "Book of Glory" (13–20)
  Farewell Discourse
  Death and Resurrection
Epilogue (21)

several significant literary points of change. For instance, John 1:1–18 is a kind of philosophic reflection on time and space and the incarnation. Then, suddenly, at 1:19, we are brought directly into the daily life of first-century Palestine, walking among crowds who are dialoguing with John the Baptizer about his identity. Clearly, a shift of some kind takes place between 1:18 and 1:19.

The flow of life in real time continues through the next several pages, as John the Baptizer points to Jesus and then steps out of the way (1:19–36); Jesus gains a following through his miracles and teachings (1:37–12:50); and then predicts his impending death (13:1–38). What transpires next seems to move into another kind of literature once again. From chapter 14 through chapter 17, Jesus is almost lost in a last reverie, a kind of mystical intimate moment with his disciples. The monologue weaves back and forth on itself until it shoots upward toward heaven in a prayer that surrounds Jesus and his disciples in a divine blanket of engulfing holiness (17). Abruptly, the light dissolves, and with a kind of staccato journalistic pedantry, the events of Jesus' arrest, trial, death, and resurrection are recorded (18–20). Chapter 20 ends with a brief, but sufficient, conclusion to the book as a whole. Yet, suddenly another story appears, and the finality of the wrap-up in chapter 20 is broken and ignored (21). The disciples are listless and almost devoid of the power revealed when they earlier had realized that Jesus was come back to life. They now decide to go off fishing, for lack of anything better to do. But then Jesus appears, and their lives are quickly refocused so that they will be his followers to the end of their days. With that said, a second brief conclusion is offered, and the gospel is finished.

Stepping back from the whole of this narrative, and reviewing the obvious literary disjunctures or sudden stylistic shifts in gospel, it becomes apparent that a significant transition happens between chapters 12 and 13 (related to the coming of "the hour" for Jesus; note 2:4, 4:23, 7:6, 12:23, 13:1, 17:1). This pivotal point is further accentuated by the grouping of all of Jesus' "miraculous signs," as John calls them, into chapters 1–12. This is why the first part of John's gospel is often called "The Book of Signs," while the last part wears well the name "The Book of Glory," because Jesus terms it so (12:23). Bookending everything, a cryptic prologue opens the gospel (1:1–18), and an epilogue, perhaps

---

Λογος—*Logos*

The philosophic meaning of "logos" was first voiced by **Heraclitus** (c. 535–475 B.C.). He believed that our normal discourse and actions were somehow part of a larger cosmic meaning and purpose, which he identified as "logos."

Sophists like **Protagoras** (c. 490–420 B.C.) continued to link "logos" to the meaning behind our daily conversations. **Aristotle** (384–322 B.C.) declared "logos" to be reasoned discourse, and worthy of study in its own right within the field of rhetoric.

Eventually, the *Stoics*, headed by **Zeno** (c. 334–262 B.C.), explained "logos" as the divine principle that animated the whole of reality. By the first century A.D., as **John** was incorporating the term into the Prologue of his gospel, Roman writers such as **Seneca** (4 B.C.–65 A.D.) and **Epictetus** (55–135 A.D.) had popularized "logos" to mean the ultimate divine thought behind the cosmos and the energizing principle that guided things to exist as they were supposed to be and interact as they had been designed. This is the connection **John** is trying to make.

written by another party and added after the initial gospel was completed (chapter 21), brings it to a close. Each of these four sections deserves a closer look.

The gospel's unique prologue highlights several ideas. First, both Jesus and the message of Christianity are tied to the comprehensive foundational values shaping common philosophic systems of the day. "Logos," to the Greek mind, was the organizing principle giving meaning and identity to everything else. By using this term to describe Jesus, John portrays him as more than just a fine teacher who said a few nice things on a Palestinian spring afternoon. Jesus is, in fact, according to John, the very creator of all things, and the one who gives meaning to life itself. Apart from Jesus, nothing makes sense or has any intrinsic meaning.

Second, "light" and "darkness" explain everything. Right up front, John helps us think through life and values and purpose in a stark dualism that is engaged in a tug-of-war for everything and everybody. Nicodemus will come to Jesus in the darkness of night (chapter 3), only to be serenaded by Jesus' fine teachings about walking in the light. The blind man of chapter 9 is actually the only one who can truly see, according to Jesus, because all of the sighted people have darkened hearts and eyes. Judas will enter the room of the Last Supper basking in the light of the glory that surrounds Jesus (chapter 13), but when he leaves to do his dastardly deed of betrayal, the voice of the narrator ominously intones "and it was night." Evening falls as Jesus dies (chapter 19), but the floodlights of dawn rise around those who understand the power of his resurrection (chapter 20). Even in the extra story added as chapter 21, the disciples in the nighttime fishing boat are bereft of their netting talents until Jesus shows up at the crack of dawn, tells them where to find a great catch, and is recognized by them in the growing light of day and spiritual insight. Darkness, in the gospel of John, means sin, evil, and blindness and the malady of a world trying to make it on its own apart from its Creator. Light, on the other hand, symbolizes the return of life, faith, and goodness, and health and salvation and hope and the presence of God.

Third, as a corollary to these ideas, John shows us that salvation itself is a kind of re-creation. Using a deliberate word play to bind the opening of the gospel to the sentences that start Genesis, John communicates that the world once made lively by the Creator has now fallen under the deadly pall of evil, and needs to be delivered. The only way that this renewal can happen is if the Creator reinjects planet Earth with a personal and concentrated dose of the original Light by which all things were made. Although many still wander in blindness or shrink back from the light like cockroaches or rodents who have become accustomed to the inner darkness of a rotting garbage dump, those to whom sight is restored are enabled to live as children of God once again.

This leads to a fourth theme of the prologue, namely that the New Testament era is merely the Old Testament mission of God revived in a new form. Jesus, the Logos, comes to earth and "Tabernacles" among us (verse 14), just as the Creator did when covenanting with Israel, and commissioning her to become a witness to the nations. Furthermore, those who truly recognize Jesus for who he is, see in him the "glory" of the Father. This is a direct link to the *Shekinah* glory light of God that filled the Tabernacle and the Temple, announcing the divine presence. The mission of God continues, but it will now be experienced through the radiance that glows in all who are close to Jesus. The "Tabernacle" that houses the glory of the divine presence is on the move into the world through this "only begotten Son of God" (1:14) and all who become "children of God" (1:12) with and through him.

What Significance Do the "Signs" Have?

On this philosophic foundation, John organizes a very deliberately shaped encounter with Jesus. The seven "miraculous signs" of chapters 2–11 not only provide healing and hope to those who were first the objects of divine grace through Jesus, but they also dig deeper into biblical history to replay major scenes of the Old Testament in a way that reasserts the mission of God, while shifting its agency from Israel to Jesus. For instance, just as sin first disrupted the marriage of Adam and Eve in the Garden of Eden, so Jesus first displays his regenerative powers by restoring the celebration at a wedding (chapter 2). Again, while Adam and Eve mourned the loss of their son through murder brought about by sin, a new nobleman (John deliberately sets this character above national, tribal, or ethnic limitations that are otherwise used to identify all other persons in the gospel) receives back his son from the dead (chapter 4). Next, Jesus encounters a man who has been ailing for thirty-eight years (chapter 5), and who can only otherwise be healed by passing through waters that have been divinely disturbed. Interestingly, Moses, in Deuteronomy 2:14, gives the only other reference to the number thirty-eight in all of the Bible, mentioning it as the amount of time that the Israelites have been wandering in the wilderness, waiting for the shalom that can come to them only if they pass through the waters of the Jordan River, which will be divinely disturbed in order to make the crossing possible.

In this way, John continues to portray Jesus as the new agent of divine redemption, functioning in parallel to the manner in which God dealt with Israel of the Old Testament. Jesus, too, feeds the people of God in the wilderness (chapter 6) and tames the raging waters that in the darkness prevent God's people from entering the Promised Land (chapter 6). Furthermore, as Isaiah was told about the blindness of the people in his day (Isaiah 6), Jesus contends with similar dysfunctional eyes (chapter 9). And just as Ezekiel had to preach to the

---

Careful Reading of the Text

It is important to read the text of this gospel closely and carefully. In doing so, new clues to John's more subtle themes and meanings can be found. For instance, the narrative of Jesus' life begins in what we might see as an awkward compilation of meaningless references to days:

- 1:29—"the next day …"
- 1:35—"the next day …"
- 1:43—"the next day …"
- 2:1—"on the third day …"

But if we track John's calendar, and count the announcement of John the Baptizer about Jesus as the first day, the succession of daily references suddenly identifies Jesus' first miraculous sign of turning the water into wine at the wedding feast in 2:1–11 as occurring on the gospel's narrative seventh day. This, of course, is the great Sabbath of God, and the day on which God's people are supposed to rest and enjoy God's presence among them.

In other words, John subtly shows us that Jesus is himself the great blessing of God's presence, now come among us. The Sabbath has arrived!

dead nation of Israel in order to resurrect it from the grave of exile (Ezekiel 37), so Jesus brings back to life one of his dear friends who has died (chapter 11), symbolizing the ultimate goal of divine grace.

It is only when the seven signs have been published to the world in this manner, that the "Greeks" (John's notation for the whole world out there, beyond our tiny Jewish enclave) come seeking Jesus (12:21). Then, immediately, Jesus declares that his "hour" has come. Why? Because the salvation of God sent to this world (John 3:16–17) has been recognized through the signs, and has been received by the world. It has begun to make an impact, and the world will never again be merely content with darkness. Dawn is breaking.

Charted out, with intervening parallels of texts or themes, the signs look like this:

Sign & Reference	Event	Notes	O.T. Parallel	Intervening Parallels
#1 2:1–11	Water into Wine	Creation Days Paralleld	Genesis 3	Lives from Genesis
#2 4:43–54	Nobleman's Son Raised	No Ethnic Identity Given	Genesis 4	
#3 5:1–15	Man at Pool Healed	"38 years"	Deuteronomy 2:14	Lives from Exodus
#4 6:1–15	Crowds Fed	"in wilderness"	Exodus 16	
#5 6:16–21	Waters Tamed	Water Threat	Exodus 14–17 Joshua 3–4	Lives from Numbers
#6 9:1–41	Blind Man's Eyes Opened	Ejected from Synagogues	Isiah 61	Teaching of Prophets
#7 11:1–44	Lazarus Raised	"Good Shepherd"	Ezekiel 37:1–14	Then Come the Greeks

What Is the "Book of Glory" About?

Once the transition takes place from the "Book of Signs" to the "Book of Glory," only two major events happen. First, Jesus meets for an extended meal and conversation with his disciples (chapters 13–17). This lengthy monologue seems somewhat meandering and repetitive until it is viewed through the Hebrew communication lens of chiasm. Then, the "Farewell Discourse," as it is known, takes on new depth, as it weaves back and forth and climaxes in the middle. This parting exhortation becomes an obviously deeply moving instruction to Jesus' followers to remain connected to him by way of the powerful "Paraclete" (a Greek term meaning "counselor" or "advocate"), in the face of the troubling

Was Jesus' "Last Supper" a Passover Meal?

Following Mark's lead, the Synoptic gospels clearly identify the final meal that Jesus shared with his disciples as a Passover celebration. Strangely, for all the other symbolism in the fourth gospel, John clearly steers away from that connection in chapter 13. Why?

The answer appears to have several parts to it. First, John deliberately times the events of Jesus' final week so that Jesus is tried and sentenced to death on Friday morning (at the same time as the unblemished Passover lambs were being selected), and crucified during the precise hours when the Passover lambs were being slaughtered in the Temple courtyard. In this way, John accomplishes a purpose that he indicated at the beginning of his gospel, to portray Jesus as the "Lamb of God" (1:36). Thus, it is important for John *not* to identify the Last Supper as the Passover, since Jesus must die with the lambs who were being slaughtered prior to that meal.

Second, this does not immediately mean that either John or the Synoptics are telling the story wrong. Instead, there were actually several different calendars functioning among the Jews of the day, marking the celebration of the Passover with slight variations. These came into being due either to the chronological ordering of each new day (Roman: sunrise to sunrise, or Jewish: sundown to sundown), or the perceived occasion of the new moon that began the month (adjusted differently by Babylonian and Palestinian rabbis).

Thus, Jesus and his disciples probably ate a Passover meal together, as the Synoptics identify it, but one which was tied to a different calendar than that used by the bulk of the Jerusalem population. In this way, John could leverage the different schedule to communicate a particular emphasis in his portrayal of Jesus' symbolic identity.

that will come upon them because of his imminent physical departure, and the rising persecutions targeted toward them by the world that remains in darkness. In chiastic summary, the Farewell Discourse can be portrayed in this manner:

Gathering experience of unity *13:1–35*
  Prediction of disciple's denial *13:36–38*
    Jesus' departure tempered by Father's power *14:1–14*
      Promise of the "Paraclete" *14:15–24*
        Troubling encounter with the world *14:25–31*
          "Abide in Me!" teaching *15:1–17*
        Troubling encounter with the world *15:18–16:4a*
      Promise of the "Paraclete" *16:4b–15*
    Jesus' departure tempered by Father's power *16:16–28*
  Prediction of disciple's denial *16:29–33*
Departing experience of unity *17:1–26*

Every element of this "Farewell Discourse" is doubled with a parallel passage, except for Jesus' central teaching that his disciples should "abide in me." Furthermore, these parallel passages are arranged in reverse order in the second half to their initial expression in the first half. At the heart of it all comes the unparalleled vine-and-branches teaching, which functions as the chiastic center and ultimate focus of the discourse as a whole. In effect, John shows us how the transforming power of Jesus as the light of the world is to take effect. Jesus comes into this darkened world as a brilliant ray of re-creative light and life. But if he goes about his business all by himself, the light will have limited penetrating value, against the expansive and pervasive darkness that has consumed this world. So, a multiplication and amplification have to happen. Jesus himself spoke about this at the end of the "Book of Signs." He said:

> The hour has come for the Son of Man to be glorified. I tell you the truth, unless a kernel of wheat falls to the ground and dies, it remains only a single seed. But if it dies, it produces many seeds. The man who loves his life will lose it, while the man who hates his life in this world will keep it for eternal life. Whoever serves me must follow me ... (12:26)

In this chiastic "Farewell Discourse," Jesus makes clear the meaning of everything. His disciples have been transformed from darkness to light (and thus from death to life) through Jesus' incorporation of them into fellowship with himself and the Father (chapters 13 and 17). This does not free them immediately from struggles, as seen in Judas's betrayal and the coming denial of them all. But the connection between the Father and the disciples is secure, because it is initiated by the Father, and will last even when Jesus disappears from them very shortly, because the powerful "Paraclete" will arrive to dispense Jesus' ongoing presence with them all, wherever they go and in whatever circumstances they find themselves. Of course, that will only trigger further conflicts and confrontations with "the world." So (and here's the central element of the discourse), "abide in me!" Either you are with the darkness, or you are with the light. Either you are dead because of the power of the world, or you are alive in me. And, of course, if you "abide in me," you will glow with my light, and the multiplication of the seed sown will take place. Eventually, through you, the light that comes into the world through Jesus will bring light to everyone. It is a picture of the mission of God, promised to Abraham, enacted geographically through Israel, but now become a global movement through Jesus' disciples who "abide" in him through the power of the "Paraclete."

The second half of this "Book of Glory" shows Jesus as he moves through his Passion into the resurrection. While the details of Jesus' trial and crucifixion are virtually identical with those given in the Synoptic gospels, there are a number of little incidents reported that could only have been written by an eyewitness—the name of the servant of the high priest who is wounded by Peter's sword (18:10); the reason for Peter's access into the area where Jesus was being tried (18:15); the words of the conversation between Annas and Jesus (18:19–24); the transfer of Mary's care from Jesus to the beloved disciple (19:27). These are reminders again that the fourth gospel was authored by someone who was with Jesus at every turn, and remained Jesus' deep friend right through the end.

When describing the events of resurrection morning, John gives us some wonderful analogies to see its meaning on several levels. For one thing, when Mary looks into the empty tomb (20:10–12), the scene as John describes it immediately calls to mind the Ark of the Covenant that symbolized Yahweh's presence in the Tabernacle, and later the Temple. While the other gospel writers tell of angels being present, John views them through Mary Magdalene's eyes, and sees two such creatures in exactly the same position as the cherubim that stood guard over the Mercy Seat throne. This time, however, the divine presence was missing, indicating the dawning of a new age, in which the Creator's power and presence would not be confined to or limited by a particular geographic location. The second strategy in the divine mission had come, and the gospel was now to be preached to the whole world through Jesus' disciples.

Then, when Mary Magdalene weeps because she misses her "Lord" (which is the Greek version of "Yahweh"), a man appears on her periphery, and she assumes that he is "the gardener." Of course, Mary's perception is incorrect, because the man is actually Jesus. But is she really wrong? John never says that she was mistaken; only that Mary Magdalene had assumed he was the gardener. In fact, John appears to want his readers to get the subtle message that Jesus is *indeed* the gardener. After all, at the beginning of time, the Creator placed Adam and Even in a garden and came to walk and talk with them (Genesis 2). Now, in the re-creation of all things, it is quite appropriate for new life to begin anew in a garden where the great Gardener is again meandering and sharing intimacy with those who are favored friends. John confirms this symbolic intent when he tells

Jesus and His Mother

In John's gospel, Jesus' mother only appears twice, and is never called "Mary." On both occasions, Jesus addresses her as "woman," not in a condescending or demeaning manner, but as a term of respect and endearment.

In the first story told, Jesus' mother appears to be the caterer for the wedding in Cana (John 2:1–11), and enlists Jesus to replenish the supply of wine. In the second story, at the cross (John 19:25–27), Jesus passes the responsibility of care for his mother from himself as the oldest son to his best friend.

When these stories are viewed next to the imagery of Revelation 12, they seem to take on an even deeper significance. The first incident portrays Mary as the woman who gives birth to the Messiah, standing in as the representative for the whole Old Testament people of God. The second incident situates Mary as the one who comes under the care of the apostles, or symbolically assuming a role as the New Testament people of God. In this way, as with other elements of John's gospel, the mother of Jesus is both a participant in the things that happen in Jesus' life, and also a larger metaphor for the meaning of the matters being communicated.

"My Lord and My God!"

With these words of Thomas (20:28), John finalizes the link between the man Jesus and the deity worshipped by Israel in the Old Testament. Though John never gives a nativity story in which Jesus' miraculous birth is told, here he announces the full and complete incarnation; Jesus is both human (physical wounds) and divine (the acknowledgement of worship reserved otherwise only for Yahweh), and thus the true Messiah of Israel.

about Jesus speaking Mary's name. Just as Adam and Eve, along with all the animals and all elements of creation, came into being when they were named in the first beginning, so now Mary is restored to life in a new way as her identity is regenerated when Jesus speaks her name. Jesus, however, cannot be held in this garden (20:17) as partner in only one local friendship, for the process of re-creating all things is only just beginning, and he must leave to finish the task. Only when he goes, as he said in the "Farewell Discourse," will he be able to multiply his presence through the gift of the "Paraclete."

This coming of the "Paraclete" is enacted next, when Jesus meets with the rest of his disciples later that day. John tells us that he "breathed on them" (20:21), imparting to them the divine Spirit, and sending them out as his ambassadors, exactly in the manner of which he prayed in chapter 17. Is this, as some have suggested, John's different version of Pentecost (Acts 2)? No; it is a final expression of the re-creation process. Just as Adam only came alive to his life and livelihood at the beginning of time when God breathed into him the divine breath (Genesis 2), so now this tiny gathering of the new humanity cannot function until they are divinely enthused in a similar, very literal manner. The Creator who breathed the breath of life into Adam in the first creation now breathes the same breath of life into his disciples in this re-creation. The dead of the world are coming back to life!

John ends his gospel with the story of Thomas, who demands the proof of physical evidence in order to believe this good news. Although Jesus provides Thomas' requested touch, Jesus commends those others who can become reborn human creatures through faith—which is not dependent upon direct experiential contact with Jesus' physical body. In this, the missionary nature of John's gospel message is confirmed, for John ends by issuing an invitation to the same trust and belief to all who read it (20:30–31), even though they do not have opportunity to touch the physical features of Jesus.

What Is the Significance of the Epilogue?

The epilogue (chapter 21), possibly added later, does several things. First, it reveals the uncertainty that plagues the disciples and the Church, wanting to be witnesses of Jesus, but caught up in the cares and demands of the times. Second, it reaffirms the missionary character of the apostolic Church, particularly when 153 fish are caught in the disciples' net only at the instigation of Jesus (this was the number of the nations of the world as described by at least some Greek teachers of the day). Third, it provides a way for Peter to be fully restored to leadership graces, since he will become the key communicator and witness among the disciples. Fourth, it announces both Peter's early death (by crucifixion under Nero's persecution, around 65 A.D.) and John's longevity, each of which contributes in different ways to the formation of the Christian Church in the first century.

Jerome wrote that when John was a very old and feeble man living in Ephesus, he was brought each Sunday to the front of the congregation's gathering on a pallet carried by others. Invariably, John would be asked to speak a word, and just as constantly, he would raise himself on one elbow. With great effort, he would whisper out with a hoarse rasp, "Little children, love one another." When asked why he always said the same thing, he would reply that this message was enough; that it was all that was necessary.

It was during those final years of John's life, according to Jerome, that others urged him to write another gospel, in addition to the Synoptics, which were by then widely circulated and read. Since John was the last of Jesus' original disciples still living, it would be a final direct link with the One who had changed the world. So it is that we have this amazingly crafted testimony of the light and life of the world.

Discussion Points

- How does the structure of John's gospel differ significantly from that of the Synoptics? What does the literary development of the Fourth Gospel indicate about its dominant themes?
- How does the Prologue to John's gospel provide an introductory explanation of the person and character of Jesus? In what ways is this prologue linked to the early books of the Old Testament? How do the themes of the Prologue recur throughout the rest of the gospel?
- What are the seven "miraculous signs" that John relates as Jesus' key displays of divine authority? How do these relate to other incidents or concepts in the Old Testament?
- In what manner do "light" and "darkness" pervade the gospel of John as normative themes? What do they express? How do they identify moral qualities of situations or persons?

- How does the chiastic structure of Jesus' farewell discourse (John 13–17) point to its key elements for interpretation? What stands at the literary center? How do the rest of the literary elements flow out from that normative passage?
- In what ways does the gospel of John portray the salvation that Jesus brings as a kind of re-creation?
- How are Nicodemus (chapter 3) and Judas (particularly in chapter 13) reverse images of one another? What message might John be seeking to communicate through this pairing?

The Meaning of Jesus in the Gospels

The historical presence of Jesus on Earth is hard to question. The specific events of Jesus' life are less clear, but many have been attested to in the four gospels of the New Testament. More importantly, these witnesses each explore at least one significant aspect of the meaning of Jesus' coming into this world.

Matthew clearly shows Jesus to be a great deliverer of God's people, in the tradition of other miraculously born leaders scattered throughout Israel's history. Jesus finds his identity in his connection to the two great covenants that shaped Israel, the Sinai Covenant and the Covenant with David. The first provides the basis for Jesus as the one who relives the life of the nation in summary form, and the latter testifies to Jesus' identity as the great and eternal king promised in a culmination of David's royal dynasty. As Matthew remembers Jesus' teachings and miracles, he organizes them into five books, so that Jesus becomes the source of new scriptural revelation for this new age of the Church's witness and evangelism.

Mark shows Jesus to be a divine whirlwind of action and hope for a world under the oppressive dehumanization caused by evil powers. Jesus, as the "Son of God," blasts his way through, bringing freedom and healing. Because people might misinterpret what is going on, and too quickly try to crown him as local king, Jesus tries to downplay his growing popularity until the final showdown occurs in Jerusalem. Although evil forces seem to win the day, Jesus turns the world upside down through his resurrection, and nothing is ever the same again.

Luke carefully investigates the story of Jesus' life and teachings, emphasizing the miraculous character of his coming, the clarity of his teachings, the power of his healings, and the missionary witness that pervades his legacy in the church. Luke testifies that Jesus is the Savior of all people, not just the Jews, and especially of the marginalized in every society. Those who were not able to meet Jesus while he was on Earth are now able to connect with him through the Church and its liturgical practices.

John sees in Jesus the re-creation of the world. After God made this universe, it fell under the deadly contagion of sin, evil, and darkness. Rather than simply allowing it to self-destruct or be burned in cleansing judgment, God chose instead to re-create all things, sending Jesus as the advance transforming ambassador of heaven. Jesus deals with sin by serving as the ultimate Passover Lamb; with evil by undoing its historical encroachment through seven "Miraculous Signs"; and with darkness by revealing the divine glory housed in mortal flesh. He plants this glory in the dark recesses of earth through his death, so that it might spring up like a new harvest of life. Then, he binds himself to his followers with the gift of the "Paraclete," enabling them to be a spreading flame of divine light after he leaves.

Bible "Big Picture"

Covenant Making: God establishes a covenant relationship with a missional community by way of a redemptive act

Old Testament: The Exodus and Sinai Covenant

Genesis—Why is the covenant necessary?

Exodus—What is the covenant all about?

Leviticus—How does it affect daily living?

Numbers—Who is in the covenant community and why?

Deuteronomy—How long will the covenant be in force?

New Testament: The Person and Work of Jesus

Matthew—Jesus is the Messiah King who relives the life of Israel, and becomes Savior King of the Nations

Mark—Jesus is the powerful Son of God who releases people from the many evils that enslave them

Luke—Jesus is the heaven-sent Teacher and Healer who brings hope through the ministry of the church

John—Jesus is the ultimate Passover Lamb who recreates the dark world through the witness of his disciples

Covenant Living: God guides the covenant relationship with the missional community by way of authorized spokespersons

Old Testament: The Prophets, with Their Interpreted History and Sermons

Stories: The interpreted history of Israel

- *Joshua*—Possessing the Land with missional significance
- *Judges*—Nearly losing the Land through covenant failure
- *Ruth*—The model of covenant obedience that restores
- *1 & 2 Samuel*—Establishing the monarchy that might fulfill the covenant mission
- *1 & 2 Kings, 1 & 2 Chronicles*—Failure of the Old Testament covenant community mission experiment
- *Ezra and Nehemiah*—Restoring the covenant community in anticipation of Yahweh's next major act
- *Esther*—Responding to the warning that Yahweh's people have a covenant identity and purpose

Sermons: the verbal declarations of Yahweh's designs and intents

- *Isaiah*—Divine deliverance from Assyria, coming global renewal
- *Jeremiah*—Doom and gloom in Judah's final years, promises of restoration
- *Ezekiel*—God on the move, bringing judgment and promises of a new age
- *Daniel*—Struggles of faithful exilic living, plus visions of God's growing kingdom
- *Hosea*—The divine/human soap opera
- *Joel*—Hints of "the Day of the Lord" found in a locust plague
- *Amos*—Imminent divine judgment because of social covenantal disobedience
- *Obadiah*—Edom condemned for harming Judah at the time of deportation
- *Jonah*—Missionary trek to Assyrian enemy capital showing global divine favor
- *Micah*—Yahweh's faithfulness, Israel's unfaithfulness, and imminent judgment

- *Nahum*—God will destroy Assyria because of its cruelty to other nations
- *Habakkuk*—Dialogue with Yahweh on the mysteries of social sins and divine judgment
- *Zephaniah*—Brief notes on impending divine judgment and future redemptive restoration
- *Haggai*—"Let's get that Temple rebuilt!" and "God bless Zerubbabel!"
- *Zechariah*—Visions of judgment on the nations and visions of glory on restored "Israel"
- *Malachi*—Dialogues between Yahweh and the people on failures and the future

New Testament: The Apostles, with Their Ecclesiastical History and Letters

Covenant Questions: God nurtures the covenant relationship with a missional community by way of spiritual wisdom and insight

Old Testament: The Poetry and Wisdom Literature; Questions of Fundamental Human Identity as Illuminated by the Theology of the Covenant

  Job—"Why do I suffer?"
  Psalms—"How do I pray?"
  Proverbs—"What is true wisdom?"
  Ecclesiastes—"What is the meaning of life?"
  Song of Songs—"What is the meaning of love?"
  Lamentations—"What is the meaning of divine election?"

New Testament: The Comparison of the Two Covenant Expressions

For Further Investigation

Brouwer, Wayne. (Atlanta: SBL, 2001). *The Literary Development of John 13–17: A Chiastic Reading.*

Brown, Raymond E. (Garden City: Doubleday, 2003). *An Introduction to the Gospel of John.*

Carson, D. A. (Grand Rapids: Eerdmans, 1990). *The Gospel According to John.*

Köstenberger, Andreas J. (Grand Rapids: Baker, 1999). *Encountering John.*

Köstenberger, Andreas J. (Grand Rapids: Baker, 2004). *John.*

Covenant Living (2)

The Creator guides the covenant relationship with a missional
community by way of authorized spokespersons

29.

From Centripetal to Centrifugal

The New Era of the Old Divine Mission

There is something wonderfully paradoxical about the Christian Church. Its origin as a unique social phenomenon clearly dates from the Pentecost events described in Acts 2. Yet, at the same time, Jesus' disciples, who were at the center of the Church from its very beginning, would say that this "new" community of faith was simply part of a centuries-old already existing people of God, stretching back all the way to Abraham and his family. The connection between the old and the new is rooted in several theological axioms.

First, it is built upon the confession that there is a God who created this world and uniquely fashioned the human race with attributes that reflected its Maker. Second, through human willfulness, the world lost its pristine vitality, and is now caught up in a civil war against its Creator. Third, intruding directly into human affairs for the sake of reclaiming and restoring the world, the Creator began a mission of redemption and renewal through the nation of Israel. Fourth, Israel's identity as a missional community was shaped by the suzerain-vassal covenant formed at Mt. Sinai. Fifth, in order to be most effective in its witness to other nations, Israel was positioned at the crossroads of global societies, and thus received, as its "promised land," the

One Divine Mission, Two Missional Strategies

In God's initial encounter with Abram, recorded in Genesis 12, it is clear that the relationship between God and Abram was missional in character. The creator wished to "bless" all nations of the earth, but would enact that blessing through Abram and his descendants. This became the source of Israel's unique identity: bound to Yahweh through the Sinai covenant, and positioned on the great highway between the nations in the territory known as Canaan. For the mission to work, people would have to flow to and through this piece of property, and Israel would have to be the visible face of God and God's intentions.

But the world is expanding, and "Canaan" is no longer the center of civilizations. Also, the witness of Israel to the nations had become muted through historical circumstances and internal challenges. So the Creator became a creature (John 1:1–14), taught and showed and expressed the divine mission, and then initiated the Christian Church from among the people of Israel, to become an international community of witness within every culture.

What began as a centripetal force, pulling all nations into Israel's witnessing orbit, was now flung out as a centrifugal spray, invading and influencing every territory on earth.

territory known as Canaan. Sixth, the effectiveness of this divine missional strategy through Israel was most evident in the eleventh and tenth centuries B.C., during the reigns of David and Solomon, when the kingdom grew in size and influence among the peoples of the ancient Near East and beyond. Seventh, this missional witness eroded away—almost to oblivion—through a combination of internal failures and external political threats, until most of the nation of Israel was wiped out by the Assyrians, and only a remnant of the tribe of Judah (along with religious leaders from among the Levites, and a portion of the small tribe of Benjamin) retained its unique identity as the people of Yahweh. Eighth, because of the seeming inadequacy of this method of witness, as the human race expanded rapidly, the Creator revised the divine missional strategy, and interrupted human history in a very visible manner again in the person of Jesus. Ninth, Jesus embodied the divine essence, taught the divine will, and went through death and resurrection to establish a new understanding of eschatological hope, which he passed along to his followers as the message to be communicated to the nations. Tenth, Jesus' teachings about this arriving messianic age were rooted in what the prophets of Israel called the "Day of the Lord," a time when divine judgment for sins would fall on all nations (including Israel), a remnant from Israel would be spared to become the restored seed community of a new global divine initiative, and the world would be transformed as God had intended for it to be, so that people could again live out their intended purposes and destinies. Eleventh, instead of applying all aspects of this "Day of the Lord" in a single cataclysmic event, Jesus split it in two, bringing the beginnings of eternal blessings, while withholding the full impact of divine judgment for a time. Twelfth, the Christian Church is God's new agent for global missional recovery and restoration for the human race, superseding the territorially bound witness through Israel with a portable and expanding testimony influencing all nations and cultures. Thirteenth, since the "Day of the Lord" is begun, but not finished, Jesus will return again to bring its culmination. Fourteenth, the church of Jesus exists in this time between Jesus' comings as the great divine missional witness.

Each of these themes is implied or explicit in the first two chapters of the book of the Acts of the Apostles. God and sin and the divine mission are all part of the fabric of the narrative, while Israel's role in the divine mission, along with the changing strategies, is declared openly. Jesus is at the center of all these things, but the unique divine intrusion he brought into the human race is now being withdrawn, as he ascends back to heaven. Now the church must become the ongoing embodiment of Jesus' life and teachings, so that it may live out the divine mission until the remainder of the "Day of the Lord" arrives when Jesus returns.

The Structure of Acts

The book of Acts is the second of Luke's two volumes on the life and work of Jesus, presented first through his immediate person in the gospel, and now through his extended "body," the Church. There are several guiding forces that shape the way in which Luke tells this second part of Jesus' story. One of them is clearly stated by Jesus in Acts 1:8: "You will receive power when the Holy Spirit comes on you; and you will be my witnesses in Jerusalem, and in all Judaea and Samaria, and to the ends of the earth." With that in mind, Luke describes the way in which this witness emerged first in Jerusalem (chapters 2–7), then swept through Samaria (chapters 8–12), and finally began its push toward the ends of the Earth (chapters 13–28). Jesus' declaration provides the big outline of Acts.

But there are other themes that group these materials as well. For instance, because the witness of the church in Palestine was first guided by Peter, and that beyond Palestine gained its momentum from Paul, these two figures are central to the contents in each major section of Acts, in succession:

- Peter and the Jewish/Palestinian Witness (Acts 1–12)
- Paul and the Gentile/Mediterranean Witness (Acts 13–28)

This pair is often joined by other leading figures who play dominant roles in fits and spurts. We see, in Luke's unfolding narrative, a succession of key "witnesses:" Peter (1–5), Stephen (6–7), Philip (8), Saul (9), Peter (10–12), Paul and Barnabas (13–14), James (15), Paul and Silas (16–17), Paul and his companions (18–20), and Paul (21–28).

The initial organizing structure of Jesus' missional command in Acts 1:8 seems to be further developed by Luke in a clear series of Church expansions that are tracked throughout the work. Each successive wave of missional outreach is built upon the previous field of witness, but pushes the engagement one step further:

Pentecost Symbols

Sound of wind: A single word, both in the Hebrew (*ruach*) and Greek (*pneuma*) languages, serves to designate "wind," "breath," and "spirit." T hus, the sound of a rushing wind captured the attention of all who were about to breathe in the Spirit of God.

Single blaze of fire becoming multiple flames above heads: Jesus' cousin John had said that he baptized with water, but that Jesus would baptize with the Holy Spirit and with fire (Luke 1:16). This vision represented the single divine Spirit baptizing all at the same time.

- The witness to Jerusalem (2:1–6:7)
- The witness to Judaea and Samaria (6:8–9:31)
- The witness to the Gentiles (9:32–12:24)
- The witness to Asia Minor (12:25–16:5)
- The witness to Europe (16:6–19:20)
- The witness to the ends of the Earth by way of Rome (19:21–28:31)

All but the last of these regional (or, in the case of the move to a gentile audience in 9:32–12:24, ethnic) expansions is brought to a similar conclusion of the type: "And the word of God grew and multiplied ... " It appears that Luke perceived of the missional witness of the Church in each of these sections as having pervaded those regions sufficiently enough that all persons within them had access to the message about Jesus. In the last section, however, the gospel is again briefly stated to both the Jews (Acts 22) and the Gentiles (Acts 26), but there is no concluding progress report of completion. Some believe this indicates that Luke was planning a third volume, intending to track Paul's next series of journeys once he was released from Rome after his appeal to Caesar had been adjudicated. A more likely theological hypothesis, however, is that Luke deliberately leaves the story of the expanding witness open-ended. The mission work begun at Pentecost has reached worldwide levels of impact by the close of Acts. But it has not yet succeeded in reaching "the ends of the Earth," or bringing all of the world's citizens back into relationship with their Creator. So, the testimony put forward in the book of Acts is never complete, but continues on in the life of the Church. Viewed in this way, the Church is always writing chapter 29 to the book of Acts, so that any attempt at a final "progress report" is only partial and interim.

Pentecost and Babel

Although not explicitly stated, there seems to be a conscious undoing of the troubles that started at Babel through the miracle of multiple-language communications at Pentecost. In Genesis 11, the human race was becoming unified against its Creator, and the divine solution to dissipate this rebellion was to multiply the languages spoken, forcing the community to become segmented into competing groups. At Pentecost, this action is reversed, and the many people who communicated in their diverse local languages suddenly all hear the same message of grace at once, and are knit together into a new common humanity of the Church. Babel was undone by Pentecost!

Acts and the Mission of God

The momentum of the stories told in the book of Acts is derived from a single critical incident that took place in Jerusalem during the Jewish religious festival known as Pentecost. Jesus' instruction for his disciples to stay in Jerusalem and wait for a special gift (Acts 1:4) must have seemed vague at the time, but the arrival of the explosive power of the Holy Spirit during the Pentecost feast made sense. This celebration was both a harvest festival and a time for recalling the gift of the original covenant documents to Moses at Mt. Sinai. These two themes intersect marvelously with what is taking place. First, there is the dawning of a new age of revelation and divine mission, paralleling the first covenant declaration in the book of Exodus. Second, during the Pentecost harvest festival, the first sheaves of grain are presented at the Temple, anticipating that God would then bring in the full harvest. This expression of faith serves as a clear analogy to the greater missional harvest of the Church, which was begun through a miraculous "first fruits" in Jerusalem that day.

Peter capitalizes on these themes when he preaches a sermon explaining Joel's prophecy of the "Day of the Lord." Peter ties together God's extensive mission, the history of Israel, the coming of Jesus, and the splitting of the Day of the Lord so that the blessings of the messianic age could begin before the final divine judgment fell. The pattern for entering the new community of faith was clearly outlined: repent and be baptized. The former indicated a transforming presence of the Holy Spirit in individual hearts, while the latter became the initiation rite by which the ranks of this missional society were identified (replacing the badge of circumcision in its unique application to the nation of Israel—see Colossians 2:11–12).

Reaction to the rapidly developing Christian fellowship was swift and sharp. Within Jerusalem's dominant religious community, there was consternation about the apostles' identification of Jesus as the Jewish Messiah (Acts 4), creating tensions and divisions. Inside the newly organizing Church itself, there were ethical issues that needed to be addressed (Acts 5–6). Soon, the followers of Jesus needed to expand their leadership team (the deacons of Acts 6), and found themselves the targets of increasingly organized persecutions (Acts 8:1–3). Although this disrupted the close fellowship of the Jerusalem congregation, those who moved elsewhere to find safety brought the message of Jesus' teachings, death, and resurrection with them (Acts 8:4).

An amazing turn happened, however, when the leading persecutor, a zealous Pharisee named Saul, suddenly went through a miraculous conversion (Acts 9), and began to preach that Jesus was indeed the Messiah. When Peter's exploits with the Roman centurion Cornelius at Caesarea nurtured the new Gentile mission of the church (Acts 10–11), Diaspora-born Paul (Saul by his other name) became the perfect candidate to partner with Barnabas in establishing an international congregation in the

---

Why the Negative Reaction to Stephen's Sermon?

Among the many millions of Christian sermons that have been preached, Stephen's homily in Acts 7 comes across absolutely tame and almost boring. Why was there such a negative response from those who heard it, so much so that they stoned the preacher to death?

The answer seems to be in the illustrations Stephen uses, and their implications. As he retells the history of Israel, Stephen notes the places where God showed up: to Abraham in Mesopotamia, to Joseph in Egypt, to Moses in the land of Midian. Stephen reminds his listeners that God did not act according to their prescribed religious practices, nor was the deity confined to the Temple as some kind of magical talisman they could use and control. Precisely because in the past, God had been seen and found in a myriad of places around the world, so now it should not come as a surprise that God was showing up in a very different form than what they expected—in the person of Jesus. Furthermore, just like their ancient forebears, the current generation was rejecting the initiatives of God, to their own hurt.

That was a sermon with barbs, and those who were pained because they understood its implications took matters into their own hands: They made certain that Stephen would never preach like that again.

eastern Roman capital city of Antioch (Acts 12). Soon, this congregation served as the launching pad for the great mission journeys of Paul and his companions (Acts 13–19) that would forever relocate the expansion of the Christian Church outside of Jerusalem and Palestine.

What had been a centripetal energizing motion during the first phase of God's recovery mission on planet Earth (that is, drawing all nations toward a reengagement with their Creator through the strategically placed people of Israel), was now shifted into a centrifugal motion of divine sending out these blessings of testimony to the world, in ever-widening circles of witness. The Christian Church, born as a Jewish messianic sect, became a global religion.

The Strange Food Stories of Acts 12

There seems to be a symbolic strangeness in the stories of Acts 12 that connects them to the exodus of Israel from Egypt. Luke tells us:

- "This happened during the Feast of Unleavened Bread" (3)—the time of the Passover (release from Egypt)
- Peter is released from prison and goes "home" (Mary and John Mark's home)
- People praise Herod as a god because he provides food
- Herod is struck down by disease, "eaten by worms," and dies!
- "But the word of God continued to increase and spread" (24)

There appears to be a kind of mirror reflection in the Christian Church's dispersion from Jerusalem and the release of ancient Israel from Egypt. Each event takes place under the totalitarian control of a ruler who provides food and enslaves God's people. Each results in the death of that tyrant by divine judgment. Each involves the celebration of the Passover meal. In each case, the released folks go "home," and the purposes of God grow and multiply, in spite of challenges and opposition.

"Covenant living"

The book of Acts functions in the New Testament in a similar manner to the way in which the "Former Prophets" or historical books did in the Old Testament. It is neither a complete nor impartial history of the first years of the Christian Church. Rather, it is an interpretive commentary on the manner in which the Church was either a faithful community of witness, or where it became sidelined when it forgot its essential nature. While the span of time the book of Acts covers is rather brief (roughly 30 A.D. through 58 A.D.), the basic model of Church life is established, and the content of its missional message clearly articulated.

In fact, Luke seems deliberately to draw parallels between the early days of the nation of Israel and these first years of the Christian Church. For instance, the critical sin of Achan that nearly compromises the conquest of Canaan in Joshua 7 finds a striking counterpart in the ethical failure of Ananias and Sapphira in Acts 5, which causes the marvelous openness and sacrificial grace of the early Jerusalem Church to become momentarily tarnished. Similarly, the horrible enslavement of Israel by Egypt, along with its miraculous deliverance to live out a higher purpose, appears to be intentionally backgrounded, as Luke tells of Peter's divine deliverance from prison and the freeing effects it has on the Church (Acts 12).

All in all, Acts provides the context in which the more pointed instructions of the apostolic letters can be understood. Together, they form the prophetic pair for this new era of the divine redemptive mission.

Discussion Points

- What are Jesus' disciples asking in Acts 1:6 when they inquire whether he is "going to restore the kingdom to Israel" at this time? How does Jesus respond? What is the significance of Jesus' response for the message of the book of Acts?
- How does Jesus' instruction to his disciples in Acts 1:8 serve as a guide to the literary structure of the book of Acts as a whole? What other elements of literary development can be found in its pages? How do the "progress reports," scattered throughout the book, also serve to move along the narrative and its theological message?
- What was the significance of the feast of Pentecost for the Jews of the first century? How does this meaning play into the new experience of the arrival of the Holy Spirit in power? In what way did the symbols displayed on that day complement the message communicated to and through the disciples of Jesus?
- Why do persecutions quickly erupt against the new fellowship of Jesus followers? What are the critical points of division that separate the rest of their society against this small and fervent band?
- Why is Peter's visit to Cornelius in Acts 10–11 so significant? How does it alter the perception of the first Christians about their connection to ethnic identity? How does it change the understanding of non-Jews toward the meaning and message of Jesus' life, death, and resurrection?

For Further Investigation

Bruce, F. F. (Grand Rapids: Eerdmans, 1988). *The Book of Acts*.

Stott, John. R. W. (Downers Grove: InterVarsity, 1994). *The Message of Acts: The Spirit, the Church, and the World*.

30.

First New Testament Letters

Galatians and James, and the Crisis of Christian Identity

Figure 30.1 Syrian Antioch: site of the first intentional new church development outside of Palestine.[1]

The story of the expansion of Christianity is intimately connected, at its beginnings, to the person of Paul. While the specific details of his conversion are told in Acts 9, a larger portrait of Paul emerges in snippets from his letters. A paragraph in Philippians 3 tells us that Paul's parents were strict observant Jews ("circumcised on the eighth day"), openly religious ("of the people of Israel"), conscious of their family history and lineage ("of the tribe of Benjamin"), and careful to maintain ethnic purity ("a Hebrew of Hebrews"). Added to these bits of information come notes found in Paul's personal testimony in Acts 22–23. He was raised in a Diaspora Jewish community in Tarsus (22:3), a Roman citizen from birth (22:8), and aligned through parental influence with the Pharisees in the sociopolitical mix of first-century Jewish culture (22–23:6).

---

1 Adapted from: Copyright © by J B Phillips Estate. Source: http://www.ccel.org/bible/phillips/JBPhillips.htm

281

Gamaliel

While most local Jewish leaders were called rabbi (which means "my teacher"), Gamaliel had achieved such a revered status in the community that he was addressed as rabban ("*the teacher*"). In the *Talmud*, the central text of rabbinic Judaism, Gamaliel is also identified as Nasi ("prince") of the Sanhedrin, or president of that ruling body.

Gamaliel was the grandson of one of the previous standout Jewish teachers, Hillel the Elder. Both are credited with being the key spiritual leaders among the Jews of their day. This is affirmed about Gamaliel in Acts 5:34–40, where he is identified as "a Pharisee" and "a teacher of the law" and a leading figure of the "Sanhedrin," who "was honored by all the people." In that passage, Gamaliel actually changes the disposition of the rest of his Sanhedrin ruling comrades through a reasoned speech that causes all to view a tense situation from a different angle. In the end, Gamaliel defuses overheated passions, and provides a calming new leadership direction.

Paul was very fortunate to have studied under Gamaliel. Aspects of Gamaliel's rabbinic teaching methods likely reveal themselves in some of Paul's exegetical arguments, such as Galatians 4:21–31 and 1 Timothy 2:11–15.

Paul's Hellenic name (meaning "small" or "humble") was popular throughout the Roman world, and may have been a simple cognate to his familial Hebrew name, "Saul" ("asked for" or "prayed for"). This name might have shown the family's pride in its Benjamite roots, since Israel's first king (likely the person after whom Paul was named) was from that tribe. Paul seems to have taken great pride in his vocational training outside of the religious instruction he received, for he reminded the Corinthian congregation that while he was with them, he "worked with [my] own hands" (1 Corinthians 4:12). When Luke reports on Paul's stay in Corinth, he mentions that Paul was busy in the marketplace plying his trade as a "tentmaker" (Acts 18:3).

In his religious education, Paul's instruction was at the top of the Jewish mountain, literally and figuratively. Although born in Tarsus (at the northeastern corner of the Mediterranean Sea, near Antioch), his family must have had high hopes for him in religious leadership, for he told a Jerusalem audience that he was "brought up in this city" and that "under Gamaliel I was trained in the law" (Acts 22:3). It appears likely that Paul showed early promise in synagogue studies in Tarsus, and that his rabbi or the community thought he was a prime candidate to learn from the leading Jewish teacher of the day, Rabban Gamaliel in Jerusalem. Paul's older sister, probably married at the time, was either living in Jerusalem, or was sent to live there and create a home for the young lad while he studied with Gamaliel. When Paul was later arrested in Jerusalem in 54 A.D. (Acts 21) and imprisoned there, we learn that his nephew ("the son of Paul's sister," Acts 23:16) was coming and going from the jail, taking care of his uncle's needs, and serving as the link with the rest of Paul's family.

Gamaliel was a leading figure in the Jewish ruling Sanhedrin, and the brightest light among the Pharisees of his day. Not surprisingly, under the influences of both Paul's father and Paul's great teacher, Paul himself forthrightly adopted the Pharisaic religious perspective and lifestyle as well (Acts 23:6). Paul excelled in his studies, for he said that it was out of his religious zeal that he began to persecute the Church (Philippians 3:6). Even more, in his words, "as for legalistic righteousness," Paul judged himself "faultless" (Philippians 3:6) in his day-to-day behaviors. Paul lived and breathed his religious identity with a passion that was true and straight and unyielding.

But then Jesus confronted him (Acts 9), and suddenly Paul needed to rethink the whole of his theology and practices (Galatians 1:13–17). The outcome was a synthesis between zealous conservative Judaism and energetic Christian missionary engagement. Soon, Barnabas took Paul along as a partner in the planting of a cosmopolitan missional congregation in the heart of Antioch (Acts 12), the third largest city of the Roman Empire. It was the administrative capital of Rome's eastern district, close to Tarsus (Paul's family home), and also near Cyprus, where Barnabas's family lived (Acts 4:36). During those years, a large colony of Jews made their homes in Antioch, perhaps as many as 20,000 out of a total metropolitan population of around half a million.

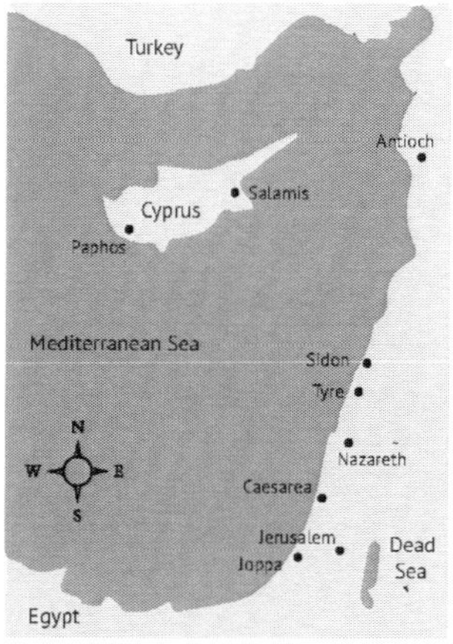

Figure 30.2 Cyprus (Barnabas' home) in relation to Antioch.

The First Mission Journey

During a prayer meeting in the Antioch church, probably in early 48 A.D., the group received a very strong divine message that their primary leadership team was supposed to be sent on a missionary journey (Acts 13:1–3). We do not have details about how the plans were laid, but it is reasonable to suppose that they arranged a trip into familiar territory. Cyprus was Barnabas's home turf, and it may well be that after they blitzed across that island, they intended to travel back to Antioch along the Pamphylian coast, stopping briefly in Tarsus along the way.

Indeed, they traveled the length of Cyprus, preaching in various Jewish synagogues, and then boarded boats for the mainland. But at the seaport of Perga, John Mark left them and "returned to Jerusalem" (Acts 13:13). Also, it seems that Paul might have gotten quite sick at that juncture in their travels. What the illness was is not certain, but when Paul later wrote to those whom he and Barnabas met in the highlands of central Asia Minor, Paul reminded them that "it was because of an illness that I first preached the gospel to you" (Galatians 4:13). A further clue to these events is found in Paul's additional cryptic testimony that something was wrong with his eyes (Galatians 4:15). Since the

Dating Paul's Life

While we have no resources to determine Paul's birth date or year, there are a number of references made either by Luke in Acts, or by Paul himself in his letters, that help us build a fairly coherent chronology of his life after becoming a Christian:

- 34—Conversion (Acts 9)
- 34–43—Reflections, Training, and Introductions (Galatians 1:18–2:1)
- 43–47—Establishing a new Church in Antioch with Barnabas (Acts 11:19–30)
- 48—First Mission Journey (Acts 13–14)
  - Writes his Letter to the Galatians
- 49—Jerusalem Council (Acts 15)
- 49–51—Second Mission Journey (Acts 16–18)
  - Writes his *Letters to the Thessalonians*
- 51–54—Third Mission Journey (Acts 18–19)
  - Writes his *Letters to the Corinthians and Romans*

- 54—Arrest in Jerusalem (Acts 21)
- 54–56—Imprisonment in Caesarea (Acts 23–26)
- 56–57—Voyage to Rome (Acts 27–28)
- 57–59—First Imprisonment in Rome (Acts 28)
  - Writes his *Letters to the Philippians, Philemon,* the *Colossians,* and the *Ephesians*
- 59–67—Later Travels and Mission Journeys (Philemon, 1 Timothy 1, Titus 1, 2 Timothy 4)
  - Writes his *Letters to Timothy* and *Titus*
- 67—Second Imprisonment in Rome and Death

The Legend of Baucis and Philemon|

An old legend told of the gods Zeus and Hermes coming down from Mt. Olympus to see the true character of the Greek people. The gods disguised themselves, and wandered from village to town, asking for hospitality. Unfortunately, all were too busy to be bothered by poor strangers. As the ire of the gods was heating up, they chanced upon a mean hovel at the edge of a small settlement. It was the home of Baucis and Philemon, an old couple who lived quietly by themselves, but were willing to share their meager possessions with these travelers. Philemon even tried to catch and kill their only duck, but it took refuge between Zeus's legs. At that point, the gods revealed themselves to the kind pair, led them up into the hills, and saved them from the fires of judgment which the gods then rained down upon the nasty town. The remains sank until a beautiful lake was formed,

Figure 30.3 Paul's first mission journey.[2]

Pamphylian coastline is marshy and mosquito ridden, it might have been malaria that laid Paul low. That would explain why the team went immediately up into the highlands, rather than continuing along the shore toward Tarsus and Antioch.

There are hints that a switch in leadership was taking place during this time. Until the travelers arrived in Pisidian Antioch (not to be confused with Syrian Antioch, from which they had come), Barnabas was always listed first by Luke. He was the one who had met Paul in Jerusalem sometime after Paul's conversion, and introduced him around to the skittish apostles, who thought this might be a double-agent ploy to have them arrested or killed. It was Barnabas who had searched for Paul, asking him to come as a colleague to plant the new international congregation in Antioch. And across the island of Cyprus, it was Barnabas who seemed to have taken the lead on his home turf.

Now, however, in Acts 13:14, the leadership mantle suddenly shifts to Paul. He determines where the group will go, and stands to deliver the message of Jesus. In Pisidian Antioch, Paul preaches a historical review of God's work in the synagogue,

---

2   Adapted from: Copyright © by J B Phillips Estate. Source: http://www.ccel.org/bible/phillips/JBPhillips.htm

leading finally to a message about Jesus being the Messiah. A week later, "almost the whole city" comes out, for this new gospel was creating quite a stir. While many believe, jealous Jews incite a riot that forces Paul and Barnabas out of the synagogue. They spend the next days in the marketplace, speaking to Gentiles as well as Jews. But animosity is building, and soon the travelers are forced from the city (Acts 13:14–31).

Down the road, at a smaller town named Iconium, Paul and Barnabas again preach in the Jewish synagogue to good response. Just as before, however, growing Jewish resentment causes them to turn to the Gentiles. Soon, a plot against them is discovered, and they move on once again (Acts 14:1–7).

At Lystra, the pair encounter a crippled man immediately outside of town. He is begging for alms, but Paul raises him up with a miraculous healing. This causes a serious commotion in town, and the entire population mobs out to worship Paul and Barnabas as Hermes and Zeus, key leaders among the Greek gods. When Paul convinces the crowds that he and his companions are only human, their worship quickly flips over to disgust. Meanwhile, enemies who had dogged their heels from Antioch now turn the frenzied tumult against them. Paul and Barnabas are stoned and left for dead. Fortunately, some sympathetic care providers nurture back the almost-extinguished sparks of life in them, and after a short while of secretive recovery, Paul and Barnabas move on again (Acts 14:8–20).

Traveling over to nearby Derbe (Acts 14:21), the team again preaches about Jesus, and then begin to wend their way home. Paul and Barnabas stop briefly in each highland community where they had recently spent a few days or weeks, and appoint elders in the new Christian congregations (Acts 14:22–25), carrying on the ages-old Israelite practice of local leadership. Returning to Syrian Antioch, Paul and Barnabas bring a report of their mission journey to their home congregation (Acts 14:26–28).

And that's when the trouble starts (Acts 15; Galatians 2). Reports of Gentile converts to Christianity sizzle toward Jerusalem. Peter comes up to Antioch to celebrate this exciting mission work (Galatians 2:11), but others with less enthusiasm

with Baucis and Philemon's cottage at its side. This, then, was transformed into a magnificent temple, and the elderly couple became priest and priestess of the shrine. When they neared death, they stood next to one another with loving smiles, and the gods morphed them into an oak and linden tree, whose branches still entwine.

Galatians in Broad Outline 📖

- **Chapters 1–2:** Paul reviews his personal journey to freedom in Christ, and laments the recent developments that have pitted "Jewish Christianity" against "Gentile Christianity," with regard to the keeping of ritual ceremonies from the Mosaic laws.
- **Chapters 3–4:** Paul uses rabbinic argumentation to show how Abraham was declared righteous by God prior to engaging in the acts of circumcision; how the "Law" is like a teacher who is no longer needed after a child becomes fully mature; and how Hagar and Ishmael typify slavery (Law) over Sarah and Isaac, who portray freedom.
- **Chapters 5–6:** Using very strong language, Paul urges the expression of true freedom in Christ, which is neither Law nor License, but Liberty.

"Large Letters"

Paul closes his message to the Galatians with a personal greeting, scrawled in large letters in his own handwriting. This shows that Paul often used others (professional letter-writers are called amanuenses) to write out his letters as he dictated them orally. The size of his handwriting may be due to his poor eyesight, a leftover reminder of the illness that first brought him to these people.

Who Was This James?

There are three persons in the New Testament who are identified by the name "James":

- Jesus' disciple, the brother of John and son of Zebedee (Mark 1:19–20).
- Another of Jesus' disciples called James, son of Alphaeus (Luke 6:15).
- Jesus' brother (Matthew 13:55; Galatians 1:19).

The first of these was killed by King Herod around 44 A.D. (Acts 12:2). The second is so obscure that he is never mentioned again. The third appears to have become the leader of the early Christian Church in Jerusalem, for when Paul first becomes a believer, it is to this James that he is introduced (Galatians 1:19). This is the James who presides over the Jerusalem council.

are soon sent by James (the brother of Jesus and leader of the Jerusalem congregation) to ensure that all was happening in an appropriate manner (Galatians 2:12). These representatives announce that Gentiles have to become Jews in belief and practice before they could become part of the Christian Church. After all, Jesus was Jewish, and was being acclaimed as the Messiah foretold by Israel's prophets.

These ambassadors of the Jerusalem church institute separate meal and communion practices (Galatians 2:12–13), making it clear that only those who are ceremonially pure could take positions of leadership in the community. Much to Paul's surprise, even Peter and Barnabas ally themselves with those advocating these discriminating practices. Paul, of course, is anything but timid, and accosts Peter publicly (Galatians 2:14), creating even stronger polarization among the congregations on these matters.

The disease of Jewish superiority spreads to the churches of Paul and Barnabas's recent mission journey, and threaten to split the infant Christian community before it even had an opportunity to get started. In response, Paul dashes off a letter to the churches of "Galatia," the Roman district through which they had traveled on their mission trek.

Paul's Letter to the Galatians

In the first part of this passionate letter (Galatians 1–2), Paul reviews his personal journey to an understanding of freedom in Christ, and laments the recent developments that had seemingly stolen away this freedom from many of them. Next, Paul goes into a lengthy Jewish rabbinic argument about how Abraham was counted as "righteous" in his relationship with God already before he entered into the rituals of circumcision. Paul concludes that neither circumcision nor any other ceremonial expression is essentially necessary for a meaningful relationship with God, and that Jesus' recent teachings, death, and resurrection only reaffirmed and expanded this truth. In fact, said Paul, the "Law" (that is, the ceremonial dimensions of the Sinai Covenant) is like a teacher who is no longer needed after a child becomes fully mature. Using a rabbinic allegory, Paul points to Hagar and her son, Ishmael, as representations of Abraham's "slave" side of the family, regulated by the social codes from Mt. Sinai. Sarah and her son Isaac, on the other hand, were symbols of Abraham's "free" side of the family, and lived out of the delight that was expressed through ecstatic worship in Jerusalem. In the final portion of his letter (Galatians 5–6), Paul uses very strong language to urge the expression of true freedom in Christ. This is found in neither the legalism of ritual religious regimens which bind and burden, nor in licentiousness, which turns us evil and ugly. Rather, true Christian freedom is experienced when we no longer consider ourselves under external demands that have no important ends in themselves, but when we voluntarily give ourselves as slaves to God and others out of love. In this context, there can be no division between "Jewish Christians" and "Gentile Christians," for the Church of Jesus Christ has become the new "Israel of God" (Galatians 6:16).

The Jerusalem Council

Wisely acknowledging the seriousness of this burgeoning conflict, leaders of the Jerusalem congregation call representatives from all the churches to come together for a prayerful conversation, probably in the fall of 49 A.D. (Acts 15). James, the brother of Jesus, presides over the event, and reports are received from both the Pharisaic Jewish Christians, who demanded that Gentiles become Jews before they could be Christians, and also from Paul and his companions, who told of the marvelous faith exhibited by those who had believed within the Gentile communities of Antioch and Galatia. The

---

The Four Stipulations

- Don't eat meat offered to idols (this would later become a matter of contention that Paul would address again in Romans 14 and 1 Corinthians 8)
- Don't eat blood
- Don't be sexually immoral (probably intended to discourage the common practice of sexual relations with temple prostitutes, which was part of business life)
- Don't eat flesh from strangled animals

Palestinian Jewish Authorship

James refers to Abraham as "our father" (2:21), and calls places of worship "synagogues" (2:2). He uses the Jewish term "Gehenna" to name the place of divine punishment (3:6); this indicates a Jerusalem connection, for "Gehenna" is Aramaic for "valley of the Hinnom," which was the garbage dump for the city. James uses a specifically Jewish name for God ("Lord of Armies") in 5:4. Moreover, he is aware of the climate of Palestine that includes hot, burning winds (1:11), as well as early and latter rains (5:7). Placing himself in Palestine and writing to Jews outside of it, he declares that he is addressing "the twelve tribes scattered among the nations" (1:1).

Why the Order of New Testament Books?

Although most of the letters of the New Testament were written before the gospels, the gospels tell the story of Jesus, which logically precedes the teachings of the letters. Since most of the letters collected into the New Testament were written by Paul, these have been gathered as a group, and were eventually copied as New Testament documents in order of size, from longest to shortest (possibly as encouragement to scribes who tackled the most massive projects first). This means that Paul's letters are not found in chronological order in the New Testament. The rest of the letters and writings were mainly grouped by author, with the future-anticipating Revelation reasonably positioned at the end.

most critical testimony, however, appears to be Peter's tale of the visions that led to his encounter with the Roman centurion, Cornelius, in Caesarea (Acts 10–11). Although Peter is by nature inclined to side with the "Judaizers," he gives his full conviction to the perspectives of Paul and Barnabas, and this tips the final outcome clearly in that direction.

The Jerusalem council of Christian leaders adopted a clear resolution, stating that Gentile believers in Jesus did not have to first become Jews through the process of proselytizing, but could be received on equal footing with Jewish believers in any Christian congregation. Four behaviors were urged (though not commanded). If the Gentile Christians would practice these, it would help observant Jews associate more comfortably with Gentiles in the same congregations. Then, these decisions were communicated to the churches by way of a short letter.

The Letter of James

James probably wrote his letter to the congregations at this time as well. He may have sent it as a public way of affirming the solid Jewish background and lifestyle among those who were the earliest believers in Jesus. Not surprisingly, coming from one who had grown up with Jesus, there are a good number of similarities between the contents of this letter and the teachings of Jesus. Many parallels have been noted, especially with the Sermon on the Mount in Matthew 5–7.

It is clear that James is addressing social tensions within the congregations to which he is writing. While some of these conflicts had to do with discrimination on the basis of wealth or power (James 5:1–6), others seem to have resulted from judgments made by some about how to rank people when preparing seating charts at community gatherings for table fellowship (James 2:1–14). This would fit with the description of Paul in Galatians 2 about how communities had become divided over whether or not Gentiles had to keep the ceremonial laws regulating the Jews in order to sit with them at meals or Last Supper remembrances.

The letter itself is not highly organized by topic. It seems to be more a stream-of-consciousness exhortation. A good portion of James's letter contains strong ethical instructions, especially about social relations. Unmistakable throughout, however, is the deep piety of the author, who constantly calls for his reader to pray, fast, and hold to absolute trust in God. The main groupings of themes appear to be these:

- Dealing with trials from without (1:2–12)

- Understanding trials from within (1:13–18)
- The difference between merely hearing and actually doing good (1:19–27)
- Honoring one another without preference (2:1–14)
- The sinful power of the tongue must be controlled (3:1–4:12)
- Uncertainties of life call for humility (4:13–17)
- Caution against the horrible demoralization often caused by wealth (5:1–6)
- Encouragements to patient faithfulness (5:7–12)
- Advice about mutual care in the community (5:13–20)

In summary, by the end of the Church's second decade (the late 40s), Paul had become a leading figure in the early Christian community, particularly after Barnabas took him to be a partner in establishing the missional congregation in Antioch. That church launched Paul and Barnabas on their first mission journey to Cyprus and the highlands of Asia Minor (late 48–early 49 A.D.). Soon, it became clear that not all Jews wanted to acknowledge Jesus as the promised Messiah, and that many Gentiles were eager to believe. Bringing these divergent ethnic groups together in Christian congregations forced Jewish believers to rethink their understanding of religious identity and its practices, as Paul urged in his emotional letter to the Galatians (mid 49 A.D.). The resulting arguments caused James, the acknowledged primary leader of the Church, to gather representatives in Jerusalem for a prayerful council on the matter (late 49 A.D.). In the end, the liberating new behaviors taught by Paul and Barnabas—and surprisingly affirmed by Peter because of his divine vision at Joppa and engagement with Cornelius at Caesarea—carried the day, and letters explaining the council's decisions were sent by way of personal messengers to all the churches. James wrote his longer letter of encouragement, focusing on piety and social care, and probably included it in the distribution packages that were sent out (late 49 A.D.). These letters of Paul and James became the first documents of the New Testament.

The early Christian Church honored the Hebrew scriptures (most often read in the Septuagint Greek version) as their own authoritative texts for worship, theology, and moral behavior. What has come to be known as the "New Testament" did not begin as "scripture." These

Did Paul and James Disagree?

While James affirmed the directions taken by Paul and Barnabas in their organizing of Jews and Gentiles together into Christian congregations, he is sometimes viewed as having a different theological perspective on the relationship between "faith" and "works." Paul made it clear in his letter to the Galatians that faith is central, and that works do not play any part in achieving our relationship with God. James, however, stresses in his letter that works are the means by which faith is expressed, and therefore must be done. Most theologians believe that Paul and James agreed on the essentials of salvation, but emphasized different aspects of the human response as they addressed alternative needs in the community. Paul wanted to ensure that no Gentile was excluded from fellowship because he or she did not engage in ritual Jewish ceremonial activities. James, on the other hand, wanted to encourage devout Jews to continue their practices of piety, even as Christians, in order to remain rooted in faith and its public expressions.

documents achieved scriptural designation over time, as the Church recognized in them the normative authoritative witness of Jesus' first followers and other authorized spokespersons who had received helpful new revelations from God. In this manner, the New Testament began to take shape in collections similar to those that emerged in the earlier Old Testament library.

Just as the Sinai Covenant was central and normative to Israelite identity and purpose, so the teachings and actions of Jesus became the heartbeat of the new Christian community. Although most of the letters of Paul and the other apostles were written slightly before the Synoptic gospels, the gospels themselves became the foundational new covenant platform, upon which were raised the other writings of significance. Jesus himself, just before dying, had testified that who he was and what he was doing was the "new covenant" (Mark 14:24; Matthew 26:28; Luke 22:20; 1 Corinthians 11:25).

Paralleling the proclamations of the Old Testament prophets, the writings of the New Testament apostles became a supportive commentary on the meaning of Jesus for those who were part of the new community of faith attached to him. The authority of the gospels resides in their communication of the life, teachings, death, and resurrection of Jesus. The authority of the letters of the apostles (along with the book of Acts) comes from the unique calling of these people as divinely appointed spokespersons for Jesus (cf. 1 Corinthians 1; 4; 7:25; 9; Ephesians 3:2–13), just as was the case for the Old Testament prophets.

Finally, in a kind of miscellany of supportive materials, are found the "Writings" of the Old Testament, and the materials of the New Testament which do not fit neatly into either of the other categories. Virtually nothing new is garnered about either the Sinai Covenant or the life and teachings of Jesus in these works. Instead, they testify to issues that linger in each religious community, and further encourage believers to remain faithful, even through challenging times.

In this way, both Testaments are structured in similar fashions. The great redemptive acts of God in early Israel's existence, and again in the person of Jesus, provide the foundational "Covenant Documents," upon which the rest of scripture is built. As the initial communities of faith began to live out their missional purpose among the nations of the world, God raised up authorized spokespersons to give guidance and clarity about the meaning of God's covenanted relationship with them and their evangelistic lifestyle. The history lessons, sermons, and letters of these prophets and apostles became the literature of scripture "Covenant Living." And the additional supportive and instructional resources form a third collection of "Covenant Documents" for both Israel and the Christian Church, as the poetry and wisdom literature and apocalyptic visions nurture faith and spiritual depth.

The writings of the Bible become scripture for the divinely created missional communities of faith because of both their contents and their functions. This is the unique character of scripture in the Israelite and Jewish traditions, very different from that in any other faith community.

Discussion Points

- What is the critical issue to which Paul responds with his letter to the Galatians? How does Paul address that issue? What arguments does he use to get his point across?
- Why is a conference of Church leaders assembled in Jerusalem, according to Acts 15? What is the key topic under discussion? What information is brought about on that topic?
- What resolution comes to the body, and why? What advice was disseminated from the gathering to the congregations scattered abroad? How have the decisions of this council shaped the character and membership of the Christian Church?
- Who was likely the James who wrote the New Testament letter named after him? What do we know about him? What clues are there in the letter itself about his identity?
- What are the key topics addressed in the letter of James? What information can we glean from this letter about the practices and problems of the early Church?

For Further Investigation

George, Timothy. (Nashville: Holman, 1994). Galatians.

McRay, John. (Grand Rapids: Baker, 2003). *Paul: His Life and Teaching.*

Moo, Douglas. (Downers Grove: InterVarsity, 1986). *The Letter of James.*

31.

Eschatological Ethics

Will Jesus Come Back This Week or Next?

After the Jerusalem council, Paul and Barnabas were eager to visit the Galatian congregations, and inform them personally of the good outcomes in this early Christian theological debate which had affected them so deeply (Acts 15:36). But tensions flamed between them when they argued whether John Mark should be invited along (Acts 15:37). Paul was still very upset that the younger man had suddenly "deserted" them on their first mission journey (Acts 13:13). In the end, Barnabas felt a family obligation to give it a try with Mark again, while Paul chose a new partner, named Silas, to join him in these travels (Acts 15:39-41).

It was probably late in 49 A.D. when Paul and Silas left Syrian Antioch, their home base. They traveled overland to the communities in central Asia Minor, where Paul and Barnabas had established Christian congregations more than a year earlier. At Lystra, they were joined by Timothy (Acts 16:1-2), a promising young man whose mother was Christian, but whose father was not. Together, this growing company of itinerant preachers had in mind an itinerary taking them farther north in Asia Minor (Acts 16:6-8). There were other new areas where Jewish settlements in Hellenic cities might give them an open door for talking about Jesus.

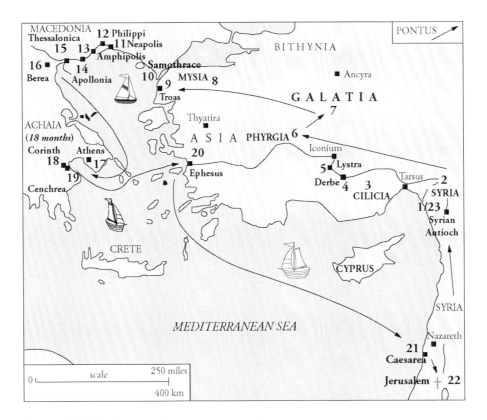

Figure 31.1 Paul's second mission journey[1]

While pondering their options at Troas, Paul may have had some medical problems. The text of Acts 16 shows a shift at that point from third-person references to first-person recollections (note verses 6–10). It seems obvious that doctor Luke, the man who would author this book, joined the band at Troas. It might well be that he came to Paul as a healer, and stayed with Paul as a new believer and fellow evangelist. Also in this city, a divine directive illumined Paul in a vision (Acts 16:9–10), with the result that the company headed next across the Aegean Sea to Macedonia. Philippi was their first major stop, a fairly new Roman colony established by military personnel who received parcels of land as their pensions. As of yet, there was no sizable Jewish population in the city, since Paul and Silas found a small group of Jews worshipping at the river's edge on a Sabbath (Acts 16:13). Once there were ten Jewish males in any town, a synagogue had to be established, so the river gathering meant that Jews had not come to Philippi in any significant numbers. As was his custom, Paul spoke to the small group about Jesus, and a new Christian congregation was formed in the home of Lydia (Acts 16:14–15).[1]

Paul and Silas stayed in Philippi for some time, but eventually encountered trouble that landed them in jail. A young fortune-teller began to follow them, shouting out to the crowds about them (Acts 16:16–17), perhaps in a mean-spirited or nasty manner. Paul was aggrieved by her evident demonic possession, and exorcised her (Acts 16:18). The girl's masters were very

---

1   Copyright © by J B Phillips Estate. Source: http://www.ccel.org/bible/phillips/JBPhillips.htm

Paul's Message in Athens

The speeches recorded by Luke in the book of Acts carry essential information about the theological perspectives of the Church's first leaders. Paul's address to the Athenians in Acts 17:22–31 is masterful in its contextualization of the gospel message.

Paul begins by noting the large place that religion appears to have among the Athenians, pointing to the shrines in the city, including an altar with the fascinating inscription, "To an Unknown God." Pausanius, a Greek geographer who lived a century later (c. 110–180 A.D.), wrote about seeing the same altar on the main road into Athens from Piraeus. His contemporary, the historian Diogenes Laertius, explained how the altar came to be, in Lives and Opinions of Eminent Philosophers. In 632 B.C., Olympic hero Cylon received a message from the oracle at Delphi to seize power in Athens. The coup was ill-fated, and Cylon's group fled their pursuers to take refuge in Athena's temple on the Acropolis. Although the city archons promised the rebels a fair trial, these men were not convinced. They linked themselves by ropes to the altar of the temple, claiming Athena's protection as they were marched to court. The ropes broke, according to Diogenes, and the archons took it as a sign that Athena had judged the men guilty. They were immediately killed.

But justice may have been perverted in this assassination. Immediately, a plague fell on Athens and threatened to annihilate its citizens. No ceremonies or sacrifices worked relief. Finally, in desperation, the city leaders sent for Epimenides of Crete to bring wisdom and release from this apparent divine judgment.

Epimenides was a philosopher and poet. He surveyed Athens in its crisis, and then asked that two flocks be brought out to the Areopagus, one all white sheep and the other all black. Raising a prayer to the "unknown God" whose displeasure had been stirred, Epimenides told those tending the flocks to sacrifice the sheep who lay down. Makeshift altars were built, animals were burned, and the plague was lifted.

Diogenes notes that the remnants of these altars continued to serve as holy sites, just as Paul found them seven centuries later. Now, Paul uses the ideas of pervasive religious sentiments, sin and healing, and a transcendent God who creates, sees, and governs all peoples, to bring the good news about Jesus. Paul even quotes Epimenides ("For in him we live and move and have our being") from one of his famous poems, along with a Greek poet named Aratus ("We are his offspring."), using the literary sources of the day to bring home his point.

Paul's short message is brilliant. Using touchstones in his contemporary culture and literary productions, Paul identifies the needs and perspectives of his listeners, and then shows how the great Creator, God, has provided hope and healing and meaning for all, confirming these things through Jesus.

upset, and threw Paul and Silas into prison (Acts 16:19–24). A midnight earthquake rocked the place, and led to the jailer's conversion (Acts 16:25–34). In the morning, the Roman citizenship of Paul and Silas was discovered, and the magistrates were beside themselves in efforts to undo the unlawful treatment these two had received (Acts 16:35–40).

It was on to Thessalonica next, for Paul and Silas and their team (Acts 17:1–9). For three weeks, Paul preached about Jesus in the Jewish synagogue. When Gentiles swelled the crowd of Christ-believers, however, some Jews became jealous and formed a mob to disrupt civic life. The uproar caused city officials to arrest leading members of the new Christian congregation, and the group sent Paul and Silas out of town that evening under cover of darkness. With brief stops in Berea (Acts 17:10–15) and Athens (Acts 17:16–34), Paul eventually arrived in Corinth, where

Dating Paul's Journeys

There are only a few references to dates and rulers in the New Testament, and one of them occurs in the story of Paul meeting Aquila and Priscilla. This couple had recently resettled from Rome to Corinth "because Claudius had ordered all the Jews to leave Rome" (Acts 18:2). In his *Lives of the Caesars*, Roman historian Suetonius wrote that Emperor Claudius expelled the Jews because they were constantly causing disturbances in their arguments over a man named *Chrestus* (many believe this might be a misunderstanding of *Christus*, and the arguments in Jewish communities over whether Jesus was the Christ). The edict occurred in 49 A.D., which allows us to pin Paul's arrival in Corinth to late 49 or early 50 A.D.

1 Thessalonians in Summary

—The marvelous witness of this young church even through oppressive circumstances (1–3)

—Living faithfully because Jesus is coming soon (4:1–12)

—What about those who have recently died? (4:13–18)

—Jesus is coming soon! (5)

he met Aquila and Priscilla for the first time (Acts 18:1–3). This couple would become fast friends with Paul, keeping in touch for the rest of his life.

The Thessalonian Correspondence

Although Paul would spend the next year and a half in Corinth, at the outset, his heart remained back in Thessalonica. Already when he was traveling through Athens, Paul worried about how the fledgling Thessalonian congregation was faring (1 Thessalonians 2:17–20), and sent Timothy back to find out more and make a report (1 Thessalonians 3:1–5). Paul had already continued on to Corinth by the time Timothy caught up with him, and was elated at the good word his younger associate brought (1 Thessalonians 3:6–10). With emotions running high, Paul dashed off a letter of appreciation and encouragement to his new friends (1 Thessalonians).

Most of this short letter is given to expressions of praise for the great testimony already being noised about from those who observed the grace and spiritual energy of this newborn congregation. Paul rehearses briefly (1 Thessalonians 1–3) the recent history that has deeply connected them, and tells of his aching heart now that they were so quickly "torn away" from one another (1 Thessalonians 2:17). Only after these passionate confessions does Paul spill some ink on a few notes of instruction (1 Thessalonians 4–5). While most of what Paul has to say are typical exhortations toward quiet and godly living, a surprising topic suddenly jumps out as prelude to a new and unique trajectory in Christian doctrinal development. Paul writes:

Brothers, we do not want you to be ignorant about those who fall asleep, or to grieve like the rest of men, who have no hope. We believe that Jesus died and rose again and so we believe that God will bring with Jesus those who have fallen asleep in him. According to the Lord's own word, we tell you that we who are still alive, who are left till the coming of the Lord, will certainly not precede those who have fallen asleep. For the Lord himself will come down from heaven, with a loud command, with the voice of the archangel and with the trumpet call of God, and the dead in Christ will rise first. After that, we who are still alive and are left will be caught up together with them in the clouds to meet the Lord in the air. And so we will be with the Lord forever. Therefore encourage each other with these words (1 Thessalonians 4:13–17).

The central message of Paul's missionary preaching focuses on the resurrection of Jesus. This is, for Paul, the astounding confirmation of Jesus' divine character. It is the undeniable proof that Jesus is the Messiah, and that his words and teachings have ushered in the new age of God's final revelation and redemptive activity.

Paul understood that Jesus was the great "Day of the Lord" event foretold by the Old Testament prophets (1 Thessalonians 5:1), and that out of gracious forbearance, Jesus had split this cataclysmic occurrence in two, so that the beginning of eternal blessings could be experienced before the final judgment fell (1 Thessalonians 5:2–11). This meant that Jesus had gone back to heaven only briefly, and would be returning to earth very soon—probably next week, but maybe next month. It was the generous grace of God which had provided this brief window of opportunity, allowing Jesus' disciples a chance quickly to tell others the good news, so that those who believed would also reap the benefits of the looming messianic age. Neither Paul nor God want anyone to be destroyed in the judgments that were still ahead.

The response of the Thessalonian church to this insistent focus on Jesus' imminent return apparently echoed back to Paul through Timothy's report in a way he had not expected. Rather than energizing the new believers in Thessalonica, with anticipations of divine vindication after the painful struggles they had recently endured, some had instead become deeply discouraged. In the few intervening weeks or months since they had come to faith in Jesus under Paul's passionate preaching, several members of the congregation had died. The grief of those who survived was heightened, because they supposed that their lost loved ones had come so close to sharing in the powers and perfections of the new age, only to succumb to death virtually on its threshold. They assumed that the dead were excluded forever from the messianic kingdom.

Paul corrects this mistaken notion with a brief eschatological teaching. Jesus will return soon, to be sure, and those of us who are alive when that happens will enjoy renewed direct interaction with him. But those who have already died will not be left behind. Their bodies will be raised and restored, just as happened with Jesus himself on resurrection morning. Assurance of this comes from "the Lord's own word," according to Paul. Although none of the gospels records this exact teaching from Jesus, evidently it had become part of the oral tradition already being passed along from one believer to another.

Paul then goes on to reaffirm the central imminent-return-of-Jesus proclamation that had precipitated these reflections in the first place (1 Thessalonians 5:1–11). Jesus will come back very soon, most likely in the foreseeable future. Paul fully expected that he himself, and most of his readers there in Thessalonica, would experience this event firsthand, and probably nearer on the calendar than more distant.

---

2 Thessalonians in Summary 📖

–Glad for the good report (1)

–Don't stop living responsibly while you wait for Jesus' return (2–3)

Christian Ethical Foundations

Both the Old and New Testaments contain a lot of moral instruction and guidelines to ethical behaviors. While these address many dimensions of life and behavior, they are invariably established on four primary foundational principles:

- **Creational Norms:** How did God intend for things to be?
  - Note the portraits of life on earth in Genesis 1–2
- **Restraint of Sin:** What evil has infested the world that needs to be restrained and counteracted?
  - Note the negative expression of the Ten Commandments and the laws for Israel
- **The Mind of Christ/God:** What is the heart and passion and will of God?
  - Note the unique revelation of God in Jesus Christ
- **Eschatological Hope:** What goals or plans or expectations is God drawing us toward in the consummation of all things?
  - Note Paul's ethical urgings here in 1 and 2 Thessalonians, and throughout the apostolic writings, with a message that Christian behavior should be tempered by the confidence that Jesus will return soon

---

The letter closes with a quick litany of moral and ethical exhortations, urging faithful living regardless of circumstances (1 Thessalonians 5:12–28). It was probably sent in early 50 A.D., just as Paul was getting started with his work in Corinth.

A month or two later, Paul receives a follow-up report on the Thessalonian congregation. It may have been written as a result of another visit by Timothy, but we do not know for sure. What is certain is that Paul's letter had increased the climate of expectation for Jesus' return very dramatically, to the point where a significant number of the Thessalonian Christians had either stopped working their careers, believing that these were no longer necessary because Jesus was coming so soon (2 Thessalonians 3:6–12), or came to the conclusion that the messianic age had already arrived, and they were free to carry on with no normal social restraints or obligations (2 Thessalonians 2:1–3). Paul's second letter to the Thessalonians addresses both issues. After a rousing note of appreciation for their growing faith (2 Thessalonians 1), Paul tempers his imminent-return-of-Christ teachings by injecting a likely waiting period, during which a "man of lawlessness" will appear (2 Thessalonians 2:3–4). Who this person will be or when it will happen remains unclear. For a moment, Paul's writing verges on apocalyptic speculations (2 Thessalonians 2:5–12), but then it settles quickly back into exhortations of moral behaviors consistent with the "sanctifying work of the Spirit" (2 Thessalonians 2:13–17).

In his final instructions (2 Thessalonians 3), Paul urges the Thessalonian Christians to live lifestyles of faithful service toward others, not getting caught up in the disease of idleness which seems to have sprung among some from overzealous expectations of Jesus' imminent return. A closing line, apparently in Paul's own handwriting, indicates that once again, he has used an amanuensis for creating this document (2 Thessalonians 3:17).

Paul's Eschatology

Paul's letters to the Thessalonian congregation occurred early in his ministry, with both epistles most likely penned in 50 A.D. These writings are very short, and do not spell out a fully explored eschatology. But in their brief exhortations, they contain some of Paul's most direct and explicit eschatological teachings.

First, it is clear that the emphasis in Paul's preaching is on the resurrection of Jesus. This was the confirmation that Jesus was the Messiah foretold by the prophets. It was also the most profound sign that the new messianic age had arrived. Since the messianic age was part of the promised "Day of the Lord," a time of divine judgment was sure to arrive soon.

Second, Jesus' first coming brought the beginnings of the blessings of the messianic age, but it delayed the judgments of God for a time, so that the followers of Jesus could spread the news of salvation far and wide. Splitting the "Day of the Lord" in two was an act of kindness on God's part, providing more opportunity for people to respond in faith. It also placed upon the church a missionary urgency. The reason Jesus left his followers behind during the gap between his ascension and return was to send them as ambassadors of hope to the nations.

Third, the return of Jesus was imminent, and likely to take place within weeks or months. This was the expectation that made any trials, persecutions, or difficulties endurable. Knowing that one can outlast an opponent, no matter how nasty or strong, gives great resilience to hang on and survive with dignity.

Fourth, all who trusted in Jesus when he returned would share in his glory and power. But so too would those who had believed in Jesus, and then died before Jesus had made his return. This teaching profoundly changed the burial habits of Christians, and altered expectations at dying. Rather than closing doors to human existence, death instead opened them to eternal life. Many early Christians welcomed death by martyrdom, knowing that through this act they were immediately secure in resurrection hope.

Fifth, the yawning gap of time that had been widening since Jesus' ascension required meaningful explanations for the delay of his return. Answers came in three major varieties. Some saw this lengthening "in-between" age as evidence of divine grace: God was not going to bring final judgment until more people could respond to the gospel message in faith. Others declared that the delay was a tool for testing the faithfulness of those who said they believed in Jesus. A final group called to mind Jesus' words about signs that would appear before the final days, and tried more closely to define the number of specific events must still take place prior to his return.

Intertwined together, these three dimensions of eschatological expectations became hardwired into the Church, and infused it, for Paul, with a missionary urgency and an uncompromising ethic. The church must speak to everyone with loving passion about Jesus. At the same time, Christians were responsible to live in a profound moral simplicity that assessed every behavior by the question, "What should we be doing when Jesus returns?"

Discussion Points

- Who are the new participants in the company of Paul as his second mission journey ensues? What is the unique indication in the book of Acts that doctor Luke joined the troupe at Troas? How does the text of Acts indicate some of the ways in which the members of this group interacted, and how they envisioned Paul as their leader?
- What was the initial makeup of the Philippian Christian congregation? What were the social roles of those who first became members of that church?
- How do Paul and Silas's Roman citizenship benefit them as they travel deeper into the heartland of the empire?
- What was the central focus of Paul's missionary preaching? How is this theme explored further with the Thessalonian church through Paul's letters? What were the critical issues at stake when trying to understand the implications of this theological point?
- How did the early Church deal with the delay in Jesus' promised return? What were the major options available, and how do these still inform Christian theology today?

For Further Investigation

Bruce, F. F. (Downers Grove: InterVarsity, 1982). *1 & 2 Thessalonians.*

Green, Gene. (Grand Rapids: Eerdmans, 2002). *The Letters to the Thessalonians.*

32.

Life in a First Christian Congregation

Paul Wrestles for the Soul of Corinth

P aul wrote his letters to the Thessalonians while he was staying in Corinth. This city, located at the southwestern end of the narrow land bridge between Greece's northern and southern mainland regions, played a vital role for the region in both land and sea trade. It was a wealthy metropolis during the first century A.D., and coupled that abundance of resources with many social vices. Sexual openness and experimentation, in particular, oozed out of Corinth, until the rest of the Mediterranean world began to use its name to identify lascivious lifestyles.

Paul's stay in Corinth is quickly told in Acts 18:1–17. He began his missionary sojourn there as usual, with a time of teaching about Jesus to the Jews in the local synagogue. Paul is eventually forced out by vigorous opponents, who refuse to acknowledge that Jesus could have been the promised Messiah. Although Paul is no longer permitted to speak in the synagogue, the leader of the synagogue becomes a believer, as did a good number of its members. From a new location in the house adjacent to the synagogue, and also from his workspace as a tentmaker in the Corinthian market, Paul broadens his preaching dialogues with people, until a thriving congregation is formed of both Jewish and Gentile converts.

Figure 32.1 Paul's third mission journey.[1]

Encouraged by a vision that affirmed divine blessing on his ministry in Corinth (Acts 18:9–11), Paul remains in the city at least a year and a half (virtually all of 50 A.D., and well along into 51 A.D.). Then he decides to make a report back at his sending church in Syrian Antioch, and takes his new friends, Priscilla and Aquila, along (Acts 18:18). Stopping briefly in Ephesus across the Aegean Sea, Paul feels a strong pull to engage in a similar church-planting effort there. But he is already committed to his travel plans, so he leaves Priscilla and Aquila in Ephesus, and vows to return soon (Acts 18:19–21).

It was probably a couple of months later that Paul traveled overland through Asia Minor, and set up shop in Ephesus (Acts 19:1). Priscilla and Aquila had already established a solid core of converts and new leaders. Among their number was Apollos, a keen and well-schooled Jew from Alexandria, who was able quickly to understand how Jesus could be the Jewish Messiah (Acts 18:24–28).

Paul stays on in Ephesus for more than two years (Acts 19:8–10), carrying out a number of regional mission journeys (note the various travel itineraries listed in 2 Corinthians 1:15–7:16), and growing a significant Christian presence in the city itself. It is during this time that members from his former congregation in Corinth begin to contact Paul with questions about theology, ethics, and church practices. Paul's responses will eventually become his most passionate and profound letters of Christian instruction. We know them today as 1 and 2 Corinthians.

The Corinthian Correspondence

Probably sometime in late 51 A.D. or early 52 A.D., Paul sends a letter of strongly worded reproof to the Corinthian congregation. No copies have survived, but from what Paul himself says about this communication in 1 Corinthians 5:9, it is easy to see why some might take exception to it. Indeed, it appears that a number of people in the congregation began to disown Paul's authority after reading that letter, and then began to instigate factionalism in the community. Cliques grew, based upon personal preferences about which leaders were better preachers, and who had a right to claim greater sway among them (see 1 Corinthians 2–4). Meanwhile, a delegation of three men (Stephanus, Fortunatus, and Achaicus), all highly respectful of Paul's apostolic authority, travel from Corinth to Ephesus, bringing to Paul an oral report about the difficulties going on in the church. They also carry a written list of questions that members of the congregation are raising.[1]

---

1   Copyright © by J B Phillips Estate. Source: http://www.ccel.org/bible/phillips/JBPhillips.htm

1 Corinthians

Paul quickly writes a letter of response. Although it is actually his second letter to the Corinthian congregation, because the earlier communication has been lost, this one survives as 1 Corinthians in our New Testaments. Immediately, in the opening passages, Paul addresses the difficulties some have at his continued influence in the congregation. He chastises the members for dividing up into parties, where each waves a banner acclaiming the worthiness of a different leader. These groupings were sinful and disruptive, according to Paul, for they denied the honor that ought to be given only to the true head of the Church, Jesus Christ. Such schisms also played favorites among human leaders, setting them against each other, rather than recognizing their complementary gifts for helping the Church as a whole to grow. By chapter 4, Paul is ready to give a declaration for his own apostolic authority, pleading with the Corinthians to receive his teachings as God's own initiatives toward them.

In chapters 5 and 6, Paul painfully rehearses some of the examples of immorality within the congregation that must have been the focus of his earlier letter. Several social sins, including blatantly inappropriate sexual relations and lawsuits between Christians, are marched out onto the platform in descriptions that must have left little doubt as to whom Paul was talking about. The reflections about sexual behaviors may have reminded Paul of the queries on the list brought by Stephanus, Fortunatus, and Achaicus. To these he turns next. Apparently there were eight questions raised:

> ### 1 Corinthians in Summary
>
> - Reproof for Divisions and Sins (1–3)
> - Reminder of Apostles' Authority (4)
> - Specific Pastoral Problems: (5–6)
>   - Blatant sexual immorality (typical of Corinth)
>   - Lawsuits between Christians
> - Responses to Questions:
>   - About marriage, singleness, and divorce (7:1–24)
>   - About the conduct of virgins (7:25–40)
>   - About meat dedicated to idols (and apostolic authority) (8:1–11:1)
>   - About worship practices, especially the Lord's Supper (11:2–33)
>   - About spiritual gifts (12–14)
>   - About Jesus' resurrection and ours (15)
>   - About the collection for the poor in Jerusalem (16:1–11)
>   - About Apollos (16:12)

- Is singleness a more appropriate Christian lifestyle than being married, and if so, what should married folk do about it? (7:1–24).
- How should unmarried people handle their sexual desires? (7:25–40).
- When we are offered meat that originates in local religious ceremonies involving other gods, what are we to do (and who gives you a right to tell us)? (8:1–11:1).
- What is the most appropriate way to celebrate the Lord's Supper, especially with the diversity of our congregational population? (11:2–33).
- The expression of spiritual gifts is becoming a conflict among us. How do we deal with this? (12–14).
- Did Jesus really come back to life after his death, and does it matter? (15).

- Is there a standard practice about sharing our possessions and financially contributing to the needs of others? (16:1–11).
- When is Apollos coming to provide some leadership among us? (16:12).

It is in Paul's reflections on marriage, singleness and virginity that some have found him a misogynist. He advocates singleness as preferable to marriage, and sexual abstinence as a sign of spiritual strength. But this letter must be viewed alongside Paul's recent correspondence with the Thessalonian congregation, where his concern for the return of Jesus shapes all other dimensions of his theology. The same is true here. Paul would later write more tenderly about marriage and family relations (Ephesians 5:22–33). At this time, however, he is concerned that the freedom in Christ which people are experiencing should not lead them to licentious behaviors. Christian identity and morality, according to Paul, must be eschatologically conditioned: Live always as if Jesus were coming back tomorrow, and give no reason for others around you to be offended unnecessarily by your actions.

The matter of meat offered to idols in chapters 8–10 is very interesting, because it arises from confusion about the instructions issued by the Jerusalem council several years before (Acts 15). Gentiles were told that they did not have to first become practicing Jews in order to become believing Christians. But some social and dietary suggestions were offered, so that Gentiles and Jews might be able to share table fellowship, particularly when commemorating the Last Supper together. The brief instruction issued by the Jerusalem council several years before was to "abstain from food sacrificed to idols" (Acts 15:29).

But already now, that command was being interpreted in various ways. When animal sacrifices were made at cultic shrines, particularly on well-attended public occasions, there was often too much flesh, either for burning or for eating at the time. Without refrigeration, since the meat was destined to spoil quickly, much of the excess was dumped into the markets at bargain-basement prices. Because many of the Christians in Corinth were slaves or from lower classes, this inexpensive meat offered a lot of meal for the money. And that is where the controversy began.

Some folks, who had taken strong hold on the freedoms offered by Christ, knew that idols were not rival gods, and therefore any meat purchased in this way was simply a wise use of funds. Others, however, who had emerged into Christianity from prior work

Why Does Paul Think He Can Speak with Authority?

Paul uses a strange twist on words in 1 Corinthians 7:10 and 12. In the first, he says that his words are the direct command of the Lord. In the second, he says that he is speaking from his own authority, and not from the Lord. What does he mean?

It seems that Paul was very conscious of elements of doctrine or moral behavior about which there was a direct command in the Old Testament, or concerning which Jesus had distinctly spoken. In new situations where there was not a clearly articulated mandate from God of these kinds, Paul often felt he had the authority as an apostle to give reasonable religious direction. This he does in 1 Corinthians 7:12. Further confirmation of this understanding seems evident in 1 Corinthians 7:25, and is likely the manner in which other ethical pronouncements from Paul are to be read (for instance, 1 Timothy 2:12).

at the shrines and former participation in the cultic practices of these non-Christian religions, found it scandalous for Christians to buy and eat such meat. Another group remembered the instructions of the Jerusalem council, and thought it a matter of principle not to engage in this act that had specifically been prohibited by the church leaders.

Paul's response sorts through these differing reflections on Christian freedoms and interpersonal responsibilities, and leaves the final decisions up to maturing believers who are wise enough to understand how their behaviors can impact others. Once again, as with his instructions in his letter to the Galatians, Paul places the goal of a loving response to Jesus as primary in the making of all moral and ethical choices, and follows that closely with a sense

> ### 2 Corinthians in Summary
>
> –Praise to "the God of all comfort" (1:1–11)
>
> –Paul reminisces nostalgically: travel plans, apostolic authority, difficulties and eternal hopes, and the ministry of reconciliation (1:12–7:16)
>
> –Encouragement to give in the offering for the poor in Jerusalem (8–9)
>
> –Paul defends his authority and ministry (10–12)
>
> Closing notes of care and concern (13)

of obligation to serve and help others. In effect, Paul's ethical code is essentially that which Jesus espoused: Love God above all, and love your neighbor as yourself (Matthew 22:37–40).

It is while addressing this situation that the secondary issue of Paul's apostolic authority comes into question. He uses the question raised by the congregation, along with the different views about the topic that were circulating among its members, to reaffirm his own divine calling, and to restate the wisdom that has been granted to him by the Lord of the Church for adjudicating in these matters. Just as the Corinthians need to probe with wisdom the underlying issues to social and ethical mores, so they need to assess Paul's own leadership qualifications as they continue in or reject a relationship with him.

Paul's response to questions about worship practices (11:2–33) contains a reflection on two social value systems. First, with regard to differing roles for women and men in society, Paul wants to ensure that the genders are not blurred. There is a creational distinction between females and males, according to Paul, and this must not be erased, even by the freedoms found in Christ. At the same time, this gender distinction ought not to undermine the broad equality by which the gifts of the Spirit are distributed. Both women and men can and should prophesy. Spiritual leadership in the church is not limited by gender.

Second, in a review of the church's celebration of "the Lord's Supper," as it was becoming known, another facet of social interaction was addressed. The "differences" within the congregation were not only of the kind where parties became loyal to different leaders (1 Corinthians 1–3), but also the manifestation of divergent socioeconomic groupings present in Corinthian society. The reason why some who attended these Lord's Supper gatherings "go ahead without waiting for anybody else" and others "remain hungry," was due to the divergent lifestyle practices of the rich and the poor among them. Wealthy people were able to come and go as they pleased, including showing up to worship services, potluck dinners, and Lord's Supper celebrations right at the start. The poor and the slaves, however (some likely coming from the same households), were often late to arrive because they had to fulfill their domestic work obligations first. Paul declared that "recognizing the body of the Lord" was necessary if the Lord's Supper was to be celebrated properly. This did not mean having the capacity to understand an appropriate theological theory of the atonement, or some other such cognitive ability. Instead, it amounted to remembering that all who belong to Jesus are welcome at his table, and none have more rights than others. If this socially and economically diverse group of society was indeed the body of Christ, each must live and act accordingly, making room at the table for all.

This reflection on the expression of the body of Christ at the communion meal may have significantly shaped Paul's next reflections. When answering the Corinthians' question about spiritual gifts (1 Corinthians 12–14), Paul further develops the body of Christ metaphor, making it the core analogy by which both the identification and expression of unique gifts were to happen. At the center of this discussion, Paul pens one of the most beautiful hymns about love ever recorded (1 Corinthians 13). Although it is often lifted from its context to become a wedding text, this passage is actually the glue that holds together all of Paul's testimony concerning spiritual gifts. Only when these are used out of love, and expressed through love, is the true community of faith formed and nurtured.

Next follows Paul's powerful reflections on the meaning of Jesus' resurrection, and its implication for each of us who lives and dies (1 Corinthians 15). Beginning with eyewitness testimonies about the reality of Jesus' return to bodily life, Paul traces out the necessity of Jesus' physical resurrection for the affirmation of human existence itself. Then Paul goes on to explain the metamorphoses that all of us will go through, when we one day share in both Jesus' death and his resurrection. Paul's final words on this subject are a marvelous bit of encouragement: "Therefore, my dear brothers, stand firm. Let nothing move you. Always give yourselves fully to the world of the Lord, because you know that your labor in the Lord is not in vain" (1 Corinthians 15:58).

Drawing the letter quickly to a close, Paul explains the collection for the poor in Jerusalem that he had organized and how he wished for the Corinthians to take a part in this sharing of the blessings of God with those in need (1 Corinthians 16:1–11). Paul includes in these instructions his intended travel itinerary, so that they would have their gifts ready when he arrived.

Finally, there is a brief and cryptic note about Apollos. Evidently some were asking when this renowned preacher and teacher would come to Corinth, possibly to take up the primary congregational leadership position that Paul had vacated. There were many in Corinth who appreciated Apollos's gifts, and some even preferred him to Paul (1 Corinthians 1, 3). Paul apparently wanted to accommodate these needs and wishes of this congregation, for he was urging Apollos to go back to Corinth, even though Apollos seemed unwilling at the time, possibly because of his warm bonds with Priscilla and Aquila, or because of the growing tensions in the Corinthian congregation that were causing Paul and others to experience severe leadership headaches. Serving as pastor in the Corinthian congregation was a monumental challenge, and Apollos apparently knew that going there as senior pastor was no enviable job!

2 Corinthians

The letter we call 1 Corinthians was not well received by its original readers. Their relations with Paul apparently deteriorated rapidly after it arrived, and many more among them began to call into question Paul's presumed ongoing authority. In response, Paul decides that he needs to make a personal visit, both to address the immoral behaviors to and renew his pastoral ties with the church as a whole. Paul's return to Corinth was anything but triumphant, however, and actually turned out to be a bust. Later, he would call it a "painful visit" (2 Corinthians 2:1).

After this debacle, Paul limps back to Ephesus confused and hurt, and writes a severe letter of reproof that later caused him regret because of its caustic tone and content (2 Corinthians 7:8). Although we might wish to know more specifically what Paul said in that correspondence, no copies have survived. Still, Paul's strongly worded pastoral medicine apparently worked, at least to a degree, for when Titus made his report after delivering the letter, he told of great and pervasive repentance and sorrow among the Corinthians (2 Corinthians 7:6–16). Humility was breeding healing and hope.

About the same time that Titus was back in Corinth, Paul apparently has a near-death experience during a preaching trip to Troas (2 Corinthians 1–2). This scare seems to have been the trigger which initiated Paul's fourth letter, a letter of comfort and tenderness to the Corinthian congregation. Evidently, Paul needed to confirm the renewal of his relationship with the Church, lest, if he should die soon, the lingering memories of their interaction would only be pain and conflict. Paul's last letter to Corinth survives as our 2 Corinthians.

It is a passionate, tender, personal and encouraging communication. Paul can hardly repeat the word "comfort" often enough in his opening paragraph (2 Corinthians 1:3–7). Then he reminisces nostalgically, telling of his travel plans, his apostolic authority and how it came to him, the difficulties he has faced over the years of dedicated service to God and the Church, and the ministry of reconciliation that motivates him (2 Corinthians 1:12–7:16).

Next, Paul injects another note about his organization of the massive offering for the poor in Jerusalem (2 Corinthians 8–9), and uses the occasion to nurture expressions of authentic gratitude. Then, once again, he defends his apostolic authority and ministry (2 Corinthians 10–12), basing these in his divine calling, his servant lifestyle, his different motives from the "false apostles" who are circling about as if to create names and kingdoms for themselves; his profound vision of God's glory, coupled with the humbling weakness of his body; and his passionate concern for the Corinthians. Paul closes this otherwise engaging letter with somewhat fearful anticipations of the confrontations he might again face when he arrives in Corinth. He ends, though, with a clear sense of longing for the warmth he expects on the occasion of their reunion (2 Corinthians 13).

There is no other congregation of the first-century Christian Church about which we know more than the one in Corinth. Paul's constant contact with this troublesome fellowship over half a decade produced the New Testament's clearest teachings concerning the church's ministry practices, and a host of intimate reflections on the development of life and leadership in a local outpost of the kingdom of God. For this reason alone, 1 and 2 Corinthians are a priceless treasure, always being mined and refined by later generations of Christians who continue to wrestle with the same issues and problems, and who seek to claim similar joys and hopes.

In summary, Paul's interaction with the Corinthian congregation may be charted in the following manner:

I	Paul forced from Thessalonica, has a stopover in Athens, goes on to Corinth for year-and-a-half stay	50-51	Acts 17-18
II	Paul travels to Jerusalem & Antioch, then establishes new mission in Ephesus	51	Acts 19
III	Paul stays in Ephesus for more than two years, writes his first letter to Corinth (no longer extant)—a strong reproof against immoral connections	51-53	1 Corinthians 5:9
IV	The Corinthian congregation sends Stephanus, Fortunatus & Achaicus with a letter of concerns & questions	52	1 Corinthians 7:1
V	Paul responds with his second letter to the church, now known to us as 1 Corinthians	53	1 Corinthians
VI	Relations with the Corinthian congregation deteriorate; Paul's authority is questioned during his "painful visit" to Corinth	53	1 Cor. 4:18; 2 Cor. 2:1, 12:14, 21, 13:1-2
VII	Returning to Ephesus, Paul writes a "severe letter" (no longer extant), delivered by Titus, hoping to address this dark situation	53	2 Corinthians 7:5-16
VIII	Paul leaves Ephesus on an evangelism trip to Troas, has a near-death experience, becomes concerned about his unreconciled Corinthian relationship	53	2 Corinthians 1-2
IX	Paul finally meets Titus in Macedonia, hears good & bad news from Corinth, and sends his fourth letter (our 2 Corinthians)	53	2 Corinthians
X	Paul makes a third (final) visit to Corinth (stays with Gaius); writes letter to church in Rome	54	Acts 20:2-3; Romans 16:1-2, 23

Figure 32.2 Chronological chart of the interactions between Paul and the Corinthian congregation

Discussion Points

- Summarize the journeys of Paul that brought him into contact with the congregation in Corinth, and outline the correspondence and other contacts that transpired between them. How do the letters of 1 and 2 Corinthians in the New Testament fit into this picture?
- What were the primary difficulties being experienced in the early Corinthian congregation? How does Paul address these matters?
- What were the questions on the list of issues that the delegation from Corinth brought to Paul while he was living in Ephesus? What are Paul's primary responses to these questions?
- How did the matter of the instruction from the Jerusalem council in Acts 15 become a new source of conflict in the Corinthian congregation? What is Paul's advice to those who wrestled with these matters?
- What are some of the worship practices and public ceremonies typical of the early Church that we can deduce from 1 Corinthians? What lingering rites of the Christian Church emerge from actions already in vogue at that time?
- How is the tone of 2 Corinthians significantly different from that of 1 Corinthians? What might account for the divergence? What are the primary issues Paul talks about in 2 Corinthians?

For Further Investigation

Barnett, Paul. (Grand Rapids: Eerdmans, 1997). *The Second Epistle to the Corinthians.*

Blomberg, Craig L. (Grand Rapids: Zondervan, 1995). *1 Corinthians.*

Fee, Gordon D. (Grand Rapids: Eerdmans, 1987). *The First Epistle to the Corinthians.*

Garland, David E. (Grand Rapids: Baker, 2003). *First Corinthians.*

Garland, David E. (Nashville: Holman, 1999). *2 Corinthians.*

33.

Summarizing Christian Testimony

Paul's Letter to the Roman Congregation

S omewhere around late 53 A.D., the social and economic impact of the Christian gospel began to be felt acutely in Ephesus. Among the many cultural and civic resources of that city was its shrine to Artemis (known among the Romans as Diana). This temple was considered to be one of the Seven Wonders of the World. In fact, a great portion of the economy of Ephesus was derived from the cultic activities surrounding the temple, along with the religious tourist trade it brought to the city. As Christian adherents multiplied in Ephesus, and numbers of participants in the religious and social services related to the temple decreased, the local business world felt deeply challenged.

In response, "a silversmith named Demetrius" called together other craftsmen, and incited a public riot that brought the city to a standstill (Acts 19:23-41). Local government officials eventually defused the situation, but Paul believed the time had come for him to move on. He traveled around the Aegean Sea, collecting the offerings that had been set aside in the churches for the large benevolence gift he was planning to bring to Jerusalem. Paul arrived in Corinth either late in 53 or early in 54, and stayed three months with his friend, Gaius (Acts 19:1-3;

Paul's Letter to the Roman Congregation in Summary 📖

Theme: "The Righteousness of God" (1:1–17)

Sin: It is pervasive and crippling (1:18–3:20)

Salvation: It is a gift like that received by Abraham, and while we wrestle with it, God never lets go of us (3:21–8:39)

Interlude: But what about the Jews? (9–11)

Service: (12–15)

    The service of love (12)

    Service in society (13)

    Weak and strong: Meat offered to idols again (14–15:13)

Closing Notes: Paul's authority and travel plans; many personal greetings (15:14–16:27)

Romans 16:23). When he found that another acquaintance (and a leader in the Christian congregation located in Cenchrea, one of Corinth's seaport suburbs) named Phoebe was making a trip to Rome (Romans 16:1), Paul quickly penned what has become the most orderly summary of early Christian theology.

Because Paul had not yet made a visit to Rome, this letter is less personal and more rationally organized than was often otherwise true. Paul intended this missive to be a working document; the congregation, already established in the capital city of the empire, would be able to read and discuss it together, in anticipation of Paul's arrival, which was planned for some months ahead (Romans 1:6-15). Paul summarized his working theme and emphasis up front: A new expression of the "righteousness of God" had been recently revealed, with great power, through the coming of Jesus Christ (Romans 1:17).

Theme: "The Righteousness of God"

Paul moves directly from his brief declaration about the righteousness of God into an extended discourse on the wrath of God as revealed against wickedness (Romans 1:18). Because of this, many have interpreted Paul's understanding of God's righteousness as an unattainable standard, against which the whole human race is measured and fails miserably. Only then, in the context of this desperate human situation, would the grand salvation of Christ be appreciated and enjoyed.

But more scholars believe that Paul's assertions about the righteousness of God actually have a positive and missional thrust. In their understanding of what Paul says, it is precisely because of the obvious corruption and sinfulness in our world, which are demeaning and destroying humanity, that God needed again, as God did through Israel, to assert the divine will. In so doing, the focus of God's righteousness is not to heap judgment upon humankind; instead, God's brilliant display of grace and power in Jesus ought to draw people back to the creational goodness God had originally intended for them. In other words, the Creator has never changed purpose or plan. The divine mission through Israel was to display the righteousness of God, so that all nations might return to the goodness of Yahweh. Now again, in Jesus, the righteousness of God is revealed as a beacon of hope in a world ravaged by evil bullies. The power of God is our only sure bodyguard against the killing effects of sin and society and self.

Sin and Its Pervasive Demoralization of Human Life

This more positive perspective on the righteousness of God fits well with the flow of Paul's message. In chapters 1:18–3:20, Paul describes the crippling effect of sin. We are all alienated from God (1:18–25). But we are also alienated from each other (1:26–32), so that we begin to treat one another with contempt and painful arrogance, and destroy those around us in the malice which blinds us. We are even, says Paul, alienated from our own selves (2:1–11), not realizing how tarnished our sense and perspectives have become.

We make excuses about our condition (2:12–3:20), claiming that we are actually pretty good people (2:12–16), or accusing society and religion of raising moral standards to levels that are simply unrealistic (2:17–3:4), or even blaming God for all the nastiness around us and within us (3:5–20). Yet, the result is merely self-deception, and continued rottenness in a world that seems to have no outs.

Once the stage has been set for Paul's readers to realize again the pervasive grip of evil in this world, Paul marches Abraham out onto the stage as a model of divine religious reconstruction. God does not wish to be distant from the world, judgmental and vengeful. Rather, Jesus come, the fullness of God's healing righteousness revealed.

Salvation and Its Powerful Transforming Initiatives

The story of God's righteousness as grace and goodness begins with Abraham. God has always desired an ever-renewing relationship with the people of this world, creatures made in God's own image. Paul describes God's heart of love in 3:21–31, using illustrations from the courtroom (we are "justified"–3:24), the marketplace (we receive "redemption"–3:24), and the Temple ("a sacrifice of atonement"–3:25). Moreover, while this ongoing expression of God's gracious goodness finds its initial point of contact through the Jews (Abraham and "the law" and Jesus), it is clearly intended for all of humankind (3:27–31).

This is nothing new, according to Paul. In fact, if we return to the story of Abraham, we find some very interesting notes that we may have glossed over. "Blessedness" was "credited" to Abraham before he had a chance to be "justified by works" (4:1–11) In other words, whenever the "righteousness of God" shows up, it is a good thing, a healing hope, an enriching experience that no one is able to buy or manipulate. God alone initiates a relationship of favor and grace with us (4:1–23). In fact, according to Paul, this purpose of God is no less spectacular than the divine quest to re-create the world, undoing the effects that the cancer of sin has blighted upon us (Romans 5). It feels like being reborn (5:1–11). It plays out like the world itself is being remade (5:12–21). This is the great righteousness of God at work!

Now, Paul gets very practical. Although we might think that we would jump at the opportunity to find such grace and divine favor, Paul reminds us that our inner conflicts tear at us until we are paralyzed with frustration and failure (Romans 6–7). Sometimes we deny these struggles (6:1–14). Sometimes we ignores these tensions (6:15–7:6). Sometimes we grow bitter in the quagmire of it all (7:7–12). And sometimes we even throw up our hands in despair (7:13–24).

Precisely then, says Paul, the power of the righteousness of God as our bodyguard is most clearly revealed Thankfully, God's righteousness grabs us and holds us, so that through Jesus and the Holy Spirit we are never separated from divine love (Romans 7:25–8:39). Hope floods through us because we know Jesus and what He has done for us (8:1–11). Hope whispers inside of us as the Holy Spirit reminds us who we truly are, and whose we will always be (8:12–27). Hope thunders around us, as God's faithfulness is shouted from the heavens right through the pages of history (8:28–39): "… we are more than conquerors through him who loved us. For I am convinced that neither death nor life, neither angels nor demons, neither the present nor the future, nor any powers, neither height or depth, nor anything else in all creation, will be able to separate us from the love of God that is in Christ Jesus our Lord."

Interlude: The Knotty Problem of Election

This powerful testimony seems to cause Paul to reflect ruefully, however, on a truly knotty theological problem. If Paul can be so certain about God's strident grace toward us in this new age of the Messiah, why did God's declarations of favor toward Israel in the previous age of revelation seem to fail? Why did Israel lose its privileged place in the divine plan, while the spreading church of Jesus Christ is suddenly God's favored child?

These questions become the research matters for Paul's internal intellectual debating team in Romans 9–11. First up comes the standard reflection that God is Sovereign. This means, for Paul, that God's special relationship with Israel was God's choice to make, and is not undone now that God wishes also to use a new tactic in the divine attempt at recovering the whole of humanity back into a meaningful relationship with God.

Nevertheless, according to Paul, there has been something amiss about Israel's side of this relationship with God. Rather than understanding its favored position as enlisting it into the divine global mission, the nation tended to become myopic and self-centered. Instead of believing that she, too, needed to repent and find God's care through grace, Israel supposed that she had an inherent right to divine favor.

In the end, Paul believes that partly through Israel's false presumptions, and partly because of God's temporary change of strategies in order to better fulfill the original divine redemptive mission, Gentiles have come to the center of God's attention, while Israel, though not forgotten, is partially sidelined for a time. But even this alteration in the temperature of God's relationship with Israel is a lover's game: Israel needs to feel the good jealousy for a partner that she has too long taken for granted, so that she will recover her passions of great love. In the meantime, however, all win. God wins in the divine missional enterprise. The Gentiles win because they have a renewed opportunity to get to know God. And Israel wins because she is never forgotten, and is coming round to a renewed love affair with her beau. No wonder Paul ends these reflections with a passionate doxology culled from Isaiah 40:13 and Job 41:11:

> Oh, the depth of the riches of the wisdom and knowledge of God! How unsearchable his judgments, and his paths beyond tracing out! Who has known the mind of the Lord? Or who has been his counselor? Who has ever given to God, that God should repay him? For from him and through him and to him are all things. To him the glory forever! Amen.

Service and Its Loving Expressions

Paul may well have had to wrestle his way through that problem of divine election, at least in part because of the mixed Jewish-Gentile makeup of the Roman congregation. This possible tension seems to reassert itself again in Paul's applications of Christian behavior in the chapters that follow. First, Paul urges a lifestyle of service rooted in sacrifice to Jesus (12:1-2), shaped by spiritual giftedness (12:3-8), and energized by love (12:9-21). Then Paul makes this servant behavior even more specific, by nodding to its public expressions (Romans 13): Obey the government as a tool of God's care in the restraint of evil (13:1-6), and live as good neighbors who glow with the righteousness of God in some pretty dark neighborhoods (13:8-14). Finally, Paul revisits the issues surrounding the matter of the purchase and consumption of meat offered to idols (Romans 14:1-15:13), just has he had probed it in 1 Corinthians 8:1-11:1. Here, though, the overt tensions between legalistic and licentious extremes of Christian behavior seem less consuming than they did when Paul wrote to the Galatians and the Corinthians. Instead, his instructions flow more gently out of his social ethic of love and service.

In his letter's concluding notes, Paul gives rather detailed travel plans (Romans 15:14-32), followed by a massive and interesting string of greetings to specific individuals who had become Paul's friends over the years (Romans 16). Included are words of appreciation for Priscilla and Aquila, now returned to their former home in Rome; a nod to Epenetus, whom Paul identifies as "the first convert to Christ in Asia" (which would mean that he probably was originally from Antioch of Pisidia, and encountered Paul on the first mission journey); family greetings to a couple who together are both acknowledged as "apostles," Andronicus and Junias; a reference, probably as a nickname, to a "dear friend" called Stachys ("Big Ears!"); and affirmations about Rufus, who may well have been the son of Simon of Cyrene, the man who carried Jesus' cross on the route to Golgotha (see Mark 15:21). From Paul's location in Corinth, greetings are sent by Timothy, Paul's family, the amanuensis (Tertius) who scribed Paul's letter, the head of the Corinthian congregation (Gaius), and even the director of public works for the city of Corinth (Erastus).

Paul's letter to the Roman congregation has become the sourcebook for much of Christian theology. It describes the mission of God in a grand sweep, addresses certain difficult problems associated with anthropology and culture, and focuses strongly on appropriate ethical and moral behavior. But most importantly, it speaks with passionate assurance about the love of God, and the grand divine desire to have intimacy with us.

> And we know that in all things God works for the good of those who love him, who have been called according to his purpose. For those God foreknew he also predestined to be conformed to the likeness of his Son, that he might be the firstborn among many brothers. And those he predestined, he also called; those he called, he also justified; those he justified, he also glorified. What, then, shall we say in response to this? If God is for us, who can be against us? He who did not spare his own Son, but gave him up for us all—how will he not also, along with him, graciously give us all things? Who will bring any charge against those whom God has chosen? It is Jesus, who died—more than that, who was raised to life—is at the right hand of God and is also interceding for us. Who shall separate us from the love

of Christ? Shall trouble or hardship or persecution or famine or nakedness or danger or sword? ... No, in all these things we are more than conquerors through him who loved us. For I am convinced that neither death nor life, neither angels nor demons, neither the present nor the future, nor any power, neither height nor depth, nor anything else in all creation, will be able to separate us from the love of God that is in Christ Jesus our Lord (Romans 8:28-39).

Discussion Points

- Where was Paul when he wrote his letter to the Romans? What significant ministry had he recently concluded, and what were his plans for the future? How did the congregation in Rome factor into these intentions?
- How is Paul's letter to the Roman congregation structured? What are its key points? How are these explained and developed?
- What is the meaning of Paul's theme phrase, "the righteousness of God?" How has it been variously interpreted, and why?
- What is the problem of divine election, set out positively in chapter 8, and then probed more negatively with regard to the history of Israel in chapters 9–11, with which Paul wrestles? How would you explain it to someone else who has never thought about it?
- What are the social implications of the Christian gospel, according to Paul, in Romans 12–15? How does the matter of "meat offered to idols" again enter the picture?

For Further Investigation

Moo, Douglas J. (Grand Rapids: Eerdmans, 1996). *The Epistle to the Romans.*

Schreiner, Thomas F. (Grand Rapids: Baker, 1998). *Romans.*

Zetterholm, Magnus. (Minneapolis: Fortress, 2009). *Approaches to Paul.*

34.

Two Testimonies on the Road to Prison

Unfinished Acts

After Paul sent his letter to Rome from Corinth, in early 54 A.D., a plot on his life was discovered (Acts 20:3). Paul left town quickly, but apparently altered his intended itinerary to avoid the assassination attempt. Instead of taking a ship directly to Syria, he went overland through Macedonia, making stops at Philippi and Troas (Acts 20:3–11). His brief stay in Troas, the hometown of Luke, proved quite eventful. During a marathon service of greetings, reports, and preaching in a hot upstairs room, one of the younger fellows in the crowd sat on a window ledge to catch cooler air, dozed off, and fell to the street below. Although the crowds shrieked at finding him dead, Paul was able to restore Eutychus's life.

Paul is in a hurry to get to Jerusalem, but the journey takes him right past Ephesus. Since he has invested so much into that congregation, he feels he could not ignore it as he traveled. Instead of making the trek inland to the city itself, though, Paul sent word on ahead, asking for the elders of the congregation to meet him in the port town of Miletus. There, in April of 54 A.D., Paul gives them a tearful farewell message, believing that they would never be face to face again (Acts 20:38). Then, Paul and his companions press on quickly to Jerusalem, even though ominous signs indicated that arrest and possible torture lay ahead for Paul (Acts 21:1–16).

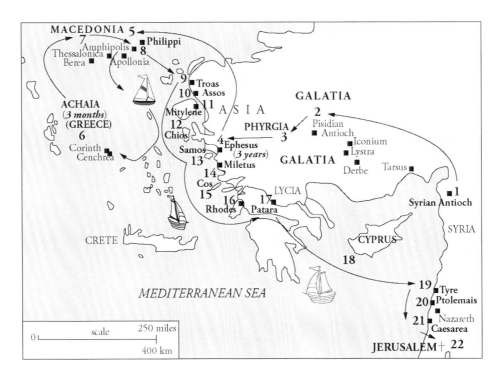

Figure 34.1 Paul's third mission journey.[1]

Arriving in Jerusalem, Paul is warmly welcomed, and makes a report to the church leaders about all that had happened in his last trip to the west (Acts 21:17–26). They share his excitement for the spreading witness of God's grace, but also inform Paul that rumors were rampant about his teachings. The "many thousands of Jews" who had believed in Jesus as Messiah were receiving propaganda from some folks who were jealous about Paul's missionary success. Others, also, have no use for Paul's perspective that the divine redemption strategy included Gentiles, who did not have to become Jews in order to be made Christians. In order to take the sting out of all this gossip and harmful rumor-mongering, the elders of the congregation in Jerusalem urge Paul to join four other Jewish men who are about to engage in weeklong rites of purification at the Temple. Paul gladly goes, and even agrees to pay the expenses of the others. This should make clear that Paul had not given up his Jewish roots and religious commitments, even though he saw God's mission widening in its scope.

But Paul's antagonists do not want to make peace. Instead, they stir up a riot in the Temple under the ruse that Paul is violating the place by bringing ritually impure Gentiles into its exclusively Jewish courts (Acts 21:27–32). The mob mania spreads, and only quick action on the part of the Roman commander stationed in the Fortress of Antonia, abutting the Temple, prevent Paul's death.

Although the Roman authorities do not view Paul as a criminal, there is so much confusion swirling around him that they decide to keep him under protective custody. This allows time

---

1 Copyright © by J B Phillips Estate. Source: http://www.ccel.org/bible/phillips/JBPhillips.htm

for the Jewish officials to bring formal charges against Paul, and for Paul to give his testimony to both the Jewish population of Jerusalem (Acts 22), and also the Gentile leaders stationed in Palestine at the time (Acts 26). While each of these testimonies is slightly altered to engage uniquely its particular audience, they are together very consistent about the actual details of Paul's conversion experience, and clearly mirror the original incident itself (Acts 9).

It seems likely that Luke believes that Paul was nearing the end of his ministry, and he wanted to make it clear that Paul's testimony was exactly the same in both Jewish and Gentile circles.

Figure 34.2 A modern miniature recreation of the fortress of Antonia overlooking the Temple courtyard in first century Jerusalem.[2]

Jewish antagonists, especially among the Pharisees (to whom Paul appealed as a comrade; Acts 23:1–10), could not fault Paul for his theology. Yet they disliked his easy interaction with the Gentiles, and believed that his notion of God's promiscuous favors toward these people was at best misguided, and at worst appallingly heretical.

Plots from the Jews, and political ploys from the Roman authorities, result in Paul's transfer to a prison in Caesarea, where his confinement continues for two years (Acts 23–24). Finally, when regimes change, Paul is given the opportunity to tell his story again, this time to the Roman rulers (Acts 25–26). Frustrated by the lack of movement in his case, Paul takes advantage of his rights as a Roman citizen, and appeals directly to the emperor. Ironically, King Herod Agrippa told Governor Festus that there really was no case against Paul, and that had he not appealed to Caesar, he should have been set free.

But the appeal now took over, and dictated Paul's next several years. Paul is shipped with other prisoners on a boat leaving Caesarea for Rome in late 56 A.D. (Acts 27). The winds at first work in their favor, but sometime near the end of 56 A.D., a violent storm tosses their boat around for a while, and eventually smashes it against the shoals of Malta. Once again, Paul is protected from several threats against his life (Acts 28), and actually becomes a favored refugee on the island.

Three months later, in early 57 A.D., the prisoners are put on another ship that had wintered at Malta, and the journey to Rome resumes. Word of Paul's imminent arrival spread quickly through the Christian community, and people came long distances to meet him, forming an entourage that accompanied Paul the rest of the way to Rome. At last, Paul arrives in the great city, under circumstances much different than he had hoped or imagined. Nevertheless, he gives thanks that God had fulfilled the earlier promise made (Acts 27:23–24), that Paul would indeed get to Rome, and bring the message of the gospel there as well.

---

2   Copyright in the Public Domain.

Figure 34.3 Paul's journey to Rome.[3]

Paul stays in Rome under house arrest for two years (57–59 A.D.), waiting for his appeal to be heard. During that time, he remains busy, preaching and teaching, and sharing his personal testimony (Acts 28:17–31). The rather abrupt ending to the book of Acts has provoked questions about Luke's intentions. Was the historian of the early Church intending to write volume 3? Did Luke document the later travels of Paul, but this text has been lost to us? Or was there, perhaps, a more satisfying conclusion to the book of Acts that has gone missing?

No evidence has been discovered for any of these possibilities in any manuscript tradition. Nor are there reports to support any such theories from among other early Christian sources. Instead, there is growing appreciation for the careful literary planning that Luke put into the book of Acts. In an organized manner, it unpacks the critical message of Jesus early on (Acts 1:8) about the expanding witness of his disciples, until the entire Earth has access to the good news. Luke's own literary clues reveal how he makes use of this flow, setting it out in growing circles of gospel penetration, each concluding with a progress report that indicates a measure of completion.

Now, through Paul's arrival in Rome, the gospel is entering the gateway to the entire world, "the ends of the Earth," as Jesus put it. But the task of witnessing to the world is ongoing, and cannot be accomplished merely by Paul's presence in the great city. For that reason, Luke gives no "progress report" at the end of Acts 28, in the way he did at the conclusion of each of the other sections, highlighting the spread of the gospel. Instead, he seems to imply that the next chapter is always being written by those who continue traveling to the ends of the Earth. In fact, we become the living testimony of Acts "29." We continue to write the story.

---

3   Copyright © by J B Phillips Estate. Source: http://www.ccel.org/bible/phillips/JBPhillips.htm

Discussion Points

- How does Paul express both his confidence in Gentile freedom not to have to live according to Jewish law as Christians and his personal practices of adhering to Jewish ritual traditions? Is Paul inconsistent in these things? Explain.
- What are key points of Paul's personal testimony? How do the two renditions, first to the Jews in Temple square (Acts 21) and then to the Roman leaders in Caesarea (Acts 26), show both similarities and differences? How closely do they match the initial record of Paul's conversion experiences in Acts 9?
- How does the abrupt ending of the book of Acts present a possible literary problem? What is a possible theological solution to that problem?

For Further Investigation

Stott, John R. W. (Downers Grove: InterVarsity, 1994). *The Message Acts: the Spirit, the Church, and the World.*

35.

Countercultural Revolution

Children of Light in an Awfully Dark Night

Four of Paul's letters mention that he is a prisoner at the time of their writing: Ephesians (3:1; 4:1; 6:20), Philippians (1:13-17), Colossians (4:10; 4:18), and Philemon (1; 23). According to the book of Acts (and a brief reference in 2 Corinthians 12:23), Paul was imprisoned a number of times. On most of these occasions, however, his incarceration was very brief (e.g., in Philippi; Acts 16:16-40). Two imprisonments, though, were of significant duration: Paul's two-year stint in Caesarean confinement (Acts 24) and the doublet of years he spent in Rome while waiting for Caesar to hear his appeal (Acts 28:30). Paul's prison letters could have been written from either of these, though there are good reasons to opt for Roman origins.

For one thing, it is clear that Paul's letters to the Colossians, Ephesians, and Philemon were written at the same time. They are sent by way of the same human carriers, Tychicus (Ephesians 6:21; Colossians 4:7) and Onesimus (Colossians 4:9; Philemon 8-19). They refer to the same people surrounding Paul in prison (Timothy, Aristarchus, Mark, Epaphras). And they deal with identical theological and pastoral issues in almost verbatim repetition of words (cf. Ephesians 5:21-6:9 and Colossians 3:18-4:1; Colossians 1:3-6, Philemon 4-6 and Ephesians 3:14-19). Such hints not only confirm the connections among these letters, but they also contain clues as to where Paul was when he wrote them. It is highly unlikely that Philemon's slave, Onesimus, would run away from the Lycus and Maeander river valleys in Phrygia (southwest Asia Minor) toward Palestine. Conversely, with trade and communications moving between that region and the capital of the

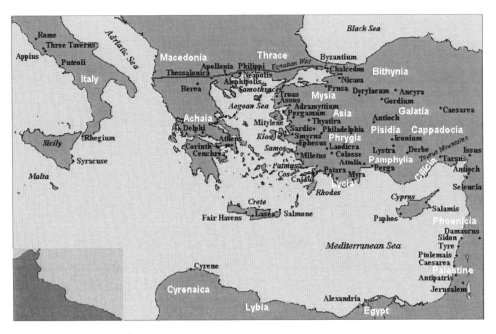

Figure 35.1 Key places in Paul's ministry.

empire, it is very likely that Onesimus would end up in Rome. So it is very reasonable to believe that Paul wrote his letters to the Colossians, Ephesians, and Philemon from Rome.

"Joy" in Philippians

- "I always pray with joy because of [you]" (1:3–8)
- "I rejoice" (1:18)
- "I will continue to rejoice" (1:18)
- "your joy" (1:26)
- "my joy" (2:2)
- "I am glad and rejoice" (2:17)
- "You too should be glad and rejoice with me" (2:18)
- "You may be glad" (2:28)
- "Welcome him in the Lord with great joy" (2:29)
- "Finally, my brothers, rejoice in the Lord!" (3:1)
- "my joy and my crown" (4:1)
- "Rejoice in the Lord always! I will say it again: Rejoice!" (4:4)
- "I rejoice greatly in the Lord" (4:10)

Similar arguments can be made about Philippians. Paul's reference to the "whole palace" in 1:13 could possibly indicate that he was in Caesarea, among the court officials who created a small replica of Roman governance in that provincial town. But it is highly unlikely, especially when Paul goes on to talk about fellow Christians "who belong to Caesar's household" (4:22). This can hardly be taken as anything other than a mention of the royal courts in Rome. Because of these clues, it seems obvious that all of Paul's prison letters were written while he was in Rome, between 57 and 59 A.D.

When looking at the contents of the letters themselves, it appears that Philippians was written earlier in Paul's Roman stay, while the other three were likely penned near the end of it. Paul seems to be somewhat settled into prison life when he writes to the Philippians; but in Paul's note to Philemon, he makes it clear that he expects to be released soon, and free again to travel. This would date Colossians, Ephesians, and Philemon to sometime in 59 A.D., while Philippians probably was sent in late 57 or early 58.

Paul's Letter to the Philippians

In spite of its brevity, Paul's letter to the Philippians contains a number of notes about Paul's changing situation and the people who are in and out of his social circle. Paul is "in chains" (Philippians 1:13), and around him are a number of preachers who testify about Jesus (Philippians 1:14–18), some for more noble reasons than others. Paul may have been depressed about his circumstances (Philippians 1:22–24), and maybe even thought at one time that he was about to die (Philippians 2:16–17), but he believes there is still a future ministry ahead of him in this life (Philippians 1:25–26). Recently, the Philippians had sent their pastor or key leader, Epaphroditus (Philippians 2:25–30), to bring a gift of food and clothes to Paul (Philippians 4:18), along with their warm wishes. Now Paul is sending this letter of thanks, and will soon commission his trusted associate, Timothy, to bring Epaphroditus home to Philippi (Philippians 2:19–30).

Pulling together these bits of information, a reasonable chronology surrounding the writing of Paul's letter to the Philippians might look like this:

- Sometime in the spring of 57 A.D., Paul arrives in Rome. While he is clearly a prisoner awaiting adjudication before
  Caesar himself, Paul is also a Roman citizen with rights and freedoms. And since the charges against him are sectarian (related to Jewish religious practices) rather than capital crimes, Paul is able to establish his own living circumstances within the larger palace precincts, while remaining under a type of house arrest.
- Probably late in 57 A.D. or early in 58, Epaphroditus, who has been serving as pastor or congregational leader in Philippi, brings Paul a rather significant gift from that church (Philippians 2:25; 4:10). It may have included both money and supplies; in any case, it greatly enhances Paul's comfort in his limited circumstances.
- Epaphroditus stays on with Paul for some time, assisting him as a servant. Unfortunately, Epaphroditus became ill and nearly died (Philippians 2:25–30), and only very recently has returned to full health.
- Paul believes that homesickness for Philippi and the congregation there might have contributed to Epaphroditus's grave malady, and vows to send him back home as soon as he is able to travel. Of course, a letter of appreciation and encouragement is a necessary part of all these things, so Paul pens Philippians, probably sometime in early 58 A.D.

Philippians in Summary 📖

–Praise and thanksgiving from prison (1)

–Great hymn of Jesus' humility and witness, plus the ministry of Timothy and Epaphroditus (2)

–Paul's old testimony and his new one (3)

–Much joy and much appreciation (4)

Paul's letter to the Philippians is the most joyful and uplifting note of the entire New Testament. Even in Paul's confinement, he is filled with delight in his relationships, and amazed at what God is doing (Philippians 1). Almost without needing to do so, Paul reminds the congregation of the great example of Jesus, who gave up everything in order to express the love of God to us (Philippians 2:1–18). Another example of this selfless care is found in both Timothy and Epaphroditus, each of whom had sacrificed much in order to serve others, especially the faith community in Philippi (Philippians 2:19–30). More encouragement to serve follows, with Paul reflecting on his own changes of behavior and value systems once he was gripped by the love of God in Jesus (Philippians 3). A few personal instructions and notes of appreciation round out the letter (Philippians 4).

Although other letters of Paul are more intentionally "theological," this small epistle has a particularly wonderful poetic reflection encapsulating the entire ministry of Christ in a few lines (Philippians 2:6–11). Because of its condensed and hymnic character, some think Paul brought these verses into his letter from an early popular Christian song or creedal statement. Perhaps so. Nevertheless, the whole of this short book is lyrical, and reaches for the superlatives in life through lines that are both economical and majestic:

Finally, brothers, whatever is true, whatever is noble, whatever is right, whatever is pure, whatever is lovely, whatever is admirable—if anything is excellent or praiseworthy—think about such things (Philippians 4:8).

Paul's letters Known as Philemon, Colossians, and "Ephesians"

Sometime after the letter to the Philippians was sent, and Epaphroditus had made the journey home, accompanied by Timothy (probably near the end of 58 A.D.), another visitor arrived. His coming would eventually elicit a whole new spate of letters from Paul:

• Onesimus, a runaway slave from Paul's friend Philemon, came to Rome and found

---

People in Philippians

- Timothy (with Paul in Rome, but not imprisoned)
  - Joint author with Paul (1:1)
  - Paul's junior partner, soon to be dispatched to Philippi (2:19-23)
- Epaphroditus (from Philippi, possibly Elder or Pastor)
  - "my brother, fellow worker and fellow soldier, who is also your messenger, whom you sent to take care of my needs" (2:25)
  - "For he longs for all of you and is distressed because you heard he was ill. Indeed he was ill, and almost died." (2:26-27)
  - "…I have received from Epaphroditus the gifts you sent." (4:18)
- Euodia and Syntyche (leading women, first converts)
  - "women who have contended at my side" (4:3), but who are now at odds with each other (4:2)
- Clement (evangelist and co-worker with Paul)
  - "fellow worker" (4:4)

The reference to Epaphroditus as a "fellow soldier," and his role as lead elder or pastor for the Philippian congregation, may indicate that he is the one who operated the jail in which Paul and Silas were imprisoned when they first came to Philippi (Acts 16). Similarly, one or the other of Euodia and Syntyche might be the young girl out of whom Paul cast the demonic spirit in his first encounter with her.

Paul. Perhaps Onesimus was overwhelmed by the alien environment of the big city, and heard that Paul, someone he had met a few years earlier, was in town. Or maybe Onesimus came to Rome specifically because he knew Paul was there, remembering how kindly Paul had treated him while the itinerant evangelist was staying at Philemon's home. In any case, Onesimus and Paul had a joyful reunion, and for a time Onesimus lived with Paul, acting out the true meaning of his name: "useful."

- After a while, however, Paul began to have qualms about ignoring the property rights that bound Onesimus to Philemon. Paul was sure that sometime soon he would run into his old friend again, and this secret of Onesimus spending time with him would not come to light without great damage to their relationship. In fact, Paul was beginning to make plans for his next travels, since he expected to be released from prison very shortly. Evidently, Paul had received word that his case was soon to be on Caesar's docket, and knew from Herod Agrippa's testimony (Acts 26:32) that royal judgment would clearly be in his favor. When freedom did come, Paul wanted to spend time with Philemon, as one stop on the next journey.

> **Philemon in Summary** 📖
>
> –Greetings, old friend! (1–7)
>
> –I'm sending "Useful" back to you as a brother, not a slave (8–21)
>
> –I hope to visit you soon (22–25)

- So, probably in early 59 A.D., Paul made plans to send Onesimus back to Philemon, accompanied by a trusted friend named Tychicus. Paul penned a short note to Philemon, explaining Onesimus's circumstances of both frustration and faith, and pleading with his friend to treat the young man well.

- About the same time, news came to Paul regarding a doctrinal controversy that was threatening the church in Colossae. This congregation had been established under the ministry of Epaphras (Colossians 1:7–8), a local believer who had originally come to faith through Paul's ministry in nearby Ephesus (Colossians 4:12–13), just down the Lycus and Maeander river valleys.

- Since Colossae was very close to Philemon's home, Paul decided to send a letter to that congregation, addressing these threats to the church's faithfulness and stability. Tychicus was asked to deliver this letter at the same time as he brought Paul's personal note to Philemon (Colossians 4:7–9).

- While he was in the writing mood, Paul also dictated a third letter, to be sent in the same direction at the same time. It was less personal and more general in the themes that it ex-

> **Colossians in Summary** 📖
>
> –You are great, and Jesus rules! (1)
>
> –Some of you are putting too much emphasis on rituals and disciplines; trust Christ! (2)
>
> –Get the view from above in order to set your values and practices in order (3:1–17)
>
> –Treat one another with respect (3:18–4:6)
>
> –Final greetings (4:7–18)

To Whom Was "Ephesians" Written?

Oldest manuscripts do not have "in Ephesus" in 1:1.

Contrary to Paul's universal practice, there are no personal references in the letter to individuals among its intended recipients.

At the conclusion of his letter to the Colossians, Paul writes: "After this letter has been read to you, see that it is also read in the church of the Laodiceans, and that you in turn read the letter from Laodicea" (4:16).

There is some early church testimony identifying "Ephesians" as Paul's letter to the "Laodiceans."

Ephesus became the operational center of the church in Asia Minor, and many documents were eventually collected there, including Paul's letters.

"Ephesians" in Summary

- Jesus is Lord of All! (1)
- Jesus has broken down the barrier between God and us (2:1–10) and between Jews and Gentiles (2:11–22), uniting all by grace
- Paul's Gentile ministry explained (3:1–13)
- Paul' magnificent prayer (3:14–21)
- Building up Christ's body (4:1–16) and living as witnesses of God's goodness (4:17–5:20)
- Respecting one another in social relationships (5:21–6:9)
- Putting on the "Armor of God" (6:10–20)
- Final greetings (6:21–24)

pressed than either of the others, and may well have been intended as a more generic epistle of encouragement to be circulated around the area churches. This letter seems to have arrived first in Laodicea (Colossians 4:16), and began a circuit around the regional congregations. Because Ephesus had been the launching pad for mission efforts throughout the region, the Christian congregation in Ephesus soon became recognized as the "mother church" of the rest, and probably came to be the official caretaker and repository of important documents. For that reason, this circular letter from Paul eventually ended up in Ephesus, and became known as Paul's letter to the "Ephesians."

Paul's short letter to Philemon consists mostly of kind greetings and personal good wishes. At its core, however, is a brief note about Onesimus's recent situation, and Paul's hopes for the slave's future honorable and brotherly treatment. This note from Paul precipitates centuries of lively debate and ultimately strong tensions and divisions in the Christian church. Since Paul affirms Philemon's right to own Onesimus as a slave, some have argued that slavery as a social institution is not intrinsically wrong, so long as the slaves are well cared for. Others, of course, have argued that the logical implication of Paul's letter is a mandate for Philemon to release Onesimus from slavery, and make him a paid employee, while treating him as a social equal. If so, Paul's letter to Philemon is actually diametrically opposed to slavery, and Paul is only making polite requests in a spirit of friendship and according to established social conventions.

The irreconcilability of these views eventually split Christian denominations in the United States into "northern" and "southern" factions over slavery. What seems to be a short, kind innocuous letter, has, unfortunately, produced a maelstrom of whirling controversy that continues to engender debate. Fortunately, Paul and Philemon did not seem to come to blows about the matter. At the close of that letter, Paul told Philemon to get the guest room ready, for Paul was sure he would be traveling soon to visit both Philemon and Onesimus.

Paul's letter to the Colossians is quite short, but it packs a big punch of theology and perspective. First, Paul celebrates the faithfulness of these disciples of Jesus, and also the great majesty and power of the one they serve (Colossians 1:1–23). After a short declaration of Paul's immense care for the Colossian congregation (Colossians 1:24–2:5), he addresses the problem that was beginning to divide the congregation (Colossians 2:6–23). Although it is difficult for us to know exactly what were the specific elements of the false teaching that some were embracing, it appears to have included the worship of angels, certain forms of asceticism, and possibly a unique version of how the commands given through Moses were to be kept. These slim details suggest to some that an early form of Gnosticism was taking root. Others find a Jewish connection, with certain leaders pushing for a Palestinian ritualistic legalism of the kind that Paul had reacted against so strongly in his letter to the Galatians. Whatever the case, Paul's response was to urge the congregation to focus on the superlative transformation brought by Jesus, which did not need to be supported with secondary rules and regulations.

Thus, it is reasonable to conclude that Paul's let-

Did Paul Write Colossians and "Ephesians?"

In a world without copyrights, agents, ISBN numbers and book publishers, some first- and second-century writers forged documents, claiming authorship under well-known names in order to put forward their ideas. This happened in the Christian Church as well as the rest of society.

Because of this, some scholars question whether all of the letters attributed to Paul were actually written by him. No dispute is raised about Romans, 1 and 2 Corinthians, Galatians, Philippians, 1 Thessalonians, or Philemon. But Ephesians, Colossians, and 2 Thessalonians are mildly debated, and the letters to Timothy and Titus are rejected as Pauline by a significant number of theologians.

For Ephesians and Colossians, the primary literary elements that spur this discussion are some unusually long sentences in these letters, a use of many words not found in Paul's writings, and a question as to whether some terms are given different theological meanings than what is considered the standard Pauline view.

ter to the "Ephesians" was actually a general letter intended for reading in all the area churches, that it is the document he referred to in Colossians 4:16, and that it became known by its current title because it ended up in the collection of documents held by the church in that city.

In an almost counterintuitive move, Paul then goes on to give what might be termed "rules" for Christian living. But these commands about marriage, family, and work relationships are more a projection of the social outcomes that should emerge when everyone's focus remains on Jesus (Colossians 3:1–4:1), rather than a new set of legalistic instructions. It is interesting that after brief statements about the responsibilities of wives (Colossians 3:18), husbands (Colossians 3:19), children (Colossians 3:20), and fathers (Colossians 3:21), Paul's advice to "slaves" is rather extended (Colossians 3:22–25). Philemon's slave, Onesimus, might well be carrying this packet of letters, and would certainly know many of the slaves who were part of this nearby congregation! Paul does include a brief challenge to "masters" as well (Colossians 4:1), exactly in line with the contents of his letter to Onesimus's master, Philemon. A few personal notes and many

Magnificent Ephesian Themes

- Prayer pervades this letter:
  - A prayer of praise (1:3-6)
  - Paul's junior partner, soon to be dispatched to Philippi (2:19-23)
  - Prayers on behalf of the readers (1:15-23)
  - A magnificent prayer (3:14-21)
  - A call to prayer (5:19-20)
  - Another call to prayer (6:18-20)
- The matter of Jews & Gentiles together in the church is addressed again, this time with glaring clarity (2:11-22). Here, however, the tone Paul sets is the most positive ever. The problems of divisions may be a human sociological issue, but Jesus has triumphed over all of them, and aggressively destroys our petty alienations while assertively establishing a new human community of faith and love.
- Paul's apostolic authority continues to be challenged or questioned (3:1-13), although he does not seem as self-conscious about his unique commissioning as when he was in the difficult times of his tumultuous relationship with the Corinthian congregation.
- Paul writes about Christian behavior in terms of ethical dualism which is both separatist and evangelical (4-5). It is separatist in that those who are transformed by the gospel of Jesus change their behaviors and no longer live in the unredeemed manner of the rest of society. It is evangelical in that the very change of behaviors provides an opportunity to call out to neighbors and former associates, bringing them also into the light of Jesus while there is still time.
- Eschatological expectations drive the urgency of both lifestyle and mission (5). Paul remains confident that Jesus is returning soon, and our energies must always be focused on not wasting time on frivolous matters, and on bringing others to faith in Jesus.
- Paul sees in marriage a mutual submission (5:21), but expresses the relationships between husband & wife analogically, therefore giving somewhat unique descriptions of relational roles to each (5:22-33). These roles may seem limiting or inappropriately defining, but in response to the culture of the times, they were extremely liberating.

personnel reports bring Paul's letter to a conclusion (Colossians 4:2-18).

Paul's third letter in the same dispatch is shaped in nearly the same as his letter to the Colossians. Jesus is Lord of all, Paul fairly shouts at the beginning, producing wonderful new life in all who are part of the Church (Ephesians 1). In place of Paul's instructions about the false teaching at Colossae comes a brief reminder that Jews and Gentiles are together on the same footing before God because of the powerful redemptive work of Jesus (Ephesians 2). As he begins to celebrate this amazing grace of God through prayer (Ephesians 3:1), Paul interrupts himself, reminding his readers of the specific calling he has received to know and communicate this divine revelation (Ephesians 3:2-13). Then, Paul resumes his powerful and profound prayer of praise (Ephesians 3:14-21), and launches into an extended metaphor on what it means for the living body of Christ to function in a dark world (Ephesians 4:1-5:20). Very similar to his instructions in Colossians 3, Paul outlines specific behaviors that are expected in Christian households (Ephesians 5:21-6:9).

These variations are rather easily explained by acknowledging Paul's rich literary and theological training, and remembering that he used an amanuensis to write his letters. This secretarial assistance likely influenced syntax and word choice.

In a brief, but scintillatingly clear, analogy, Paul dresses up the Christian warrior in full battle gear (Ephesians 6:10-20). Only one final note, telling of Tychicus's mission on Paul's behalf (Ephesians 6:21-22), and a short word of blessing (Ephesians 6:23-24), bring this letter to a close.

Paul's letters from prison address a couple of specific issues—the nature of a relationship between master and slave, for instance, when both are Christians, and a proper response to the false teaching that was being promulgated at Colossae. But mostly, these writings paint, in vibrant colors, the character of moral choices in a world that is compromised and broken. Darkness and light are the key metaphors. Evil has wrapped a blanket of pain and harm around all that takes place in the human arena. Jesus is the brilliant light of God, penetrating earth's atmosphere with grace and reconciliation. Because of Jesus' physical departure at the ascension, his followers now must step in and become a thousand million points of light, restoring relationships and renewing meaning. Jesus is great, and because of our connection with him, we can be great too. Not for our own sakes, of course, but as witnesses of the eschatological hope that tomorrow's amazing future of God is something we already participate today. That is why Christianity is the religion of the dawn.

Discussion Points

- What are the likely circumstances under which these "Prison Epistles" were written? How do Paul's letters to Philemon, Colossae, and "Ephesus" show literary and chronological connections?
- What is the theological message of the "hymn" about Jesus in Philippians 2? What are its implications for the Christian doctrine of "Christology" (how one views the person and work of Jesus)?
- What can we learn about Paul from his brief personal reflections in his letter to the Philippians?
- Who are Philemon and Onesimus? What is their relationship with Paul? How are these social dimensions explored theologically in the letter Paul writes to Philemon? Do Paul's instructions to Philemon and his relationship with Onesimus encourage or allow slavery as a legitimate expression of Christian social morality?
- What are the common themes expressed by Paul in his letters to the Colossians and the "Ephesians?" How are these themes nuanced in unique directions within each letter? What might have been the "heresy" to which Paul reacts in his letter to the Colossians?

For Further Investigation

Fee, Gordon D. (Grand Rapids: Eerdmans, 1995). *Paul's Letter to the Philippians*.

O'Brien, Peter T. (Grand Rapids: Eerdmans, 1999). *The Letter to the Ephesians*.

O'Brien, Peter T. (Waco: Word, 1982). *Colossians-Philemon*.

Wright, N. T. (Downers Grove: InterVarsity, 1989). *Colossians and Philemon*.

36.

Passing the Torch

Inspiring the Next Generation of Leaders

The question of Pauline authorship has become central to theological discussions about the "Pastoral Letters," 1 and 2 Timothy, and Titus. Though no scholars dispute the rightful place of these documents in the New Testament, and their theology is never considered to be non-Christian, a good number of reviewers believe that other leaders in the early Church penned these epistles. There are essentially five reasons for possibly taking this view:

- The events and travels mentioned in these letters do not fit with any chronology found in the book of Acts.
- There is a high concentration of words in these letters that are not used in any of Paul's other writings that have become part of the New Testament (306 out of the total of 848 Greek words in these letters are not found elsewhere).
- The structures of congregational life and the leadership roles that are

Figure 36.1 Key sites where Paul traveled.

identified appear to some to be more akin to ecclesiastical developments in the second century, rather than the middle of the first century.

- The writing style seems different from that in Galatians and Romans and Corinthians, including the manner in which some terms are used.
- Some of the wrong teachings which are warned against in these letters seem to presuppose a more fully developed official Church doctrine than was likely during Paul's life.

While these are weighty matters that will continue to stimulate scholarly discussion for years, there are a number of countervailing responses that need to be taken seriously. First, the letters to Timothy and Titus were pervasively received in the early Church as genuinely from Paul, without qualm or dispute. While other forgeries were discussed—and caught—the Pauline authorship of these letters was never questioned.

Second, the differences in vocabulary, between these letters and others that are universally acknowledged as authentically from Paul, can be attributed to the unique emphases, concerns and topics that were in focus. Any author's letters will vary greatly, depending on the relationship he or she has with the addressees and the circumstances that shape the reason for writing. When Paul wrote to congregations that were struggling with certain issues of doctrine or practice, he kept those particular matters central to his response. Here, unlike with the others, Paul is writing to long-time friends and pastors he has mentored, and his vocabulary expresses the unique relationship he has with these younger men.

Third, the unusual elements of style can be attributed to Paul's use of different amanuenses (writing scribes) for the various letters. While letter writing involves dictation, it is also influenced by the literary skills and vocabulary of the persons who actually put the pen to paper.

Fourth, there is a very obvious reason why the events noted in these letters do not fit the chronology of Paul's travels and contacts in Acts: that record ends at 59 A.D., while Paul was still a prisoner in Rome; these letters, on the other hand, were written sometime in the 60s, well after Paul had been released and had begun to travel once again. They came into being after Luke had finished the book of Acts, and so simply are not part of its chronologies.

Fifth, organizational developments in the church took shape rather rapidly, as is true of any social group. These letters were written more than a decade after Paul's early letters, and ought to reflect the changing leadership systems that evolved as Christian congregations matured. Beside, these letters were very specifically focused on leadership training in established congregations under the direction of second-generation pastors, a topic that was not addressed by Paul before this time.

To deny Pauline authorship for these "Pastoral Letters" goes against the perceptions of those who knew Paul and his successors, and produces many problems. Who would have written these letters, if not Paul, and why would they have been written? What would be gained by such forgeries, particularly if no alternative Christian group or sect laid claim to them as holding a "better" Christian theology? Why would so many of the key leaders of the early church accept them as from Paul if they mysteriously appeared in questionable circumstances? Little is gained and much is lost to move against the strong evidence of Pauline authorship.

A Possible Chronology

Assuming these pastoral epistles are genuinely Pauline, how do they fit into Paul's later life? Because we have no journal or historical record of Paul's travels after Acts 28, we have to admit more speculation than clarity. There are the strong bookends for dating the last decade of Paul's life, of course: his release from prison in Rome in 59 A.D. and his death around 67 A.D. In between, we have to arrange the pieces with the few clues ferreted out of Paul's writings, buttressed by a number of hints from other early church testimonies.

Because of Paul's promise to visit Philemon, made sometime during 59 A.D., along with our knowledge of the typical flow of traffic around the Mediterranean and the bits of travel reports that Paul makes to Timothy and Titus, it seems reasonable to assume that Paul traveled with Titus and Timothy from Rome to the island of Crete, soon after Paul's release in 59 A.D. There, he installed Titus as pastor, and then continued his journey to the mainland of Asia Minor. By late 59 A.D., Paul was likely enjoying the warm hospitality of his friends, Philemon and Onesimus, just outside of Colossae.

Around the turn of the next year, Paul probably headed down the Lycus and Maeander river valleys to Ephesus, which had been his base of missionary operations six or seven years before. The congregation in Ephesus was large and growing, and Paul assisted in installing as pastor there his most promising protégé, Timothy. Perhaps sometime during the year 60 A.D., Paul traveled on to Macedonia (1 Timothy 1:3), probably wanting to spend time with his friends and ministry supporters in Philippi (Philippians 1:25–28, 2:24).

From that city, many have speculated, Paul traveled on to Spain. This was certainly his plan a few years earlier, when he wrote to the church in Rome (Romans 15:24). Also, in 96 A.D., Clement of Rome (1 Clement 5:5–7) reflected on Paul's travels to the "farthest bounds of the West," a term used in the Roman Empire to designate Spain. There are other supportive references in the *Muratorian Fragment*, Chrysostom's Tenth Homily on 2 Timothy, and Cyril of Jerusalem's Lecture 17:26 of his *Jerusalem Catecheses*.

Paul's First Letter to Timothy

That kind of journey would have required at least a year or two. It was probably sometime during these travels, early in the decade of the 60s, that Paul wrote 1 Timothy. It is a warm and encouraging letter, filled with the advice of a mentor, and the seasoned reflections of a man who has observed the strengths and weaknesses of congregational life.

In the first half, Paul addresses Timothy primarily as a pastor, urging him to watch out for false teachers (1 Timothy 1), establish appropriate practices in worship gatherings (1 Timothy 2), and appoint spiritually mature persons as leaders within

---

1 Timothy in Summary

- Instructions for Timothy as a Pastor (1–3):
  - Watch out for false teachers (1)
  - Worship practices and propriety (2)
  - Character and duties of church leaders (3)
- Instructions for Timothy as a Person (4–6):
  - Keep on the right track (4)
  - Treat people in the church with respect (5)
  - Beware the temptations of wealth; final notes (6)

the congregation (1 Timothy 3). Woven throughout these instructions are a number of personal notes: Paul rues his early persecution of the Church (1 Timothy 1:12–13) and uses God's grace on his unworthy self as an illustration of the immeasurable quality of divine mercy (1 Timothy 1:14–17). Paul reminds Timothy of the prophecies that had once been spoken about the younger man in a public worship setting (1 Timothy 1:18), and how reflecting on this divine testimony can keep Timothy from making some of the same mistakes that have fallen on other leaders (1 Timothy 1:19–20). And Paul expresses his intended travel plans to visit Timothy soon (1 Timothy 3:14).

The second half of Paul's letter is much more personal in its general contents. Paul gives wise counsel about how to deal with difficult members of the congregation, even though many consider Timothy too young to wield leadership authority (1Timothy 4). At the same time, Paul reminds Timothy to treat each person with respect, and suggests strategies for nurturing healthy pastoral care and wholesome congregational life (1 Timothy 5). Finally, in a very strongly worded warning, Paul cautions Timothy about the insidious leeching character of wealth. He uses this indictment to encourage Timothy to practice disciplines of restraint and moderation, advising others to do so as well for the sake of their spiritual health (1 Timothy 6).

While this letter has generally been very formative for the organization of pastoral ministry throughout the Church's history, one short teaching in it has probably caused more debate than any other New Testament passage. At the conclusion of several paragraphs suggesting public behaviors and fashions appropriate to Christians who are the countercultural citizens of the kingdom of God, Paul briefly defines the social place of women, as he perceives it. In 1 Timothy 1:11–15 Paul writes that, "a woman should learn in quietness and full submission," that he does "not permit a woman to teach or to have authority over a man," and that women "will be saved through child-bearing."

These verses have often been interpreted as misogynistic and socially reductionistic. How should they be understood, if received as part of the prophetic/apostolic revelation of God in the New Testament age? Several considerations help to keep our interpretations focused and meaningful.

First, Paul is writing to Timothy, who is pastor of the Christian congregation in Ephesus, a city known for its religious cult surrounding the Temple of Artemis, or Diana. In that social arena, there was a clear cultural expression of female religious behavior, and it did not involve modesty, submission, or child rearing.

Second, Paul's earlier instructions in this passage are aimed toward a general form of Christian social behavior that neither causes public offense, nor calls to itself unnecessary attention. Third, Paul's use of the Genesis creation story as an illustration of his pronouncements appears to be shaped in the allegorical style of Jewish rabbinic teachings, in which the theme is not necessarily rooted in specific events, but rather in implications drawn.

Fourth, Paul's line of argument about childbearing does not seem logically to insist that only women who bear children can be "saved." Instead, it appears that Paul is writing about salvation itself coming to the human race through the childbearing qualities of the female branch of humanity. This was the process by which Jesus, the Savior, entered the human race, fulfilling the great promise to Eve in Genesis 3:15.

Fifth, Paul uses terminology that is related to personal opinion, in much the same way that he did when writing about sexuality, marriage, and virginity in 1 Corinthians 7. There, in a more extended discussion, Paul distinguished between those commands which were clearly given by the Lord (e.g., 1 Corinthians 7:10) and those which Paul deemed appropriate, based upon spiritual insight and current circumstances (e.g., 1 Corinthians 7:6-7, 8, 12, 18, 25).

It is true that a case can be made for assuming that Paul believed women of all ages and situations were to be submissive, childbearing wives, and that he believed such a perspective was the command of God, grounded in the very structures of creation. But such a position is neither consistent with the rest of Paul's teachings about roles or the expression of spiritual gifts in the Church, nor fully in tune with the instructions that immediately precede these specific verses (as noted above). Rather, it is more likely that, in the crisis of religious turmoil in Ephesus, Paul was urging Timothy to do what was necessary to prevent any seekers of truth from misinterpreting the gospel of Jesus because of offenses or barriers created by unnecessary or inappropriate public behavior. Because the cultic worship of Artemis was a prominent dimension of Ephesian culture, and since its habits and public practices were embedded in the civic mind-set, Paul urges, through pastor Timothy, that the Christian congregation clearly distance itself from the displays people knew so well. In this setting, men should lead quiet and upright lives (1 Timothy 2:1–8), and women should distinguish their clothing, adornments, and lifestyle from that exhibited by the females who scampered through the Temple and city market.

Paul's instructions about congregational leadership roles, immediately following (1 Timothy 3), may well be influenced by the same emphases. If men are to lead "peaceful and quiet lives in all godliness and holiness" (1 Timothy 2:2), and are to take the initiative in public rites of worship (1 Timothy 2:8), they would be the expected leaders of congregational life. When 1 Timothy 3 is viewed as a description of how this works out for the Ephesian congregation, rather than a prescription of absolutized gender roles in all times and places, Paul's words make good sense, and do not contradict his other writings, which affirm equal access and participation in leadership for both females and males.

Paul's Letter to Titus

It is possible—and indeed probable—that Paul wrote his letter to Titus around the same time as he did his first epistle to Timothy. Although Titus is much shorter, it deals with most of the same themes: the young pastor should appoint good leaders to prevent false teachers from destroying the church (Titus 1); he should treat with respect the various social groups in the congregation, and urge them to express godly piety (Titus 2); he should encourage members of the church to live in peace and faithfulness (Titus 3:1–11). Some of the wording, especially

---

Titus in Summary 📖

Appoint good leaders to prevent false teachers from destroying the church (1)

Primary teachings for various social groups in the church (2)

Living in peace and faithfulness (3:1–11)

Final warnings and greetings (3:12–15)

related to the qualities of character required for those in leadership, is almost identical between the letters to Titus and Timothy.

Paul ends his letter to Titus with a few personal notes, announcing that he will soon be in Nicopolis, on the east side of Greece, anticipating "winter" (Titus 3:12–15). Since there is no reference in these letters to grave persecutions that might be developing, or any indication of the apostle Peter's death (which probably happened early in the attack on Christians that followed Rome's burning in July of 64), Paul probably authored 1 Timothy and Titus around the middle of 63 A.D.

Paul's Second Letter to Timothy

Paul's next years were likely quite hectic. When the fires began burning Rome in the middle of 64 A.D., Emperor Nero was quick to point the accusing finger toward Christians. As a leading figure in the Christian movement, Paul soon became a hunted man. It is probable that the winter of 63–64 A.D., spent in Nicopolis, was the last peaceful time in his life. Nero would die in 68 A.D., but not until he had killed thousands of Christians, including both Peter and Paul.

In his attempts to stay ahead of warrants for his arrest, Paul probably flitted from location to location from late 64 through early 66 A.D. His travel notes to Timothy, in the second letter sent to the young pastor, certainly have the air of haste and mobility about them. During that year or so, Paul spent time in Corinth (2 Timothy 4:20), Miletus (2 Timothy 4:20), and Troas (2 Timothy 4:13), at minimum, and probably a number of other places as well. But Troas was to be his last voluntary stop. There, in the city where he had first come to know doctor Luke sixteen years before, Paul was arrested and hauled off to Rome, without even being able to take along his few personal belongings (2 Timothy 4:13).

Evidently there were several different arraignments and trials during the legal process that would lead to Paul's death (2 Timothy 4:16). After all, Paul's Roman citizenship provided him with protections that Peter and others did not enjoy. In between some of these court matters, Paul sent a final letter to his younger friend, Timothy. It is warm and passionate, urgent and reflective, pessimistic and optimistic, all at the same time. Paul encourages Timothy to live faithfully as a pastor, carrying on the tradition of his godly forebears, grandmother Lois and mother Eunice, and learning from the example of Paul's own life as his spiritual mentor (2 Timothy 1:1–2:13). Paul also reminds Timothy of some of the key teachings that are critical for church leaders to espouse regularly (2 Timothy 2:14–3:9). Finally, Paul lapses into tender reminders of the times they spent together, and offers his strong personal testimony of faith and trust in Jesus, even as he senses his execution looming (2 Timothy 3:10–4:8). Some final greetings and urgent instructions end the letter (2 Timothy 4:9–22).

---

2 Timothy in Summary

Live faithfully, as you have learned from me (1:1–2:13)

Pastor faithfully, as you have learned from me (2:14–3:9)

Final tender reminders and testimony (3:10–4:8)

Closing instructions and greetings (4:9–22)

The last words of Paul are quite moving. First he sums up his life in athletic metaphors:

> For I am already being poured out like a drink offering, and the time has come for my departure. I have fought the good fight, I have finished the race, I have kept the faith. Now there is in store for me the crown of righteousness, which the Lord, the righteous judge, will award to me on that day—and not only to me, but also to all who have longed for his appearing (2 Timothy 4:6–8).

Then, he ends his many years of communication and correspondence with a caring and concise blessing: "The Lord be with your spirit. Grace be with you" (2 Timothy 4:22). Paul was executed by beheading, probably sometime in 67 A.D.

Retrospect

It is hard to exaggerate the impact of Paul's life and theology on the Christian Church. More than anyone else, he urged and practiced intentional mission outreach as an essential aspect of Christian life. Moreover, Paul saw his primary target audience as the large Gentile community that extended well beyond Palestine and the Jewish communities tucked into the corners of the Roman Empire. In reaching for the nations, Paul saw the fulfillment of what God had intended to do through the seed of Abraham. The Church was, for Paul, God's next major strategy in reclaiming the human race for its original relationships and purposes.

Because of the vision of Christ that captured him on the road to Damascus, and the startling news of Jesus' resurrection, Paul nurtured in his converts an apocalyptic ethic and lifestyle. Paul's message was deceptively simple: Jesus came a little while ago and shook things up; now Jesus is coming again soon, so live as if that matters.

Paul also was the key figure in helping the Church transition from its original temporary mission outposts, into an organization with adaptable, but supportive, structures. In this way, he clarified the meaning of Christ's life, death, and resurrection, and crafted a perspective that started as personal testimony and ended as comprehensive worldview theology. By the time congregations exhausted their conversations with Paul, they had a tool kit of core theological and ecclesiastical concepts that could be applied to most situations they would encounter.

Added to these things was the intensive and extensive mentoring, through which Paul multiplied his gifts and passions in dozens of other key figures who would carry on, long after he was gone. Not only did Paul teach and model well, but he sustained contact with congregations and individuals who were part of his journey. In so doing, he helped to knit together the early

Paul in Retrospect

- Urged intentional mission, especially to Gentiles
- Nurtured apocalyptic ethic and lifestyle
- Helped transition church from mission to organization
- Clarified the meaning of Christ's life, death, and resurrection
- Mentored a generation of leaders
- Created ecclesiastical communications network

communities of believers that eventually made the Church of Jesus a global enterprise, rather than merely a few isolated religious philosophy clubs scattered around the major cities of the Mediterranean world.

God created all things, with humankind as the heartbeat and pinnacle of life on planet Earth. Israel was God's witness to the nations of the ancient world. Jesus came to permanently weld God's redemptive designs to human history. And Paul organized the spreading missional Church that emerged from among Jesus' followers.

Some claim that Paul is really the founder of Christianity, since Jesus was merely a good teacher who never left a record or an organizational plan. But this is to misread both Jesus and Paul. What God did in Jesus changed human history forever, with or without Paul. In fact, apart from Jesus, there could be no Paul as we know him (Galatians 2:20; Philippians 1:21; 3:1–21). At the same time, however, it is hard to imagine the growth and spread of Christianity separated from Paul. Jesus is "the way and the truth and the life" (John 14:6), the "foundation" (Matthew 16:18; 1 Corinthians 3:11) and "cornerstone" (Ephesians 2:20–22; 1 Peter 2:4–8) of the Church; and Paul was its first prominent building supervisor and CEO (Ephesians 3:1–13).

Discussion Points

- Why do some Bible scholars question the authorship of Paul for the pastoral letters? What are possible responses to their challenges? How might these letters fit into the chronology of Paul's life and travels?
- What are the key concerns of Paul's first letter to Timothy? What implications are made for early Church practices? How have Paul's instructions continued to function as guidelines for ecclesiastical organization?
- What are the parallels between 1 Timothy and Titus? What are the unique elements of each letter? How do these letters provide a picture of the social groupings within the early church?
- How does 2 Timothy provide a fitting conclusion to Paul's writing ministry and Church leadership development? What are its key themes?
- In reflecting on Paul's ministry as a missionary, Church developer, leadership mentor, and theologian, what are some of the ways in which Paul left a permanent influence on the Christian Church?

For Further Investigation

Mounce, William D. (Waco: Word, 2000). *Pastoral Epistles*.

Towner, Philip H. (Grand Rapids: Eerdmans, 2006). *The Letters to Timothy and Titus*.

37.

The World and Life of Paul

A Closer Look

While the names of many biblical figures are widely familiar (e.g., Abraham, Jacob, Esau, Moses, Joshua, Ruth, David, Solomon, Daniel, Esther, Peter, John), we actually know very little about the day-to-day lives of most of these people. We have become more aware of Jesus' life (at least the events surrounding his birth and the years of his public ministry), because of the details given in the gospels. But no person in the Bible can be known as well to us as Paul of Tarsus, the great champion for the Christian gospel. The New Testament writings provide us with a fuller picture of his existence than is possible for anyone else on the pages of either Testament. In addition, there are a good number of references to Paul and his travels in early Christian literature, some more trustworthy than others, but all giving us portraits of the time in which he lived. Moreover, daily life in the Roman world has been exhaustively explored and explained, providing additional understandings of how Paul would have experienced the world.

Paul died in the latter part of the Neronian persecution, which lasted from July of 64 A.D. through Nero's death in mid-June 68. Paul was probably executed by beheading, in late 67 or early 68 A.D. This provides us with a clear end point for Paul's life. While we are not as certain about the exact date of his birth, there are clues to help us determine a reasonable biographical sketch.

Since Rabban Gamaliel was the leader of the Jerusalem Sanhedrin and a recognized teacher from about 30–50 A.D., Paul probably came to Jerusalem as a mature boy or young man sometime between 25–33 A.D. Paul seems not to have met Jesus in the flesh until the unique encounter on the road to Damascus, meaning that he would not likely have been in Jerusalem long before Jesus' death in 32 or 33 A.D. Since Paul was able to take a leadership role in persecuting Christians by 33 or 34 A.D. (Acts 9), he was likely in his early 20s by this time.

So, the dates of Paul's life might well be something like this:

- 12 A.D.—Born as Saul Paul (both names were likely given him by his parents, as was typical in Jewish families of the day) in Tarsus
- 28 A.D.—Sent to Jerusalem to study with Gamaliel in mid-teen years
- 33 A.D.—Observing Stephen's death and taking a leadership role in persecuting Jesus' followers, at around 20 years of age. Converted to a Jesus follower himself that year
- 33–34 A.D.—Time in Damascus, Arabia, and in early contacts with the Church leadership
- 34–48 A.D.—Spent time in Tarsus and Antioch, participating in the leadership and development of the Antioch congregation
- 48 A.D.—Traveled to south central Asia Minor for the first mission journey with Barnabas, followed by the writing of Galatians
- 49 A.D.—To Jerusalem for the Jerusalem Council of Acts 15
- 49–51 A.D.—The second mission journey, with Silas, through Asia Minor, around the Aegean Sea, and a two-year stay in Corinth; the writing of the Thessalonian letters
- 51–54 A.D.—The third mission journey, with Silas and others, based in Ephesus; authoring the Corinthian and Roman correspondence
- 54–56 A.D.—Under arrest in Jerusalem and Caesarea
- 56–57 A.D.—Travels to Rome
- 57–58 A.D.—Under house arrest in Rome, awaiting an appearance before Caesar; writing of the Philippians, Philemon, Colossians, and Ephesians correspondence
- 58–59 A.D.—Travels to Crete, Ephesus, and other places around the Aegean
- 59–63 A.D.—Journeys to Rome and Spain; writing of letters to Titus and Timothy (1 Timothy)
- 63–65 A.D.—Travels around Greece and Asia Minor, evading Nero's soldiers and visiting the churches and pastors
- 66 A.D.—Arrested in Troas, transported to Rome; the writing of 2 Timothy
- 67/68 A.D.—Executed in Rome in his mid-50s

We might wish to know more about Saul/Paul's younger life, even though that information is not given by Paul anywhere in the New Testament writings. But it is possible for us to reconstruct a likely impression of many of Paul's experiences from what we glean elsewhere.

What Was Life Like in a Rabbinic School?

Synagogues emerged after the destruction of Solomon's temple in 586 B.C. They were usually independent structures, built in the architectural style of local environs, consisting at minimum of a single room with benches, for reading scripture in community. As synogogues developed, some included hostel quarters for traveling rabbis and scholars, and later, community halls for Jewish social gatherings.

From earliest times, synagogues were used for instruction in the scriptures, usually facilitated by communal recitation. At first, this seems to have been a practice primarily for adult Jewish males, but in time included instruction for younger males, who would each become a *bar mitzvah*, a "son of the Commandment." Recognition of the passage from childhood into adult stature happened at around twelve years of age (thus the experiences of Jesus in Jerusalem, as told in Luke 2:41-52).

Great Jewish centers like Jerusalem and Alexandria developed schools that were known for particular lines of scripture interpretation as developed by particularly astute and revered teachers. During the first half of the first century A.D., the key teacher in Jerusalem was Gamaliel the Elder, descended from grandfather Hillel and father Simeon, both of whom were considered to be the primary Jewish teachers in their own days. Hillel was of particular stature among Jewish scripture exegetes, and is referred to often in the Talmud as the head of a renowned school of biblical interpretation. Gamaliel was the lead scholar of this school from around 30–70 A.D., and was called *Rabban* (the Teacher). He is mentioned twice in Acts, first as the leader of the Sanhedrin (5:34) who brought a cautionary word defusing violence against Jesus followers, and later by Paul as his teacher in the Jerusalem school (22:3).

Saul was likely sent to Jerusalem by his family and the Jewish community of Tarsus because of his early aptitude for learning scripture in the synagogue of Tarsus. It is not clear how old he would have been at the time, but it is certainly probable that his married sister (see Acts 23:16) was either already present in Jerusalem or was sent to Jerusalem to provide lodgings for young Saul. Saul's education would involve:

- Scripture recitation leading to memorization.
- Memorization of the orally transmitted scholarly interpretations of scripture.
- Listening to the rabbis, including Rabban Gamaliel, expound upon the interpretation of scripture. The teachers and rabbis would be seated on a raised platform; hence Paul's statement about his own learning experiences "... at the feet of Gamaliel ..." (Acts 22:3).
- Listening to debates of the scholars on particular points of interpretation.
- Engaging in interpretive debates (only the older students would do this).

This educational experience seems to influence Paul's Christian teaching style in a number of places. For instance, when Paul makes a comparison between legalism and liberty in Galatians 4, he offers an allegory on the identity and offspring of Abraham's two wives, Hagar and Sarah (Galatians 4:21–31). Other similar rabbinic analogies and allegorical teachings relate the process of Abraham's relationship with God to our experience of grace (Romans 4:1–25); show the solidarity of Israel's corporate identity with its consequences (1 Corinthians 10:1–11); explain the transcendent character of marriage (Ephesians 5:22–33); and provide a commentary on public behaviors (1 Timothy 2). Paul learned his lessons well. He was an astute scholar of scripture and a keen rabbinic teacher. These gifts were further focused once Paul met Jesus, and began to understand a new key to scriptural interpretation.

Paul the Traveler

Paul's letters give us a glimpse into his teaching and preaching style. Of course, before the written documents came Paul's personal visits to dozens of cities and towns around the Mediterranean world. Our records of Paul's travels are significant—but incomplete. Still, we are able to understand a bit more of his daily activities when we keep these things in mind.

- Walking was the most common method of getting around for Paul. How fast did he travel? A lot depended on the urgency of his goal and the circumstances of the road. Here are some reasonable estimates of daily travel:

  - Easy pace—20-30 miles a day
  - Difficult terrain—5–15 miles a day
  - Strong pace, strong travelers—Up to 40 miles a day

- Roman centurions, couriers, and some of the wealthy would travel on horseback or in carts or chariots powered by large animals (oxen, donkeys, horses). While the daily distance of travel might be somewhat longer because of the endurance of the beasts, there was also a trade-off with the need to provide food and care for these animals. Carts and carriages were often not much faster than steady walking, but a person on a horse could travel more briskly:

  - Easy pace: 40-50 miles a day
  - Difficult terrain: 10-25 miles a day
  - Strong pace, determined travelers: 100-140 miles a day

- The Romans called the Mediterranean Sea their Roman lake. The bulk of the Roman Empire was on or near the Mediterranean Sea and was connected by boat travel. Boats, for the Romans, were certainly not the "ships" we often have in mind for water travel today. Most Roman ships were between 100–240 feet long, with the majority of them on the smaller side. Made of wood and powered by sail or oar, these boats were ruled by the wiles of the winds and currents. Since these ships were very small, susceptible to storms, and unable to travel at night (except under very specific circumstances), water travel hugged shorelines. Still, it is an interesting exercise to consider how much time would have been required for Paul to travel the route of his first Mission Journey (Acts 13–14), for which we have nearly every meaningful point of departure and destination:

- Antioch to Seleucia: 19 miles by foot (short day)
- Seleucia to Salamis: 150 miles by boat (one day)
- Salamis to Paphos: 100–150 miles by foot, depending on which route (5–10 days)
- Paphos to Perga: 200 miles by boat (one day)
- Perga to Antioch: 128 miles by foot (probably four days)
- Antioch to Lystra: 100 miles by foot (probably three days)
- Lystra to Iconium: 19 miles by foot (one day)
- Iconium to Derbe: 35 miles by foot (one day)
- Derbe to Iconium: 35 miles by foot (one day)
- Iconium to Lystra: (19 miles by foot (one day)
- Lystra to Antioch: 100 miles by foot (probably three days)
- Antioch to Perga: 128 miles by foot (probably three days; mostly downhill)
- Perga to Attalia: 10 miles by foot (a few hours)
- Attalia to Seleucia: 350–400 miles by boat (probably two days)
- Seleucia to Antioch: 19 miles by foot (one day)

The net result is that Paul's First Mission Journey would require approximately 30 days of travel time, plus a minimum of 10+ days of ministry time, plus at least a week of illness/beating recovery time (since we know that Paul got sick on the journey—cf. Galatians 4:13—and that he was beaten nearly to death on one occasion—cf. Acts 14:19).

Where did Paul stay when he traveled? It is clear from a number of greetings and other comments which Paul makes in his letters that most of the time he was provided hospitality by people who knew him or cared about him. Public rooming houses were available, but Paul likely did not use them. The Romans had established *castra* (rest-stop shelters) at roughly 18-mile intervals (ox-cart travel daily distance) on official Roman roads. These were sometimes later supplemented with barracks and provision magazines (*horrea*) for troops, and over time, many of these were upgraded as *mansio* (villas maintained by public funds) for traveling Roman officials, who had to show passports for access. Paul could likely have made use of these as a Roman citizen, but many of his traveling companions did not hold citizenship, and would have been forbidden to stay in such quarters.

There were also inns, usually private homes with sleeping quarters for rent. Rooms at these inns were often also used for storage and/or livestock when not rented to travelers. Many times, these were extra rooms added to structures as lean-tos on the side of a house or building. Of course, in such places, beds were comprised of either straw or straw-filled mattresses, often on the ground or floor, and sometimes on wooden frames, possibly with rope lattices or wooden slats. Meals could sometimes be bought from the innkeeper (at or from the family table), but otherwise were usually purchased from nearby vendors.

Paul and his companions, however, probably stayed with modestly wealthy families. In fact, we have hints at this and records of a number of these:
- Family and friends of Barnabas on Cyprus (Acts 13)

- Jewish families who would provide hospitality for Jewish travelers (Timothy's family home; Acts 16:1)
- New friends and converts:

  - Lydia in Philippi (Acts 16:15, 40)
  - Aquila & Priscilla in Corinth (Acts 18:2–3)
  - Christians in Ptolemais (Acts 21:7)
  - Philip in Caesarea (Acts 21:8)
  - Mnason between Caesarea and Jerusalem (Acts 21:16)
  - Friends at Sidon (Acts 27:3)
  - Publius on Malta (Acts 28:7)
  - Christians in Puteoli (Acts 28:14)
  - Gaius in Corinth (Romans 16:23)
  - Philemon (Philemon 23)
  - Onesiphorus in Ephesus (2 Timothy 1:16–18, 4:19)

There are also indications in both Acts and Paul's letters of other accommodations, including private quarters that Paul rented for himself (Acts 28:30), times in various prisons (Acts 16, 23, 24), and, of course, short periods when Paul was onboard ship en route from one place to another.

What did Paul and his companions eat? Although he never tells us the specifics of his meals, it is likely that Paul shared in the typical culinary experiences of the Roman world of his day. Romans took their main meal in the evening, and had a hurried, mandatory meal midday. Breakfast was less of a meal than a bite on the run. Here are the usual ingredients for each repast:

- **Breakfast** (*jentaculum*): If taken, breakfast was eaten very early and consisted of salted bread, milk or wine, and perhaps dried fruit, eggs, or cheese.
- **Lunch** (*cibus meridianus* or *prandium*): A quick meal, it was eaten around noon. It could include salted bread or be more elaborate with fruit, salad, eggs, meat or fish, vegetables, and cheese.
- **Dinner** (*cena*): The main meal of the day, dinner would be accompanied by wine, usually watered down. The Latin poet Horace ate a meal of onions, porridge, and pancake. An ordinary upper-class dinner would include meat, vegetables, eggs, and fruit. *Comissatio* was a final wine course at dinner's end. Most women and the poor ate sitting on chairs, while upper-class males reclined on their sides on couches along three sides of a cloth-covered table (*mensa*). The three-sided arrangement is called the *triclinium*. Banquets might last for hours, eating and watching or listening to entertainers, so the men would stretch out and relax (without shoes), which must have enhanced the experience. Since there were no forks, diners would not have had to worry about coordinating eating utensils in each hand.

Since Paul wrote that he adapted his own lifestyle to conform to the circumstances in which he found himself (1 Corinthians 9:19–23, 10:33–11:1), it is likely that these Roman meal patterns would have been his as well.

Paul the Evangelist

Paul's mission strategy had two essential parts. First came the face-to-face contacts, intended to lead people into a knowledge and trust of Jesus. Second were the letters that maintained contact over the distances, as Paul moved on and traveled elsewhere. A corollary to this second dimension of Paul's evangelistic works was his training of many apprentices and (as he called them) "fellow workers," who often became his "living letters," renewing contacts and friendships through personal representations.

Most important, among these, were the initial personal encounters. While Paul spent his adult life meeting new people, there seems to have been a change in the format for Paul's missionary engagement over time. In the early years of his travels, Paul would go to Jewish synagogues to tell fellow Jews about Jesus. After all, Jesus was the fulfillment and culmination of the whole history of Israel and her covenantal mission with God. So, it made sense to start with and build upon this common identity and theological outlook, explaining to Jews that their Messiah had come in the person of Jesus of Nazareth. If, however, the Jews in this new city rejected the message and ejected Paul and his companions from their synagogue, Paul would transition to the marketplaces of the towns, talking to both Jews and Gentiles about Jesus at their businesses and in their commercial transactions (Acts 13:5; 13:14; 13:42–48; 14:1; 16:13; 17:1–10; 18:4–8; 18:19).

Later in his career, however, Paul seems to have adopted a less frenzied hit-and-move-on missional strategy. By the midpoint of his second mission journey, and certainly as the primary method of his third, Paul began to establish a congregational base in a large, regional administrative or commercial city (Corinth and Ephesus, for example), and then make short trips out of that location to evangelize the surrounding area. It was in this second missional strategy that Paul developed a vast network of friends in ministry. From the few pages of his New Testament writings, along with the book of Acts, we find this great "crowd of witnesses" surrounding Paul, to use the language of Hebrews 11–12:

- Barnabas: A Levite from Cyprus (Acts 4:36; 11:25–230; 12:25; 13–15)
- John Mark: Cousin of Barnabas (Acts 12:25; Colossians 4:10; 2 Timothy 4:11; Philemon 24)
- Silas (Acts 15:40; 2 Corinthians 1:19; 1 Thessalonians 1:1; 2 Thessalonians 1:1)
- Timothy: From Lystra; Jewish mother and grandmother; Gentile father (Acts 16:1–3; Romans 16:21; 1 Corinthians 16:10–11; 2 Corinthians 1:1, 19; Philippians 1:1, 2:19–23; Colossians 1:1; 1 Thessalonians 1:1, 3:2, 3:6; 2 Thessalonians 1:1; 1 Timothy; 2 Timothy)
- Luke: A doctor (Acts 16:11; Colossians 4:14; 2 Timothy 4:11; Philemon 24)
- Aquila and Priscilla: Jews from Rome; tentmakers (Acts 18:2–3, 18–19; Romans 16:3–4; 1 Corinthians 16:19; 2 Timothy 4:19)

- Erastus (Acts 19:22; 2 Timothy 4:20)
- "Sopater son of Pyrrhus from Berea, Aristarchus and Secundus from Thessalonica, Gaius from Derbe, Timothy also, and Tychicus and Trophimus from the province of Asia" (Acts 20:4)
- Titus (Galatians 2:1-3; 2 Corinthians 7:13, 8:6, 16-23; 12:18; 2 Timothy 4:10; Titus)
- Apollos (1 Corinthians 16:12; Titus 3:13)
- Tychicus: Delivered the letters to the Colossians, Ephesians, Laodiceans, and Philemon (Acts 20:4; Ephesians 6:21; Colossians 4:7-9; 2 Timothy 4:12; Titus 3:12)
- Epaphroditus: Pastor or key leader of the Philippian congregation who brought a care package from that church to Paul in Rome; nearly died from illness during the trip (Philippians 2:25-30, 4:18)
- "I plead with Euodia and I plead with Syntyche to be of the same mind in the Lord. Yes, and I ask you, my true companion, help these women since they have contended at my side in the cause of the gospel, along with Clement and the rest of my co-workers, whose names are in the book of life." (Philippians 4:2-3)
- Epaphras: Probably an evangelist trained by Paul while in Ephesus on his third mission journey, who was first to evangelize and found a Christian congregation in his home town of Colossae (Colossians 1:7-8, 4:12-13; Philemon 23)
- Onesimus ("Helpful"): Runaway slave of Paul's friend, Philemon, whom Paul sent back to Philemon as a brother in Christ (Colossians 4:9)
- Aristarchus: Prisoner in Rome with Paul (Colossians 4:10; Philemon 24)
- Jesus Justice: Fellow worker with Paul in Rome (Colossians 4:11)
- Demas: With Paul in Rome (Colossians 4:14; Philemon 24), later abandoned him (2 Timothy 4:10)
- Archippus: "Tell Archippus: 'See to it that you complete the ministry you have received in the Lord.'" (Colossians 4:17)
- Crescens: "Crescens has gone to Galatia" (2 Timothy 4:10)
- "Erastus stayed in Corinth, and I left Trophimus sick in Miletus. Do your best to get here before winter. Eubulus greets you, and so do Pudens, Linus, Claudia and all the brothers and sisters." (2 Timothy 4:20-21)
- Artemas (Titus 3:12)
- Zenas: The lawyer (Titus 3:13)
- Philemon: Friend and provider of hospitality, who had been brought to Christ through Paul's personal ministry (Philemon)

This collection of friends and fellow workers is impressive, indeed, especially when one realizes that all of these people were part of Paul's life for only two decades (48-68). And the list is likely not comprehensive. Were we to actually travel with Paul, we would probably meet hundreds of others whom Paul knew by name.

Paul the Letter Writer

Once Paul moved on from a particular ministry location, the letter writing began. In the Greco-Roman world, private letters averaged around 90 words. They were usually an expression of friendship between men, or family communications. Literary letters, like those of the orator and statesman Cicero and the philosopher Seneca, were often about 200 words in length. These were generally more formal in character, with stylized rhetoric for communicating points and ideas.

Roman government letters were generally shorter than literary letters, but formal in style and structure. They communicated actions and decrees, military movements and needs, advice or instructions from senior officials to junior officials, and news from the provinces to the central government.

While clay and beeswax tablets had long been used for imprinting short lists and messages, by the time of the first century, most correspondence was on paper. Papyrus sheets, used for letter-writing, were usually about 9 ½ by 11 inches, and depending on the size of the handwriting, could contain 150–250 words. They were written only on one side. Most Roman personal and family letters, then, would be contained on a single sheet, which was often folded and sealed, or placed in an envelope and sealed. Literary compositions required the stitching together of two or more sheets, and the formation of a scroll.

Personal, family, and private letters were usually written by the authors themselves. Literary and government correspondence, however, and the letters of the wealthy, were typically dictated to an amanuensis, who would then scribe them out in full from shorthand notes. Paul appears to have used this form of letter production (see Romans 16:22, where Tertius, the amanuensis, inserts his own greetings and self-disclosure; see also 1 Peter 5:12), but often writes out the final declaration of his name in his own hand (Galatians 6:11; 1 Corinthians 16:21; Colossians 4:18; 2 Thessalonians 3:17).

Paul seems to have taken over the typical letter-writing habit of his world, but transformed it into a unique Christian form of literature:

- Paul combined the familiarity of family correspondence (with its personal greetings, notes of events in the lives of both writer and recipients, and reminders of actual events and interactions) with the formality of stylized rhetoric in literary correspondence (note especially Paul's letter to the Romans, and also chapters 3–4 of Galatians).
- Paul's shortest letter is Philemon (335 words), his longest is Romans (7,101 words), and the average among all of his New Testament letters is about 1,300 words. Only Philemon (and perhaps 2 Thessalonians and Titus) could possibly have been squeezed onto a single sheet of papyrus. Thus, Paul's letters were generally significantly longer than typical first-century letters.

Also, Paul intersperses the personal expressions of family and friendship correspondence with doctrinal treatises such as one might find in literary documents. In all of this, Paul essentially created a new form of communication, one that has given rise to a peculiarly Christian genre of literature.

Paul's Daily Life

While our dominant image of Paul is that of someone standing in a marketplace and speaking loudly about Jesus (as is described in Acts 16:16–34), there was certainly much more to his daily activities. For one thing, Paul writes that he worked hard to provide for his own upkeep, not wanting to be dependent on others (1 Corinthians 4:12). Indeed, it was in Corinth where Luke tells us that Paul plied his trade as a tentmaker, alongside Aquila and Priscilla (Acts 18:2–3).

What was tentmaking in the first-century Roman world like? Roman tents were mostly used for army shelters on the field. These were smaller shelters than the typical Bedouin tents of the Arabian deserts.

Since Roman military companies and legions were present everywhere in the Empire, tents were in constant demand. It is not clear whether the individual soldiers purchased their own tents, or if the military bought them in bulk. It is likely that if the soldiers were supplied tents, the costs were eventually deducted from their pay, as was true for most of their supplies.

Tentmakers probably did not kill and skin animals, but may have procured prepared hides from other vendors in marketplaces. Tentmakers themselves were responsible for cutting hides and stitching them together using awls for boring holes, knives for slicing leather lacings, and needles of bone, wood, or possibly iron. They would also prepare and install the ropes at the corners of the tents, but probably did not provide uprights, crossbars, or pegs, since soldiers were expected to be able to supply these in the field.

In Corinth, there was another market for tents: the biennial Isthmian Games. Similar to the Pan-Hellenic Olympic Games, but a bit smaller in scale, the Isthmian Games brought athletes and spectators from all over the Greek world. It is likely that supplying this recurring need, along with servicing military personnel getting ready for bivouac, provided steady work and income for Paul, particularly when he was in Corinth.

Supplemental to this income came funds and care packages from individuals and congregations. We know that the Antioch church, which first sent Barnabas and Paul (their key pastoral leaders) on the initial mission trek (Acts 13:1–3), continued to be a home base and supporting church for further evangelistic ventures. But there are other hints of ongoing support for Paul and his company as well. For instance, the Philippian congregation, formed on Paul's second mission journey (Acts 16), maintained its care for Paul through his first Roman imprisonment (Philippians 4:15–18) and might well be the group Paul refers to in 2 Corinthians 11:7–8 ("the brothers who came from Macedonia"). Furthermore, Paul boldly wrote to the Roman congregation (Romans 15:23–32) that he intended on traveling to see them, precisely so they could have a part in his support for his planned mission trip to Spain.

There were also individuals who appear to have contributed to Paul's care along the way. Lydia comes to mind (Acts 16:14–15), as do Tyrannus (Acts 19:9), Gaius (Romans 16:23), Paul's own family (Acts 23:16), and Onesiphorus (2 Timothy 1:16–18). While the circumstances of their investments in Paul's work are never presented, their support is unquestioned.

Paul the Roman Citizen

Paul's daily life was also colored by his Roman citizenship. Roman citizenship began as the privilege of the ruling class males of the Roman Republic. When Rome expanded its borders and moved into its empire phase, Roman citizenship appears to have been obtained in one of six ways:

- Males born to Roman citizens were automatically Roman citizens.
- Some persons were granted Roman citizenship as a gift.
- Some cities were declared to be "free Roman cities," and all of the leading men (those who were government leaders, landholders, and wealthy patrons) were automatically granted Roman citizenship. This happened at Tarsus; it was brought into the Roman Empire by General Pompey and made his administrative capital. Because it was the city of the governor, it was declared a "free city" in 66 B.C., and its prominent men were granted Roman citizenship. Most likely this is what happened to Paul's family, and thus allowed him to be born a Roman citizen (Acts 22:23–29).
- It was also possible to buy Roman citizenship (Acts 22:28).
- Noncitizens who served in the Roman army auxiliary units were granted Roman citizenship as an incentive after 25 years of military service.
- Slaves made free at the deaths of their masters were not given citizenship, but were called "freedmen." Any children born to them after they became "freedmen" were automatically Roman citizens.

What privileges were gained by having Roman citizenship? There were several levels of Roman citizenship late in the Republic, but by early in the Empire, it was commonly understood that Roman citizenship gave the following rights and protections:

- The right to vote in the Roman assemblies (*jus suffragiorum*).
- The right to stand for civil or public office (*jus honorum*).
- The right to make legal contracts and to hold property as a Roman citizen (*jus commercii*).
- Legal recognition in commercial affairs, particularly between Roman citizens and foreign persons (*jus gentium*).
- The right to have a lawful marriage with a Roman citizen, to have the legal rights of the paterfamilias over the family, and to have the children of any such marriage be counted as Roman citizens (*jus connubii*).
- The right to preserve one's level of citizenship upon relocation to a polis of comparable status (*jus migrationis*).
- The right of immunity from some taxes and other legal obligations, especially local rules and regulations.
- The right to sue in the courts and the right to be sued.
- The right to have a legal trial (to appear before a proper court and to defend oneself).
- The right to appeal from the decisions of magistrates and to appeal the lower court decisions.

- The right to not be tortured or whipped or receive the death penalty, unless found guilty of treason.
- If accused of treason, a Roman citizen had the right to be tried in Rome, and even if sentenced to death, no Roman citizen could be sentenced to die by crucifixion.

This last privilege was, of course, the key that allowed Paul to be beheaded when convicted by Nero's government, rather than suffer through the crucifixion that Peter endured a short while before.

All of this brings to mind the question of how people in various parts of the Roman world know if someone was actually a citizen, or just pretending? The answer lies in the fact that Romans were fastidious record-keepers. The name of every Roman citizen was recorded on documents kept in the Tabulorium in Rome.

This commitment to documentation meant that there were also local records of citizens and their children (this is actually the origin of the concept and office of *notary public*). Such determination to maintain ledgers served as a deterrent to scam artists. While there were instances of deception by people who presented themselves as elite or nobles or Roman citizens—but were not—for the most part, the Roman government and world functioned like an extended network of small towns, linked by local leaders who knew others, and for whom quick verifications were readily available in an informal communications system.

It was Paul's Roman citizenship that got him out of prison in Philippi and prevented some of the worst problems of travel that might otherwise have befallen him. It also placed him under the jurisdiction of the emperor in a manner that would ultimately cost him his life. In this process, Paul learned the inside of the penal system too well.

Prisons in ancient Rome were not used for punishment. They were places for holding those accused until trial or adjudication. That is why Paul was imprisoned on a number of occasions, but when he was awaiting trial in Rome, he was actually living in personally-rented quarters.

For those entering the judicial system from the general non-citizen population, prisons were most often caves (natural or carved out), with wood doors or metal gates to prevent escape; for Roman citizens and the wealthy, prisons were more likely villas with secured rooms. Chains and manacles were often a regular feature in the former, and less so in the latter. Also, the common prisons were often owned by individuals as a source of income (so the jail of the Roman centurion in Philippi in Acts 16), while the villas were owned and operated by the Roman government.

Incarceration rarely lasted more than a few days and quickly led to either release or sentencing, depending on the adjudication verdict. A guilty declaration resulted in one or more of these punishments (in increasing order of severity):

- A fine
- Loss of citizenship or social stature
- Banishment
- A term or life in one of the following:
- Sold as a slave for labor
- Placed in the gladiatorial system for sporting events

- Oarsman aboard a ship
- Life and work in a mine

- Death:

  - Beheading (Roman citizens)
  - Crucifixion (non-Roman citizens or Roman citizens convicted of treason)
  - Killing by animals or gladiators in the arena

Paul would have observed all of these, and was himself a victim of most of them at one time or another. The last he would have endured under the command of Nero, probably in 67 or 68 A.D.

Paul and the Churches

But Paul's life was not primarily about eating or drinking or working as a tentmaker, or even experiencing the protections of Roman citizenship. Paul's life was about Jesus, and the care of Jesus' people. Paul's heart was in the church.

While the church of Jesus—the "Body of Christ" (1 Corinthians 12–14)—was always flesh and blood, infused with the living Spirit of God, it took on shape in its gatherings and worship expressions. Where did congregations meet as witnesses to their Lord?

- In the Temple courts in Jerusalem (Acts 2:46; 3:1)
- In homes (Acts 2:46; 4:31, 12:12, 18:7; Romans 16:3–5; 1 Corinthians 16:19; Colossians 4:15)
- Possibly in synagogues (especially the Jewish followers of Jesus; Acts 18:7; see also Revelation 2:9)
- According to Justin Martyr, in his final interrogation before being sentenced to death, he is asked by Roman prefect Junius Rusticus: "Where do you meet?" To which Justin replied: "Wherever it is each one's preference or opportunity. In any case, do you suppose we can all meet in the same place?" At this answer, Junius Rusticus asked a follow-up question, possibly as a way to arrest other Christians: "Tell me, where do you meet? In what place?" Justin replied: "I have been living above the baths of [...] for the entire period of my sojourn at Rome ... and I have known no other meeting place but here. Anyone who desired could come to my residence, and I would give to him the words of truth."
- In restaurants or public meeting places (Acts 20:7–11)

In other words, anywhere and everywhere. What began as a small band of disciples of Jesus, walking the dusty paths of Galilee, morphed into the largest single social organization in the world. Through Paul and others, the Church of Jesus Christ grew into a global network of those who testified to the risen Christ, and lived as if God mattered most.

Discussion Points

- Using the information about travel in Paul's world, prepare a tentative time line for each of Paul's major travels, as outlined in Acts 15-28.
- How might Paul's travels with Barnabas (not a Roman citizen) on the first mission journey, and his travels with Silas (a Roman citizen) on his second and third mission journeys functioned differently in terms of cultural, social and political engagements along the way?
- What role did Jewish synagogues have in providing a launching pad for Paul's missionary travels?
- What are the common features in all of Paul's New Testament letters? What are unique features found in some but not others? How do Paul's letters compare with those of Peter, James, John and Jude? How do Paul's letters compare with the letters to seven churches found in Revelation 2-3?

For Further Investigation

Cowell, F. R. *Life in Ancient Rome* (1976)

Donfried, Karl Paul and Richardson, Peter. *Judaism and Christianity in First-Century Rome* (1998)

McRay, John. *Paul: His Life and Teaching* (2003)

Stegemann, Ekkehard W. and Stegemann, Wolfgang. *The Jesus Movement: A Social History of Its First Century* (1999)Time-Life Publications. *What Life Was Like: When Rome Ruled the World* (1997)

38.

The Badge of Suffering

An Old Fisherman's Testimony

About the time that Paul was engaged in his final communications with Timothy and Titus, Peter made his own last swing through the churches of northern and eastern Asia Minor. This was quite a trip for an older man to take (exceeding the reach of all of Paul's journeys recorded in Acts), since Peter was based in Rome at the time. He calls Rome "Babylon" (1 Peter 5:13), a code term already circulating throughout the Christian Church, hinting at the persecutions looming from the ruling center of the world in a way similar to the Babylonian pressures mounted against Judah centuries before. It may well have been that Peter was invited to officiate at a number of large baptism ceremonies in the congregations to which these letters are written, since Peter's tone is that of instruction for new believers, and baptism is a central concern (1 Peter 3:13–22).

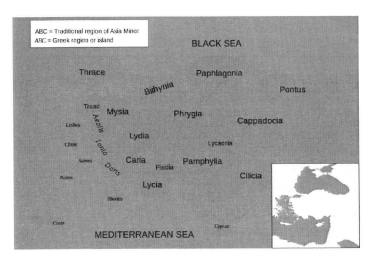

Figure 37.1 The places in Asia Minor where Peter traveled and sent letters.[1]

Peter's Dark Encouragement

Peter reminds his readers that he was an eyewitness of Jesus' life and sufferings (1 Peter 5:1; see also 2:23), and directly echoes a number of Jesus' teachings in his words (compare 1 Peter 2:12 with Matthew 5:16; 1 Peter 2:21 with Matthew 10:38; 1 Peter 3:14 and 4:13–14 with Matthew 5:10–12). Some scholars believe this letter could not have been written by Peter, since its use of the Greek language is too educated, too well crafted. But the double pairs of brothers from the fishing trade in Capernaum that Jesus called to follow him (Peter and Andrew, James and John), probably came from middle-class families, where education was important. Moreover, just as Paul had amanuenses writing out his letters, so in 1 Peter 5:12, the letter-writing skills of Silvanus (a variant of Silas) are recognized. Peter may well have been accomplished in his use of the Greek language, and certainly Peter's letter-writing scribe was.

Peter writes in powerful terms about the great salvation recently brought to humankind by Jesus. His opening image is of a gold refiner, sitting over the melting ore in the super-heated pot, obviously extremely uncomfortable by the heat and oppressive circumstances he is enduring for this process. Peering into the boiling cauldron, he gently scoops the slag off the surface of the molten metal. The process is not finished until the refiner can see his face reflected on the golden mirror of the cleansed mineral. Both the refiner and the ore are stressed by the process, but the outcome is beautiful.

This image is the first hint that Peter's letter will focus on the pressures of heated persecution. In fact, staying stalwart in faith through growing opposition and mounting persecution will be the overarching theme of this letter. Peter's readers need to be shielded by God's power (1:5) because they are suffering "grief in all kinds of trials (1:6). Some among them are slaves (2:18), and particularly prone to experiencing suffering (2:20), but all should follow the pattern of Jesus who also suffered (2:21) while leaving an example of faithful, quiet endurance. All

1 Peter in Summary

Great salvation has recently been brought by Jesus (1:3–12)

So, live holy lives because you are God's special people (1:13–2:10)

Follow the pattern of Jesus to live in humility and service (2:11–3:12)

And follow Jesus through the suffering of discipleship, especially because the end is near (3:12–4:19)

A word of encouragement to the elders (5:1–4)

Final general encouragements and greetings (5:5–14)

Christians should live exemplary lives of service (3:1-13), but even this is no guarantee of escaping the coming challenges (3:14), for all will soon be caught up in the pincers of painful persecution (4:1-19). These looming persecutions, however, are merely the temporary purification process (1:22) which will allow God and others to see the face of Jesus revealed in them.

Peter's readers are second-generation Christian, not having seen Jesus in the flesh (1:8), coming to faith through the testimony of others. Peter acknowledges that all of this is a new twist in the great redemption plans of God, having been foretold uncertainly by the prophets (1:10-11), but now made manifest in Jesus and the experiences of these folks (1:12).

Peter's Jewish identity and his connectedness with the covenant history of Israel are very obvious. He uses the central command given by Yahweh to Moses at Mount Sinai (Leviticus 19:2—"Be holy, because I am holy!") now to shape his exhortations about the Jesus-community lifestyle (2:4-10). Adapting the images of Israel as God's missional assembly to the Christian church, Peter continues the metaphors by equating Jesus to the Passover Lamb (2:24-25) that brought Israel into being, was proclaimed by Isaiah as the Suffering Servant, and now provides both salvation and behavior modeling for this gathering of God's people in a pressure-cooker world (2:11-3:12).

One of the most convoluted and difficult sentences in the whole of the Bible is found near the end of chapter 3. Verses 18-22 are two long and complex sentences in the Greek manuscripts of this letter. In our English translations we usually use at least four sentences to bring clarity to Peter's ideas:

> For Christ also suffered once for sins, the righteous for the unrighteous, to bring you to God. He was put to death in the body but made alive in the Spirit. After being made alive, he went and made proclamation to the imprisoned spirits—to those who were disobedient long ago when God waited patiently in the days of Noah while the ark was being built. In it only a few people, eight in all, were saved through water, and this water symbolizes baptism that now saves you also—not the removal of dirt from the body but the pledge of a clear conscience toward God. It saves you by the resurrection of Jesus Christ, who has gone into heaven and is at God's right hand—with angels, authorities and powers in submission to him.

But even then, the interpretation of this passage is discussed, and leads to many digressions. Some see in this passage the pre-existent second person of the Trinity appearing in different forms through biblical history, beginning with Noah. Others point to a bifurcation of Jesus' flesh and spirit, with the latter making a tour of hell (either to endure the suffering God's people would otherwise have faced, or to declare the triumph of salvation over the wiles and wishes of demonic forces) while the former rests in the grave. None of these explanations is entirely satisfying, and their discussion ought not to cloud the central message that is abundantly clear:

2 Peter in Summary

I want to tell you one last time about Jesus and the transforming power of the gospel (1)

Watch out for the growing problem of false teachers, who are compromising the message of Jesus for their own personal gain (2)

Live under the urgent expectation that Jesus is about to return (3)

Who Was Jude?

Probably Jesus' brother (Matthew 13:55; Mark 6:3), who was thereby the brother of James, the early leader of the Jerusalem Church (Luke 6:16; Acts 1:13; Jude 1). He may have been one of the ambassadors sent out to the churches from the Jerusalem council of Acts 15 with the report of the council's decision (Acts 15:27, 32)

What Sources Does Jude Quote?

Jude quotes from two apocalyptic writings that were popular during his day.

Book of Enoch:

Presumed visions of the Enoch of Genesis 5

Focus on angels, demons, and spiritual battles

Tells of spiritual conflicts that spill over into the history of Israel from the beginning of time through the inter-Testamental period

Assumption of Moses:

Presumed final testimony of Moses as dictated to Joshua

Warns of coming days when people will be led astray by lying spirits and false teachers

through his sufferings, Jesus has provided the way of salvation that available to all, and calls for believers to stand strong in whatever painful challenges are hurled at them.

The fact that Peter singles out Elders as the key leadership team of the congregations is both an affirmation of the leadership positions noted elsewhere in the New Testament (e.g., Acts 14:23; 1 Timothy 3 and 5; Titus 2) and also keenly ties him to his Jewish heritage. Elders were the recognized leaders of Israelite communities, and had become the designated officials in charge of synagogues. This form of church leadership was adapted from the Jewish social structures that birthed the early church.

Peter's final notes again return to the theme of suffering (4:12-19; 5:10). But the assurances is repeated that Jesus is in charge (5:11) and that he will return soon to make everything right and new. This will be a key idea more fully developed in Peter's next letter.

The tone of Peter's letter is far darker than any of the writings of Paul. There is an ominous pall of suffering that clouds every perspective. Jesus suffered. You will suffer, if you are faithful. You must follow Jesus in and through suffering. New trials and greater suffering are coming. Whether by way of external hints or from the inner promptings of the Spirit, Peter seems to have been anticipating the sharp clout of Nero's official pogroms, just ahead.

Yet through the murky shrieks and sinister valleys, Peter never loses confidence in God's sovereignty or care. God is judge over evil, the ever-faithful Creator, and the Chief Shepherd who will soon bring untarnishing crowns of glory for those who remain true.

Peter's Eschatological Expectations

The second letter attributed to Peter has been dogged by some controversy throughout the years. Its language and style seem different from 1 Peter, and it focuses on the second coming of Jesus (2 Peter 3) in a way that is not done anywhere else in the New Testament. Yet, the majority of the Church accepted it as Peter's letter from the very beginning. Once again, stylistic and vocabulary differences can be attributed to the secretarial assistance Peter used, and the particular false teaching that Peter wanted to address.

After all, the author identifies himself as Jesus' disciple Simon Peter (2 Peter 1:1), seems to be an old man looking back over a long career (2 Peter 1:12-15), speaks of being with Jesus during his earthly ministry (2 Peter 1:16-18), and uses these connections to confirm his teachings and authority (2 Peter 1:19-21). All of this does not prove the letter is from Peter, of course, but, together with the affirmation of the early Church, these things support its ring of authenticity.

It seems that the letter was written because a number of pseudo-Christian teachers were compromising the core message of Jesus for their own personal gain (2 Peter 2). It is not clear whether they were seeking money for their teaching ministries, or if they just wanted fame and a high standing in their communities. In light of these developments, Peter presses the same apocalyptic ethic that Paul touted so often: Jesus is coming soon, so be ready, and live appropriately (1 Peter 3). What is particularly striking about Peter's version is that he clearly identifies the times in which he is living, coupled with the imminent return of Jesus, as the "Day of the Lord" (2 Peter 3:3, 8, 10, 12). In this, Peter affirms the truth of Old Testament prophecy, links its anticipations of God's impending interruption of human affairs to Jesus, and recognizes the splitting of the "Day of the Lord" into two events, bounded by Jesus' first and second comings.

Peter anticipates his nearing death (2 Peter 1:12-15), and certainly believes difficult times are ahead for all believers. It is likely, therefore, that Peter wrote this letter sometime in late 63 or early 64 A.D., probably a year or so after his first letter, and shortly before his arrest and crucifixion under Nero's persecution.

Jude the Copycat

The bulk of Peter's second letter is symbiotically connected with the brief letter attributed to Jude. Because of their similar literary development and vocabulary, it is very likely either that both letters relied on a common source, or that one of the two borrows heavily from the other. Scholars today believe that it is most probable that 2 Peter was written first, and that Jude's reiteration of these themes was sent out later, probably sometime in the late 60s. This is based, at least in part, on a comparison of Jude 18 and 2 Peter 3:3. Jude quotes Peter's words, and declares that 2 Peter was written by one of Jesus' apostles (Jude 17). Since Jude refers often to the imminent judgment of God, but never makes reference to the destruction of Jerusalem and the Temple by the Romans in 70 A.D., he likely penned his letter prior to that event.

The major question that dogs these two letters is this: Who were the false teachers that Peter and Jude were so concerned about? While we cannot pinpoint them by name, there are a number of elements of their theology and practices that we can read backward through the lines of the biblical authors:

- By their lifestyles, these false teachers denied the power of Jesus to shape their behaviors (2 Peter 2:1; Jude 4).

- In some manner, they defiled the love-feast of "communion," or the "Lord's Supper" (Jude 12).
  - They were themselves immoral in lifestyle, and then they encouraged similar immorality in others (2 Peter 2:18–19; Jude 11).
  - They minimized the place of law in the Christian life and emphasized freedom (2 Peter 2:10, 18–19; Jude 4, 12).
  - They were plausible and crafty, fond of rhetoric, out for gain, and pandered to those from whom they hoped to win favor (2 Peter 2:3, 12, 14, 15, 18; Jude 16).
  - They were arrogant, and cynical of church leaders (2 Peter 2:1, 10, 11; Jude 8).
  - They posed as visionaries or prophets (2 Peter 2:1; Jude 8).
  - They were self-willed, divisive, and confident of their own superiority (2 Peter 2:2, 10, 18; Jude 19).

All in all, they sound like very nasty people. Some aspects of these behaviors seem similar to warnings that Paul had issued to the Corinthian congregation, about inappropriate teachers among them (1 Corinthians 6:12–13, 18–20; chapter 15). Other cues could be linked with several of the allusions Paul made to the Colossians about the false teaching that was spreading in that community (Colossians 2:6–23). A number of scholars try to connect these problematic teachers with the "Nicolaitans," who show up as bad guys in Revelation 2:6 and 2:15, but that is an almost impossible stretch, simply because we do not know enough about either group to link them. In the end, we cannot draw a clear picture of these dark and cultish figures. All we can say is that they scared the leaders of the early Church enough for Peter and Jude to issue stern formal warnings against them.

The letters of Peter and Jude do not add a great amount of insight to the teachings already put forward by Jesus and Paul. They are, however, a bit like warning markers—you can move safely within this territory, but if you step beyond certain lines, great peril awaits you. Peter provides powerful encouragement from someone who knew Jesus firsthand, and could call others to join him in living faithfully through times of great stress and suffering. In his final years, Peter issues warnings against false teachers, and urges believers to live in expectation of Jesus' imminent return.

While a bit more eccentric in his twist on things, steeped as he was in the popular apocalyptic and wisdom literature of his day, Jude also did his part to keep the rapidly expanding Church true to its essential beliefs. Jude may have seen this as his mandate and legacy because of his family ties. Christianity was the movement begun by his older brother, Jesus, and it had been shepherded from Jerusalem, for some time now, by his older brother James.

Discussion Points

- What personal experiences from Peter's life are hinted at in 1 and 2 Peter? How does the writer leverage these as a source of encouragement for his readers?
- How is the theme of suffering explored in 1 Peter? What is the relationship developed between the sufferings of Jesus and those of the Christian community? What lessons can be learned by Peter's contemporaries as they reflect on the life of Jesus?

- What are the most obvious inappropriate actions and instructions of the false teachers noted by Peter and Jude? How might these wrong teachings have developed? How might these presumed leaders have gotten power and positions of influence? Who might Peter and Jude point to today, as performing similar heretical acts in the current religious environment? Why?
- How does Jude use the popular religious literature of his day to illustrate his message?

For Further Investigation

Bauckham, Richard J. (Waco: Word, 1983). *Jude, 2 Peter.*

Grundem, Wayne. (Downers Grove: InterVarsity, 1998). *1 Peter.*

Jobes, Karen H. (Grand Rapids: Baker, 2005). *1 Peter.*

Marshall, I. Howard. (Downers Grove: InterVarsity, 1991). *1 Peter.*

39.

Battling Self-Centered Variations on Christianity

John and the Proto-Gnostics

I t is obvious that 1 John is not a letter, at least not of the variety that we have become familiar with in the New Testament. It carries no identification of the author, puts forward no greeting, offers no personal notes or reminiscences, includes no travel plans, responds to no particular life situations encountered by either the writer or the readers, and offers no concluding blessing. It is not a letter.

Still, it fits well within the kind of teaching material that makes up the bulk of the letters in the New Testament. It is precisely this subliminal "feel" of 1 John, along with the two letters that accompany it, that has placed 1, 2, and 3 John in the company of the "epistles." Part of the premise of considering together the writings of Paul, Peter, James, Jude, and John—all similar in status among the people of God in the New Testament age, as were the prophets of the Old Testament—is their literary grouping as authoritative teachings from Jesus' first-team leadership group to the growing and expanding missional Church that was rapidly unfolding around them.

Occasion

What makes 1 John part of this collection is that it seems to be the doctrinal portion within a collection of letters. The occasion that triggered the writing of these three documents from John was a crisis forming in a church to which John was closely tied, and with whose pastoral leader he had a deep bond of friendship.

Over the months or years prior to the writing of 1, 2, and 3 John, a critical separation fractured the congregation between two parties and their leaders. On the one side are "the Elder" (John himself), Gaius, Demetrius, and the bulk of this particular congregation. On the other side are Diotrephes and a group of false teachers, who were at one time allies and part of the congregational leadership team, but are now abrasively identified by the Elder/John as "antichrists." From the bits of sociological data in these writings, we can confidently say several things about the church that was experiencing these polarizing disputes:

- The congregation is likely to be quite large, since there are multiple leaders lining up on both sides.
- Its members seem to be fairly well educated, because the teachings being espoused by both the false teachers and John himself are often quite technical and philosophical.
- The church must have been established for some years by the time of this controversy; long enough, certainly, to have had a gradual evolving of leadership teams, and doctrinal development that has become highly nuanced.
- Moreover, the congregation was located not very far from Ephesus, since John was quite an old man by this time, and yet seems to have had regular personal contacts on-site with Gaius, its pastor.

It is probable that 1, 2, and 3 John were part of a single packet of correspondence, written together in one setting, and delivered all at one time, by a man named Demetrius. Demetrius was being sent by the Elder as his personal representative. 3 John forms the cover letter for the collection as a whole. In it, the Elder commends Demetrius to Gaius, identifying Demetrius as the chosen ambassador of the Elder, who was trusted to act on the Elder's behalf in resolving this crisis. 2 John is the introductory letter from the Elder to the congregation as a whole, encouraging faithfulness during these stressful times of dispute and tension, and setting the stage for a public reading of the summary teaching, also enclosed. 1 John forms that brief, but substantive, teaching itself. It was intended to be read and discussed by the congregation, outlining correct and incorrect theologies that have surfaced in this debate, and pointing to next steps in dealing with these matters.

Author

While "the Elder" is never actually identified as John, the disciple and close friend of Jesus, John's name has been associated with these writings from their earliest appearance in the Church. Not only did those who knew John well testify that these writings are his, but there is confirming internal evidence as well. The vocabulary and writing style of these documents are very similar to both the Gospel of John and also the Book of Revelation. In fact, these writings use many nearly identical statements and phrases to explain life and perspective and theology, as are found in those other books. Along with that, the very structure of reality, a kind of dualistic worldview of light versus darkness, good versus evil, pervades them all.

The earliest confirmed appearance of these documents is in Asia Minor (Turkey today). This supports the likelihood that "the Elder" truly is John, the disciple of Jesus. John lived at Ephesus for the last half of his life, during which time these writings appeared, and he served as a key figure in the development of early Christian theology from that location. Because Emperor Domitian reigned from September of 81 through September of 96, and was probably responsible for sending John from Ephesus into exile on the nearby prison island of Patmos, the correspondence packet of 1, 2, and 3 John was likely written either during the years surrounding 80, before John's deportation, or otherwise much later, after John's release in the last half of the 90s. Since "the Elder" (2 John 12; 3 John 13) appears to be mobile, intending to travel and visit Gaius soon, the earlier time frame seems more probable, allowing for the younger John (already about 80 at that time) to actively pursue such a journey. Yet the developing doctrinal controversy highlighted by 1 John is of the kind that would eventually rupture into competing forms of Christianity in the second century. This leads many to propose a later date. If it is indeed John, the disciple and friend of Jesus, who writes these treatises, most likely they came into being in the early-to-mid-80s, before John was taken away as a prisoner.

False Teaching

What is the heretical teaching that this competing group is putting forward? Although we do not have any actual writings that might have been circulated by the false teachers, or first-person written reports of their oratory, we can read backward through John's main points of emphasis, and decipher nuances of the heresy propounded. Against what the others must have been teaching, John stresses these things:

- There is clear continuity between Old and New Testament ages (1:1–4)
- God has given a recent new revelation, the person of Jesus (1:2–3)
- There is only one God, and this divine Being is entirely unified in character (1:5)
- Sin is an obvious reality, and cannot be ignored or presumed out of the human picture (1:6–10)
- Jesus actually died, and this happened as a sacrifice that had religious transactional qualities; it was redemptive (1:7, 2:1)
- There is a unity of theology and ethics; what you believe must come out in your practices, or it is not truly held at all (2:3–6)
- Followers of Jesus are, by their very nature and calling, concerned about the physical well-being of others (2:9–11)
- Godly people need to deny worldly desires that constantly plague the human race (2:15–17)
- The highest value of all is love expressed in relationships (3:10–15, 4:21)
- Jesus actually died, and this was an atoning sacrifice (3:16, 4:10)
- The Holy Spirit is one with the Father and the Son (3:21–4:6)
- Jesus is and remains truly flesh and blood (4:2, 5:6–8)

When these emphases in John's teaching monograph are consolidated, they appear to be a reaction to early Gnosticism. Gnosticism was a philosophic worldview that often parasitically attached itself to various religious expressions, twisting their key concepts in complex and mystical directions. During the second century, a number of Gnostic communities sprang up in the Christian Church, particularly in its eastern regions. Clement of Alexandria (c. 150-c. 215) and his pupil, Origen (c. 185-254), were among the most articulate spokespersons of Gnostic-influenced Christian theology who remained within the orthodox faith. Irenaeus (c. 140-c. 202), Tertullian (c. 160-c. 220), and Hippolytus (170-235) all wrote extensively against the heresy of Gnosticism, and their explanations often parallel John's earlier teaching on these things.

Gnosticism saw the world as cosmologically dualistic. All of physical reality was bad and degraded, while spiritual dimensions of life were good and empowering. The ultimate deity was like that of the Greek Stoics—nonrelational, dispassionate, impassive, unchanging, and transcendent. But since the material world actually existed, an emanation (called the Demiurge) from the transcendent god must have served as a secondary or subordinate creator. Of course, any god which would bring into being material things was already compromised. So, clearly, the deity of the Jews, the Creator God of the Old Testament, had to be a bad god. This distinguished Christianity from Judaism. Like the Demiurge (or identified with the Demiurge), the god of Genesis (and therefore all of the Hebrew scriptures) was certainly less than perfect, and may well have been an ogre with a sadistic mean streak. Human beings, after all, are at best an evil joke. Many of us (but not all), have a divine spark trapped within our material shells, imprisoned almost to extinction by the loathsome attachments we have to passion and appetites.

Christianity, however, is the religion of Jesus, the liberator. Obviously, if Jesus is to bring salvation, He needs to transcend the material world, which is inherently bad. So Gnostic forms of Christianity took one of two approaches when theologizing about Jesus. The Docetists (from the Greek word meaning to "seem" or "appear"), believed that Jesus was only a divine projection into our world (like a hologram), who was not actually human and did not really interact directly with material substance. It was precisely because of His intrinsic difference from us that He was able to speak to our condition, and provide a means of spiritual escape.

The Adoptionists, on the other hand, believed that Jesus was a very good human being, who was then adopted by God to be used as a temporary transmitter of divine teachings. When Jesus was baptized by John, the Holy Spirit came upon him, granting to the man Jesus the ability to see, know, and understand transcendent, spiritual things. Later, when Jesus was being crucified, he himself acknowledged what had happened, for he raised his face toward heaven and cried out, "Father, into your hands I commend my spirit!" This, of course, was the release, or separation, of the divine spirit from the human Jesus. Many of the Adoptionists believed that God was deeply grateful to Jesus (the man) for his faithful service and partnership for a time with the divine spirit, and that after Jesus (the man) died, God raised him up as a new kind of creature. This resurrected Jesus was the prototype that true Christians should emulate, and toward which they should aspire.

If we as humans are to gain release from our material prisons and become truly liberated spirits, we need several things. First, we must gain the appropriate knowledge. This is the origin of the term Gnosticism, which is simply taken from the Greek word, γνωσις, meaning "knowing" or "knowledge." Since we are all trapped in the same material muddle, only a transcendent, divine spirit can communicate this necessary knowledge to us. Jesus' life was all about this, whether as a projection into our experiences who was not himself fully, materially human, or by way of the unique divine insights and abilities granted the man who was adopted by God, and endowed with a special spiritual connection. So we need to learn the teachings of Jesus, because these will help us shed the claws of materialism that dig into the divine sparks many of us are beginning to realize that we have. Of course, the sayings and parables of Jesus would be interpreted differently by Gnostic teachers than they would by John and those who followed in his steps. That was the reason for the controversy which erupted in Gaius's congregation in the first place.

Second, we must engage in rituals of purification, through which we learn to transcend our own evil flesh, and purify the growing power of our spirits. These may be negations of bodily functions, or solitary mystical reveries. In any case, they are very myopic and self-focused: "I am on a spiritual quest ..." "I am seeking truth, which you might not be privy to ..." "I cannot be bothered by your needs or concerns, since I have moved into transcendence ..."

Third, we must release the divine spark within us, ultimately through the death of our physical bodies. This is why, in the Gnostic *Gospel of Judas*, for instance, Jesus tells Judas that Judas's planned betrayal of Jesus is of supreme importance, and constitutes the most necessary task that any of the disciples could accomplish. Judas is the hero of the story, for Judas alone understands that Jesus cannot be a fully blessed immaterial spirit until his physical flesh and blood dies. Only this will release the divine spark within him. So Judas is praised by Jesus as the one who does the very best thing in having Jesus killed. Physical death is the only guaranteed way to get rid of the material substance that diminishes true human life. Thus, Jesus' death and resurrection are at the center of Gnostic theology, but their purposes are strikingly different than expressed in the rest of Christian hope and understanding. For Paul and John and the rest of the New Testament writers, Jesus' death was a scandal and a tragedy, even if it was part of the divine purpose and will. Jesus' resurrection was an affirmation of the goodness of human life restored, precisely in its material state. For Gnostics, however, things were exactly the opposite. Jesus' death was the great release, and the resurrected Jesus was fully spiritual, completely separated from physical influence or limitation.

These opposing perspectives about the intended or best expression of human life produced the ethical concerns that John addresses. Some Gnostics evidently believed that since we are powerless to transform our bodies or material substance into anything good, we might as well allow our flesh to enjoy its pitiable quest for passion, and indulge ourselves in any gross sensuality that our bodies might lead us into. After all, our truest beings are not really engaged in these things; it is only our weak and self-destructive bodies that are so inclined. Meanwhile, our spirits are set on higher goals and purposes.

A second element of Gnostic behavior, apparently, was that of ignoring the plight of others. Why should we try to alleviate the suffering which others experience in their flesh, since comfort only buttresses the pretense that their bodies have some meaning. We ought not to care for others, because such investments mess us up with material reality. These actions, in turn, only pull us away from our truest spiritual goals, strengthen the capacities and resolve of the material prisons of our bodies which hold our spirits in check, and prevent others, whose flesh is weakening, from gaining more quickly the blessed release that will happen to their spirits when their bodies actually die.

All of this seems to have fostered a kind of Gnostic elitism. If some of us know these things, and others do not, we who know are better than those who do not know. We who have true knowledge from Jesus are on the track toward illumination and release, while those others are dumb dodos. Too bad they aren't like us, but there is not a thing we can do about it. We are enlightened; they are not.

True Christian Beliefs and Response

In the face of these teachings, which were dividing at least this one congregation and threatening the gospel that John knew so well and had taught for so long, John gives some very pointed instructions. Right at the start of his short lecture, he affirms that the God of the Old Testament is also the true Creator God (1 John 1), and that there is no cosmological dualism in which good and evil coexist in the eternal forms of spirit and matter. Evil is not an inherent part of human identity; it is an intruder (1 John 1:6–10). Nor is evil automatically connected only with the material dimension of human existence; our spirits can be sinful, just as our hands can be engaged in things that are good and right and noble (1 John 2:9–11).

When focusing on Jesus, John declares without qualification that he is the divine Son of God, who actually became flesh and blood (1 John 2:20–23). Jesus is neither a holographic spiritual projection into our world, untouched by material plight or passionate feelings, nor an adopted superman, who is so divinely charged that he no longer fully participates in the experiences of the rest of us. This counters the Gnostic ideas about their supposed divine teacher, and turns the testimony of the incarnation into the critical test for defining which teachings are true and which are not (1 John 4:1–3).

Furthermore, since God cares about us as fully integrated flesh-and-blood-and-spirit creatures (after all, we are brought into being by the true and good Creator), we must also care about each other (1 John 3:7–24). Since God loved us so much that God entered our world in the person of Jesus, we ought also to fully engage in each other's lives for help, encouragement, and care (1 John 4:7–21). In fact, the test of love is whether one has learned to care about the physical needs of a sister or brother (1 John 4:19–21). Christianity does not remove us from pain, but causes us to enter into it on an even deeper level, just as it brought Jesus into his stormy and tortured existence with us, and ultimately crucified Him (1 John 5:1–12).

Thus, salvation is both physical and spiritual. We are already "children of God" (1 John 3:1), and we are also becoming more fully the family of the Creator (1 John 3:2–3). Love is the highest moral good, the truest expression of "Light" against the "Darkness" that evil and sin have brought into our world. This is why the last line of John's teaching ("Dear children, keep yourselves from idols"), often considered cryptic or ill placed, is actually the summation of the entire teaching. It is the idolatry of self or spirit that misled these false teachers. They were neither superior spiritual gurus nor better human beings than those who did not believe in their proto-Gnostic teachings. In the end, they were false messiahs (thus, "antichrists") of the cult which, in its most dastardly expressions, was merely self-absorbed childishness, where "I" stands at the center of the universe.

John believes that God does a better job in that location, and that our lives are meant to radiate the divine glory wherever we find ourselves. After all, "we love because he first loved us" (1 John 4:19).

Discussion Points

- What is the probable context in which these three documents were written? How do the life and times of John, the apostle, fit into this possible picture?
- What are the critical concerns that John has about the teachings of the deviant leaders? How does John address these false assumptions?
- How do the views of Gnosticism continue to exist in our societies? How are they evident in some forms of religious teaching? What is the Christian response to them?

For Further Investigation

Kruse, Colin G. (Grand Rapids: Eerdmans, 2000). The Letters of John.

Logan, Alastair H. B. (Edinburgh: T & T Clark, 2006). The Gnostics.

Stott, John R. W. (Downers Grove: InterVarsity, 1988). The Letters of John.

Bible "Big Picture"

Covenant Making: God establishes a covenant relationship with a missional community by way of a redemptive act

Old Testament: The Exodus and Sinai Covenant

  Genesis—Why is the Covenant necessary?

  Exodus—What is the Covenant all about?

  Leviticus—How does it affect daily living?

  Numbers—Who is in the covenant community, and why?

  Deuteronomy—How long will the Covenant be in force?

New Testament: The Person and Work of Jesus

  Matthew—Jesus is the Messiah King, who relives the life of Israel, and becomes Savior King of the Nations

  Mark—Jesus is the powerful Son of God, who releases people from the many evils that enslave them

  Luke—Jesus is the heaven-sent Teacher and Healer, who brings hope through the ministry of the Church

  John—Jesus is the ultimate Passover Lamb, who re-creates the dark world through the witness of his disciples

Covenant Living: God guides the covenant relationship with the missional community by way of authorized spokespersons

Old Testament: The Prophets, with Their Interpreted History and Sermons

Stories: The interpreted history of Israel
- *Joshua*—Possessing the Land with missional significance
- *Judges*—Nearly losing the Land through covenant failure
- *Ruth*—The model of covenant obedience that restores
- *1 & 2 Samuel*—Establishing the monarchy that might fulfill the covenant mission
- *1 & 2 Kings, 1 & 2 Chronicles*—Failure of the Old Testament covenant community mission experiment
- *Ezra and Nehemiah*—Restoring the covenant community in anticipation of Yahweh's next major act
- *Esther*—Responding to the warning that Yahweh's people have a covenant identity and purpose

Sermons: The verbal declarations of Yahweh's designs and intents
- *Isaiah*—Divine deliverance from Assyria, coming global renewal
- *Jeremiah*—Doom and gloom in Judah's final years, promises of restoration
- *Ezekiel*—God on the move, bringing judgment and promises of a new age
- *Daniel*—Struggles of faithful exilic living, plus visions of God's growing kingdom
- *Hosea*—The divine/human soap opera
- *Joel*—Hints of "the Day of the Lord" found in a locust plague
- *Amos*—Imminent divine judgment because of social covenantal disobedience
- *Obadiah*—Edom condemned for harming Judah at the time of deportation
- *Jonah*—Missionary trek to Assyrian enemy capital showing global divine favor
- *Micah*—Yahweh's faithfulness, Israel's unfaithfulness, and imminent judgment
- *Nahum*—God will destroy Assyria because of its cruelty to other nations
- *Habakkuk*—Dialogue with Yahweh on the mysteries of social sins and divine judgment
- *Zephaniah*—Brief notes on impending divine judgment and future redemptive restoration
- *Haggai*—"Let's get that Temple rebuilt!" and "God bless Zerubbabel!"
- *Zechariah*—Visions of judgment on the nations and visions of glory on restored "Israel"
- *Malachi*—Dialogues between Yahweh and the people on failures and the future

New Testament: The Apostles, with Their Ecclesiastical History and Letters
Stories: The unfolding of the "new covenant" in Jesus through the actions and mission of the Church
- *Acts*—The power of Jesus enacted upon the Church by way of the Holy Spirit to be a missional community

Sermons: The teachings of Jesus communicated through the apostles
- *Romans*—The righteousness of God revealed against Sin, bringing Salvation, and prompting Service
- *1 & 2 Corinthians*—How to live as Jesus' followers in a compromised society and very human Church
- *Galatians*—Gospel Liberty over either Legalism or License, uniting Jews and Gentiles in faith
- *Ephesians*—God's great power at work in Jesus transforms sinners into saints who bring light into darkness
- *Philippians*—Rejoice! Knowing Jesus brings joy! Enjoy one another in true care and commitment!
- *Colossians*—Christ rules, so stop building petty parties in the church, and live as ambassadors of light
- *1 & 2 Thessalonians*—Your testimony is heard everywhere; the dead will rise, but Jesus may delay
- *1 & 2 Timothy*—Work faithfully as a pastor, live faithfully as a person, and carry on after I am gone
- *Titus*—Organize the work of ministry well, so that all may be blessed
- *Philemon*—Receive useful Onesimus back as both slave and brother, and prepare for my visit

- *James*—Learn to live as brothers and sisters of Jesus and of one another; no special treatment!
- *1 & 2 Peter*—Live faithfully, particularly in the face of growing persecutions, knowing that Jesus is coming
- *1, 2, & 3 John*—The God of Israel is the God of the Church; Jesus came in the flesh; love one another
- *Jude*—There are some nasty teachers out there; don't listen to them!

Covenant Questions: God nurtures the covenant relationship with a missional community by way of spiritual wisdom and insight

Old Testament: The Poetry and Wisdom Literature; Questions of Fundamental Human Identity as Illuminated by the Theology of the Covenant

Job—"Why do I suffer?"

Psalms—"How do I pray?"

Proverbs—"What is true wisdom?"

Ecclesiastes—"What is the meaning of life?"

Song of Songs—"What is the meaning of love?"

Lamentations—"What is the meaning of divine election?"

New Testament: The Comparison of the Two Covenant Expressions

Covenant Questions (2)

The Creator nurtures the covenant relationship with a
missional community by way of spiritual wisdom and insight

40.

Connecting Old and New

Refining the Biblical Worldview for the Faint of Heart

H ebrews is a very interesting book, filled with great theology, but structured uniquely in its style of presentation. The title reference, "to the Hebrews," was given to this nineteenth book of the New Testament at least as early as the second century. Eusebius, the Church's first major historian, had information that Clement of Alexandria believed that the document was written by Paul and addressed to Jewish Christians living in Palestine. Clement thought Paul deliberately hid his own identity, because many in the Jewish Christian community resented Paul's main focus of ministry with Gentiles, and were troubled by Paul's belief that the ceremonial regulations of offerings and purification rites were no longer necessary. Clement was further of the opinion that Paul had written this document in the Hebrew language, but that Luke had quickly translated it into polished Greek, in order to serve the many Diaspora Jewish communities where the Hellenistic language was primary (Eusebius, *Church History*, Book 3, Chapter 38).

What Kind of Literature Is This?

A linguistic and literary analysis of the book, however, undermines Clement's views, as even Eusebius recognized. First, the theology of Hebrews is certainly compatible with that which Paul expressed in his letters; its phrasing and syntax, however, are so different as to make it impossible to understand how they could emerge from the same person, even if there were amanuenses or letter-writing secretaries involved. Second, the scripture quotations found in Hebrews are all but one taken directly from the Septuagint (the Greek translation of the Hebrew Bible). In fact, the very selection of Greek texts rather than Hebrew texts provides the nuances for theological points that are made throughout the book. This means that it is highly unlikely that Hebrews was first written in the Hebrew language and then translated into Greek, since the very wording of the arguments and theories in the book depend on the Greek Septuagint. Third, Paul was never shy about identifying himself in his writings, whether to Jews, Gentiles, or mixed groups, even when his personality or teachings were being challenged. It is probably for reasons such as these that in the western regions of the early Church, where Paul had spent the bulk of his ministry, this document was rarely identified with him, although it was quoted early on as an authoritative teaching for the Church.

Such is the strange legacy of Hebrews: clear and precise in theology, even while its origins and specific audience are lost from our view. Although Hebrews concludes with a few epistolary notes (Hebrews 13:22–25), the document is not actually a letter. Nor is it a "gospel," like the Synoptics and John (though it is rigorously focused on Jesus), since it neither outlines aspects of Jesus' movements around Palestine nor summarizes his teachings. Sometimes, Hebrews seems to be a sermon, or perhaps a string of sermons stitched together; this may well have been its initial form, before an editorial reworking that created the complex, but cohesive, document we now have. The final version appears to be an extended written teaching that was designed to be read in public. It is a tightly woven rhetorical interaction between exposition (explaining the meaning of scripture passages) and exhortation (applying those meanings and values to life situations).

> ### Rhetorical Interweaving in Hebrews
>
> **Exposition** (*explaining the meaning of scripture passages*): 1:1–14; 2:5–8; 3:2–6; 3:14–19; 4:2–10; 5:1–10; 6:13–15; 7:1–22; 8:3–9:10; 9:16–22; 10:1–18; 11
>
> **Exhortation** (*applying meanings and values to life situations*): 2:1–4; 3:1; 3:7–13; 4:1; 4:11–16; 5:11–6:12; 6:16–20; 7:23–8:2; 9:11–15; 9:23–28; 10:19–39; 12–13]

What Is Its Worldview?

Whatever one might call the literary genre, Hebrews is unquestionably built upon the foundation of Old Testament linear thought. It tells of the progression in God's activities with human history, pointing to specific events like the revelations at Sinai, the construction of the Tabernacle, and the ministry of the prophets. This unfolding redemptive work of God has recently reached its apex, according to Hebrews, in the coming of Jesus (Hebrews 1:1-4). Everything—past, present, and future—becomes meaningful only as it intersects with Jesus Christ. Jesus' entrance into human time has changed even our understanding of time, and we are now living in the new, messianic era.

Although there are many smaller sections and parenthetical notes, the thrust of Hebrews as a whole is on explaining the unique identity and role of Jesus, and drawing out the implications this has for all who know Him:

- Jesus is the Superior Way to God (Hebrews 1-6):
  * Angels delivered the Torah, but Jesus is Himself the Living Word (chapters 1-2).
  * Moses received the Torah, but Jesus is a new and living symbol (chapters 3-4) of God among us.
  * Aaron and the priests sacrificed daily and yearly, but Jesus sacrificed himself once for all (chapters 5-6).
- Therefore, Jesus is like Melchizedek, uniquely filling a mediatorial role (Hebrews 7-10).
- So keep following him, in spite of challenges and tribulations (Hebrews 10-13).

One of the most critical passages expressing this view in summary is found in Hebrews 8:

Who Was Melchizedek?

Melchizedek is a shadowy figure who only emerges three times in the Bible. First, there is a brief mention of Abram's encounter with Melchizedek, the "king of Salem" and "priest of God Most High" (Genesis 14:18), after rescuing Lot from neighboring kings. Because Abram has a unique relationship with God, and yet receives a blessing from Melchizedek and honors this king and priest by giving a tenth of his goods, Melchizedek gains distinction as standing above Abraham (and his descendents) in spiritual authority.

Second, this heightened sense of Melchizedek's mediatorial role is played out in Psalm 110, which might be David's response to the promise made by God in 2 Samuel 7, that one of his descendants will always be king over God's people. Melchizedek was somehow divinely commissioned outside of the Mosaic/Aaronic family appointments, and the unique gift given to David's family had the same qualities about it.

Third, this becomes the source of allegorical material for the author of Hebrews. Like Melchizedek, Jesus stands outside the ordinary priestly system of Israel, and therefore can function in a unique way as a mediator. There is even a play made on the limited information about Melchizedek in Genesis (his parentage is not noted) and the special circumstances of Jesus' birth (the miracle of the incarnation).

But the ministry Jesus has received is as superior to theirs as the covenant of which he is mediator is superior to the old one, and it is founded on better promises. For if there had been nothing wrong with that first covenant, no place would have been sought for another. But God found fault with the people and said: "The time is coming, declares the Lord, when I will make a new covenant with the house of Israel and with the house of Judah. It will not be like the covenant I made with their forefathers when I took them by the hand to lead them out of Egypt, because they did not remain faithful to my covenant, and I turned away from them, declares the Lord. This is the covenant I will make with the house of Israel after that time, declares the Lord. I will put my laws in their minds and write them on their hearts. I will be their God, and they will be my people. No longer will a man teach his neighbor, or a man his brother saying, 'Know the Lord,' because they will all know me, from the least of them to the greatest. For I will forgive their wickedness and will remember their sins no more." By calling this covenant "new," he has made the first one obsolete; and what is obsolete and aging will soon disappear (Hebrews 8:6–13, quoting from Jeremiah 31:31–34).

In making the comparison between the old and new expressions of the covenant, the author does not criticize the former, but turns common perceptions on their head. He assumes that the recent developments, related to Jesus' coming, were intended all along, with the cultic ceremonies of Israel functioning like a prelude or a preamble:

> The law is only a shadow of the good things that are coming—not the realities themselves. For this reason it can never, by the same sacrifices repeated endlessly year after year, make perfect those who draw near to worship. If it could, would they not have stopped being offered? For the worshipers would have been cleansed once for all, and would no longer have felt guilty for their sins. But those sacrifices are an annual reminder of sins, because it is impossible for the blood of bulls and goats to take away sins (Hebrews 10:1–4).

Since Jesus has entered our history as the definitive revelation of God's eternal plans and designs, he has fulfilled the intent of the sacrificial system, and thus made it obsolete. This message, along with the enthusiasm of the divine Spirit, energizes the community of faith that now spreads its witness in this messianic age as the Christian Church:

> Therefore, brothers, since we have confidence to enter the Most Holy Place by the blood of Jesus, by a new and living way opened for us through the curtain, that is, his body, and since we have a great priest over the house of God, let us draw near to God with a sincere heart in full assurance of faith, having our hearts sprinkled to cleanse us from a guilty conscience and having our bodies washed with pure water. Let us hold unswervingly to the hope we profess, for he who promised is faithful. And let us consider how we may spur one another on toward love and good deeds. Let us not give up meeting together, as some are in the habit of doing, but let us encourage one another—and all the more as you see the Day approaching (Hebrews 10:19–25).

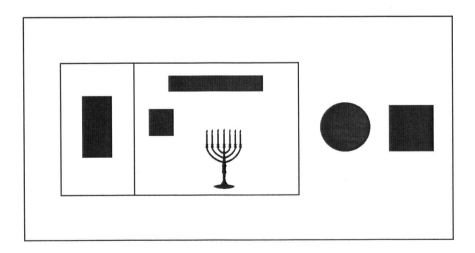

Figure 39.1 The floor plan and primary furnishings of both the Tabernacle and the Temple.

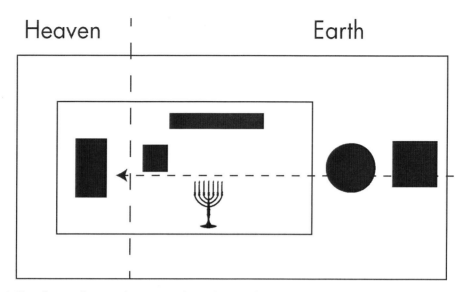

Figure 39.2 The floor plan and primary furnishings of the Tabernacle as used by the writer of Hebrews to diagram and symbolize his theology. Jesus is the "great high priest over the house of God" who travels from heaven to earth in order to take us back to heaven with him. The route traveled transforms each piece of furnishing into a new Christian symbol: Altar of Burnt Offering/ Jesus' Cross; Bronze Sea/Baptism; Table of Showbread/the Lord's Supper or Eucharist; Golden Lamp/Light of Jesus through the Spirit among the Churches; Altar of Incense/Prayers of God's people; Ark of the Covenant/God's throne.

Steeped as he is in Jewish culture and covenantal outlook, the author reduces all of life to the symbolic representations of the Tabernacle. When God took up residence on earth, the furnishings of the Tabernacle were designed to provide a means by which sinful human beings could approach a holy deity. In the Tabernacle courtyard, on the **Altar of Burnt Offering**, a sacrificial transaction took place, atoning for inner sin and alienation from God. The **Bronze Sea** standing nearby, although used only by the priests and Levites, symbolized the external cleansing necessary when making contact with Yahweh. In the Holy Place, the first room of the Tabernacle proper, were the visible representations of fellowship—a **Table** always prepared for mealtime hospitality, a **Lamp** giving light for Yahweh and his guests, and the **Altar of Incense** which, with its sweet smells, overcame the stench of animal sacrifices outside, and created a pleasant atmosphere for relaxed conversation. Finally, intimacy with God could be had by passing through the curtain, and stepping into the throne room itself, the Most Holy Place. Here,

Why Was Hebrews Written?

- New threats of persecution are looming (2:14–18; 10:32–34; 12:4)
- Many in this community are experiencing a loss of spiritual nerve (2:1; 6:1–12; 10:19–25; 10:35–39; 12:12)
- These are thus in danger of losing faith in Jesus (3:16–4:16)
- This loss of faith in Jesus appears to nurture a tendency to go back to Hebrew/ Jewish expressions of religious identity, which do not need Jesus (10:26–31; 12:18–29)]

the **Ark of the Covenant**, with its **Mercy Seat** throne, was the actual place where Yahweh appeared to his people. Because this spiritual journey was too large a leap for most sinfully compromised humans to make, access was granted and taken only once a year in the person and representative acts of the high priest. Israel, as a people, met Yahweh in the Tabernacle (the "House of God") through these symbolic representations.

What Jesus has recently done, according to Hebrews, is short-circuited these feeble and repetitious efforts at renewing human relations with God. He did this by fulfilling all of the deep-down meaning of these practices in the grand once-and-for-all activity of his death and resurrection. Now the old meanings, good and proper as they were, are connected to new symbols: the **cross** becomes the Altar of Burnt Offering; **Baptism** is the cleansing washing that replaces the waters of the Bronze Sea; the **Lord's Supper** is the ongoing experience of the hospitality Table; the **Holy Spirit** is the illuminating presence previously offered by the Lamp; **prayers** (both ours and Jesus') form the new Incense that sweetens the atmosphere when we seek God; and the Most Holy Place, with its Mercy Seat atop the Ark of the Covenant, is nothing less than God's grand throne room in **heaven** itself. Indeed, if the microcosm worldview of the Tabernacle is expanded and inverted, we can sketch out the meaning of Jesus and the true religion of our lives as a journey from outside the camp into the holy presence of God.

> Therefore, since we have a great high priest who has gone through the heavens, Jesus the Son of God, let us hold firmly to the faith we profess. For we do not have a high priest who is unable to sympathize with our weaknesses, but we have one who has been tempted in every way, just as we are—yet was without sin. Let us then approach the throne of grace with confidence, so that we may receive mercy and find grace to help us in our time of need (Hebrews 4:14–16).

> Therefore, brothers, since we have confidence to enter the Most Holy Place by the blood of Jesus, by a new and living way opened for us through the curtain, that is, his body, and since we have a great priest over the house of God, let us draw near to God with a sincere heart, in full assurance of faith, having our hearts sprinkled to cleanse us from a guilty conscience and having our bodies washed with pure water (Hebrews 10:19–22).

It is obvious from the writer's argument that he and those he is addressing are deeply steeped in the worldview, culture, practices, and religious rites of Judaism. Not only so, but theirs is a conservative, orthodox, historical understanding of the religion of Israel. The Old Testament is the revelation of God, and Israel holds a special place in transmitting the divine outlook and purposes with the human race. Israel's identity was shaped around its religious ceremonies, which themselves emanated from the Tabernacle, its furnishings, and its symbolism.

What Was the Occasion for Writing Hebrews?

Although the author of Hebrews shares these perspectives with his audience, there is one significant difference between them: He fully believes Jesus has ushered in a culminating change that transcends and makes obsolete these previous expressions of religious identity, while they, due to cultural pressures around them, are not so sure of that. This document is written to convince a community that is on the verge of slipping away from Jesus, back into a pre-Jesus Jewish ritualistic context—that such a move would be both unwise and inappropriate (Hebrews 10:19–39).

All of this asks the question: Who were the first recipients of this document? Where were they living? What was their background? When were they caught up in these things?

There are a number of clues that come through the author's notes about the experiences they have faced:

- These are second-generation Christians (2:1; 2:3; 13:7)
  - who had come through tough times (10:32):
  * Many were publicly ridiculed (10:33)
  * A number of their leaders apparently were killed (13:7)
  * At least some of them had their property confiscated (10:34)
  * Although most had not been martyred, many had spent time in prison (10:34; 13:3)
- They knew the Hebrew scriptures well (obvious from the continual stream of scriptural quotes and allusions)
- They had practiced Hebrew religious ceremonies in the past (13:9–10)
- But they were likely Gentile in ethnic background, having come into Judaism in the first place by way of conversion (10:32)

When all of these things are considered together, subtle demographic lines emerge. Because they are well educated, communicate in Greek, and appear to have come to Judaism from a Gentile background, it is likely that these people were proselytes to Judaism who had been seeking moral grounding in an increasingly debauched—and debasing—Roman society. There were many instances in the first centuries B.C. and A.D., where non-Jews became enamored of the rigorous lifestyle found in Jewish communities scattered around the Roman world. After going through years of nonparticipating observation and instruction, these converts were then officially declared to be Jews through ritual entrance ceremonies.

New adherents of any cause or religion are often the most zealous for their newly adopted perspectives and philosophies. It certainly seems to have been the case with these folks. So, it must have been quite exciting and shocking when news about Jesus circulated, announcing the arrival of the Messiah and the coming of God's final act of revelation and transformation. No doubt many of these Gentile proselytes to Judaism were quick to take the next step in exploring the messianic fulfillments of the religion they had recently adopted.

Of course, it did not take long before tensions within the Jewish community, and later persecutions from without, took the glow off these exuberant times. Now, in the face of renewed threats against Christians by the Roman government, a complicating twist had been added. All Christians, whether Gentile or Jewish in background, were specifically identified as participants in an illegal religious cult, while Jews who did not believe in Jesus retained official protections as part of an already sanctioned religion.

This heightened the confusion of identity issues for proselyte Jews. If they continued to profess Jesus as messiah, they would be separated from the rest of the Jewish community and persecuted by the Roman government, perhaps losing their property, their families, and even their lives in the process. If, however, they gave up the Jesus factor in their messianic

Judaism, they would be able to return to the safety and camaraderie of the general Jewish community, with all of its religious rigor and righteousness, and at the same time, escape threats from the Roman officials. The latter option was a very tempting choice to make. This seems, in fact, to be the background of one of the last and most specific exhortation of Hebrews:

> Therefore, since we are surrounded by such a great cloud of witnesses, let us throw off everything that hinders and the sin that so easily entangles, and let us run with perseverance the race marked out for us. Let us fix our eyes on Jesus, the author and perfecter of our faith, who for the joy set before him endured the cross, scorning its shame, and sat down at the right hand of the throne of God. Consider him who endured such opposition from sinful men, so that you will not grow weary and lose heart. In your struggle against sin, you have not yet resisted to the point of shedding your blood ... Therefore, strengthen your feeble arms and weak knees (Hebrews 12: 1–4, 12).

The writer of Hebrews points to others, of both Old Testament times and recent difficult circumstances, who chose to keep in step with the messianic progression of God's activities, culminating in the coming of Jesus, the Messiah. If these followers of the right way could keep their faith, even when it cost them everything, you can do it too! And look! They are the ones who are cheering you on! They believe you can remain faithful. In fact, Jesus Himself stands at the end of your journey and beckons you on to the finish line! So don't give up now, just when you are achieving a newer depth in your relationship with God! You can continue on! You can make it!

To Whom Was Hebrews Written?

If this is indeed the context that nurtured Hebrews into being written, it is possible to reflect more intelligently on the location of the community in question, and the times during which the document was authored. Although the writer of Hebrews talks at length about the sacrifices offered regularly by the priests, there is no indication that either he or his readers were watching these things take place, day in and out. The ritual systems of the Tabernacle are used like intellectual building blocks of a worldview system. They are deeply ingrained in the culture, but not necessarily constantly experienced by those familiar with them, any more than is true for Christians who talk easily about the crucifixion of Jesus.

Because the scripture passages quoted and exegeted by the author are consistently from the Septuagint, it appears reasonable that the readers were not living in Palestine. The references to Timothy, prison, and people from Italy in Hebrews 13:23–24 make a Roman connection likely, but do not help in determining whether the author or the audience was located there. What is beneficial, however, is the series of hints about successive waves of persecution. In the remembered past, according to the author, an official government pogrom cost many of them their property and material possessions, landed some in jail, and brought about the death of a few of their leaders. Now they were facing a greater threat, and distinctions were being made between Jews who identified with Jesus as messiah and those who did not.

The three periods of significant government persecution against the Christian Church during the first century were under emperors Claudius (48-49 A.D.), Nero (64-68 A.D.), and Domitian (81-96 A.D.). If this document is written after one attack and shortly before another is reaching its climax, Hebrews was probably penned in either the early 60s or the early 80s. The more limited persecutions under Claudius seem better suited for the past troubles faced by this group, since most of them had come through and were restored to their usual social experiences. Also, it is interesting that the destruction of the Temple is nowhere mentioned in this document. Since so much of the theological argument in Hebrews is based upon the idea that the ritual ceremonies of Judaism are no longer needed, the destruction of the Temple would have been a perfect illustration of the author's point. If the Temple had been destroyed, it would seem to confirm God's own intent to make null and void the ceremonies at the center of Jewish religious practice. In fact, the very choice made by the writer of Hebrews to talk only about the *Tabernacle*, and not the *Temple*, may be an indication that the Temple was still standing. After all, the author does not want to cast aspersions against the cultic rituals that were taking place daily in Jerusalem, but only to go back to their roots and meaning. So he uses the Tabernacle as his point of reference, knowing that it would serve his theological analogies better than the still-visible rites and customs experienced in the Jerusalem Temple by many of them on their pilgrimages. Together, these clues seem to push toward an original date of writing in the early 60s, possibly from Ephesus, where Timothy was pastor. Since Apollos had gone there as well, he would be a prime candidate for authorship, but there is simply not enough evidence to make a wise decision about that.

Like the "Covenant Questions" documents of the Old Testament, Hebrews brings a word of wisdom to the New Testament community. It compares the two great redemptive interruptions of God into human history, and shows how these were paired aspects of God's one primary desire: to reassert the divine presence and care among an alienated humanity. Setting these two pivotal acts of God against each other makes no sense; but neither does remaining handcuffed to the former when its greater replacement has come. True religion is not about how humans can become better people through the ritual acts of even the best of systems; rather, it is about how we can follow Jesus with confidence, especially during times of persecution, since he is the latest and greatest expression of the kindness and majesty of God.

Discussion Points

- What is the historical context producing so much anxiety among the readers of Hebrews? What actions were they taking, or not taking? How does the author address these concerns?
- What is the worldview of the author of Hebrews? How does this person define history, God's mission, and the role of the successive waves of Hebrew/Jewish identity? How are these related to Jesus?

- What are the unique elements of the life of Melchizedek which become part of the writer of Hebrews' theology about Jesus? How is Jesus like Melchizedek, and what does this mean for Jesus' life, work, and redemptive sacrifice?
- What outcomes are desired from his readers by the writer of Hebrews? How does he encourage them toward these ends?

For Further Investigation

Lane, William L. (Waco: Word, 1991). *Hebrews.*

Schenck, Kenneth. (Louisville: Westminster John Knox, 2003). *Understanding the Book of Hebrews.*

41.

The Awful Pains of Labor

Dying for a World Waiting to Be Reborn

The name of the final book of the Bible is associated with an entire genre of literature. Its first word in the original Greek text is transliterated into English as "apocalypse," and is most often translated as "revelation." This term literally means to uncover, or to take out of hiding, and explains the primary feature of what has become known as "apocalyptic literature." Scenes, ideas, and information that have been hidden from human view for long ages are now brought out into the open. But this does not mean that the details of the "revelation" are easily understood. The "revealing" process itself is often arduous, and produces at least as many questions as it suggests to answer. The process of revealing usually happens through a special communication link which pairs a heavenly messenger, who knows or understands the significance of the dreamlike scenes, with a divinely selected human correspondent, who is particularly attuned to spiritual realities, or who has passed through refining trials that make him specially prepared for the sensory overload involved.

The Revelation of Jesus Christ brought to John at Patmos is both mysterious and majestic. It contains one of the most powerful scenes of worship recorded anywhere (Revelation 4-5), and yet remains complex and mysteriously cryptic to the general reader. Because of this, four major strategies of interpretation have developed:

Characteristics of Apocalyptic Literature

- Temporal dualism: strong distinction between current and coming ages
- Pessimism about current age, optimism about future age
- History is to be understood as occurring in eons or segments (4, 7, 12), reflecting a divine plan
- Imminent arrival of God's reign, which will destroy current temporal powers
- Cosmic vantage point and global impact of unfolding events
- Vindication of "the righteous" and restoration of natural perfections and harmonies
- Involvement of supernatural beings in current conflicts, as well as future "gories" and glories
- Clear messianic figure, who is at the center of all things and events

---

- **Preterist**: Revelation is a coded document designed to give comfort and encouragement to those in John's day, but its specifics largely escape us today. Both John and his readers understood all of the symbolism in the words he was writing, since it was aimed at people, places, and events in their own experiences. The encoding was necessary to keep Roman officials from understanding, and thus minimize the possibilities of reprisals and more martyrdoms.

- **Historicist**: Revelation outlines the history of the church through the centuries, and close analysis of its contents can actually pinpoint events taking place at any given time since Jesus ascended to heaven. Because Jesus has not yet returned, there are mysterious incidents still to come, and these are symbolized in the strange tellings of Revelation's last pages. We must try to decipher the meaning of these cryptic scenes if we wish to read the signs of the times more clearly.

- **Futurist**: Revelation mostly foretells the specific events which will lead to the end of the world and Jesus' second coming. Beyond the first three chapters, which were notes of encouragement given to the Church in John's day and remain beneficial as promises and warning for churches everywhere, the rest of the book is probably talking about a single generation of people who will live shortly before the return of Jesus. Many believe that the reestablishment of the modern state of Israel is linked to an imminent fulfillment of these things, and that the crises portrayed graphically in Revelation are rapidly unfolding around us.

- **Idealist**: The book of Revelation is nonhistorical, in that it does not, for the most part, try to identify specific, recordable experiences of persons or cultures either past, present, or future. Instead, it is a type of allegory which powerfully pictures the perennial and ongoing combat between God and the Devil, between the Church and the world, and between good and evil generally. Instead of trying to find contemporary or past events linked to certain scenes in the book, we should interpret every situation of human history in light of the overarching themes of the book:
  * Jesus is the powerful resurrected and ascended Savior.
  * Evil is constantly trying to usurp God's authority and destroy God's creation and God's people.
  * We are living on a battlefield in which all people are affected by the scars and wounds of war, and few signs of victory are ever seen.
  * All human beings must choose to confess Jesus as Lord and Savior, and stand firm to that testimony—no matter what the cost—or they will slip into an alliance with evil that will eventually destroy them.

* Jesus is returning to make all things new, but before that happens, this world will undergo even more powerful and threatening advances of evil.
* One day, the faith of the faithful will be rewarded, and the dead and living together will enjoy the perfections of the new creation, in which all evidence of parasitic evil will have been removed.

While each of these approaches to the book of Revelation has merit, the last ("Idealist") is most directly connected to the literary development of the text itself. Although the paragraphs and scenes may seem convoluted and unrelentingly dense in many parts, there is also an obvious movement to the flow of its passages. Driven by sevens, the images and happenings are grouped into clearly defined sections. And when these collections of sevens are marked out from one another, it becomes apparent that they are triggered by exactly three critical scenes, in which Jesus is shown to play a pivotal role. Here is how the text of Revelation unfolds:

Why These Seven Churches?

Ephesus stands at the head of the list among these congregations to whom John is instructed to send letters from Jesus. This was John's home congregation, so it makes sense that the series would begin there. Furthermore, Ephesus was the regional center of commerce and distribution, placing all of the other cities in direct trade connection with it. The order of the letters is like a normal distribution pattern fanning out from a base of operations in Ephesus.

- **Jesus Addresses the Church Living in the City of Humanity** (1–3)
  * *Vision of Jesus as Risen Lord* (1)
  * *Letters of Jesus to Seven Representative Churches* (2–3)
- **Jesus Delivers the Church out of the Destruction of the City of Humanity** (4–18)
  * *Vision of Jesus as Lion/Lamb Redeemer* (4–5)
  * *Three series of sevens:*
    - Seven Seals anticipate divine judgment (6–7)
    - Seven Trumpets announce divine judgment (8–11)
      - Interlude: Clarifying the Combatants (12–14)
    - Seven Bowls of Plagues accomplish divine judgment (15–18)
- **Jesus Restores the Holy City** (19–22)
  * *Vision of Jesus as Bridegroom/Conquering King* (19:1–10)
  * *Seven Actions of Restoration* (19:11–22:5)
    - Epilogue (22:6–21)

When observed in this manner, carefully responding to the literary movements of the text itself, greater clarity emerges. John has three major visions of Jesus (1, 4–5, 19), and each is followed by one or more series of sevens. Overall, the progression moves from local congregations that are experiencing persecution, heresy, and compromise (2–3); to a global battlefield, in which all citizens of planet Earth are caught up in the horrible conflict between evil and good (6–18); and finally, on to a transcendent victory brought about by the return of Jesus and the divine renewal of creation itself (19–22).

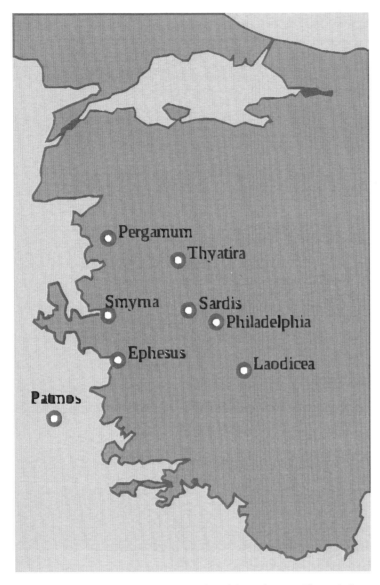

Figure 40.1 Location of Patmos Island (Revelation 1), and the seven churches of Revelation 2-3.[1]

Jesus addresses the church living in the city of humanity

John writes that he is on the island of Patmos as he receives these visions. Patmos is about fifty miles to the southwest of Ephesus, where John had been pastor and church leader for the previous three decades. Although the book of Revelation does not mention the Roman emperor Domitian, early Church sources indicate that an empire-wide persecution of Christians took place during his reign (81–96 A.D.). Tertullian adds a note about this in Chapter XXXVI of his *On the Prescription of Heretics*, stating that, in Rome, "the Apostle John was first plunged, unhurt, into boiling oil, and thence remitted to his island-exile."

There is evidence on Patmos today that the island had been a quarry for building stones during Roman times, and that slave labor was used in this arduous work. However it came to be that John was on Patmos, he remained vitally connected to both his resurrected friend Jesus, and to the congregations back on the mainland of Asia Minor, who were praying for him.

In the opening vision, Jesus is identified as the Creator and Consummator ("the first and the last"), and is shown symbolically in the Temple (walking among the lamp stands), bringing the glory of God into the human arena. While Jesus is clearly human in his physical features, these have been translated by his resurrection (Revelation 1:18) so that they pummel the observer with transcendent power and glory.

Each of the seven letters that follows (Revelation 2–3) begins with a self-description by Jesus, in which some aspect of his revealed glory in chapter 1 is reiterated. The letters are a mixture of

---

1 Copyright in the Public Domain.

warning and encouragement, clearly articulating the experiences of actual congregations living in the first century. They appear to be representative messages, so that even as they speak directly to these seven churches, they communicate Jesus' ongoing relationship to all congregations generally.

The location of these churches and the order in which the letters are dictated are very interesting. Ephesus is first on the list, for good reason. John has been the key pastor and leader at the church in Ephesus for at least three decades by this time, so his congregation comes first into view. The next church is directly north of Ephesus, about fifty miles directly overland, but much further by sea, also on the coast of the Aegean. Today, "Smyrna" is the large Turkish port of Izmir. "Pergamum" ("Bergama" today) lies another seventy-five miles directly north of Smyrna, a little inland up a broad agricultural valley. Fifty miles east-southeast is Thyatira ("Ahkisar" today), on the ancient trade route from the Hellespont to Ephesus. Sardis ("Salihli" today), the ancient capital of Persia in its western province, is another thirty-five miles almost due south of Thyatira. Its commanding perch on the mountainside above a broad and fertile farming valley made it a key military site. Only twenty-five miles up the valley to the southeast stood Philadelphia ("Alesehir" today), with Laodicea ("Denizli" today) another seventy miles in the same direction. From Laodicea, by way of the Meander River valley (the whimsically slow and wandering river that has given us the term "meander"!), Ephesus was just a hundred miles directly to the west.

So the loop formed by the roads connecting these seven churches followed three significant trade routes. Ephesus was the cultural and commercial pivot, while directly opposite on the circle, Sardis was the political and military bastion of the region. Paul, Timothy, and John had probably traveled this "ring road" a good number of times while each was stationed in Ephesus.

The letters to each church are also quite telling:

- **Ephesus** had the first church in the district, and enjoyed a place of ecclesiastical prominence, but seems to have grown sophistically indifferent to Jesus over time.
- **Smyrna** was a wealthy city, but its first Christians were among the poor and the slaves; Jesus notes their oppressed condition.
- **Pergamum** was a wealthy city with a medical school, and was renowned for its famed Altar of Zeus, which Jesus seems to refer to in his letter.
- **Thyatira** was a thriving commercial center, whose citizens cannily played the markets, in bed with whichever prophetess would predict the next windfall (note Jesus' warnings!).
- **Sardis** was the mountaintop political and military command post. Although impregnable by reputation, Persian troops had scaled its

Pictures and Images in Revelation

Virtually all the images in Revelation draw upon similar images in several Old Testament books:

Exodus: The plagues

Ezekiel:

   The scroll of prophecy/judgment

   The war with Gog and Magog

   The restored Temple and new creation

Daniel:

   The use of terms ("Son of Man," "seven")

   Tour of spiritual visions by way of angelic guide

unguarded cliff and surprised the sleeping inhabitants, just as Jesus now threatened to do in the church there.

- **Philadelphia** had experienced devastating earthquakes which caused doors and gates to seize up. Jesus uses that imagery to declare a future stability based upon the unshakable foundation of his Temple.
- **Laodicea** had both hot and cold running water, brought in by aqueducts from cold mountain rivers and nearby mineral springs. The fertile valley at its feet was known for its sheep industry, and the production of short black wool jackets. Jesus plays on the water theme, and offers white tunics to cover spiritual nakedness.

Jesus delivers the church out of the destruction of the city of humanity

In John's second major vision of Jesus, the scene shifts from Earth to heaven (Revelation 4–5). God is not represented by creatures or beings or shapes or symbols, but only as the shimmering of pure light itself, in pulsating and changing hues covering the whole spectrum. The throne from which God rules is not backed against the wall of some palace room, but is at the center of all things, so that all of created reality flows out from it, and surrounds it with worship, and receives its light and life from God. Everything everywhere participates in synchronized waves that emanate out from this point of origin, and the pulsating undulations send back to the throne of God choruses of praise and songs of reverence.

Occupying the key places of honor closest to the divine throne are the twenty-four elders, representing the combined leadership of the people of God through biblical history—twelve patriarchs in the Old Testament, twelve apostles in the New. As the rhythms of worship resound, and catch everything in heaven and on earth and in the seas in their vibrations and beats, a new element is suddenly introduced: a scroll is extended out from the indescribable light of the One on the throne. This parchment is covered with writing, and appears to be of critical importance for whatever has to happen next. Yet no one seems to have access to it, so John weeps.

Quickly, however, John is told that the "Lion of the tribe of Judah, the Root of David," is approaching, and that he will unfasten the seals that bind the scroll. Expecting a roaring and powerful beast, John is amazed to see instead a "Lamb, looking as if it had been slain." It was "standing in the center of the throne." Subsequent lines make

---

Face-off of the Superpowers

In Revelation 12–14, evil is personified in three ways, each of which mirrors one of the Persons of the Holy Trinity by which Christianity apprehends the Being of God:

Father:	*Dragon:*
Creation	Destruction
Providence	Terrorism
Son:	*Beast from the Sea:*
Ruler of Nations	Ruler of Nations
Died and Rose	Healed "Fatal Wound"
Holy Spirit:	*Beast from the Earth:*
Fire and Signs	Fire and Signs
Nurtures worship	Commands worship

it clear that this One is Jesus. In these quick descriptors, John tells us several things. First of all, Jesus is human, a king in the line of David. Meanwhile, He is also the "root" of that whole royal family, giving the rest of its members their royal authority. At the same time, He is the One who died as the true Passover Lamb, fulfilling the meaning of that ritual right which gave identity to the nation of Israel. But He also came alive again in the resurrection of Easter Sunday, and rules over all things with supreme and unequaled authority. He is, in fact, truly God (notice that He stands at the center of the throne, which is a position that can solely be claimed by the Creator Deity of the universe).

Jesus slowly, but deliberately, opens the seven seals in succession. As they are cracked, scenes of partial devastation wreaked upon earth and human societies provide anticipation of the coming comprehensive judgment of God. Before the full impact of these things annihilates humanity, however, a group symbolically numbering 144,000—but visually identified as "a multitude that no one could count"—is ceremonially protected from the combined destructive power of evil and the awful judgment of God (Revelation 7). It is important to pay close attention to the manner in which John records his vision here, because the symbolic 144,000 and the innumerable host are identified as one and the same group. Since John brings this number back again in Revelation 14:1, it is critical to understand 144,000 as a descriptive collective, rather than an itemized tally.

Numbers in Revelation

4: dimensions of created reality ("four corners")

7: number of God; perfection

Half of 7 plus half of 7: complete history of humanity (half before Jesus, half after):

"A time, times and half a time"

3 and a half years

42 months

1,260 days

24: symbolic union of Old Testament (12 tribes) with New Testament (12 Apostles)

1000: symbol of completeness in human realm

144,000: symbol of complete gathering of God's people

The opening of the seventh seal (Revelation 8:1) triggers the beginning of the blowing of seven trumpets that announce the near arrival of holocaustic divine judgment. New visions accompany these blasts, and with each, the seismic tremors on Earth increase in intensity, as more profound destruction ensues. Just prior to the blowing of the seventh trumpet, John is given a scroll to eat (Revelation 10), clearly marking him as a prophet like Ezekiel (Ezekiel 3), whose earlier visions provide many of the themes and expressions that are part of the revelation to John.

Before the bowls of plagues are poured out (Revelation 15–18), accomplishing the final judgments of God and the time of transformation into the eternal age of renewal, there is what appears to be a kind of face-off between the superpowers who are behind the scenes, and who shape the battlefield skirmishes of this conflict. In Revelation 12 and 13, evil in personified form is shown to mirror the identity and activities of the Holy Trinity. As the Father is Creator and Sustainer of all things, so the dragon tears at these material wonders, skewing and destroying them in a wild rage to harm God's people and God's plans (Revelation 12). Defeated in a bid to kill the divine Messiah born of the woman (symbolically drawing together the representation of the great mother, Eve of Genesis 3:15, the nation of Israel that was God's bride

What is the "Millennium?"

Revelation 20:2–6

AMILLENNIALISTS:

Metaphor of the complete period between Jesus' first and second comings

Should not be taken literally (hence *a-millennial*)

POSTMILLENNIALISTS:

Period of great gains for the Church, preparing the way for Jesus' return to usher in messianic age

Literal thousand years, beginning:

At the Reformation?

With the Enlightenment?

With the social and scientific revolutions of the 19th Century?

PREMILLENNIALISTS:

Period of future reign by Jesus on earth from Jerusalem

Literal thousand years (Dispensationalists: "Age of Kingdom")

---

and gave birth to the Messiah, and the Church of the New Testament age which is under attack, all combined into a single descriptive package), the dragon conjures up helpers from the human arena. The beast from the sea (Revelation 13:1–10) is an unholy counterpart to Jesus, receiving power and authority from its wicked master, and displaying a "fatal wound" that had been healed, mimicking Jesus' own death and resurrection. Because it takes up residence in the human realm, this beast begins to receive worship from all of humankind. Its authority is enhanced when the beast from the Earth emerges, eliciting fire from heaven and miraculous signs at its appearance, just as happened when the Holy Spirit of God came to Earth on Pentecost (Acts 2). And like that third Person of the holy Trinity, this unholy entity turns the attention of the human race to the one who came before, which is, in this case, the beast that had the fatal wound that healed.

In striking images, John portrays the nasty game of imitation that evil tries to play, in a bid to win humanity away from its true relationship of worship with the Creator. In fact, Revelation 13 ends with the great and mysterious marking ceremony, in which all of humanity is branded with 666. While many interpretations swirl about, in reality, John makes it clear that this is a devilish counterpart to baptism, since the only ones who escape the trauma of this identification are those who wear instead the names of God (Revelation 14:1–5). The 777 mark of belonging to Father, Son, and Spirit is the only antidote to the mesmerizing and dehumanizing promises issued by the great enemy of God and of God's people. While they glow with tantalizing power, they end up short (only a 666) and are destined for the ultimate trash bin, where everything imperfect is consumed or purified by fire.

Despite the power and wily maneuvering of the dragon and his helpers, they are no match for the true God. Revelation 14 concludes with a harsh indictment upon the unholy trinity and all who fall under its sway, and a great promise that soon the final judgment will begin. Indeed, in chapters 15–18, the stored-up wrath of God upon evil and sin is poured out from seven bowls which replay the majority of the devastations brought on Egypt during the days of Moses (Exodus 7–11). In the end, the personification of evil as it coalesces in the human community is destroyed, doomed—just as ancient Babylon was ruined because of its part in attacking the people of God (Revelation 17–18).

Jesus restores the holy city

Then comes the third vision of Jesus, who now appears both as conquering King and ravishing Bridegroom (Revelation 19:1–10). Before the victory and wedding celebrations can begin, however, a mopping-up operation takes place, in which seven aspects of judgment and restoration are sorted out (mostly introduced by John with "then I saw"):

- The King appears to fulfill his destiny (Revelation 19:11–16).
- The last battle is fought, in which all the evil in the human arena is focused and repelled (Revelation 19:17–21).
- Satan is bound for a certain period of time (Revelation 20:1–3).
- The dead are raised to life for good or for ill (Revelation 20:4–6).
- Evil is destroyed (Revelation 20:7–10).
- The final judgment, determining the eternal destiny of all humankind (Revelation 10:11–15).
- Earth is re-created and restored in its relationship with the Creator (Revelation 21:1–22:5).

Revelation ends where it began, with a call to faithfulness in the face of mounting opposition. While its details provide endless fodder for teachers, preachers, and theological speculators, a consistent core message emerges: During times of crisis, when evil seems to dominate the human scene, don't lose heart, because God is still in control of all things, and Jesus is returning soon to annihilate evil and transform creation into all that God intended for it to be.

Obviously, this was a necessary message late in the first century, when first Nero's and then Domitian's persecutions of the Church killed many, and caused thousands of others to huddle in fear. Since the language and cosmological perspectives in the book are very similar to those in the Gospel of John and the Letters of John, there is every reason to suppose that they, along with this book, were written by the disciple of Jesus who pastored the congregation in Ephesus late in the first century. This John was exiled to Patmos by Domitian as a way of undermining the courage of the Christian Church, which he despised. Since Domitian ruled from September of 81 through September of 96 A.D., the revelation of Jesus to John was probably penned and sent sometime in the mid- to late-80s.

Its message is timeless:

- To be a Christian is to be in conflict in this world.
- If one tries to opt out of this conflict, one automatically joins the other side, and will be trapped by the powers of evil.
- Faithfulness to Jesus almost invariably leads to martyrdom, because this conflict is all or nothing.
- But those who trust in God will find the strength to remain faithful through suffering, die in hope, and have their confidence rewarded by Jesus' ultimate victory and the renewal of creation, which includes the resurrection and glorification of all God's people.

Discussion Points

- What are the major approaches to interpreting the book of Revelation? How do these differ from one another? What outcomes for the theology of the book of Revelation are expected by each?
- What is the literary structure of the book of Revelation? How do the unique sightings of Jesus help shape the contents? How might these be used to understand the flow of the message in the book?
- What are the critical points of exhortation or encouragement that can be deduced from the book of Revelation, regardless of the overall theological approach taken?

For Further Investigation

Boring, M. Eugene. (Louisville: Westminster John Knox, 1989). *Revelation*.

Mounce, Robert H. (Grand Rapids: Eerdmans, 1997). *The Book of Revelation*.

Osborne, Grant. (Grand Rapids: Baker, 2002). *Revelation*.

Bible "Big Picture"

Covenant Making: God establishes a covenant relationship with a missional community by way of a redemptive act

Old Testament: The Exodus and Sinai Covenant

Genesis—Why is the Covenant necessary?

Exodus—What is the Covenant all about?

Leviticus—How does it affect daily living?

Numbers—Who is in the covenant community, and why?

Deuteronomy—How long will the Covenant be in force?

New Testament: The Person and Work of Jesus

Matthew—Jesus is the Messiah King who relives the life of Israel, and becomes Savior King of the nations

Mark—Jesus is the powerful Son of God who releases people from the many evils that enslave them

Luke—Jesus is the heaven-sent Teacher and Healer, who brings hope through the ministry of the Church

John—Jesus is the ultimate Passover Lamb, who recreates the dark world through the witness of his disciples

Covenant Living: God guides the covenant relationship with the missional community by way of authorized spokespersons

Old Testament: The Prophets, with Their Interpreted History and Sermons

Stories: The interpreted history of Israel

- *Joshua*—Possessing the Land with missional significance
- *Judges*—Nearly losing the Land through covenant failure
- *Ruth*—The model of covenant obedience that restore
- *1 & 2 Samuel*—Establishing the monarchy that might fulfill the covenant mission
- *1 & 2 Kings, 1 & 2 Chronicles*—Failure of the Old Testament covenant community mission experiment
- *Ezra and Nehemiah*—Restoring the covenant community in anticipation of Yahweh's next major act
- *Esther*—Responding to the warning that Yahweh's people have a covenant identity and purpose

Sermons: The verbal declarations of Yahweh's designs and intents

- *Isaiah*—Divine deliverance from Assyria, coming global renewal
- *Jeremiah*—Doom and gloom in Judah's final years, promises of restoration
- *Ezekiel*—God on the move, bringing judgment and promises of a new age
- *Daniel*—Struggles of faithful exilic living, plus visions of God's growing kingdom
- *Hosea*—The divine/human soap opera
- *Joel*—Hints of "the Day of the Lord" found in a locust plague
- *Amos*—Imminent divine judgment because of social covenantal disobedience
- *Obadiah*—Edom condemned for harming Judah at the time of deportation
- *Jonah*—Missionary trek to Assyrian enemy capital showing global divine favor
- *Micah*—Yahweh's faithfulness, Israel's unfaithfulness, and imminent judgment
- *Nahum*—God will destroy Assyria because of its cruelty to other nations
- *Habakkuk*—Dialogue with Yahweh on the mysteries of social sins and divine judgment
- *Zephaniah*—Brief notes on impending divine judgment and future redemptive restoration
- *Haggai*—"Let's get that Temple rebuilt!" and "God bless Zerubbabel!"
- *Zechariah*—Visions of judgment on the nations and visions of glory on the restored "Israel"
- *Malachi*—Dialogues between Yahweh and the people on failures and the future

New Testament: The Apostles, with Their Ecclesiastical History and Letters

Stories: The unfolding of the "new covenant" in Jesus through the actions and mission of the Church

- *Acts*—The power of Jesus enacted upon the Church by way of the Holy Spirit to be a missional community

Sermons: The teachings of Jesus communicated through the apostles

- *Romans*—The righteousness of God revealed against Sin, bringing Salvation, and prompting Service
- *1 & 2 Corinthians*—How to live as Jesus' followers in a compromised society and very human Church
- *Galatians*—Gospel Liberty against either Legalism or License, uniting Jews and Gentiles in faith
- *Ephesians*—God's great power at work in Jesus transforms sinners into saints, who bring light into darkness
- *Philippians*—Rejoice! Knowing Jesus brings joy! Enjoy one another in true care and commitment!
- *Colossians*—Christ rules, so stop building petty parties in the Church, and live as ambassadors of light
- *1 & 2 Thessalonians*—Your testimony is heard everywhere; the dead will rise, but Jesus may delay
- *1 & 2 Timothy*—Work faithfully as a pastor, live faithfully as a person, and carry on after I am gone

- *Titus*—Organize the work of ministry well, so that all may be blessed
- *Philemon*—Receive useful Onesimus back as both slave and brother, and prepare for my visit
- *James*—Learn to live as brothers and sisters of Jesus and of one another; no special treatment!
- *1 & 2 Peter*—Live faithfully, particularly in the face of growing persecutions, knowing that Jesus is coming
- *1, 2, & 3 John*—The God of Israel is the God of the Church; Jesus came in the flesh; love one another
- *Jude*—There are some nasty teachers out there; don't listen to them!

Covenant Questions: God nurtures the covenant relationship with a missional community by way of spiritual wisdom and insight

Old Testament: The Poetry and Wisdom Literature; Questions of Fundamental Human Identity, as Illuminated by the Theology of the Covenant

Job—"Why do I suffer?"

Psalms—"How do I pray?"

Proverbs—"What is true wisdom?"

Ecclesiastes—"What is the meaning of life?"

Song of Songs—"What is the meaning of love?"

Lamentations—"What is the meaning of divine election?"

New Testament: The Comparison of the Two Covenant Expressions

Hebrews—"What is the relationship between the first and second expressions of the Covenant?"

Revelation—"What will be the culmination of all things, and how will that relate to its beginnings?"

42.

Conclusion

We shall not cease from exploration
And the end of all our exploring
Will be to arrive where we started
And know the place for the first time.
T. S. Eliot

As the parents of three wonderful daughters, my wife and I can sympathize with the couple who sent their child off to college, only to find out a few months later that she was dating another student, and that the two of them were already talking about marriage. The worried parents urged their daughter to bring her boyfriend home so they could meet him. When the college twosome arrived, and hurried and worried greetings were made at the door, Mom shunted Daughter off to the kitchen, while Dad guided Boyfriend firmly into the family room for a little heart-to-heart.

"So," Dad said at last, trying to find out more about this young man, "what are your plans for your future?"

"I'm not sure, sir," the boyfriend replied, "but I know that your daughter and I were destined to be together, and that God will provide."

"Well, what about finances? How do you intend to pay the bills if you should get married?"

"To tell you the truth, sir, we haven't given that much thought yet. But we are deeply in love, and we are confident that God will provide."

This was not giving the father much confidence, so he pressed on. "Do you have any ideas about careers and where you will live, and whether you will both finish college?"

"We're planning to take it one day at a time, sir," came the reply, "and we're sure that God will provide."

Later that night, Mom and Dad were finally alone together, and she said to him, "Well, what do you think?"

"I have mixed feelings," he told her. "On the one hand, the fellow seems to be a deluded, shiftless, irresponsible fool who hasn't even begun to understand how life works. Yet, on the other hand, I get the sense that he thinks I am God!"

The Human Quest

There is much of that family's conundrum in the way we all live out our existences here. Partly, we breeze through our days and experiences, believing that we can make it on our own, no matter what. At the same time, we wrestle with resources and responsibilities, knowing that there are some moral values and cosmic principles which affirm certain directions and activities in life, while denying and negating or punishing others. Caught somewhere in between is our mixed hope and dread, that a higher power out there will fill in the gaps and accommodate our weaknesses and make things right when we mess up. We truck along, blissfully in love with others or ourselves, or our careers or our daily duties, trusting that "God will provide," whatever we assume "God" to be or mean.

From a historian's viewpoint, it is obvious that the human race is incurably religious, and cannot seem to free itself from god-talk, or the language of mystery and transcendence. At the same time, no religion has been able to argue clearly, from within the system of human experience, that a particular deity is inescapably present, or that any peculiar worldview is undeniably true or coherent or all-encompassing. Thus, for several religious systems, divine revelation is a necessary corollary, even though what is needed by humanity, and what is offered from above, are both hotly debated.

Is revelation a form of clarity and insight that rightly discovers the true nature of things, which we are unable to investigate without transcendent help? Or is revelation the accumulating experiences of those who have sought meaning, helping us to stand on the shoulders of others, until we can see further? Or is revelation an injection of supernatural knowledge into our limited reasonings, from outside the system, by the one who created the system? Or is revelation an intrusion of divine activity into the human arena, leaving clues, fossils, and symbols which must then be interpreted and applied?

The religion of the Bible assumes that all of our experiential reality had a beginning, a big-bang explosion that fashioned everything we encounter out of previous nothingness. It also declares that this rigging of substance out of matter and energy was the act of a benevolent and all-powerful Creator. And, the Bible declares this deity desires an ongoing relationship with the worlds that have been brought into being. More particularly, according to both Old and New Testaments, this God nurtures a special longing to engage the human race as a partner in the journey of life. Humankind is, so we are informed, God's unique and crowning species within the grand complexity of molecules and moons, of fish and fowl, of galaxies and granite, of emotions and electrons.

But in its understanding of this ongoing friendly arm-wrestling between Creator and Creature, biblical religion is deeply rooted in human history. The Bible does not merely talk about values and ideas or morals on which to construct easier lives. Nor is it a set of centering exercises, which will keep the imminent more fully tuned to the transcendent. Instead, the story put forward in biblical literature is that the creatures of earth have lost their ability to apprehend or understand their Creator, and that the Deity must necessarily take not only the first, but also many recurring steps, in an effort to reconnect with them. So revelation is a concept involving both action and content. God must somehow interrupt the normal course of human affairs in a way that will catch our attention. And when we have stopped to notice or ponder, or even recoil in fright, there must be some information that we can use in a way that allows and encourages us to rethink the meaning of all things.

Reading the Bible again for the First Time

It is in this sense that I have tried to explain the literature of the Bible. It is rooted, it seems to me, in two major divine interruptions into human history—first, through the events of the exodus and Sinai covenant that created Israel as a missional nation, and then second, in the unusual and unrepeatable incarnation of deity into the Person of Jesus Christ. All of the literature of the Bible is gathered around these two redemptive events and their implications. For this reason, the Pentateuch and the gospels are the critical elements shaping the biblical religion. They are not codes of law or wise ethical teachings from a distinguished school of thought; they are the documents articulating an unusual intrusion of divine will into the human arena for the threefold purpose of actively transforming lives by redemptive transactions, teaching the Creator's original worldview, and establishing a missional community that will live out and disseminate those perspectives.

Appended to these central documents are the ongoing declarations of guidance provided by divinely authorized and spiritually attuned spokespersons, who called others to remember the redemptive events and their significance, and challenged them to live as if these things matter. In the Old Testament expression of biblical religion, these persons are identified as "prophets"—those who speak on behalf of God; in the New Testament they are called "apostles"—those who are *sent* by God.

Finally, accreted to these collections are a few other writings that became recognized by the faith community for their depth of spiritual insight, or for their helpful clarification of recurring issues. Whether by divine determination or political maneuvering or the whims of history (or even, perhaps some combination of all of these), the resulting literary product came to its current shape, and is known as the Bible. It cannot be fully understood apart from its assumptions about divine revelation. Yet at the same time, it does not presume to be merely a transhistorical injection of supernatural mysteries into the human arena, for the use of those who alone are inducted into secret societies, where the mind of God is supposedly explored.

If the Bible is to have any ongoing religious value, its two historical nodes of divine redemptive activity have to be taken seriously. Stripped of the exodus/Sinai Covenant, or of the redemptive divinity of Jesus, the Bible makes little sense. Suddenly, its moral codes are no better than others that have been formed and articulated at various points throughout history; its pilgrimage images are little different from other quests for significance and the sacred; and its personalities become only another bunch of interesting heroes and drifters, who give moral lessons through their flawed frolicking.

But if there is a God, and if that God wished to reclaim, by creatorial right, a relationship with those brought into being as an extension of the divine fellowship and heavenly energy, the Bible makes a good deal of sense. It is a collection of covenant documents which trace the divine redemptive mission through two stages: its early history in locating a transformed community at the crossroads of human society in order to be seen and desired, and its later expression through an expanding and transforming presence in every culture, that tells the story of God along with the other tales of life.

Like the rest of literature, the Bible can be ignored, misread, or improperly used. But like the best of literature, when allowed to speak from its own frame of reference, and respected as a collection of documents that are inherently seeking to enhance human life, rather than deviously attempting to exploit it, the Bible is truly—in a very powerful and exciting way—the Word of God.